THE BLADE RUNNER EXPERIENCE

THE BLADE RUNNER EXPERIENCE
THE LEGACY OF A SCIENCE FICTION CLASSIC

edited by WILL BROOKER

WALLFLOWER PRESS LONDON & NEW YORK

First published in Great Britain in 2005 by
Wallflower Press
6a Middleton Place, Langham Street, London W1W 7TE
www.wallflowerpress.co.uk

A catalogue for this book is available from the British Library.

ISBN 1-904764-30-4 (pbk)
ISBN 1-904764-31-2 (hbk)

Book design by Elsa Mathern

Printed by Replika Press Pvt Ltd., India

CONTENTS

SECTION 4: IDENTITIES

SECTION 5: THE CITY

EDITOR'S NOTE

This anthology discusses both Ridley Scott's *Blade Runner* and Philip K. Dick's *Do Androids Dream of Electric Sheep?* In the former, the main female replicant is named Rachel, and in the latter Rachael. For convenience, the spelling 'Rachel' is used throughout this book even when referring to the character in Dick's novel or in K. W. Jeter's *Blade Runner* sequels. Other spellings, such as 'Voigt-Kampff', are taken from Paul M. Sammon's *Future Noir: The Making of Blade Runner* (1996).

My thanks as editor go to Yoram Allon at Wallflower Press for his support and guidance; to Mark Kermode and Andrew Abbot for the interviews; to Ben Mund and Don Solosan for their email testimonies, ideas and feedback; and to all the contributors, who gave so much and so selflessly.

'This is for Zhora ... This is for Pris'. This is for Fiona.

NOTES ON CONTRIBUTORS

DOMINIC ALESSIO is Associate Professor/Head of History at Richmond the American International University in London. He is also Vice Chair of the New Zealand Studies Association (NZSA) and Review Editor for the *British Review of New Zealand Studies*. He has written on science fiction for *ARIEL*, *The European Legacy*, *Foundation*, *Journal of New Zealand Literature*, *Science Fiction Studies* and *Utopian Studies*.

BARRY ATKINS is Senior Lecturer in Digital Games at the International Centre for Digital Content, Liverpool John Moores University, where he runs the MA Digital Games programme. He is author of *More Than a Game: The Computer Game as Fictional Form* (Manchester University Press, 2003) and co-editor of *Videogame, Player, Text* (Manchester University Press, forthcoming 2006).

AARON BARLOW is Assistant Professor of English, Kutztown University of Pennsylvania. He is author of *The DVD Revolution: Movies, Culture, and Technology* (Praeger, 2005) and *Cuánto te asusta el Caos? Política, religión y filosofía en la obra de Philip K. Dick* (Grupo Editorial AJEC, 2003). He is currently completing *The Rise of the Blogsphere* (Praeger, forthcoming 2007).

PETER BROOKER is Professor of Literary and Cultural Studies at the University of Nottingham where he is Director of Research in the Department of Critical Theory and Cultural Studies. He is the author, most recently, of *Modernity and Metropolis* (Palgrave, 2002), *Bohemia in London: The Social Scene of Early Modernism* (Palgrave, 2004) and *A Glossary of Cultural Theory* (Arnold, 2002). He is co-editor of *Geographies of Modernism* (Routledge, 2005), co-founder of the Modernist Magazine Project, and co-editor of a forthcoming three-volume cultural history of Modernist Magazines to be published by Oxford University Press.

WILL BROOKER is Senior Lecturer in Film Studies at Kingston University in London. He is the author of several articles and books on cultural icons, fandom and interpretation, including *Batman Unmasked* (Continuum, 2000) *Using the Force* (Continuum, 2002) and *Alice's Adventures* (Continuum, 2004), and is co-editor of *The Audience Studies Reader* (Routledge, 2003).

CHRISTY GRAY graduated from Richmond University in 2003 with a BA in Communications and Creative Arts. Since then she has worked on numerous television productions from commercial shoots to live studio broadcasting. She currently works in post-production, co-ordinating graphic design and access services for Flextech Television. Her research interests include gender and audience studies, particularly in relation to science fiction and fantasy film and television.

JONATHAN GRAY is Assistant Professor of Communication and Media Studies at Fordham University, New York. He has published on various issues of text/audience interactions in *Intensities: Journal of Cult Media, Critical Studies in Media Communication, International Journal of Cultural Studies* and *American Behavioral Scientist*. His first book is *Watching With The Simpsons: Television, Parody, and Intertextuality* (Routledge, 2005).

MATT HILLS is Senior Lecturer in Media and Cultural Studies in the Cardiff School of Journalism, Cardiff University. He is the author of *Fan Cultures* (Routledge, 2002), *The Pleasures of Horror* (Continuum, 2005) and *How To Do Things With Cultural Theory* (Hodder Arnold, 2005).

DEBORAH JERMYN is Senior Lecturer in Film and Television Studies at Roehampton University. She has published widely on women and popular culture and is co-editor of *The Cinema of Kathryn Bigelow: Hollywood Transgressor* (Wallflower Press, 2003), *The Audience Studies Reader* (Routledge, 2003) and *Understanding Reality TV* (Routledge, 2004).

JUDITH KERMAN is Professor of English at Saginaw Valley State University in Michigan, where she served as Dean of Arts and Behavioral Science for six years. She is the author of several books of poetry; editor/translator of *A Woman in Her Garden: Selected Poems of Dulce Maria Loynaz* (White Pine, 2002); co-editor and publisher of *Uncommonplaces: Poems of the Fantastic;* (Mayapple Press, 2000); and editor of the scholarly anthology *Retrofitting Blade Runner: Issues in Ridley Scott's 'Blade Runner' and Philip K. Dick's 'Do Androids Dream of Electric Sheep?'* (Popular Press, 1991; second edition, 1997). She is editor/publisher of Mayapple Press.

NICK LACEY is Head of Media Studies at Benton Park Technology College in Rawdon, Leeds. He is the author of a series of three Media Studies textbooks: *Image and Representation; Narrative and Genre; Media Audiences and Institutions* (Palgrave Macmillan, 1998, 2000, 2002). He has also published *Introduction to Film* (Palgrave Macmillan, 2005), *Blade Runner* (York Film Notes 2000) and *Se7en* (Ultimate Film Guide 2001).

SEAN REDMOND is Senior Lecturer in Film at Victoria University, Wellington. He is co-editor of *The Cinema of Kathryn Bigelow: Hollywood Transgressor* (Wallflower Press, 2003) and editor of *Liquid Metal: The Science Fiction Film Reader* (Wallflower Press, 2004). He is also co-editor of *Stardom and Celebrity: a Reader* (Sage, forthcoming 2006) and *Understanding Celebrity Culture* (Routledge, forthcoming 2006).

STEPHEN ROWLEY is an urban planner working in Melbourne, Australia. He studied cinema studies and urban planning at the University of Melbourne, and spent time living on the fringes of Los Angeles while studying film at the University of California, Irvine. His work on conventions of realism in animation is to be published in *Animation Journal* (2005).

SUSANA P. TOSCA is Associate Professor at the IT University of Copenhagen, where she is a member of the Center for Computer Games Research. Her PhD on Digital Literature was awarded the *summa cum laude* distinction at the Complutense University of Madrid and has recently appeared in book form (Universidad de Extremadura Press, 2004). Susana has been a very active member of the digital literature and computer game academic scene since the early 1990s, participating as a reviewer in conferences such as Hypertext or DAC, and has published numerous articles about computer games narrative. She is a director at the board of the Electronic Literature Organization, and an editor for the *Journal of Digital Information and Gamestudies*, the first peer-reviewed academic journal for computer games research which she co-founded with Espen Aarseth.

INTRODUCTION: 2019 VISION
WILL BROOKER

> Walking up Roppongi Dori from the ANA Hotel, where she's had the cab
> drop her, into the shadow of the multi-tiered expressway that looks like the
> oldest thing in town. Tarkovsky, someone had once told her, had filmed parts
> of *Solaris* here, using the expressway as found Future City. Now it's been
> Blade Runnered by half a century of use and pollution, edges of concrete
> worn porous as coral.
>   – William Gibson (2003: 146)

In 2003 *Blade Runner* became a verb. Twenty years after the film's release, William Gibson had no need to italicise the title, or note the director's name as he did with *Solaris*; every reader would know what he meant and call to mind the right image. 'Blade Runner', in this context, refers not so much to a film as to an aesthetic, a styling, *a look*.

But as Barry Atkins points out in this volume, *'Blade Runner'* has been an umbrella term for decades:

> It has been some time since it was possible to discuss *Blade Runner* as if
> it were a single and fixed text that might be considered in isolation from its
> history of multiple prints, or detached from its vast array of intertexts, para-
> texts, references and allusions. Even before the release of Ridley Scott's
> authorised Director's Cut in 1992, the film was already caught in a web of
> references to other texts, from its credited relationship to Philip K. Dick's *Do
> Androids Dream of Electric Sheep?* and its appropriation of the term 'blade
> runner' from William Burroughs' screenplay title, *Blade Runner: A Movie*
> (1979), to its density of intertextual allusion to a range of cinematic genres.

In 1992 that web split and reformed into a more complex network, as viewers announcing they were going to see *Blade Runner* could expect to be answered 'which one?' Beyond the two official versions were shadowy, phantom edits that to most viewers remained objects of hearsay and speculation: the Work-print, also known as the Denver/Dallas Sneaks, with its subtle differences in sound and vision; the San Diego Sneak, shown only once in May 1982, and the censored Broadcast Version (see Sammon 1996: 394).

Phillip K. Dick's original novel *Do Androids Dream of Electric Sheep?*, markedly different from the film in significant respects, has been published as *Blade Runner* since 1982, and as Christy Gray documents in her chapter here, the title *Blade Runner* has since become a brand for K. W. Jeter's three sequels (1995, 1996, 2002) that attempt to amalgamate and rationalise those variations in film and novel. In the late 1990s *Blade Runner* had also to be distinguished from 'Westwood's *Blade Runner*', the PC game that enabled players to enter the film's diegesis and work as a detective while Deckard is hunting his replicants.

Blade Runner online fandom, as well as turning inward to perform its own detection on the several film texts with their slight variations, has to look to 'sidequels' like *Soldier* (1998) and other movies that borrow from or spin off *Blade Runner*, whether influenced by its tone and design, sharing its themes or linking back to a common source in Philip K. Dick (PKD) fiction. While DVD technology enables fans to study the film more closely and precisely, their hushed discussions about the potential for an improved DVD featuring documentaries, different voice-overs, director and cast commentaries create, through online discourse, an additional, ultimate and as-yet-nonexistent version of *Blade Runner*. Academia, as Matt Hills suggests in this volume, practices *Blade Runner* fandom on a different cultural level but with similar obsession, generating a body of work on the film's treatment of identity, postmodernity and society. Scott Bukatman's monograph in the British Film Institute's 'Modern Classics' series, *Blade Runner* (1997), remains an outstanding example for its rich complexity and imaginative, unexpected angles.

This book is, of course, an addition to that body of work, making the claim through its very existence that there is something more – a lot more – to say about this endlessly-analysed film and its surrounding intertexts. Judith Kerman's anthology, *Retrofitting Blade Runner* (1997), while still a key collection, is inevitably a study of the film's meanings at a specific cultural moment (it was first published in 1991), before 'Blade Runner' splintered and warped into such a host of different forms; the essays do not and could not consider websites, PC games or DVD editions, and even in the 1997 second edition the focus is primarily on the original version rather than the Director's Cut.

Many of the chapters in this volume deliberately explore the newer texts of *Blade Runner* and those who engage with them, while others discuss the 'after effects' of Ridley Scott's film, in terms of its considerable influence on the science fiction cinema of the last twenty years. A third approach is represented by the chapters that manage to find a new and original angle on the core texts of *Blade Runner* and *Blade Runner: The Director's Cut*; for instance, by examining Deckard as a working-class man and comparing his behaviour to that of the male protagonists in British social realist cinema, or taking a feminist perspective on the under-examined character of Rachel, reconsidering her as a variation on the female roles in film noir.

The book is divided into themed sections for convenience, although as will become apparent, many of the arguments and observations from one chapter weave through several others, picked up independently by different contributors and examined in different lights.

Following my opening study, in the next chapter, of *Blade Runner* fan-pilgrimage, Judith Kerman discusses the film in a new and unexpected cultural context, as the panic-stricken rumours of societal and technological break-down that circulated in the last months of 1999 lead her to consider it in terms of eschatology – the doctrine of the last or final things, the end of days. As she notes, *Retrofitting Blade Runner* was written at a time when 2000 (or 'the year two thousand' as it was quaintly called) seemed a long way off, but a reading prompted by pre-millennial hysteria and based on Biblical images of disaster, destruction and divine punishment yields fascinating parallels, and reveals that, just as its pyramids and ziggurats tower over the seedy, rain-soaked streets, *Blade Runner* resonates with archetypes dating from many centuries prior to the noir 1940s. The chosen ones have enjoyed an exodus to Off-World colonies, while the corrupt Earth below, punished by flood, also serves in replicant eyes as an Eden, site of their creation. Kerman shows that the film is layered with myths both ancient and modern: the canyons between skyscrapers in which we first find Deckard can be seen as both the confined realm of the noir detective and as Mitzrayim, the Hebrew term for the 'narrow place' of slaves and 'little people'. The problem with apocalyptic visions of the future, Kerman concludes, is that they free us of responsibility for resolving or avoiding them; either we will be saved or damned, and both possibilities offer a kind of liberty.

In the first section, Dominic Alessio and Aaron Barlow then trace shared concerns and imagery through the many films inspired by or based directly on the work of Phillip K. Dick, showing *Blade Runner* to be both a companion piece to recent movies such as *Minority Report* (2002) and *Paycheck* (2004) and an inspiration for many others such as *Strange Days* (1995), *Dark City* (1998) and *The Matrix* (1999). Barlow's intensive analysis of film texts and their production history finds uncredited borrowings or homages to Dick and *Blade Runner* in a vast range of examples, from *Brazil*'s images of humans overcome by 'kipple'[1] through to *Twelve Monkeys*' (1996) focus on the human eye and *Soldier*'s in-joke about the Shoulder of Orion to the terminatrix ap-pearing among shop mannequins in T3. Barlow concludes that Ridley Scott's engagement with Dick has shaped both the surface design and the fundamen-tal nature of science fiction over the last two decades.

Taking a slightly different tack through a comparison with *Total Recall* (1990) and other lesser-known PKD adaptations such as *Screamers* (1995) and *Impostor* (2002), Alessio finds intriguing tropes and themes in *Blade Runner* echoed and amplified. He draws out parallels with the Nazi far-right, elabo-rates on Kerman's religious analogies and argues that, in many of these films, humankind is far less humane than its artificial equivalent. Deckard can be seen as a brutal, cold assassin of 'skin-jobs', comparable to a bounty hunter rounding up black slaves in pre-Civil War America, while Batty, by contrast, exhibits love for his comrades and compassion for his opponent. Similarly, the deadly simulacra in *Screamers* are ironically judged more 'human' as they learn to slaughter each other rather than just their military enemy, and the mu-tants in *Total Recall*, like *Blade Runner*'s gang of replicants, show a sense of community and loyalty absent among their human counterparts. The Department of Pre-Crime's callous attitude to its precogs in *Minority Report* – 'better if you don't think of them as human' – echoes the Rep-Detect Department's euphemism of 'retirement', and the Earth militia of *Impostor*, dressed in Nazi-style uniform, are far less sympathetic than the alien-built replicants who flee them.

Barry Atkins and Susana Tosca then explore the 1997 Westwood PC game *Blade Runner*, considering the way it – like Jeter's novels – combines elements from the separate but similar worlds of the Scott film and the PKD novel, creating its own vision of LA 2019 and offering players the chance to explore that world more deeply, though with a limited degree of independence. In addition to successfully and pleasurably 'replicating' the film's diegesis, Atkins suggests, the game 'remediates' it, entering into dialogue with the original. Deckard's voice-activated use of the Esper, for instance, is adapted into a mouse-controlled interface whose ability to delve into an apparently flat photograph makes it a perfect microcosm of the game as a whole. One of *Blade Runner*'s outstanding features, according to Barlow, is its sense of a fully coherent, detailed environment, a tantalising glimpse of which is presented to the cinema viewer; Atkins proposes that the game gives the illusion of entering into that screen environment, the process of clicking, examining and zooming transforming a flat screen into 'depth' that only returns to mere surface when we, as player-detectives, have exhausted its possibilities and unearthed all its clues.

Tosca argues that the issue of humanity and empathy, as well as the film's key question of the protagonist's identity, is not just paramount within the game but becomes, in the absence of a genuine liberty to make choices about plot, the source of its main appeal. After completing the narrative, players return to complete it in different ways that alter the relationships between characters and explore the different emotional and psychological positions open to the protagonist, transforming him from cold-blooded 'rep killer' to sympathiser, to escaped replicant himself. Just as it allows us to peer more closely at details that, in the film, flitted quickly out of frame, the game allows us not just to consider debates around human identity but to enter into them and act them out.

The third section explores *Blade Runner* by learning from those who arguably know it best: its fans, whether amateur – with its meaning of intense love – academic, or straddling the flimsy boundary between the two. Jonathan Gray turns his attention to a version of the film more desirable and unattainable than any of the workprints, interviewing online fans about the as-yet-nonexistent Special Edition DVD, a 'text that is ... not yet a text' and finding out who they are through what they want in this ultimate edition. Gray discovers that these dedicated viewers also value the film for its power to immerse them in a detailed fictional world, which they want to keep alive and active through an improved re-release that both preserves the text, enriches it through additional material and, crucially, maintains its sense of *aperture* and ambiguity rather than closing down its meanings and resolving its debates.

Atkins quotes the film's screenwriters as claiming 'there is no definitive draft of *Blade Runner* and there never will be. Because it's not finished yet'; it is this open-endedness that Gray's group of fans cherish.

Matt Hills extends the definition of 'fan' to include those whose close study of the film text is traditionally dignified as 'theory' and distinguished from the supposedly geeky pursuit of the same practice when it occurs outside academia. He suggests that for scholars – just as Gray discovered with online fans – it is *Blade Runner*'s 'irresolution', its contradictions and mysteries, that lend it so readily to analysis, debate and 'poaching'. Hills points out that the film's appropriation by postmodern theorists leads to a situation where new academic work on the film refers more to the existing body of writing than to the film itself, even when they contradict each other, but also suggests that theoretical analysis of *Blade Runner* follows the fan practice of detection and examination, pleasurably echoing Deckard's role.

Christy Gray approaches yet another branch of *Blade Runner* fandom, comparing those who dedicate themselves primarily to the film with other groups devoted to Philip K. Dick and his novels. She finds reservations among the latter community towards *Blade Runner* as adaptation, with some criticising it for its loss of key elements such as Mercerism, mood organs and Deckard's longing for a real animal. Some of the ideas and characters cut or changed in the transition from novel to movie were reinstated by K. W. Jeter's series of sequels, which PKD fans treat with a mixture of sceptical resistance and guarded acceptance, regarding them as 'copies of a copy', and valuable primarily for their possible role in bringing readers to Dick's work. Aficionados of Ridley Scott's film, on the other hand, seem caught between a drive to devour any new *Blade Runner* text, eagerly taking every opportunity – faced with a lack of motion-picture sequels – to explore the film's extended universe, and a disappointment in the books as a cynical prostitution of the film's premise and concepts.

Jeter's novels, the Westwood PC game, recent adaptations and the potential offered by the DVD format clearly invite fresh perspectives on *Blade Runner* that would have been impossible at the time of the Director's Cut release, let alone at the original movie's inception. Questions of identity, on the other hand, have always been at the heart of the film, and in the next section the contributors face the challenge of approaching the central text, rather than its sidequels, spin-offs and other intertexts, in a new way.

Deborah Jermyn points out that it is Rachel's arrival, as much as Deckard's voice-over, that first signals *Blade Runner* as a 'future noir'. She argues that the character, largely neglected in existing academic analyses, warrants greater recognition for the role she plays in the film's central philosophical preoccupation with what it is to be human. Returning to feminist theories that celebrated the femme fatale and 'spider woman' in the 1970s, Jermyn's close reading positions Rachel at the core of the film. Her analysis illuminates *Blade Runner*'s heroine as an ambiguous figure who destabilises patriarchal categories of either predatory schemer or sexual innocent, while her appearance and behaviour at different moments evoke 1940s film heroines such as *Mildred Pierce* (1945) and *Gilda* (1946). Jermyn concludes that Rachel's unsettling role as both replicant and rescuer, interrogator and interrogated, haunts our memories of the film in complex ways, making her one of *Blade Runner's* most poignant and resonant characters.

Sean Redmond notes *Blade Runner's* noir influences, but also identifies a fascinating parallel between Deckard and the angry young men of British Social Realist cinema. Like the protagonists of *Saturday Night and Sunday Morning* (1960), *Naked* (1993) and *Nil by Mouth* (1997), Redmond proposes, Deckard is tormented by his working-class roots and his inability to escape them; hating the city streets though he knows he belongs there, hating those he hunts though he knows he is one of them. This interpretation finds both physical and emotional class struggle beneath the technological glitter of Los Angeles 2019, with Deckard as the blue-collar hero of noir desiring the replicant daughter of the technocrat, briefly rising above the 'little people' but always returning to the ghetto where we first discover him. The film is in part a story of people trying to find their place in society – a history and a future – but Redmond concludes that Deckard's transgressive relationship with Rachel is short-lived, doomed to failure.

Redmond's themes are, to an extent, picked up by Nick Lacey's description of Deckard as an alienated worker finding no reward in his job, hitting the bottle too often and bordering on assault in his attempts at romance. Rather than focusing primarily on masculinity or the role of women in *Blade Runner*, though, Lacey is concerned with the union of the two, and the formation of the heterosexual couple. He argues that despite *Blade Runner's* continued role as a primer of postmodernism, the film only engages with postmodernism as an aesthetic, and fails to follow its implications through to a more fundamental, political level. *Blade Runner* exhibits pastiche and eclecticism on the surface, but puts all its faith in the power of romantic love between fully-formed human subjects, allowing them – in the original version at least – to escape the city and enjoy a redemptive happy ending. Lacey identifies a similarly traditional, timidly bourgeois trajectory in other recent 'postmodern' cinema, including *Dark City*, *The Matrix* and *The Truman Show* (1998). While Barlow notes the visual and thematic connections between these films and *Blade Runner*, Lacey groups them together for their inability to show the deeper consequences of postmodernism – a decentred self without history or identity, incapable of romantic union – and finds the true nature of the 'posthuman', resisting easy closure, only in independent cinema such as *Crash* (1996), *Memento* (2000) and *Donnie Darko* (2001).

When William Gibson used the film's title as a verb, though, he did not mean that Tokyo was a site of working-class masculinity or noir women, that it questioned humanity's values or felt like a computer game with a limited, branching narrative. *Blade Runner*, to Gibson, implies the city: Ridleyville, with its retrofitting, used technology, grubby add-ons and pollution damage. It was *Blade Runner's* vision of the city, escaping clichéd images of an implausibly clean utopia or impossibly changed urban environment, that most shaped the design of subsequent science fiction like *Minority Report* and *Strange Days*, and inevitably, many of the chapters in this collection return to Los Angeles 2019, often from different directions.

Of course, one of the key points of reference is noir, which as Judith Kerman notes, treated LA as its 'home locale'; while she sees Biblical flood and flaming towers in what the film's effects team named the 'Hades landscape' (Sammon 1996: 231), Kerman acknowledges that the hero of the hard-boiled 1940s detective story would soon feel comfortable here. Noir, in Kerman's view, also lends the film its sense of apocalyptic helplessness, as the private-eye protagonist has no hope of changing the system itself or seeing it changed, whether by act of God or revolution: his victory is merely to understand and then to survive. Aaron Barlow argues along similar lines that the earlier film movement invested *Blade Runner* with paranoia and ambiguity; the danger always close to home in the form of the friend or the femme fatale, rather than easily-identified in a distinctly alien Other. It was this blurring of distinctions between good and evil, Barlow suggests, that shifted science fiction from the clear-cut dichotomies of *Star Wars: Episode IV – A New Hope* (1977) to *Cube* (1997), *Twelve Monkeys* and even *Star Wars: Episode I – The Phantom Menace* (1999), where the series' villain Darth Vader is transformed into an innocent child.

To Nick Lacey, the city's aesthetic of recycling, its architecture a visual echo of Gaff's cut and paste dialect, illustrates the film's surface-level spectacle of postmodernism. Atkins, as noted above, describes the game as a means for investigating the depths and details beneath this flatness, in a way that the cinema's screen denies. Redmond also finds Los Angeles to be a patchwork of postcards and travel images from other places, other films, but his reading of *Blade Runner* in class terms leads him to focus on its references to *Metropolis* (1927), with the city's rulers far above street level and the workers teeming on the lower levels. For Redmond, the eclectic mix of styles and periods makes for a fluidly shifting, 'leaky' city where the characters find it hard to get a grip on history and identity, and are denied any social bonding or comradeship.

It is perhaps one of the film's greatest ironies, then, that a city with such an influence on both cinema production and analysis has so little basis in reality. Kerman recognises the paradox when, after describing the real-life Los Angeles of 2004 as 'arguably the most American (or least European) of all major American cities, the one most designed by and for the automobile and the suburb' she turns her attention to the film and muses that 'this LA appears changed almost beyond recognition...'. In a sense, the lack of resemblance is hardly surprising, given the history of *Blade Runner*'s fictional city before it was filmed. Philip K. Dick's novel had Deckard working for the San Francisco police department, which Scott, during the film's development, relocated to 'San Angeles', a megalopolis along the Western Seaboard 'with giant cities and monolithic buildings at either end, and then this strange, kind of awful suburb in the middle' (Ridley Scott quoted in Sammon 1996: 75).

In a 1982 interview with *Cinefex*, Scott was still promising that the movie would be set 'on the East Coast because it's raining so much' (see Sammon 1996: 76). The reasons for the shift to New York, then, were pragmatic – the city's location had to match the look, and climate, of the film – and a similarly practical rationale lay behind the final move back to Los Angeles, as the production team cut a deal to shoot on the Warner Bros. lot and on select locations within the city. Ridleyville ended up as an unnerving compromise, resisting real-life geography: East Coast weather drenched distinctive LA landmarks like the Bradbury Building, and Manhattan-style towerblocks replaced the more authentically West Coast 'awful suburb'. The lack of congruence between Rick Deckard's beat and the real Los Angeles of either the 1980s, 1990s or twenty-first century becomes especially clear when we compare *Blade Runner* with other movies set in the city – not just noir like *Double Indemnity* (1944) and *Mildred Pierce*, but the Richard Gere remake of *Breathless* (1983), near-future science fiction like the *Terminator* trilogy (1984, 1991, 2003), neo-noir like *LA Confidential* (1997) and gangster movies like *Pulp Fiction* (1994) and *Heat* (1995) – all of which show an LA that maps onto the real thing and proves recognisable from one film to the next, while bearing only remote resemblance to Ridley Scott's creation. Even *Who Framed Roger Rabbit* (1988) and *Shrek 2* (2004), nominally set in Toontown and Far Far Away,[2] are obviously Los Angeles through a distorting mirror: *Blade Runner's* city, by contrast, could be anywhere from New York through London's Canary Wharf to, as Gibson illustrates, contemporary Tokyo.

Stephen Rowley neatly sums up this contradiction early in his chapter, opening the final section on 'The City'; he places 'Los Angeles 2019' in quotation marks, indicating the unlikelihood of this particular future ever coming to pass. While the setting remains central to the film's appeal and identity, and has become so entrenched, in his words, as the definitive screen dystopia – he names *The Fifth Element* (1997), *Batman* (1989) and *Star Wars: Episode II – Attack of the Clones* (2002) as examples of its influence – 'what is interesting is that *Blade Runner's* future should continue to have such purchase despite not showing any particular signs of materialising'. A thorough search for geographical references in Ridleyville, Rowley argues, could find traces of Los Angeles in the smoggy vistas outside Tyrell's windows, but overwhelmingly the film's locale recalls a future New York, crammed with skyscrapers on a World Trade Center scale and commercial neon in the style of Times Square. Its most immediate cinematic echoes are to be found in New York fictions like *Taxi Driver* (1976) rather than noir, which, he argues, tended increasingly to send its hero out to the LA suburbs rather than have him trudge a dark downtown.

Rowley, like Lacey, also reconsiders the assumption that *Blade Runner* epitomises the postmodern city, and points out that by failing to conform to the clean lines and ordered networks of the International Style, Los Angeles 2019 serves as a modernist dystopia, a blueprint for what to avoid; he further reminds us that, as Scott Bukatman pointed out, another form of modernism identified and embraced the street-level dynamic and thrilling chaos of

Deckard's Animoid Row. Drawing on theories of urban planning, Rowley reaches the intriguing conclusion that while present-day Los Angeles falls nightmarishly short of contemporary models of community-based, pedestrian-friendly, vibrant urban living, *Blade Runner*'s Los Angeles 'doesn't look too bad after all': unlike LA in 2005, it has a downtown with great bars and restaurants, a street-life where people know your name and an effective public transportation system. Scott's vision is unlikely to come true on the West Coast, but as Rowley wryly proposes, this is real-life's loss.

In this collection's last chapter, Peter Brooker's discussion of *Blade Runner*'s LA as an 'urban imaginary' chimes with themes from the diverse chapters that precede it. Like Matt Hills, Brooker suggests that *Blade Runner*'s fiction is not just referred to alongside theoretical texts, but deferred to as an authoritative vision of future geography and an exemplar for understanding our own cities. As such, *Blade Runner* blurs the distinction between real and imaginary – non-fiction theory and speculative storytelling – just as it refuses clear-cut separation between other binaries like apocalyptic Hell and sunny paradise, West and East, utopic and dystopic metropolis, 'cold' replicant and 'empathetic' human being.

Brooker, in common with Rowley, cites the complaint of cultural geographer Mike Davis that Los Angeles has already developed beyond *Blade Runner*'s now-outdated vision of the city. Davis – finding shared ground here with Edward W. Soja – looks to a different model of future urban living, based on localised communities and co-operative labour, and prefers the near-future fictions of William Gibson's *Virtual Light* (1993) and *All Tomorrow's Parties* (1999). Gibson's close extrapolations from 1990s culture provide a more relevant template for considering the West Coast in the twenty-first century, Davis argues, than the 'gothic romance' of Ridley Scott's speculation.

As a re-release of an early-1980s film, *Blade Runner: The Director's Cut* inevitably failed to engage with the racial tensions of Los Angeles in 1992, and offered no comment on or reflection of the city's descent into a different type of nightmare: gated communities barricading rich from poor, gang warfare, and decades of resentment and frustration exploding into the LA riots. Yet Brooker argues, in a revisiting of the debates around the protagonist's status, that the relationship between the two blade runners Deckard and Gaff reveals a 'post-human' affinity and shared experience; Gaff may seem to read Deckard's mind, but Deckard also hears Gaff's voice in his own head, replacing the hard-boiled commentary. Gaff's origami unicorn in the film's final moments becomes not a taunt from a superior position but a sign of brotherhood, and Deckard's nod shows he recognises their kinship: the white cop and his 'American-Japanese-Mexican' colleague are not ethnic others but joined in a hybrid territory between replicant and human, their unconscious populated by the same archetypes. Gaff, within this interpretation, also dreams of unicorns. By reopening this moment in the film, Brooker shows that *Blade Runner*'s urban imaginary still has provocative insights and suggestions to guide our contemporary understanding of the city and the way we live within it.

NOTES

1 'Kipple' is Philip K. Dick's invented term for junk, clutter and accumulated trash that slowly invades human environments, seeming to reproduce itself.
2 *Shrek 2* includes a 'Far Far Away' pastiche of the Hollywood sign, and the 'Toontown' section of Disneyland has the same visual joke.

THE *BLADE RUNNER* EXPERIENCE: PILGRIMAGE AND LIMINAL SPACE
WILL BROOKER

> Part of *Blade Runner*'s genius lies in the creation of such an elaborately re-
> alistic vision of the future LA. What made that vision so realistic was the in-
> corporation of elements from the past, and their elaboration. By now, pretty
> much everyone knows that shit is never going to look like *The Jetsons*. The
> people who made *Blade Runner* knew that any future Los Angeles, in addi-
> tion to looking 'futuristic', will also look old.
>
> – Brian Webb (2004: 21)

Brian Webb, writing in the *LA Alternative Press* during late July 2004, shows the grip that Ridley Scott's future metropolis still holds on the popular imagination, even among hip young Los Angelenos who might be expected to regard the movie sceptically if they remembered it at all. As noted in the Introduction, the *Blade Runner* city shifted from coast to coast throughout the film's development; built around Manhattan skyscrapers, showered with Eastern climate, shot primarily on the Warner Bros. 'Old New York Street', and only nominally set in California for pragmatic reasons of location permissions. *Blade Runner* is not a symphony to the real Los Angeles; the title card identifying the city was a necessity, not an aesthetic choice. As production executive Katy Haber explained to Paul Sammon, 'you couldn't set a film in New York and then show Harrison Ford driving up to the Bradbury Building without people in Los Angeles laughing us out of the theater' (Sammon 1996: 76).

Reading Webb's review during a ten-day research trip to LA, I was surprised that a local journalist would still see *Blade Runner* as representing a possible future for the real city, would still treat its speculations as relevant, worthy of respect, and above all, would consider it 'realistic'. Los Angeles, July 2004 was worlds away from 'Los Angeles, November 2019'. My last visit to the city had been in 1979, before Ridley Scott even committed himself to the project, and *Blade Runner* had, in the decades following, begun to edge into my memories of the real LA, its dense, richly-textured fictional world almost coming to seem a stylised but plausible version of the actual location. I arrived in Los Angeles expecting to recognise something of the film's diegesis – if not actual landmarks, then a more general culture and atmosphere.

Within hours I realised the extent to which *Blade Runner*'s LA is divorced from the real city of today. The temperature was in the nineties, and the Southern California forests into which Deckard and Rachel escape in the original cut were raging with wildfire. Instead of vast Japanese advertisement hoardings, the billboards along the endless avenues varied with the neighbourhood, passing through English to Korean and Spanish. A mere half-dozen skyscrapers clustered in the business district Downtown – one of them, the tall cylinder of the US Bank, matching up vaguely to *Blade Runner*'s police tower – but most of the city was low-level sprawl. Elderly Asian women stepped carefully along the sidewalks carrying parasols, rather than neon umbrellas. *Blade Runner* offers a single glimpse of blue sky through the rain and steam; here it was a constant behind the silhouetted lines of palm trees. This was more Superman's Metropolis than Gotham City.

This chapter is a case study in cultural pilgrimage. I examine my own, sometimes naïve, responses to the real LA in relation to *Blade Runner*'s fiction, with specific reference to the four key sites in Los Angeles where scenes from the film were shot – the 2nd Street road tunnel, Union Station, the Ennis-Brown House and the Bradbury Building – and compare my responses to the testimonies of three other pilgrims: Ben Mund and Don Solosan, two online fans whom I interviewed by email, and the broadcaster Mark Kermode, whose documentary *On the Edge of Blade Runner*, directed by Andrew Abbot, was screened by Channel 4 in 2000.[1]

My key theoretical reference here is Roger C. Aden's model of pilgrimage in his book *Popular Stories and Promised Lands* (1999), and specifically the concept of the liminal (or 'liminoid'), which he develops from the work of anthropologist Victor Turner. While Turner applied the term to tribal rites of passage and Aden, perhaps surprisingly, deals mainly with 'symbolic' pilgrimages – watching a television show and losing oneself in it, rather than trekking to an actual location – their insights also provide a strong basis for examining the physical travel of fan pilgrimage. My understanding of my own, and others', *Blade Runner* experience benefited significantly from Aden's research, but it also threw up new ideas, suggestions and avenues for further discussion.

Broadly speaking, Aden, following Turner,[2] views pilgrimage as a three-part process. We depart from the habitus – Pierre Bourdieu's term (1986), implying the common-sense norms and conventions that confine us in everyday life – and transcend our normal existence through popular narratives that transport us to a 'promised land', often in the company, whether literally or symbolically, of a fan community. Returning, we are newly equipped to gain perspective on and deal with the structures of dominance and containment, perhaps evading them through 'tactics' and 'micropolitics', to use terms favoured by Michel de Certeau (1984) and John Fiske (1989) respectively, and possibly making significant material changes.

On our journey to and from the 'promised land', where we lose ourselves and become immersed in the favoured text or site, we are in a stage of inbetweenness, a state of transition. It is this idea of a neither-nor zone, outside the everyday but not overwhelmed by total connection to the sacred, that proved most relevant to my study of *Blade Runner*'s real-life locations and their relationship to the fictional, on-screen construction of those places. Turner calls this state the liminal, from the Latin '*limen*' or threshold:

During the ...'liminal' period, the characteristics of the ritual subject (the 'passenger') are ambiguous; he passes through a cultural realm that has few or none of the attributes of the past or coming state. (1969: 94)

Aden elaborates on this concept:

In rites of passage liminality refers to the indescribable time when the individual has left the past but has not yet arrived at his/her destination. This passage of time also marks a spatial change, for completing a rite of passage typically allows the participant to claim a new place in the cultural terrain. Liminality is the time of the journey encompassed by the leaving, arrival and return – exclusive of the moment of separation upon leaving and the moment of reaggregation upon return; departure and return mark not only points of time outside of the liminal but points in a cultural space where one's place or position is settled. Liminality is 'a movement between fixed points [that] is essentially ambiguous, unsettled, and unsettling'; it is 'a no-place and no-time that resists classification'. (1999: 81)

Accepting Turner's argument that 'liminal' implies a mandatory social ritual, Aden takes on the term 'liminoid' to describe an optional, more playful search for alternatives to everyday life. Strictly speaking, as fan pilgrimages are a matter of personal choice during leisure time and a deliberate decision to seek out other ways of seeing, the latter term would apply to my study; but I am using 'liminal' and 'liminality' here for their greater elegance and less specialised meaning.

I am arguing two initial points about the experience of pilgrimage to the Los Angeles locations where *Blade Runner* was shot. Firstly, that because of their coding as either everyday places – a railway station, a road tunnel – or as architectural sites of interest, and because of the extent to which Ridley Scott's production team transformed and set-dressed them into LA 2019, these locations do not offer a fully immersive, transcendent experience, a sense of fully 'losing oneself' such as Aden describes in relation to other pilgrimage sites. Instead, they can only provide a less heightened feeling of inbetweenness, of an ambiguous, liminal state bridging the real LA of the present and the fictional city of the future. While these travellers do achieve distance from their everyday lives and partially escape the 'real' world, they never reach the peak of intense connection with the 'promised land'. They are, in Turner's words, 'betwixt and between' (Turner & Turner 1978: 249): they stand on the threshold of *Blade Runner*.

Singling out this distinct experience – where pilgrims never quite make a sacred connection but instead hover on the borders between actual and fictional, holding both in a double-vision of alternate realities – provides a basis for thinking about a distinct category of pilgrimage locations, where total immersion is difficult or impossible. As opposed to the *Field of Dreams* cornfield described by Aden (1999: 219–49), where the real site is carefully preserved and presented exactly as it was in the movie, allowing a departure from the real world into the myth – as opposed, also, to simulacra-sites like the *Coronation Street* 'Rover's Return' pub (see Hills 2002: 146; Urry 2002: 130), which offer a convincing experience of entering a fictional diegesis despite being mere reconstructions of the 'real' shooting set – sites like the *Blade Runner* locations demand a significant amount of emotional commitment and imaginative work on the pilgrim's part to even approach a sense of communion with the fictional text.[3] This category, comprising an important sub-genre of pilgrimage sites, would include the otherwise-unremarkable hills of Tunisia that became Tatooine homesteads in the *Star Wars* saga, the Scottish landscapes filmed as Hogwarts and its environs in the *Harry Potter* series, the stretches of New Zealand where *Lord of the Rings* townships were built, then taken down, and mundane houses that become special only when a fan drives past and projects upon them the knowledge that their idol once lived there (see Cavicchi 1998: 171 on Bruce Springsteen's residence, and Hills 2002: 148–9 on Vancouver as an *X-Files* location).

My second point at this stage is that the three testimonies of *Blade Runner* fan-pilgrimage I am using for my study seem unconsciously to recognise this liminal state, and explicitly, though I think not deliberately, capture a sense of inbetweenness, bridging the two versions of LA but never quite bringing them together.

Blade Runner's LA 2019 shifts the real city forward in time, of course, but it also blatantly warps its space. This lack of correspondence between the city's geography and the four key locations filmed as LA 2019 leads to a fundamental disorientation for the visitor – the movie was shot at 'real' locations in Los Angeles, but they become entirely different places.

The police station in *Blade Runner* is housed within a downtown skyscraper; Union Station, where this scene was shot, is a Mission-style building, a white church structure fronted with palm trees across the road from *El Pueblo*

Union Station exterior

Ennis-Brown exterior

2nd Street tunnel exterior   Bradbury exterior

de Los Angeles, the city's most visibly Spanish district. Deckard's apartment is on the ninety-seventh floor of a tower-block, accessed through an elevator; the Ennis-Brown house, used for the apartment's exteriors, is an imposingly eccentric Frank Lloyd-Wright construction, a crumbling Mayan temple built into a North Hollywood hill with luxury mansions for neighbours. The tunnel Deckard traverses on his way home is nowhere near the Ennis-Brown; in the film it looks like a long subterranean conduit, while today's daylight reveals it as a modest passage, located in view of Disney Hall's gleaming curves, that takes less than a minute to drive through. Finally, the Bradbury, which became J. F. Sebastian's abandoned block of residences, is tucked unassumingly into a street of downmarket wedding dress outlets and cut-price chapels offering both marriage and divorce. *Blade Runner* has not lifted the real LA to cinema, respecting its layout and spatial relationships between places; it has selectively picked out interiors and transferred them into an entirely new creative geography that makes no sense in 'real' terms.[4]

I would make another suggestion: in cases such as this, where the fictional location is a mismatch with the real, *it is the real that feels 'wrong'*. The pilgrim approaches the actual site with a template of expectations based on the fictional representation, and if the destination fails to measure up, the real location, not the fantastical construction of set dressing, props, lighting and effects built on that site, is found wanting. This is a similar phenomenon to that described by John Urry with regard to postcard and brochure images of a location and the sometimes-disappointing revelation when the tourist arrives:

> Much of what is appreciated is not directly experienced reality itself but representations, particularly through the medium of photography ... What people 'gaze upon' are ideal representations of the view in question that they internalise from postcards and guidebooks (and TV programmes and the internet). And even when they cannot in fact 'see' the natural wonder in question they can still sense it, see it in their mind. And even when the object fails to live up to its representation it is the latter which will stay in people's minds, as what they have really 'seen'. (2002: 78)

In Urry's example, the idealised, internalised versions seen beforehand retain their dominance in the hierarchy of images, replacing the real even in memory afterwards. I am proposing, in the case of *Blade Runner* locations, that pilgrims approach with this hierarchy in mind and judge the real places accordingly, but that the previously-internalised image then becomes dislodged and has to be held alongside the new impression: again suggesting a liminality, a position between either-or, neither-nor alternates. 'Deckard's apartment', after the pilgrimage, will call to mind a composite between the sun-baked Ennis-Brown house up on the hill and the intriguingly similar, but frustratingly different, shots in *Blade Runner* of the building's rain-soaked exterior, enhanced and disguised by matte painting. Memories of the former are satisfying and enriching in that they fill out a three-dimensional, concrete 'reality' behind the brief cinema image, but they still fail to map cleanly onto the re-viewed scene in the film. The concept of 'Deckard's apartment' after the pilgrimage becomes a stereoscopic vision of two partially-compatible versions that can, with a squint and a shift, be made to blur into a central overlap. At a later stage in this chapter I will suggest a third term that mediates between the two and helps to bridge them.

I stated above that *Blade Runner* selected interiors, lifting them from their real-world context and relocating them in a largely-imaginary LA. This disjuncture between the entirely unfamiliar exterior and the at least vaguely-recognisable inside adds to the pilgrim's sense of transition, of entering the fictional world and leaving the real behind; or, as I am arguing with the *Blade Runner* experience, finding oneself in a mid-way position between the two. In the case of Union Station, the Bradbury and the 2nd Street tunnel, the exterior surprises – and, as suggested, potentially disappoints – because of its lack of any correspondence to the screen location. The Ennis-Brown house is a different, almost opposite, case because its outside walls were used for the *Blade Runner* shots and inspired Syd Mead's production design for the studio-built interior; here the exterior is familiar and the inside, open for guided tours, shares only its Mayan tile-design with Deckard's apartment.

I further argued that these specific locations cannot offer a fully immersive experience or transcendence from the 'real' into the fictional world. This is partly due to their multiple coding as far more than merely *Blade Runner* sites. The cab drivers who took me to the Bradbury and, obligingly slowly, down the 2nd street tunnel, had never heard of the movie. Heritage signs outside the Bradbury detail its origins – architect George Herbert Wyman's instructions via Ouija board and the inspiration he took from Edward Bellamy's *Looking Backward* (1888) – its continued use by the LAPD's Internal Affairs division, and its use in the film *Wolf* (1994). The interior, far brighter, cleaner and narrower than *Blade Runner* suggests – Scott, determined to make his use of the building startling and original (Sammon 1996: 139), transformed it into a 'kipple'-ridden, searchlit warehouse – is closed to the public from the second floor upwards; apart from the security guards, those visiting the building and sharing the space with the *Blade Runner* pilgrim are residents and workers.

Bradbury interior   Union Station interior

Tourists wandering the ground floor and first flight of stairs may be fellow *Blade Runner* fans, but without any obvious way of identifying them, they could equally have been drawn to the architecture and design, to one of the city's key 'sights' or to the location's role in a variety of movies from *Citizen Kane* (1941) and *Double Indemnity* (1944) to *Lethal Weapon 4* (1998).

Similarly, information boards at Union Station's Grand Concourse – although mounted on leftover panels from Bryant's office – highlight the building's combination of architectural styles including Spanish Colonial and Streamline Moderne, and its use in *Guilty by Suspicion* (1990), *Bugsy* (1991), *House Party II* (1991) and various commercials, with 'the futuristic film *Blade Runner*' earning a single mention. Of course, the station is busy with travellers taking the Metro, most of whom walk straight past the concourse; the space is, again, closed off to the general public and used mainly for wedding receptions. For some engaged or married couples then, the '*Blade Runner* police station' will acquire a very different meaning. Finally, the Ennis-Brown house is, like the Bradbury, notable in its own right for its design and construction, with *Blade Runner* and other movies like *House on Haunted Hill* (1999) a mere footnote in its history.

Again, one site serves as an exception. The 2nd Street tunnel is a practical route for thousands of drivers every day – my cabbie was thoroughly bemused when I told him I wanted to take photos of it – primarily serving a pragmatic transport purpose like Union Station. However, its glistening, eerily green walls clearly needed no set dressing, lighting or mattes to transform it for *Blade Runner*, and as the pilgrim can closely emulate what Deckard was actually doing in the shot – driving through traffic – this location alone does offer a sense of participatory immersion, allowing the visitor to perform the text and 'become' Deckard for the length of the transit between Hill and Figueroa. Fittingly, of course, the tunnel itself is an inbetween zone, providing a brief but uncanny illusion of being swallowed into *Blade Runner*'s underworld as it bridges the sunlit streets of present-day LA.

The majority of LA's *Blade Runner* locations, however, refuse to allow the pilgrim what John Urry, after Turner, calls 'direct experience of the sacred or

2nd Street tunnel interior   Don Solosan's shot of the Grand Concourse

supernatural' (2002: 11) – in this case, a transcendent connection with the mythic world of the fictional text. They also limit the possibilities for another experience integral to the 'promised land': that of 'communitas', an intense bonding and sharing of the pilgrimage and the connection with the sacred place. Turner uses this Latin term, preferring it to the English equivalent 'community', to describe a minimally structured group of 'equal individuals' that 'emerges recognisably in the liminal period' (1969: 96) and Aden applies it widely to his own case studies.

On a solo visit to the *Blade Runner* sites, the pilgrim has no way of knowing whether the others wandering the space are there for the same reason, because each site continues to have at least one other connotation; often one that overshadows its role as a one-time location for a 1982 science fiction movie. Sharing the *Blade Runner* experience, I will suggest below, is likely to come after the fact, when the pilgrim has returned home: a symbolic communitas that Aden views as entirely valid – he uses the term broadly, to describe the sense of knowing that one's colleagues are also watching a television show, or of imagining a friend reading the same book (1999: 94–5) – but one that is likely to fall short of the intensity found in a sharing of the sacred place at the time.

The lack of opportunity for communitas at the sites themselves further restricts the possibility for the pilgrim to experience an overwhelming feeling of transcendence, and further confirms this specific type of pilgrimage experience as distinct from that described by Aden. Again, I would suggest that this form of pilgrimage, which achieves a sense of the liminal but falls short of two key conditions associated with reaching the promised land – an immersive connection with the sacred place, and communitas, a liberating bonding and comradeship with fellow-travellers – constitutes a significant sub-category that could be explored further in relation to other fan journeys.

I want to back up some of my assertions now by drawing on the testimonies of other *Blade Runner* pilgrims. Ben Mund has an article reporting on his tour and advising the best route to others on www.bladezone.com;, and Don Solosan, under the name Gnomus, took the photographs and contributed his observations for an uncredited article at www.brmovie.com.[5] I contacted both individuals by email and communicated with them extensively during June and July 2004.

The brmovie.com page on Union Station gives a distinct sense of liminal inbetweenness; there is a constant straining to emulate the film's treatment of the space, to inhabit its world, and yet a repeated falling-back to the 'real' location. Solosan's photographs, interspersed with screengrabs from *Blade Runner*, deliberately copy Ridley Scott's camerawork, but tellingly, fail to capture the exact view:

> The first picture above is emulating the scene about 12 minutes in (although of course the angle of the camera on the crane can't be duplicated). The teller windows are to the left. This shot shows the entrance to the Grand Concourse in the distance, which is blocked off so tourists can't wander in (I took this shot through a window, in case you're wondering).

> The above three photographs are of the Grand Concourse. This would be the point of view that Deckard would have had when he entered.[6]

Note that Solosan had to manoeuvre even to attempt a recreation of the film's crane shot, and despite ingeniously taking his photograph through a window was unable to reproduce its angle. The next paragraph performs a different kind of manoeuvre, one that the *Blade Runner* pilgrim will have to practice repeatedly: as the exact point of view is impossible to reach, the fan is obliged to compromise. Here we are told that rather than reproducing the film's shot, the photograph captures what Deckard would have seen as he crossed the room – apart, of course, from the fact that the distinctive lighting and set dressing, not to mention Bryant's office, are missing.[7]

Ben Mund's page 'LA 2019 on $50 A Day', written and researched independently for a different website, expresses a very similar range of reservations and recommendations around the station as a site for *Blade Runner* pilgrimage:

> I wasn't sure what to expect here. After all, it's a working bus and train station. From the outside the huge windows make it look more like a church than an oppressive, grungy center for replicant killers and riot-geared cops.

> Going through the front doors, you'll see an information desk in front of you and a large, empty room to your left. That's the 2019 LAPD headquarters. It's not open to the public, but it's still used for filming and for wedding receptions.

> The view you get is opposite from the one you see in the film. In fact, you'll be walking the same route Deckard did on his way to Bryant's office.[8]

Once more, there is an explicit attempt at emulation and immersion that simultaneously acknowledges a certain falling-short: Mund's guide encourages the visitor to 'become' Deckard, seeing his point of view, as a substitute for the fact that the familiar screen image – the director's, the camera's and ultimately the *Blade Runner* viewer's perspective on this scene – is impossible to recreate. Significantly, this does not stop both Mund and Solosan from photographing the location from the restricted available angles, trying to either reproduce the *Blade Runner* shot as closely as possible or explore what the characters would conceivably have seen.

Indeed, having a visual record of the sites seems as important to these pilgrims as photographs are to replicants and Rick Deckard. Both Solosan and Mund took stills and video footage of the locations – the latter perhaps demonstrating an even more avid need to commune with *Blade Runner* through its own medium of moving pictures. 'One of the things I did a few years ago', Solosan told me in an email interview (7 July 2004), 'was to watch the film and roughly sketch some of the framings and angles used in shooting the locations. Then I took my camera and tried to figure out where they shot from and to recreate what they did.' Mund, by contrast, chose the perspective of character, rather than director. 'I videotaped a few brief "Deckard P.O.V." segments that gave the view Deckard would have seen as he entered these locations' (email interview, 21 June 2004).

Both experiments inevitably result in a sense of not-quiteness: just as Solosan's version of Ridley Scott's point of view cannot duplicate the film's crane shot, so Mund's shot of what Deckard would have seen will look, to anyone outside this fan community and many inside it, like the ornately-tiled concourse of a railway station. His subtitle, 'LAPD 2019', seems almost incongruous beneath the picture of Union Station without the lighting and set design that would make it recognisable as Bryant's base of operations; between the caption and the image is the leap of faith required to transform these real-life locations into the spaces of *Blade Runner*. However, it is the banner heading of his tour-guide page that most explicitly, though again perhaps unconsciously, expresses this neither-nor liminal state: the words 'A Tale of Two Cities'[9] spread across a montage of LA's sunlit downtown (of 2002) on the left and the dark, hellish landscape of oil refineries that opens Scott's film. Again, the experience of standing in one of *Blade Runner*'s LA locations is echoed in the viewer's unsettled glance between these two alternatives, or in the blurred central overlap.

A remarkably similar sense of the liminal zone between contemporary LA and the fictional future-city is created by the documentary *On the Edge of Blade Runner*, presented by Mark Kermode. Through various techniques – like a close pastiche of Vangelis's score segueing into the original soundtrack, and interviews with the production team that bathe them in blinking neon or survey their faces, Voigt-Kampff style, on security monitors within the shot – the programme emulates the aesthetic of the film, drawing 'real-life' footage from the late 1990s very effectively into the cinematic diegesis. The illusion is helped by the fact that *Blade Runner* itself includes a number of interviews and shots of video screens; Deckard's police detection and Kermode's TV journalism are, in their project to uncover a 'truth' through interrogation of subjects and close examination of visual texts, not leagues apart. Indeed, it is in the documentary's appropriation of Esper technology that it most cleverly simulates the *Blade Runner* style.

Taking the example of Union Station again, the sequence opens with Kermode introducing the location in a voice-over – again, a common technique in documentary, but also, in this context, inevitably recalling the noir hero's hard-bitten, cynical narration and specifically Deckard's commentary over the original cut of *Blade Runner*. Kermode's laid-back drawl is more London gangster than Californian private eye, but his script is clearly aiming at the dry lyricism of noir: earlier in the programme he explains that 'Deckard's turf is identified simply as Los Angeles 2019, a logical extension of that pollutedly glittering skyline, but peppered with nuances of New York architecture, and drenched in typically Eastern rain.'[10]

As Kermode notes that Union Station became the police headquarters 'where Captain Bryant first sets Deckard on the trail of the errant replicants', we cut to a shot of him in the Grand Concourse, dressed in a vaguely retro grey suit with a crisp white shirt and dark tie, his hair neatly moulded into a Brylcreem quiff. This almost-1940s outfit, resisting exact period but again evoking the noir hero, is a performance like the voice-over – perhaps more subtle than that practiced by fans who parade as *Star Wars* stormtroopers, but nevertheless a dressing-up intended to bring Kermode closer to, if not actually positioning him within, the fictional diegesis. 'The suit was a constant for all the links to camera,' Kermode explained;

> I made a decision about an outfit that would work with the film, in keeping with that slightly 1940s look. The hair is just what my hair looks like normally, but the suit was cut in that specific way … it was something I thought about deliberately and bought specifically for the documentary. It had to be in keeping with *Blade Runner*, with those locations. You don't want to be wandering around in a black leather jacket and jeans. (personal interview, 20 August 2004)

The concourse, however, still barely resembles the police hall from *Blade Runner*, and it is telling that Kermode's voice-over has to explain its use in the film rather than simply presenting it and letting the location speak for itself. Also worth noting is the fact that, despite the production team's resources, they too could not reproduce Ridley Scott's crane shot from the ceiling; like Mund's photograph, they settle for a position on ground level, clearly striving to echo *Blade Runner* but falling short of the precise angle, and in so doing – intentionally or otherwise – evoking inbetweenness, almost-thereness, not-quiteness. 'With any documentary about cinema', Kermode stressed in interview, 'you have a duty to make the style appropriate, if not reflective of the original film. You can't make something that looks like Blade Runner ... but you can make something that understands it.'

The image of Kermode is suddenly captioned with white text and numbers in a recognisably *Blade Runner* font, and a graphic effect, accompanied by the distinctive beep and clicks of the Esper machine, zooms us jerkily into the shot, finishing on a small monitor screen. This screen in turn widens to become the opening crane down into *Blade Runner*'s police department. As Kermode's suit dresses the presenter into the role of a retro-future detective, so the immediately-familiar Esper effect dresses the contemporary footage of Union Station into a *Blade Runner*-style sequence. Yet this is pastiche, not precise replication. The shot of Kermode could not, despite the costume and the visuals, be mistaken for a scene from the film: it suggests, once more, an inbetween state, a version of contemporary LA in the *Blade Runner* mode, and fittingly it provides the link taking us from Union Station of 2000 to the police department of 2019.

The downward motion of the crane shot is met neatly with an upward wipe that reveals Kermode outside the Ennis-Brown house, and another Esper effect, zooming to a monitor on the kerb, takes us to a shot of Deckard's car pulling in through the gates. Another clever visual match – again, almost but not-quite precise in its angle, dissolving through a middle-stage rather than cutting from one identical image to the next – links Deckard's windshield with the windshield of Kermode's vehicle. 'As he wends his weary way home', Kermode tells us from behind the wheel, '*Blade Runner*'s bedraggled hero drives his sedan through the 2nd Street tunnel, which runs between Hill and Figueroa, and which looks as eerily exotic in real life as it does in the film.' There is a clear attempt to bridge the two versions of Los Angeles by retracing Deckard's journey; Kermode's delivery is itself world-weary, and his commentary makes an explicit link between the fictional world and 'real life'. I noted above that the tunnel provides more opportunity than the other sites for fan immersion, and here Kermode literally acts out Deckard's role, not just standing in the same location as an observer but playing the part, virtually becoming the character. Unsurprisingly, the next transition is to Deckard in the same tunnel, and here the similarity between real and fictional, presenter and protagonist, seems far closer.

The final trip, to the Bradbury, continues this blurring of roles. Kermode enters the building, seen from outside, and a match on action cut shows Deckard emerging from the inside. The passage through the doorway marks a transit between parallel worlds: the Bradbury entrance seems to take us from the real 2000 on one side to the fictional 2019 on the other, with the traveller's identity changing as he goes through the portal. However, when we cut back to Kermode in the Bradbury, the camera following him down the hall as if he were a character, rather than facing him as a presenter, the location, like Union Station, fails to resemble J. F. Sebastian's home without a leap of faith and imagination. On a pilgrimage, the fan has to make this leap, perhaps by comparing his or her own view with shots from the film and finding the closest possible visual echo by searching for the angle Scott used and attempting, often in vain, to reproduce it. In television documentary, editing can do the work of imagination, and the sequence dissolves from contemporary footage to *Blade Runner*'s establishing shots of the location.

Nevertheless, the beginning and end images remain stubbornly distinct – the gleaming ochre of the contemporary Bradbury is worlds away from *Blade Runner*'s apartment block, its misty blues haunted with silhouettes and spotlights. Only the ornate railings provide a clear visual link, overlapping in mid-dissolve: and the experience of *Blade Runner* pilgrimage is arguably captured by that moment, just as it is by Ben Mund's photoshop montage between light city and dark. The centre point of this transition between one Bradbury and another offers another visual metaphor for the sense of neither-nor ambiguity, of straining to leave one space but not quite grasping the next, of leaving the everyday but not reaching a point of complete immersion in the sacred.

Andrew Abbot, the documentary's director stated that his impressions of Los Angeles had, like my own,

> been shaped by *Blade Runner*. But you get there and discover that the reality is so different; it's so low-rise, and sunny. What Ridley Scott really did was turn Hong Kong into LA. Only at night, in the area around the Bradbury, in the downtown area, do you get the *Blade Runner* type of atmosphere ... you can imagine then how the building would look if it was wrecked and occupied by squatters. In *Blade Runner*, of course, the whole city has fallen to bits, whereas in modern LA you only see at night, in certain areas, the poverty next to immense skyscrapers ... literally thousands of people sleeping on the street, in a kind of shanty town. During the daytime, the Bradbury is so different since its restoration ... you can only get a vague sense that you're entering the film. (personal interview, 23 August 2004)

The difficulty Abbot identified in making that leap of imagination and mentally projecting Scott's future vision over the contemporary city was echoed in my correspondence with online fans. Not only are the real locations visually distinct from the end result of Scott's night shooting and post-production, but they are multiple-coded architectural signifiers, carrying a variety of connotations both mundane and specialist rather than mapping simply onto 'Deckard's house' or 'the LAPD HQ.'

Solosan stressed the continuing role of the *Blade Runner* locations as 'normal, everyday places' but also recognised their status as 'extraordinary examples of architecture. (I imagine it would be possible to track down the building where they built Chew's refrigerated set, but it is probably just a blank industrial building so I havent bothered.) So even if you're not a *BR* or a movie fan, they're worth seeing';

> I've been to the Bradbury on several occasions, and there always seems to be people just wandering in to look around ... some of them seemed aware

of the *BR* connection. I've been up to the Ennis-Brown House at least four or five times ... the other people on the tour seemed to be there because of its significance as a Frank Lloyd-Wright house.

I find an interest and appeal beyond their *Blade Runner* connection. I'm interested in architecture (art deco, streamline moderne, programmatic, googie – LA has lots of interesting buildings and I've been photographing them when I find the time) and history, and it just so happens that in this town those two things dovetail into another love of mine: movies.

This sober account plays down the locations' role as sacred places in a *Blade Runner* pilgrimage, acknowledging not only that the sites have different connotations for other visitors, but that they carry different forms of appeal for Solosan himself; without the architectural fascination, visiting a site is not worth the trouble on the basis of *Blade Runner* alone. He found little sense of communitas – 'Yes, I've heard other people at Bradbury mention *Blade Runner*. No, I haven't talked with them' – and his attempts to connect with the Union Station concourse were thwarted by the building's continued use for purposes entirely unrelated to his own – 'I actually tried to shoot a short film at Union Station, but the Grand Concourse was booked solid with weddings and stuff.'

Ben Mund's responses took a similar line, acknowledging – and again, appreciating as a bonus, rather than resenting as a distraction – the multiple levels of interest around many of the *Blade Runner* locations. The stunning architectural features of the Ennis-Brown, the Bradbury and Union Station made them 'all more rewarding than I had hoped ... a trip to the Ennis-Brown house is well worth it. As the basis of Deckard's apartment, it's instantly recognisable, but it's also a work of art that you'll enjoy on its own.' He fully accepts the fact that most visitors will take a different meaning from these sites, and wryly notes the lack of obvious potential for bonding with other pilgrims:

The group I toured with were all fans of its architect, Frank Lloyd-Wright. Although my primary reason for dropping in at these locations was to see where *Blade Runner* was filmed, I stayed longer than I expected just enjoying the look and craft of the buildings (this is especially true of the Bradbury, which is truly beautiful). At the Bradbury, one woman had a *Blade Runner* t-shirt. She was on a cell phone, and I didn't talk to her. Short of bellowing across the lobby or throwing a Snapple bottle cap to get her attention, it wouldn't have been easy. And either of those things will get you maced in LA.

Mund confirms the notion that the *Blade Runner* pilgrimage experience has to be carved out for oneself, 'poached' (following Jenkins 1992) from a range of other possible meanings and constructed by the individual through a committed act of investment and imagination:

Although two of the locations – Ennis-Brown and the Bradbury – have signs mentioning their use in *Blade Runner* and other films, none have any official *Blade Runner* related tour. Although an enterprising cabbie who wanted to outfit his car with ductwork and 2019 details could make a great experience for those *Blade Runner* fans out there. There are certainly no official trips or merchandise. There may be mentions in guidebooks, but the only 'tours' I've seen are self-guided events on various websites.

Mund's testimony certainly includes a sense of connection and immersion, but it seems compromised; modified and tempered by other factors:

A surprise was the size of the Bradbury building. It was much narrower than I had expected, despite the 'warehouse' feel I got from the film … Union Station and the Ennis-Brown house are so immediately distinctive that in many ways you feel like you are walking into a movie set. As for the Bradbury – well, it was just too clean and well-kept to feel like you were walking into a *Blade Runner* hell-hole. The only disappointment on the tour for me was that you cannot actually go into the hall in Union Station where they filmed the police headquarters – although you can stand at the entrance and view the whole area.

Solosan also notes that the preservation and improvement of the real-life sites ironically distances them further from the film's imagery – 'none of these locations is as run down and beat up as they appear in the movie' – and again, expresses a muted sense of enjoyment rather than the intense sensation of leaving the world behind to enter a promised land. 'It's been over a dozen years since my first visit to most of them, so I don't remember that much other than the fun of "Hey, I recognise this place!"'

That said, there are elements in both these fan testimonies of the kind of transcendence described by Roger Aden. 'If a movie is like a dream', commented Solosan, 'then standing in an actual location is like stepping into the dream. There's a weird kind of energy to it.' Again, there was a modifier – 'I get that sense most in the Bradbury and Union Station as it's very easy to recognise what they shot where. It's not so strong in the Ennis-Brown because it was more inspiration than an actual location … there's not a lot in those shots that you can connect to the house' (email interview, 12 July 2004). However, the implication that entering the *Blade Runner* locations can entail a shift into a dreamlike, fantasy world, removed from the everyday and free from its conventions, strongly echoes Aden's notions that pilgrimage enables a release 'into the liminal flow of an alternative world … an alternative to reality' (1999: 160).

Mund's comment on the same theme, that 'it's easy to feel that you've stepped into the film when confronted with these structures', also suggests a sensation of leaving the real and entering the fictional, again corresponding to Aden's theory of pilgrimage and the promised land. Once more, though, this hint of transcendence was dampened by pragmatism, as Mund remembered the sites' multiple connotations:

> Of course, I was unfamiliar with the locations when I visited. I imagine this isn't true of someone who, for example, has to haul himself to Union Station at 5:00am every morning to get to his job. I bet that guy's not feeling like he's escaping... (email interview, 16 July 2004)[11]

Finally, Mark Kermode's reflections on visiting the locations expressed a similar mixture of not-quiteness and almost-communion, veering from disappointed frustration to memories of near-epiphany; the flow of his conversational response aptly captures the experience of inbetweenness:

> There's something about documentaries made at the actual location, where the ghost of that film remains at the location ... it's a real pleasure. There's the sense that those places really did exist. Though it's always not quite right ... always slightly smaller or not quite how you remember, like the Bradbury for instance. But with the tunnel, you drive through there and it's exactly right. You think 'Yeah, that's it.' (personal interview, 20 August 2004)

I suggested above that during *Blade Runner* pilgrimage, a third term mediated between the two not-quite compatible versions of Los Angeles, helping to bridge them and blur the boundaries between them. The texts that link the visitor's immediate experience of LA's everyday, contemporary locations with the remembered on-screen sequences are the testimonies of previous pilgrims. Solosan and Mund's fan pages, like Kermode's professional documentary, are characterised by an inbetween ambiguity that, in their own attempts to bridge the gap between real and fictional through photoshop, carefully-angled pictures, graphic effects and editing, effectively assist the visitor who follows their guided tours to make that leap of imagination from one world to the next.

Visiting the LA sites and finding them a realm away from the *Blade Runner* scenes I pictured internally, I began to use these testimonies, or my memories of them – rather than the film – as my primary point of reference. Rather than standing in Union Station and immediately recognising it as the 2019 LAPD headquarters, my immediate satisfaction came from recognising this location *as the one I had seen in previous pilgrims' reports*. Instead of performing the imaginative negotiation that would allow me to visualise a camera's point of view on the opposite ceiling, moving slowly down to survey a dressed-up version of the concourse, my first thoughts were along the lines of 'this is the right place ... I saw it in Kermode's programme ... what I'm looking at now is just like the picture on *BladeZone*'s website.' In the absence of the instant gratification that a carefully-preserved set or precise simulation would offer, the middle-ground of Mund, Solosan and Kermode's secondary texts provided me with pragmatic reassurance that I was in the correct location and the satisfaction of seeing the images from those secondary texts in 'real life'.

As with my earlier observation about pilgrims approaching the real with their internalised image of the screen locations as the dominant visual template, and judging the former accordingly as disappointing when it fails to match up, I suggest that this is a phenomenon not unique to *Blade Runner*, and one that could be usefully applied to other, similar sites of pilgrimage. My visit to Union Station was not 'cold' but mediated by the testimonies, amateur and professional, of previous fans; and those fans had already provided some of the work that enabled me to connect the real location with its fictional equivalent.

Again, this chimes with part of John Urry's argument about the role of photography in contemporary tourism; the real has already been mediated by secondary texts, and the actual visit consists of trying to find and reproduce locations that have already been processed:

> What is sought for in a holiday is a set of photographic images, which have already been seen in tour company brochures or on TV programmes. While the tourist is away, this then moves on to a tracking down and capturing of those images for oneself. And it ends up with travellers demonstrating that they really have been there by showing their version of the images that they had seen before they set off. (2002: 129)

This hermeneutic circle undoubtedly exists in fan pilgrimage as it does in tourism; Solosan's photographs of the Grand Concourse are very similar to Mund's, but that did not stop me from taking almost identical pictures myself, and finding some satisfaction in confirming that similarity when I re-visited the websites after my trip, recognising their images from the other side of the pilgrimage. The shots in Kermode's documentary, similarly, took on a new familiarity and became moving postcards from a place I now knew, reassuring and supporting my sense of having-been-there; my own documentation of the visit now joins these existing images, a new addition to this body of testimonies, and of course may itself guide future pilgrims.

The return home represents, in Aden's study, leaving the liminal, coming back to normal life – ideally, on new terms – and gaining a new and enhanced, albeit temporary, perspective on the everyday. In this case, I suggest that the experience of *Blade Runner* pilgrimage specifically affects the fan's engagement with the primary text of the film, and again that this involves a process of bridging gaps. The memory of having occupied the space where the film was shot, of standing in a place that, while grounded in the everyday, was nevertheless the parallel-world neighbour of a site Rick Deckard had walked or driven through, provides a link between the viewer and the screen text. Just as the testimonies of previous pilgrims evoke, on the journey's return, a reassuring sense of revisiting the familiar, so the glimpses of those key locations in *Blade Runner* – however much the film disguises them – prompt a similar, though muted, pulse of recognition, connection and intimacy; even a modest sense of ownership.

The pilgrimage has given us specialist knowledge and placed us on different terms to the normal viewer; we have crossed that hall, driven that tunnel. If we have never quite occupied that diegetic world, then we have stood very close to it, and through a reverse manoeuvre of imagination, we can now make the leap that enables us to transform the film's dressed-up locations into the ones we visited. That ornate iron gate in the background when Deckard approaches his apartment complex now stands out as a feature we noticed at the Ennis-Brown house. There is the advertising blimp viewed through a glass ceiling, which we now know really exists in the Bradbury building. As Mund comments, on returning home to re-view the primary text the pilgrimage experience, with its blurring of borders, allows a reality effect – connotations of authenticity, of concrete geography and actuality – to seep from the LA locations back across the boundary, gifting the film's diegesis with enhanced credibility:

> Surprisingly, it actually makes the film feel more real. After seeing that many of the locations in the movie are firmly anchored in reality, the locations are that much more believable. (email interview, 16 July 2004)

In this chapter I have argued several related points around the central concept of the liminal state in *Blade Runner* pilgrimage, while suggesting that this specific discussion could usefully be applied to similar fan geographies and the experience of visiting them. Firstly, I proposed that *Blade Runner's* locations, for various reasons, restrict the pilgrim from achieving a complete sense of communion with the sacred place and the associated communitas of bonding with others at a shared site, and that they therefore position the visitor in a zone removed from the everyday but not fully immersed in the mythic. I argued that the three existing testimonies in this case study were characterised, intentionally or not, by this sense of not-quite, neither-nor ambiguity in their exploration of the boundary between the real LA and its fictional counterpart, and that these secondary texts will inform and guide the pilgrim, mediating between the internalised image of the screen locations and the sometimes disappointing real equivalent. With regard to the return home, I have suggested that these texts, joined with the pilgrim's memories of his or her experience in the inbetween Los Angeles locations, continue to provide a link between the two versions of the city, bridging the gap and helping to enable a feeling of connection – perhaps still through one remove – with the primary text of *Blade Runner*.

Finally, while I argued that bonding with strangers who share a common purpose is unlikely at the *Blade Runner* locations, I would conclude that opening the pilgrimage experience to others does play an important part in this specific fandom; again, it happens on the return home:

I visited and logged the sites with two things in mind – seeing for myself, and sharing it with other fans. Having plotted out my course, I wanted to make it available both to fans who were able to make it to LA (to help them streamline their visit), and fans who would never make it to LA. (Mund, email interview, 21 June 2004)

Mund explicitly states the purpose that must lie behind Solosan's willingness to let his photographs be exhibited online, and to an extent behind Kermode's choice to investigate those sites for his documentary. Though his is a professional broadcast, not a labour of love, his bursts of boyish enthusiasm as he is allowed to tour the Warner Bros. backlot – 'Oh, this is Chew's Ice House!' – express his own fan investment in Ridley Scott, and a desire to share his personal passion. Just as this chapter joins their testimonies as another document of *Blade Runner* pilgrimage, perhaps helping others to make the same negotiation between the real world and the fictional, so my writing of it is also motivated by more than just professional obligation. Matt Hills argues in this volume that the distinction between fans and academics is another ambiguous boundary, overlapping more than some would like to think: to a significant extent, I would suggest that academics write chapters like this for the same reason that Ben Mund and Don Solosan commit their free time to constructing images and posting reports for online visitors. We seek community, and we want to share our experience.

NOTES

1   These are the four sites visited by Kermode; they were suggested to me by Mund and Solosan in correspondence, and are also featured on their website reports, http://www.brmovie.com/locations (photographs by Solosan) and http://www.bladezone.com/contents/fan/articles/la_tour/la_tour.html (article by Mund). These sites are also listed in connection with *Blade Runner* in the 2003 *Rough Guide to Los Angeles* (London: Penguin/Rough Guides).

2   Turner himself draws this structure from the far earlier work of Arnold Van Gennep, citing *The Rites of Passage* (1909). See Turner 1969: 95.

3   Hills (2002: 146) argues that no site of pilgrimage allows visitors 'inside' the text, and that reality and fantasy can be neither fused nor significantly confused; his assertion is open to debate, but his stress on 'the permeable boundaries between these two realms' echoes my focus on in-between states.

4   The Bradbury is an interesting exception, as the location in *Blade Runner* includes a specially-made 'Bradbury' façade and is clearly meant to represent the actual building, gone to seed.

5   The site itself is maintained by 'Netrunner', so my reference to this online source as 'Solosan's fan page' implies only creative ownership.

6   http://www.brmovie.com/locations/police_station.htm

7   It could be argued that this imaginary shift to Deckard's point of view is actually

a form of participation and performance, enhancing the pilgrim's immersion in the film world, rather than a second-best alternative to seeing the precise image shown in the film.

8 http://www.bladezone.com/contents/fan/articles/la_tour/la_tour.html

9 Again, the title suggests the dual vision of Los Angeles as both promised land and dystopia (see Peter Brooker in this volume) in its link to Charles Dickens' famous opening 'It was the best of times, it was the worst of times...' Ben Mund stressed, however, that the banner was the work of the bladezone.com web-masters, and not his own creation.

10 'That was just me overwriting I'm afraid', Kermode commented in personal interview (20 August 2004).

11 Solosan also pointed out that as an LA resident, he lives in the 'promised land' and frequently passes by film locations or sees production in process. Strictly speaking, then, his visits to the *Blade Runner* sites cannot qualify as pilgrimage, because they do not involve a physical departure from the home environment.

POST-MILLENNIUM *BLADE RUNNER*
JUDITH B. KERMAN

When *Blade Runner* premiered in 1982, the year 2000 seemed a long way off. In 1991 a book of essays which I edited about the film and its source materials, *Retrofitting Blade Runner: Issues in Ridley Scott's Blade Runner and Philip K. Dick's Do Androids Dream of Electric Sheep?*, was published by Popular Press at Bowling Green State University (second edition, 1997). None of the essays in that first anthology explicitly considered millennial or apocalyptic issues – neither word appears in the book's index, although several authors wrote about Biblical themes in the film. Certainly, the date shown as contemporaneous at the start of the film, 2019, places the story after 'the Millennium' but it seems that no one thinking about *Blade Runner* in 1982, when the film came out, or in 1991, when my anthology was published, expected the particularly apocalyptic flavour popular culture gave to the actual years 1999 through 2001. Personally, although I wondered what it would be like to turn 55, for most of my life when I imagined the year 2000 I just envisioned a bigger-than-usual New Year's party, a high-tech reprise of the turn of the twentieth century.

Philip K. Dick's book *Do Androids Dream of Electric Sheep?*, on which the film was loosely based, was published in 1968, a year supposed to have ushered in a New Age of its own, and perhaps the role of the Prophet Mercer in the novel gives the book explicit apocalyptic content. But looking at the film with the new eye suggested by the turn of the millennium as we actually experienced it, I was struck by how well its imagery truly fits *Blade Runner* to be a cinematic apocalypse.

The pre-millennium mood of 1999 could fairly be called slightly hysterical. The Anti-Defamation League webpage entitled 'Y2K and the Apocalypse', posted by the organisation in 1999, describes belief systems that affected the general culture well beyond the evangelical groups themselves:

The year 2000, the start of a new millennium, is fast approaching. For certain religious groups that believe in an apocalyptic vision of the 'End Times', this dramatic turn of the century signals tremendous upheaval in the world, a period when chaos will prevail. In particular, a small number of Christian evangelicals and fundamentalists believe that the Second Coming of Jesus will occur in 2000 and are thus looking for 'signs' of the Last Days as prophesied in various books of the Old and New Testaments, including Revelation, Daniel, Ezekiel and Matthew. The year 2000 is also when many people expect the Y2K computer 'bug' to cause worldwide problems, including the disruption of electricity, water services, food delivery, banking systems and transportation, leading to a complete breakdown in society. In the minds of certain Christian evangelicals, the Second Coming of Jesus and the upheaval related to the Y2K bug are inextricably linked -- the Y2K bug being a sure 'sign' of the 'Tribulation' predicted in the Christian Bible. (Anon. 1999)

This old-fashioned doomsaying combined with a high-tech element which almost certainly helped to spread the anxiety into the general population. 'The "Y2K problem" concerned computers, computer chips and software that may not properly recognise or process dates after December 31, 1999. In addition there were certain other specific dates that may have been troublesome (such as February 29, 2000)' (Anon. 2000). With their anxiety perhaps driven in part by old-fashioned superstition, even sophisticated people could not be sure that critical computer-based systems were in fact secure against crashing suddenly on 1 January 2000 or on the next business day (take your pick). For instance, the jacket copy of a PBS Home Video called *Y2K: The Invasion of the Millennium Bug* reads: 'It's coming. It could be devastating; it could be a tempest in a teapot. Even the experts don't know' and then goes on to list 'all the things we take for granted ... power and water ... cash registers, answering machines, clocks', all systems possibly vulnerable to the Y2K bug.

Online journalist Chris Travers reported the prevalent catastrophic fantasies this way:

All across the nation, the mainframe computers that control hospitals, power plants, telephone companies, railroad stations, airports and harbours suddenly stop working. Soon, the transportation system breaks down as fuel begins to become scarce. The business of the nation grinds to a halt. Within two weeks, food has disappeared from the shelves of most grocery stores. Millions begin to panic. Food riots paralyse major urban areas. Predatory bands of well-armed malcontents terrorise the countryside. Civilisation as we know it is thrown backwards one hundred years ... excuse me for being a little nervous when suddenly the Godless computer geeks tell us the apocalypse is coming. The subject has made a goodly number of us nervous for two thousand years. It takes me well into March every year just to remember to add one to the previous year. Next year, I'll have to change all four numbers! I'm not the only one upset by this new math. Even the most literal minded and scientific among us are beginning to hear footsteps in the face of the year 2000. (Travers 1999)

BLADE RUNNER AND AMERICAN TRADITIONS OF APOCALYPSE

My exploration of connections between the apocalyptic tradition and the very complex, even tangled, text which is *Blade Runner* grows out of study of the Hebrew scriptures and Jewish interpretive tradition. Since many of the American apocalyptics, past and present, drew heavily on the Hebrew scriptures for their understanding of the sacred and models of sacred society, this seems entirely appropriate. I will consider to some extent both the theatrical release (mostly identical to the original video release) and the Director's Cut.

The word 'apocalypse' has a range of meanings derived from several significant canonical and apocryphal scriptures, especially the Book of Daniel (the only fully-developed apocalypse in the Hebrew Bible) and the Book of Revelations. Typically, the following characteristics mark such works:

- an apocalypse is marked by cosmic conflict between two mighty opposites, embodying good and evil.
- although it appears to be concerned with historical events, an apocalypse is really concerned with eschatology, the vision of the end-times.
- the text takes the form of a report by a contemporary observer, a wise or just man to whom ultimate truth is revealed.
- the pre-apocalypse world is so corrupt that people cannot do anything to redeem it, which validates the vengeful fantasies of the presumptive 'remnant' about destruction of their enemies when God finally intervenes.
- in some definitions, the Millennium, one thousand years of the Kingdom of God, is the beginning of yet another cycle, followed by resurgence of evil, more battles, but ultimately victory for the forces of God.
- a remnant is saved from the cosmic conflicts, to inherit the heavenly kingdom (see Harris & Platzner 2003: 340–1; Just 2004).

Apocalyptic expectations were tied to American culture from the first settlement of the continent by Europeans. When the Puritans set forth to create their new City on a Hill, they despaired of the Old World. In crossing the ocean to create a new world, they reenacted the crossing of the Red Sea (Ex 14), one of the prototypical Biblical apocalypses in the sense indicated above. I will return to this point below.

For the Puritans, America was supposed to be the New Jerusalem, the redeemed or messianic society. But it was a howling wilderness populated with red devils and wild beasts. Just as in the case of the Mosaic Exodus, people had to learn to live and to build their new kingdom in the world as it is, and the European genocide against the Native Americans certainly can be seen as an ideological descendant of the Israelite wars against the native inhabitants of Canaan.

But the millennial kingdom sought by American apocalyptics has always been a mirage, receding as we approached it, whether it was the City on a Hill or the Frontier. Perhaps the often-noted American inability to live in the present and value the past derives to a significant extent from this overvaluing of a millennial future which never arrives. Science is only the latest of the gods expected to lead us to the Holy Kingdom, with the aid of the Archangel Technology.

California is the frontier of the American frontier, the last place where the City can be built before it is pushed into the sea, or sails off to find the real Indies, the real Garden of Eden. Unlike San Francisco, where Dick located *Do Androids Dream of Electric Sheep?*, L.A. is arguably the most American (or least European) of all major American cities, the one most designed by and for the automobile and the suburb. L.A. is, appropriately, the home locale of the noir detective story, which is an obvious literary and cinematic ancestor of *Blade Runner* even without the voice-over of the theatrical release (Gray 66–75). Although this L.A. appears changed almost beyond recognition, the heroes of noir fiction would probably feel at home there.

In its own way, the noir story is apocalyptic, because its social corruption is not solvable by the hero or anyone else in the story. The only victory the hero will get is to learn the truth and then to survive. There is no expectation of a heavenly intervention and the noir story never suggests that other possible interventions, even class revolution or earthquake, are likely to meaningfully change 'the system'.

Blade Runner's other major ancestor, science fiction, has long been recognised as having roots in apocalypse literature, with its imaginings of things unseen, its monsters and cataclysms, its utopian ('millennial') societies (see Just 2005). As the noir story explores social despair, science fiction projects our ambivalent fantasies of technology as the god of a different kind of New Jerusalem.

APOCALYPTIC BIBLICAL PRECURSORS: FLOOD, BABEL, SODOM AND GOMORRAH, EXODUS

Blade Runner is notable for a variety of Biblical images, many of them derived from Genesis and Exodus. Scholars define Daniel and Revelations as the Bible's main apocalyptic books, but the pattern is set in Genesis and Exodus, with the Flood, the destruction of the Tower of Babel, the destruction of Sodom and Gomorrah, and the Exodus. In all of them, God takes a hand in history through catastrophe and revelation, because the dominant human society is too corrupt to be repaired. These stories ring different changes on the basic apocalyptic elements, variations which echo in *Blade Runner*.

After the destruction of Sodom and Gomorrah, Lot's daughters re-enact a perverse Eden, the re-creation (as they see it) of the human race. Like the Tyrell Corporation of the film, they set out to create a new human race, in their case by having sex with their own drunk father (Gen 19:30–38). Both the Flood and the Exodus end with revelation in the form of God's covenants, giving increasingly explicit directions to human beings about how to build the Holy Kingdom (Flood, Gen 8:21–9:17; Torah, Exod 20:2–14, Deut 5:6–18, but also much of Leviticus, Numbers and Deuteronomy). The Off-World Colonies, available only to the favoured few, are implicitly highly-controlled societies (we might perhaps call them covenantal), in contrast to the chaos of Los Angeles. When the Tower of Babel is destroyed, the language of human beings instantly becomes literally cryptic, sealed, each society mysterious to the others (Gen 11: 1–9) like the undigested multicultural world of *Blade Runner*'s teeming streets.

There are saved remnants from each of these apocalyptic prototypes: Noah, Lot and his daughters, the people of Israel. And also the people who are allowed to emigrate Off-World, the people who escape the Blade Runner fate of being 'little people'. I shall return to the question of the Off-World Colonies below.

Apocalypse is marked by the question of knowledge – what are people supposed to know or not know? What is revealed, and what is sealed? When will sealed knowledge be unsealed? (Dan 12:4). Revelation is precisely God telling people what he wants them to know, in order to create the Holy Kingdom. Each of the Biblical catastrophes results from God's decision that the human experiment has failed, and each marks the beginning of a New Age. But what people ultimately want to know is what the replicant Roy Batty wants to know: why am I here, and what will my fate be? As we see at the end of Job, the answer, if we ever get one at all, is rarely entirely satisfactory. Job's challenge to God, his demand to understand the reasons for his suffering, is answered only by God's demonstration of overwhelming power (Job 38–41), and Job's own recognition that he 'spoke without understanding of things beyond [him] … being but dust and ashes' (Job 42:3–6). Although Job is 'rewarded' with a new wife, children and riches, the reward is as arbitrary as the suffering. He never receives an explanation.

As the Hebrew scriptures trace the development of the human race, God is repeatedly disappointed in His expectations of human beings. Eating from the tree of the knowledge of good and evil does not lead people to choose the good, even though God keeps reminding us what the good is. With each apocalypse, God issues more and more precise instructions, and each time human beings manage to corrupt the Creation. Certainly, the high-tech world of *Blade Runner* is an apotheosis of corruption by knowledge.

APOCALYPSE IN *BLADE RUNNER*

In fact, the Los Angeles of the film echoes all of the scriptural apocalypses of Genesis and Exodus, as well as Daniel's. We have the endless rain of the Flood overwhelming the climate of the desert Southwest (especially in the final battle between Deckard and Batty). We have animals rescued from universal destruction, as on the ark, and a woman on friendly terms with a snake, although it appears that all of *Blade Runner*'s animals (like all the animals we actually encounter in Philip K. Dick's novel) are fakes.

We have the towers of perverse knowledge, the corrupt and filthy city burning in its own fire and smoke. We have the Pharaonic imagery of Tyrell's pyramid, which also echoes the hanging garden ziggurats of Babylon. The film's art deco style owes a lot to Egyptian art, although the film also uses buildings which consciously draw upon the style of another bloodthirsty pyramid-building cultural complex, that of Meso-America. The polyglot city is nothing if not a tower of Babel, in both its multilinguality and its overweening scientific ambition.

The tower of Babel is also a perversion of Jacob's ladder, where the angels went up and down (Gen 28:13), and Deckard, like Jacob, has to wrestle with an angel (Batty) to become a man (Gen 32:25–31). 'You've done a man's job, sir', says Gaff at the end. Like Jacob, Deckard loves Rachel (whose name means 'ewe', a female sheep, in Hebrew). His love for her is an important step in his becoming fully human, especially morally, as it was for Jacob. Jacob, the 'heel' (Gen 25:26), the smooth deceiver who has always been on the lookout for advantage, cries for the first time upon seeing her (Gen 29:11) and then becomes a loving husband and father in spite of being swindled by his father-in-law Laban (Gen 29–31). In his wrestling with the angel (Gen 32:25–33), Jacob becomes an upright man, the Bible's term for a moral man, although he also is wounded – from being morally crooked and physically straight, he becomes morally straight, but physically flawed by a limp.

The social order of *Blade Runner* is beyond repair, but there is no sign of a holy intervention. Although Batty might be in some sense an 'angel', and Deckard certainly wrestles with him, Batty dies of his inherent flaw. This is another way in which he mirrors Deckard – his death echoes the human flaw that led to expulsion from the Garden and the end of physical immortality for human beings (Gen 2–3). But the analogy is complicated and enriched because Batty is a manufactured product. In tort law, this flaw might be called an 'inherent vice', the weakness in a manufactured item that leads it to fail. Inherent vice is actionable, because the manufacturer is legally responsible for falling short of perfection. Thus the problem of theodicy, of the existence of evil, suffering and death in a world created by a presumably-benevolent omnipotent deity, is well-explored by the thought experiment of the replicants, who, like humans, came from their Creator's hands with a built-in flaw. The only available God is Tyrell, 'the god of biomechanics', himself a corrupt high priest who lives in an Egyptian temple and resembles photographs of Josef Mengele.

In this world, it is not clear which direction leads toward freedom. L.A. is Eden (where creation took place) and Mt Sinai (where God meets with man), but also the slave house, where 'little people' live. In Hebrew, Egypt is *Mitzrayim*, literally a strait or 'narrow place', a river valley squeezed between canyon walls. Evoked visually by views of the narrow canyons between L.A.'s skyscrapers, it is the birth canal from which the new world will emerge.

In *Blade Runner*, exodus moves in two directions. Human beings who meet the requirements (clearly a physical exam, but implicitly others as well) leave for the Off-World Colonies, marketed as a new Eden. But it is an Eden with its own slaves (the replicants), so that the people escaping in the exodus are simultaneously recreating Egypt in their new world. Although Mosaic law allowed slavery, the slaves of the Israelites had clear legal rights, based specifically on empathy, the memory that the Israelites had been slaves and strangers in a strange land (Ex 22:20). It is obvious that the replicants have no such protection, and they are even, by definition, excluded from empathy (their own, and human empathy toward them). An 'empathy test' is in fact the main method for determining who is human (presumably empathic) and who is replicant.

From the replicants' point of view, Los Angeles is Eden because L.A. is the place where they were made by the god of biomechanics before their expulsion (as opposed to exodus) to the Colonies. It is also an abortive Mt Sinai, where they hope to meet their God and receive an explanation of their purpose in the world, and the unnamed wilderness of Job's final confrontation with God. In the Blade Runner city, Eden, Egypt, Sinai and wilderness are conflated.

As mentioned, the hero of a noir story discovers the depth and complexity of the corruption of his society as a result of his detective's quest. The only rewards of the quest are his own survival, usually somewhat damaged, and knowledge of evil. He is a seer, and like all seers he partakes in the vision available to the Eye of Providence (Alter 1981: 69). In *Blade Runner*, as on the US dollar bill, the Eye of Providence is located at the top of a pyramid (see Morris 2004 for an explanation of the meaning and origin of the symbol on the dollar). This is one of the first images in the film, and a repeating theme; appropriately, we never know whose eye we have seen.

Blade Runner is marked by cosmic conflict between mighty opposites. There is a war going on, literally out in the cosmos, and Batty is a soldier angel, but it is not clear which side is good and which evil. The replicants are both angels and monsters; Batty quotes Blake (Schellenberg 1997), but it sounds like Milton – he identifies himself with Satan, or as Satan, and in the elevator after the murders of Tyrell and Sebastian, he resembles the Frankenstein monster, another Satanic incarnation whose god is a human being.

Batty seeks the knowledge that every human being wants – who he is, who his father is, when he will die, why he lives, what he should do. He has the satisfaction of taking violent revenge on his enemies, especially the person who fathered him and fucked him over. But in the end he is human and humane enough to save Deckard's life in a gratuitous act of generosity. Or is it a god-like intervention? The flight of the dove as Batty dies clearly evokes both Noah and Jesus, although it does not come to hover over him (Matt 3:16–17) but flies from his dying grasp.

In fact, the role of the perfect man, the Jacob, Daniel or Moses, is split between Deckard and Batty. Batty has prophetic vision – 'if only you could see what I've seen with your eyes! ... I've seen things you people wouldn't believe.' He is a witness and survivor of the cosmic battle, attack ships burning off the shoulder of Orion. Like Moses, he visits his God at the top of the mountain/pyramid, seeking more life. God tells Moses and the people: 'I set before you blessing and curse, life and death. Choose life' (Deut 30:19). But it appears that the life given by the God of biomechanics is more curse than blessing. And the knowledge-burdened survivor of the film is Deckard, who, like Job, can never really understand why he was cursed and why he was spared.

Although the end times of apocalypses have historically always turned out to be mirages, it can be argued that the vision of end times in the apocalypse is an important component of American popular culture's peculiar addiction to both violent conflict and happy endings. This created a problem for the makers of *Blade Runner*. American audiences are presumed to want a 'Hollywood happy ending', and so the theatrical release featured escape to an edenic wilderness for Deckard and Rachel (perhaps near L.A. but clearly outside it), complete with a reprieve from death for Rachel. The ending of the Director's Cut, with the elevator doors closing on the fleeing couple (see Kolb 1991: 141), instead certifies the claustrophobic tone of the rest of the film. There is no escape from the corrupt society, from *Mitzrayim*, the narrow place, in the noir world, and Deckard leads Rachel into the elevator, down to an unknown fate. I have sometimes thought of this as the European ending, but it is true to the logic of noir, which has a French name and which is a literature where European world-weariness and American disillusionment seem to merge.

A last aspect of apocalypse is finally worth considering. As indicated above, the real point of apocalyptic literature is eschatology, the vision of the end-times, which can also be phrased as the question of where human society is headed. Science fiction also has its roots in apocalypse.

Like both prophetic and apocalyptic religious literature, science fiction is not about the future but about the possibilities inherent in the present. It exists outside of history, in a realm of millennial hope and terror. Like most science fiction, *Blade Runner* was purposely created by extrapolation from current trends, but it was intended to make its audiences nervous (Kerman 1997: 16–18). This unease was clearly not intended to serve political or religious (that is, ameliorative) purposes, but to exploit its audience's pleasure in being uneasy and thus to make a financial success.

But both goals (prophecy and thriller entertainment) depend on plausibility. Because so much of its cultural detail is extrapolative, the film's convincing aura of historicity is not much damaged by the complex mythic texture of the details and the story. Apocalypses from Daniel to *Blade Runner* give the impression that we have seen into the future, and their momentum feeds on the despair that underlies the idea of apocalypse: the politically dangerous idea that we finally must depend on grace because we cannot save ourselves.

I call this politically dangerous because it has two results. It relieves individuals and societies from the responsibility to solve their problems, since (a) they are not capable of defeating an evil opponent which is presumed to be as powerful (or almost as powerful) as God, and which is the real cause of their problems, and (b) they will be rescued anyway because they are members of a privileged group. Further, it tempts the desperate to make matters worse, in order to evoke from God the saving response presumed to be inevitable if things get bad enough.

In the history of apocalyptic ideas and movements, this despair led to desperate acts such as the Bar Kochba rebellion against Rome. Intended to call down divine assistance, it instead resulted in the destruction of the Second Temple, the dispersal of the Jews throughout the Roman Empire, and the defeat for almost 2,000 years of Israel's national hope. Perhaps as a result of such experiences, skepticism toward apocalyptic thinking is a well-established part of Jewish tradition (Hoffman 1998: 35–6). Although scholars disagree about the canonisation process as it applies to the Hebrew scriptures, some accounts hold that the Council at Jamnia which is usually credited with the final decisions resisted apocalyptic texts, but that Daniel's popularity and its claim to being a Babylonian-era document resulted in its canonisation.

Although belief in an end-time and in Messianic redemption has been widespread in Judaism since before the Christian era, official Jewish culture primarily concentrated on the Law, the effort to find practical ways to help (or force) ordinary flawed human beings to live holy lives. (The definitive Jewish description of the Messiah is found in Maimonides, *Mishneh Torah, Hilchot Melachim XI–XII*; see Twersky 1972: 222–7) According to Jewish folk tradition, if everyone lived according to the Law, the Messiah would instantly come. Or maybe the resulting society would no longer need him, which is the same thing.

Perhaps because this tradition of idealistic pragmatism is my own, I found the theatrical release's escape into Eden entirely unsatisfactory, preferring the ending in the Director's Cut when I heard about it, long before I ever saw it. I do not hear the closing elevator doors that end the Director's Cut of *Blade Runner* as the clap of doom for Deckard and Rachel. The noir hero is a survivor, and Deckard has, in Rachel, 'help meet for him' (Gen 2:18). They have been expelled even from the dubious Eden of protection by the forces of Tyrell and his police apparatus, and now they must earn their bread in a hard world by the sweat of their brows. As in our own society and our own lives, we do not know the end of *Blade Runner*, but we can anticipate that the hard road of non-millennial reality lies ahead.

SECTION 1: THE CINEMA OF PHILIP K. DICK

REEL TOADS AND IMAGINARY CITIES: PHILIP K. DICK, *BLADE RUNNER* AND THE CONTEMPORARY SCIENCE FICTION MOVIE

AARON BARLOW

'The electric things have their lives, too.'
　　– Rick Deckard (Philip K. Dick, *Do Androids Dream of Electric Sheep?*)

Two intertwined strands of science fiction cinema, one focused on 'the spectacle of production technology' and the other on 'the impact of technology' (see Landon 1992), are represented in *Blade Runner* by director Ridley Scott's creation of a fulsome future landscape and by author Philip K. Dick's considerations of problems resulting from human creations. This combination has helped reshape the genre, influencing the likes of *Brazil* (1985), *Akira* (1988), *La cité des enfants perdus* (1995), *Strange Days* (1995) and *Dark City* (1998).

The 'standard' vision of the city of the future now comes from the Los Angeles that Scott and his 'visual futurist' Syd Mead created for *Blade Runner*, a city Scott Bukatman calls 'a richly layered futurity … which exists solely to present this urban space both bewildering and familiar' (1993: 132). Even the planet-covering city of Coruscant in *Star Wars: Episode I – The Phantom Menace* (1999) and *Star Wars: Episode II – Attack of the Clones* (2002) echoes the Los Angeles of *Blade Runner*.

The separate influence of Dick is just as extensive; six science fiction films – *Blade Runner*, *Total Recall* (1990), *Screamers* (1995), *Impostor* (2002), *Minority Report* (2002) and *Paycheck* (2003) – come from his fiction. His influence can be found in *The Truman Show* (1998), *Donnie Darko* (2001), *Vanilla Sky* (2001), *Mulholland Dr.* (2001) and *A Beautiful Mind* (2001). In each of these, the 'reality' depicted proves untrustworthy, as it often does in Dick's fiction.

The extraordinary impact of Philip K. Dick and Ridley Scott, both separately and combined in *Blade Runner*, can be illustrated by a quick look at one of the Internet lists (randomly selected via a Google search) of the top ten science fiction movies of the 1990s, this one compiled by James Oehley for The Sci-Fi Movie Page (with my comments in brackets):

1. *Twelve Monkeys* (1996) [showing influence of Dick, but with additional influence coming from Scott. The screenplay was co-written by David W. Peoples, who also co-wrote *Blade Runner*].
2. *The Matrix* (1999) [showing strong influence both of Scott and Dick].
3. *Starship Troopers* (1997).
4. *Contact* (1997).
5. *Strange Days* [showing influence of both Dick and Scott].
6. *Dark City* [showing strong influence of both Dick and Scott].
7. *Terminator 2 – Judgment Day* (1997) [showing some influence of Scott

and perhaps more of Dick].
8. *Star Trek – First Contact* (1996).
9. *Total Recall* [showing strong influence of Dick and some of Scott].
10. *Cube* (1997) [showing influence of Dick and some of
Scott, particularly through his *Alien* (1978)].

Seven out of the ten movies listed are clearly influenced by both the ideas of Philip K. Dick and the vision of Ridley Scott, and at least six owe a debt to the combination of the two in *Blade Runner*. Oehley's Ten Worst, on the other hand, includes no movies with a clear link to Dick, though a few, like *Batman Forever* (1995), do echo or parody Scott's vision of the city of the future.

The vision of Scott coupled with the ideas of Dick provided a new dynamic for the science fiction film genre, taking it away from its early focus on technology. Scott's utilisation of film noir aesthetics, Dick's questioning of perception, Scott's complex film worlds, and Dick's unease with technology all show up consistently in science fiction film today, moving the questions considered from 'our things' to 'us'. Because of these two creators, questions on the value and meaning of humanity and the place of 'reality' in life will long continue to concern science fiction filmmakers.

Film noir's sense of pervasive and impending doom is evident in *Blade Runner*, in look, narrative structure and, according to Vivian Sobchack, 'its enunciation of the future' (1987: 248). It helps Scott pose questions of culpability, presenting characters of complex moral nature whose physical beings (and the ontologies of their existences) are often ambiguous. Though the idea of a simple good/evil dichotomy continues in science fiction movies – *Total Recall*, *The Fifth Element* (1997) and *28 Days Later* (2002) continue this tradition – Scott's use of film noir has helped alter much of the genre. Bukatman writes that earlier works such as the *Star Wars* and *Star Trek* series 'dichotomised good and evil and sent them into pitched battle. *Blade Runner*'s world was neither so certain nor so resolved' (1997: 34). *Cube*, *Brazil*, *Twelve Monkeys*, *Strange Days*, *La cité des enfants perdus* and others reflect a similar ambiguity; though a few earlier films, such as *The Day the Earth Stood Still* (1951) do so, too. Though even the *Star Wars* series (Bukatman notwithstanding) deals with good and evil in its complexities at times (after all, Anakin Skywalker, hero of the 'first' trilogy, becomes Darth Vader, the villain of the 'second'), *Blade Runner*'s ambiguity and lack of overt judgement tilted science fiction film towards a more nuanced and post-structuralist approach.

In both *The Maltese Falcon* (1941) and *Double Indemnity* (1944), template noir films, evil is found close to home, within a lover, a femme fatale. The tension in the Deckard/Rachel relationship (though she is neither evil nor predatory) in *Blade Runner* recalls these films, as does the identification between Deckard and the replicants in general. Similarly, in *Total Recall*, the hero discovers that he may be the creation of the man whose body he inhabits (as is also the case in *Macroscope*, a 1969 science fiction novel by Piers Anthony, author of the 1990 novelisation of *Total Recall*); in *Impostor*, the main character is a bomb; in *Strange Days*, it is the best friend of the main character – recalling Harry Lime in *The Third Man* (1949) – who turns out to be responsible for a gruesome killing; the killers of *Screamers* are descended from creations of the 'good guys'; and *Minority Report* has as its villain the mentor of its main character.

Perhaps only Mel Gibson's Max Rockatansky in *Mad Max* (1979) and *Mad Max II: The Road Warrior* (1981) and Kurt Russell's Snake Plisskin in *Escape from New York* (1981) precede Harrison Ford's Rick Deckard as the hard-boiled noir anti-hero in a science fiction scenario – and Plisskin is much more a parody than a characterisation of a hard-boiled type. Rarely quite the best, merely the most persistent and focused, this anti-hero's moral code dominates his hard-boiled agenda. Since *Blade Runner*, characters played by Robert De Niro in *Brazil*, Peter Weller in *RoboCop* (1987) and *Screamers*, Olivier Gruner in *Nemesis* (1993), Christopher Lambert in *Fortress* (1993), Ray Liotta in *No Escape* (1994), Sylvester Stallone in *Judge Dredd* (1995), Ralph Fiennes in *Strange Days*, Bruce Willis in *Twelve Monkeys* and *The Fifth Element*, William Hurt in *Dark City*, Kurt Russell in *Soldier* (1998) and Tom Cruise in *Minority Report* have followed Ford. All of them focus myopically on a narrow range of tasks undertaken because of a moral decision, generally the result of a perceived imbalance. Their tasks are necessitated by their individual moral compasses, though not necessarily by a belief in distinct good and evil.

Like a hard-boiled character, Dick himself did not distance good and evil, seeing evil as almost banal, often the result either of ignorance or inattention, or misunderstanding – and good as almost the same thing. Thors Provoni, a possible 'saviour' in *Our Friends From Frolix 8*, is described by the book's main character: 'He is a man who did what had to be done. No, he isn't a nice man – he's a mean man. But he wanted to help' (1970: 274). Evil and good and the motivations behind them are always ambiguous. Director Terry Gilliam shares Dick's viewpoint, though here he turns it around: 'What's evil is Jack Lint [the protagonist's pal and, eventually, his torturer in *Brazil*], the person who's the best friend, the nice guy who does what he does. And that's evil' (*Brazil* DVD: Chapter 27). Both Dick and Gilliam see the appearance of evil as merely intent to *seem evil*, the appearance of good merely as an intent to *seem* good. Both seek out real evil and good elsewhere – and look for the human even in the most horrific visages. Neither ever forgets the fact that, as Gilliam puts it, there is a 'human touch even in the most inhuman moments' (*Brazil* DVD: Chapter 22).

Dick claimed that the 'two basic topics which fascinate me are "What is reality?" and "What constitutes the authentic human being?"' (1985: 2), questions that also intrigue contemporary filmmakers. Director Gary Fleder calls 'Impostor' 'the quintessential Dick story ... in which this guy wakes up one morning, goes to work, and all of a sudden is being accused of being something else. And that's ... the most terrifying conflict of all. If you aren't who you are, what is reality, what is accusation?' (*Impostor* DVD: 'The *Impostor* Files'). Director Paul Verhoeven asks, in relation to *Total Recall*, 'Is it the reality of a dream? Or is it the reality of somebody that has a dream but comes out of the dream?' (*Total Recall* DVD: *Imagining Total Recall*).

Scott 'has compared film direction to orchestration, and "every incident, every sound, every movement, every colour, every set, prop or actor" has significance within the "performance" of the film' (Bukatman 1997: 10). Though a few earlier science fiction films – notably *2001: A Space Odyssey* (1968) and the *Star Wars* series – show this kind of care, rare was the movie with visual depth or '"layering", Scott's self-described technique of building up a dense, kaleidoscopic accretion of detail within every frame and set of a film' (Sammon 1996: 47).

Following Jacques Lacan through Fredric Jameson, Giuliana Bruno describes the visual component of *Blade Runner* as 'pastiche', 'an effacement of key boundaries and separations ... intended as an aesthetic of quotations pushed to the limit' (1990: 184), adding that the 'postmodern aesthetic of *Blade Runner* is thus the result of recycling, fusion of levels, discontinuous signifiers, explosion of boundaries and erosion' (1990: 185). Critical is a lack of overt judgementalism: the landscape, environmental deterioration and all, just 'is'. According to Bukatman, part of this can be attributed to Effects Supervisor Douglas Trumbull, whose works 'reveal an ambivalence toward technology. They are neither celebratory nor condemning' (1997: 25). Not even the Tyrell Corporation can be held responsible for the state of the world; Eldon Tyrell, through the gruesomeness of his death (and his passivity in facing it), becomes as much a victim as anyone. The Earth has been ruined; people are moving off-planet. Blame must be universal, if it is to be assessed at all. Even the victims share in the responsibility.

'Scott's hallmark was a visual density that revealed as much as, or more than, the script. The characters inhabited complex worlds that provided oblique contexts for their decisions' (Bukatman 1997:14). Scott understands quite well a point Brooks Landon makes, that 'a series of images creates its own logic quite apart from the prose narrative that it conveys' (1992: 9). Just so, Hampton Francher, the first screenwriter on *Blade Runner*, recalls an incident when 'Scott suddenly looks at me and says, "Hampton, this world you've created – what's outside the window?"' (Sammon 1996: 53). For Scott, the story becomes but one of a number of elements, for he understands that the 'most significant "meanings" of science fiction films are often found in their visual organization' (Bukatman 1997: 9). As Roger Ebert says of *Dark City* but could have been saying of *Blade Runner*, 'it's almost the keystone of a movie like this, that the effects express what the idea behind the movie is and we're not simply looking at a sideshow' (*Dark City* DVD: Chapter 8).

This is particularly true of the *mise-en-scène* of *Blade Runner*, which is as much a simulacrum as the replicants, and in many of the same ways. Jean Baudrillard describes simulation as 'a real without origin or reality: a hyperreal' (1988: 166). Put another way, both the landscape of *Blade Runner* and its replicants are a hyperreal looking for an unattainable reality (a history). The 'hyperreal', however, allows for no past, so both the city and the androids are doomed to quests without resolution.

Prior to *Blade Runner*, science fiction movies generally presented worlds showing an implausible architectural continuity. Scott's complex vision reflects the hodge-podge of real cities, extrapolating from past growth to an unrealised future – in 1982, that is. Parts of today's Beijing and Guangzhou look eerily like the Los Angeles of *Blade Runner*. In John Burdett's mystery novel *Bangkok 8*, the movie is even used to help paint a picture of Kaoshan Road in Bangkok, 2002: 'Between the stalls and the cafés there is hardly room to walk … Remember the Chinatown scenes in *Blade Runner*?' (2003: 46).

In *Blade Runner* Scott creates a world that, at a distance, appears throbbing and dynamic but that, up close, shows a more squalid and jury-rigged quality. According to Paul M. Sammon, one 'early and key *Blade Runner* visual influence was artist Edward Hopper's hauntingly lonely painting *Nighthawks*' (1996: 74) where the lights glow brightly while the people reek of defeat. As Jack Boozer notes, the movie's 'unmotivated lighting and exotic, retro-futuristic scenic design call attention to expressionistic distortion and spectacle …; we are limited to a claustrophobic world of artificial lights and shadows' (1991: 214).

Contributing to the chaotic effect of *Blade Runner* is the use of what Anna McCarthy (2001) calls 'ambient television', outdoor video advertising. The sounds of such ads, very much a part of any world inspired by Philip K. Dick, had evolved a great deal by the time of *Minority Report* (based on Dick's short story 'The Minority Report'), where the audio components of the sophisticated large-screen (almost screenless) advertisements are tailored to the individual passer-by.

One notable visual aspect of the hodge-podge of *Blade Runner* is 'retrofitting', defined by 'futurist' Mead as 'upgrading old machinery and structures by slapping new add-ons to them' (Sammon 1996: 79). Scott also likes to show the underpinnings of a city, the odd mechanical devices needed to keep human life palatable, counterpoints to a smoothly-operating exterior. Along with the teeming surface of the world, these evoke what Bukatman calls a 'bewilderingly complex urbanism' (1993: 223).

Two of the most fully-evoked science fiction film cities since *Blade Runner* are the Neo-Tokyo of *Akira* and the Hong Kong of *Ghost in the Shell* (1995), animated films based on Japanese 'manga', or comic books. As in *Blade Runner*, the street level tends toward the filthy and anarchic while the heights are sleek and modern. By the end of each, the viewer has a sense of the geography of the city and a feel for its operations and complexity. There is none of the disjointed feeling one gets from *Brazil*, where the parts of the city do not seem integrally connected, or the myopia of *La cité des enfants perdus*, where only a corner of the city is presented.

In *Dark City*, the city is a pastiche. 'We fashioned this city on stolen memories, different eras, different facts, all rolled into one', says one of the movie's aliens, but it does have a *Blade Runner*-like integrity, an integrity that should not be confused with consistency. Both movies evoke a film noir vision of a city that operates on a number of competing and, in some ways, contradictory levels, from the very rich and stylish to the squalid, moving back and forth without apology. As in film noir, the levels clearly depend on and influence each other.

The design of the city of *Judge Dredd* so completely evokes *Blade Runner* that it seems, at times, as though parody were intended. Flying cars and a chaotic ground level (filled with punk rockers) are only the most obvious of the references to the earlier film. Its distinct levels, however, are more simply 'outside' and 'inside' and lack an appearance of symbiosis.

The Washington, DC of *Minority Report* contains four distinct urban settings. The first is one of government and monuments, a tall and quiet city. The second is a sedate suburban Washington of separate houses and small parks. The third and fourth, in the words of the film's Production Designer Alex McDowell, are 'this very modern, vertical city right across the river but below that is the old city which we stretched architecturally because we've really made it more like downtown LA. There's a kind of tenement, decaying dark city which exists underneath the new city' ('Deconstructing *Minority Report*', *Minority Report* DVD 2002). It is this last that is reminiscent of *Blade Runner*. Unfortunately, the four exhibit very little continuity within the movie. The parts of the domed city of *Impostor* show the same lack of integration and they fail, like that *Minority Report* Washington, to achieve or present any unity of vision in the movie.

Dick's fiction often depicts worlds ill-at-ease with their technological advances and with their inhabitants' places in the ontology of being. Lives are frequently controlled by distant corporations and advertising agencies often usurp the roles of governments. Their worlds become collages or pastiches, pieces from a number of different perceptual frameworks, perhaps even themselves 'schizophrenic' (returning, once more, to Jameson's model as Bruno uses it). This makes Dick able, as Bukatman says, to explore 'the alienation that results from seeing through the spectacle' (1997: 48). In a speech entitled 'How to Build a Universe That Doesn't Fall Apart Two Days Later', Dick explained:

> It is my job to create universes ... However, I will reveal a secret to you: I like to see them come unglued, and I like to see how the characters in the novels cope with the problem. I have a secret love of chaos. There should be more of it. Do not believe – and I am dead serious when I say this – do not assume that order and stability are always good, in a society or in a universe. (1985: 5)

Terry Gilliam and Charles McKeown shared this attitude as they reworked the script of *Brazil*. McKeown revels in the memory of their freedom, talking about 'exciting contradictions' and the pair's 'resisting the temptation to clarify' (*Brazil* DVD: 'The Screenwriters'). Gilliam shrugs off the lack of logic, claiming that 'the world is so twisted from the norm that everything is possible' (*Brazil* DVD: 'Commentary on *Brazil*', Chapter 18).

Gilliam felt enough affinity for Dick to option *A Scanner Darkly*. Dick's tale of drug addiction centres on the deterioration of a group of characters, including one who is both a drug addict and a government agent, just the sort of conflict both Dick and Gilliam thrive on. Bob McCabe quotes Gilliam:

> Wanting to do it was probably a reaction to *Total Recall* because I'm fed up with Philip K. Dick's books not being made. *The Truman Show* is Philip K. Dick – everyone steals from Dick and they never credit him. I was asked to direct *The Truman Show* and I didn't because I thought it was sub-Philip K. Dick. That writer has greater depth in him than anybody has dealt with. (1999: 158)

Nothing came of the option. Instead, Richard Linklater has made the film, with Keanu Reeves starring. Release is scheduled for March, 2006. Gilliam's desire to make a film from a Philip K. Dick work comes not only from his love of that fiction but from what he sees as the alteration of Dick's stories into action adventures along with the use of Dick's ideas without attribution. 'We Can Remember It For You Wholesale', the story behind *Total Recall*, deals less with action than with discovery that memory cannot always be believed (but that the 'self' behind cannot be successfully contained). This is true, too, of *Time Out of Joint* (1959), the Dick novel reflected in *The Truman Show*, where, as in the novel, an artificial world has been constructed to contain one individual. In *Time Out of Joint*, however, the deception is internal as well as external. Perhaps, to Gilliam, this is the key point to Dick that most adaptations miss: deceptions most always happen with the connivance of the deceived.

In *Do Androids Dream of Electric Sheep?* the 'morning air, spilling over with radioactive motes, gray and sun-beclouding, belched about him, haunting his nose; he sniffed involuntarily the taint of death' (1996: 8). Dick later explains that 'garbage collecting and trash disposal had, since the war, become one of Earth's important industries. The entire planet had begun to disintegrate into junk' (1996: 8). Nothing is left but deterioration: 'Most androids I've known have more vitality and desire to live than my wife. She has nothing to give me' (1996: 94), says Deckard. Later, he sees the androids as people, perhaps more human than those he has been living among: 'In the absence of the Batys and Pris [androids, though there is but one 'Batty' in *Blade Runner*, not the married couple of the book] he found himself fading out, becoming strangely like the inert television set which he had just unplugged. You have to be with other people, he thought. In order to live at all' (1996: 204). Still, Deckard kills the only things that are at all capable of reversing the slow process of disintegration inside and around him. The process of entropy cannot be stopped; the androids/replicants *will* be destroyed.

In *Screamers*, inspired by Dick's short story 'Second Variety', the lover of the main character is revealed to be a robot when another 'screamer', just like her, appears. The doubles fight, the lover protecting the human, for it has been growing within itself. The humans of the movie are generally a scruffy, unwholesome lot. The robots, developed simply as killers, have moved beyond their creators, just as have the androids in *Blade Runner*. Significantly, in both movies the main character develops a relationship with a 'machine' at the end.

A different human/machine tension can be found in the *Matrix* series. Here, the machines also have surpassed their creators. At no point, however, do they seem morally superior to the humans they have usurped. In *Impostor*, as in the *Terminator* series, machines have been imbued with the human will to survive and dualities dwindle.

The androids/replicants and 'screamers' represent technology at its highest – that is, at the point where it no longer needs humans to improve it, but can start improving itself – and show its limitations. In *Do Androids Dream of Electric Sheep?*, *Blade Runner* and *Screamers*, technology itself can never solve the problems facing human beings, not even when it becomes more 'human' than the humans. Unlike the situation in the *Matrix* series, technology is never simply the villain, for it is humans who are responsible for destruction, not their tools.

In *Johnny Mnemonic* (1995), a cure for a fatal disease brought on by information overload is withheld by its corporate creators. Technology causes the disease, but technology can cure it; only human greed, human failing, gets in the way. Not surprisingly, the vehicle for salvation of humanity is a dolphin (shades of Douglas Adams' *So Long and Thanks for All the Fish*, and Alan Moore and Ian Gibson's *The Ballad of Halo Jones*).

Sometimes it is not just technology or greed that causes humans problems. Like the replicants of *Blade Runner*, the mutants of *X-Men* (2000) and *X-Men II* (2003) face ostracism for difference from humans. The mutants, though, are split between those who see humans as a threat to *them* and mutants who feel that all can get along, a split echoing the one within the cyborg community of *Nemesis*. In all three cases, the unevolved humans are seen as worth protecting, even though the 'new' beings – replicants, cyborgs, and mutants – are obviously superior.

In *Gattaca* (1997) the replicants of *Blade Runner* have been replaced by genetically-enhanced humans who control human society, leaving the rest of the population, those few who were not enhanced, nothing more than marginal lives of unskilled labour. The movie centres on a 'natural' human attempting to succeed in the new world, as though the replicants have taken over and Deckard has to pretend to be one. Though the situation of the 'natural' humans is different in the two movies (in *Blade Runner* they still run the world; in *Gattaca* they have been pushed aside), both movies deal with the difficulty of a human negotiating a world that is in danger of leaving that humanity far behind.

Another side of this growing yet dissolving dichotomy appears in Dick's story 'The Electric Ant', where Garson Poole discovers that he is a machine; everything he experiences is controlled by a 'reality tape' in his chest cavity. 'I'm a freak, he realised. An inanimate object mimicking an animate one.

But – he felt alive' (1987: 228). The story is about being and perception, concepts where logic breaks down: 'Programmed. In me somewhere, he thought, there is a matrix fitted into place, a grid screen that cuts me off from certain thoughts, certain actions' (ibid.).

> Later, Poole speaks to a supposed human:
> 'You're not real', he told Sarah. 'You're a stimulus-factor on my reality tape. A punch-hole that can be glazed over. Do you also have an existence in another reality tape, or one in an objective reality?' He did not know; he couldn't tell. Perhaps Sarah did not know, either. Perhaps she existed in a thousand reality tapes; perhaps on every reality tape ever manufactured. 'If I cut the tape', he said, 'you will be everywhere and nowhere. Like everything else in the universe. At least as far as I am aware of it.' (1987: 237)

Poole does cut the tape and the focus of the story turns to Sarah, who watches the machine become inert. However, she soon finds something else going on:

> My hands, she thought. She held them up. Why it is I can see through them?
> The walls of the room, too, had become ill-defined…
> The wind of early morning blew about her. She did not feel it; she had begun, now, to cease to feel.
> The winds blew on. (1987: 239)

And so the story ends, not with logic, but with disintegration. No answers are provided or even attempted, not even Deckard's 'You have to be with other people … In order to live at all' (1987: 228). The candle, so to speak, is just blown out.

Nemesis tries to deal with the questions raised by both 'The Electric Ant' and *Blade Runner*. Its plot revolves around an attempt by cyborgs to replace humans. Some resist, working with humans against the other cyborgs. Jared, one of the cyborgs, answers when asked why she cares about the world, 'I live here, too', presupposing a conscious self. Later, she makes the point that is at the heart of 'The Electric Ant', *Blade Runner* and many subsequent science fiction films, 'It takes more than flesh and blood to be human'.

The *Matrix* series shows a world developed and controlled by software akin to the 'reality tape' of 'The Electric Ant.' Instead of disappearing when cut from the loop, the *Matrix* humans can wake up to the 'real' world, reflecting the idea behind Dick's *Time Out of Joint*, where it is written descriptions – not computers – that seem to create the illusion.

Themes from *Time Out of Joint* appear regularly in science fiction. Dick spoke to Gregg Rickman about the book, saying that it

> was the first novel I wrote in which the entire world is fake … The world you are reading about does not exist. And this was essentially the premise

of my entire corpus of writing, really. This was my underlying premise. And this is that the world we experience is not the real world. It is as simple as that. The phenomenal world is not the real world. (1984: 138)

Just so, both *The Truman Show* and the *Matrix* series present unaware characters living in worlds constructed and controlled.

In Dick's *Eye in the Sky* (1957: 52), the characters learn that they have entered an illusory world, getting through it only to enter another, and so forth. Like the characters in *Cube*, who awaken to a maze of nearly-identical rooms, they have to band together to find a way out of each 'reality' (or to survive each room). Both works progress as much through growing understanding of the characters and their motivations as through any actual movement.

eXistenZ (1999), a movie where games mimic reality, ends with a character asking, 'So tell me the truth, are we still in the game?' It is a good question, for the start of the movie has proven to be within a game already. Here, the 'realities' are created by a meld of the personalities of the game players and the game software. When they have come out of one game into what appears to be 'reality', the two main characters, Allegra Geller and Ted Pikul, discuss the seductiveness of the illusions:

Geller: How does it feel?
Pikul: What?
Geller: Your real life, the one you came back for.
Pikul: It feels completely unreal.
Geller: You're stuck now, aren't you?

Instead of being forced into an ersatz 'reality', as in the *Matrix* series, the characters here are becoming addicted to it.

A reference to Dick's 'The Days of Perky Pat' (1963) (fast food comes from 'Perky Pat's') provides one of the earliest clues in the movie that the 'reality' we are seeing is a game 'reality'. It is a perfectly appropriate clue and homage, for the movie owes a great deal to Dick's *The Three Stigmata of Palmer Eldritch* (1964), which incorporates the earlier story and its model-and-drug induced Perky Pat game. Another idea from the book to appear in the movie is the possibility of 'leakage' from one 'reality' to another. As Pikul says towards the end of the film, 'Something's slipped over the edge here, Allegra. Something's all wrong.' At the end of *The Three Stigmata of Palmer Eldritch*, characters in the 'real world' take on the artificial limb, eyes and false teeth of Palmer Eldritch.

Cronenberg's sly homages may not be limited to Dick. In a Chinese restaurant, Geller sharpens or cleans her chopsticks just as Deckard does in *Blade Runner*. She and Pikul are arguing with their waiter over the order – just as Deckard is doing in the earlier film.

Murray Pomerance sees *eXistenZ* as an example of what he calls 'elevator films': movies in which a 'character ascends or climbs to a higher level or ports to another level, or travels through some highly technological gateway' (2003: 2). He includes *Total Recall*, *The Matrix* and *Dark City* in this category. This sub-genre owes a great deal to Dick's *Eye in the Sky*, *The Three Stigmata of Palmer Eldritch*, *The Man in the High Castle* (1962), *Flow My Tears the Policeman Said* (1974), and others. *Cube* could be considered the rebellion against the genre, where the new places end up not really new 'places' at all.

Perhaps the closest Terry Gilliam comes to recognising the debt he owes to *Blade Runner* is in his commentary on the 1999 Criterion DVD release of *Brazil*, where he says that a road near the end of the movie 'reminds me of the end of *Blade Runner*' (Chapter 34). Yet Gilliam certainly knows that this ending of *Blade Runner*, the ending of the 1982 theatrical release, was not even shot by Ridley Scott (they were outtakes from Stanley Kubrick's 1980 film *The Shining*), who had lost control over the film. This is probably intentional irony, for Gilliam had had to fight to retain control of his own film.

The real impact of *Blade Runner* lies elsewhere in *Brazil*, in the importance of the video screen, the prevalence of neon (reflective of film noir), the 'retro-fitting', the further hint of film noir in the choice of 1940s costuming, the trash on the street, the pastiche of architectural styles, the use of advertising, the presentation of a totalitarian society where the top is unable to contain the bottom, and in the use of mannequins.

McCabe quotes Gilliam as saying '*Blade Runner* really excited me, and then it really disappointed me. So I react against it' (1999: 118). Gilliam goes on to say that the influence of *Blade Runner* on other films was 'designers, designers, designers. Everything was conceptual design' (ibid.). He wanted his own film to have the appearance of accident. Protective of the 'originality' of his work, Gilliam describes the process of retrofitting as applied to *Brazil*:

> There's one guy working on that and we'd build this thing as if we were building a sculpture, and he would find bits and pieces and come up with new ideas and I'd come in and say now a bit of this and a bit of this but less of that and we just built this creature and I think it's a nice way of working rather than coming in with, say, the Syd Mead approach, where you'd give it [to] a top designer [to] design everything down to every detail. Ours was a bit more like found art, growing in an organic way with all the members of the team involved in the process. (*Brazil* DVD: 'Commentary on *Brazil*', Chapter 6)

Compare this to what Mead himself says about the similar process on *Blade Runner*:

> I set up the design format for each vehicle type and then let the draftsmen and builders make changes as they went along, as they had or wanted to … I liked that sense of collaboration. What we ended up with was a curious accumulation of detail, a heuristic growth of odds and ends that the original concept didn't include. (Sammon 1996: 80)

Almost everything, in both films, purposely looks cobbled together, despite the way Gilliam contrasts his method to Mead's.

The neon of *Blade Runner* provides a connection between the world of the film and the world of 1982. Many of the products the neon promotes were real to the time of the movie's release (some, like Atari and Pan-Am, have disappeared since, leading to contemplation of a '*Blade Runner* curse'). The neon of *Brazil*, on the other hand, is used as a parody of advertising, though it does show the impact of neon on urban existence that is a hallmark of the earlier film.

As a satire, *Brazil* takes aim at all sorts of targets, perhaps even at *Blade Runner* with its heavy-handed use (especially in the theatrical release with its voice-over) of a 1940s film noir style. Much of the costuming, certainly, parodies the clothing that Rachel, for example, sports in *Blade Runner*. The horrors of *Brazil*, however, generally come under bright light, not in film noir shadow.

When Pris awaits J. F. Sebastian in *Blade Runner*, she covers herself in trash, primarily newspapers. In a dream sequence, one of the climactic scenes of *Brazil*, a character is 'consumed' by flying papers. According to an uncredited production note on the Criterion *Brazil* DVD, the intent in that movie was to present worlds 'that appear real and lived-in, and which often overwhelm their occupants'. Here, as in *Blade Runner*, what Dick calls 'kipple' (the detritus of human life) is taking over.

The connection between people (or replicants) and store mannequins is presented in both movies through scenes of death and flying glass. In *Blade Runner*, Deckard shoots the fleeing replicant Zhora and she crashes through a series of store display windows, passing by or knocking aside a number of mannequins. As she lies dead at the end of the scene, she is made to look like a mannequin herself. After an explosion in the lingerie section of a department store in *Brazil*, injured humans are interspersed with pieces of mannequins. Mannequins also show up in subsequent science fiction films, as 'dead' cyborgs in *Nemesis* sharing Zhora's mannequin-like stillness, and in *Terminator 3: The Rise of the Machines* where the T-X robot materialises in a shop window, amongst mannequins.

While preparing *Twelve Monkeys*, Gilliam stayed away from *Brazil*, just as he had tried to avoid *Blade Runner* when making *Brazil*. Production manager Jeff Beecroft says that, 'I never really remember him ever saying "Let's look at that." I know he didn't want to do *Blade Runner*, he didn't want me to do *Alien* … So we were trying to find another whole language for these people to live with.' (*Twelve Monkeys* DVD: 'On Creating the Worlds of *Twelve Monkeys*'). Nevertheless, something of *Brazil* did seep in, as did a bit of *Blade Runner*. This could hardly be helped: the co-writer of the script for *Twelve Monkeys* was David W. Peoples, who also co-wrote *Blade Runner*. Some of the elements in *Twelve Monkeys* that specifically echo *Blade Runner* are the close-up on eyes (something also seen in *Strange Days, Cube, Soldier, Dark City, Johnny Mnemonic* and *Impostor*), the importance of animals, the dark, almost film noir, atmosphere, and the sense of deterioration. Gilliam says the 'film was very much about decay and about man's stupidity in a sense, man destroying what he has made' (*Twelve Monkeys* DVD: 'Commentary on *Twelve Monkeys*', Chapter 1), much like *Blade Runner*.

The commonplace premise of *Twelve Monkeys* (it had been used, for example, in Michael Anderson's 1989 film *Millennium*) could be a turnabout of Dick's 1954 story 'Meddler', where it is the future that is accidentally altered. The people in the 'present', aware that their travels to the future have somehow changed it, want to undo the damage: 'When did it first appear? How? What were the first signs? *What is it?* Once we know, maybe we can eliminate it, the factor, trace it down and remove it.' (1954: 271–2). The questions are exactly those of the scientists in *Twelve Monkeys*, just as they are the questions behind the *Terminator* movies.

In *Twelve Monkeys*, Cole decides at one point that he has imagined the future, that he is crazy. Is he? It is possible. 'What you think you're seeing may not be exactly so', says producer Chuck Roven, 'What you think you're hearing may not be exactly so' (*Twelve Monkeys* DVD: 'On Creating the Worlds of *Twelve Monkeys*'). What if Cole is crazy *and* his worlds are real? Dick asks, 'What about the world of a schizophrenic? Maybe it's as real as our world. Maybe we cannot say that we are in touch with reality and he is not, but should instead say, his reality is so different from ours that he can't explain his to us' (1985: 3).

One movie whose makers do not hesitate at all to admit the influence of *Blade Runner* is *Soldier*, again written by Peoples. Says director Paul Anderson:

> There's a lot of references to *Blade Runner* in this film. I always saw the two movies, *Soldier* and *Blade Runner* … as existing in the same universe, so that if Kurt [Russell] ever went to Earth, he'd encounter Harrison Ford down there … *Blade Runner* was a constant influence to us during the making of this film. And also thematically, *Blade Runner* is very much about the machine that becomes as human as it possibly can be, Rutger Hauer's character, while this movie is about the man who becomes as machine-like as the military can make him. So, in a way both Kurt and Rutger are looking for their humanity. (*Soldier* DVD: 'Commentary on *Soldier*', Chapter 8)

Soldier's *mise-en-scène* only presents a random collection of items, never weaving them together into the sort of whole Scott presents. Why a mid-twentieth-century airplane, an aircraft carrier, and a number of parking meters should have been transported to a mid-twenty-first-century garbage planet is never explained, though they may be simply tongue-in-cheek references to other movies. After all, Todd's service record includes two of the battles Roy Batty mentions in his speech to Deckard in *Blade Runner* (Tannhauser Gate and Shoulder of Orion) and he has earned a Plissken Medal, after Russell's character in *Escape from New York* and *Escape from L.A.* (1996). There are also references to *Aliens* (1986), *Star Trek II: The Wrath of Khan* (1982), and other movies.

Dark City, instead of inhabiting *Blade Runner*'s universe, turns it on its head. It is the humans, not the replicants, who are provided with imbedded memories. According to director Proyas, 'All the people in the movie are playing characters that have been imposed on them' (*Dark City* DVD: 'Commentary on *Dark City*', Chapter 3). Most seem subdued, almost confused. Co-screenwriter Lem Dobbs says, 'Given the context of the story, obviously there's a kind of robotic quality that these characters have and a kind of blandness' (*Dark City* DVD: 'Commentary on *Dark City*', Chapter 4). Like Rachel in *Blade Runner*, the humans of *Dark City* rely on planted photographs as proof of their memories. Both movies ask, 'Are we more than the sum of our memories?' (*Dark City* DVD: 'Commentary on *Dark City*', Chapter 9). This is also one of the questions of *Johnny Mnemonic*, where Johnny has sacrificed his memories of childhood in order to carry data in his head.

Human John Murdoch in *Dark City* parallels replicant Roy Batty in *Blade Runner*. There is even a roof-top struggle between Murdoch and one of the aliens, evoking the climactic fight between Batty and Deckard. Just as Batty and the rest of the replicants are physically and (perhaps) mentally superior to humans, so the humans in *Dark City*, as possessors of individual souls, are superior to the aliens.

Unfortunately for the replicants of *Blade Runner*, but fortunately for the human characters in *Dark City*, human memories do not add up to human existence. Something more is needed. According to another of the characters in *Dark City*, it is love; 'you can't fake something like that'.

Dark City shows influence of a number of sources in common with *Blade Runner*, including Edward Hopper (particularly 'Nighthawks'), the German silent film *Metropolis* (1927), the French comic *Metal Hurlant* and the 'compacted urbanism' (Bukatman 1997: 17) of Moebius, one of its principal artists, where, as Proyas says, 'the images and ideas were sort of intrinsically interwoven' (*Dark City* DVD: 'Commentary on *Dark City*', Chapter 4). One Proyas comment on *Dark City* could as easily have come from Scott about *Blade Runner*: 'The atmosphere is the thing that we're all trying to create, you know, from the acting to the lighting to the sets, it's all working towards creating a mood and an emotion for the audience' (*Dark City* DVD: 'Commentary on *Dark City*', Chapter 4).

The atmosphere is the thing in *Strange Days*, too, but the Los Angeles of the movie is stilted and, for all the motion shown, unenthused. As Will Brooker writes, '*Strange Days* simply does not offer the same level of significant detail or hidden implications' (2003: 211) found in *Blade Runner*. Still, there are significant connections between the films, among them, according to Barbara Kennedy, 'Iris, flying through the frames, erotic dark-blue sequined outfit transiently displaying a masquerade of fetishistic glamour, a creature out of *Bladerunner* [sic], trying to escape the threat of cops as they hound her' (2000: 187). Brooker details a number of other instances of possible homage to *Blade*

Runner, including parallels between protagonists Lenny Nero and Rick Deckard, the use of eyes (including that name, 'Iris'), and even a possible reference in the name of the film itself to *Dangerous Days*, once *Blade Runner*'s working title. According to Brooker, these 'could be considered postmodern nods of acknowledgement to the earlier film' (2003: 213).

Of all the characters with a little Rick Deckard in them, Korben Dallas of the science fiction comedy *The Fifth Element* comes closest to the original, though as much through parody as homage. Both characters have resigned from official positions and both are forced to return to duty directly after eating Asian food. Also, both fall for women who are something other than human. Dallas also has a great deal in common with many of Dick's main characters, including Joe Chip in *Ubik* (1969). One of Dick's set pieces is the fight between the little man and the automated devices of his society. Chip, for example, is threatened with a lawsuit by a door. Dallas is constantly beset by similar problems.

Japanese *anime* films continue to show a great debt to *Blade Runner*. Though *Akira*, as Susan Napier says, was first seen in the West as 'a complex and challenging work of art that provoked, bewildered and occasionally inspired' (2000: 5) with its 'adult themes of dystopia and apocalypse and its superbly detailed, viscerally exciting animated style' (2000: 41), its relation to *Blade Runner* was obvious. Napier describes two of *anime*'s genres, cyberpunk (whose godfather was Philip K. Dick) and *mecha* (certainly a cousin to *Blade Runner*), both utilised in *Akira*:

> Cyberpunk ... is a genre focusing on dystopian futures in which humans struggle in an overpoweringly technological world where the difference between human and machine is increasingly amorphous. *Mecha* (a shortening of the English word 'mechanical') privileges a favorite form from Japanese popular culture, the robot. (2000: 11)

Instead of replicants, *Akira*'s universe contains stunted children with extrasensory powers. Tetsuo, runt member of a motorcycle gang, begins to gain powers like those of the children but of greater extent. Immature and full of anger, Tetsuo cannot control his new powers and ends up destroying himself and much of his world.

Though Tetsuo's demise is earth-shattering, unlike Batty's in *Blade Runner*, both die in lament and failure. Both reach for a power they could not achieve; both recognise their loss. Tetsuo, however, may have a rebirth, while Batty's end is irrevocable.

Perhaps what Roy Batty needs, and fails to find in his confrontation with Eldon Tyrell, is connection to a 'being' akin to the artificial-intelligence Puppet Master of *Ghost in the Shell* who offers 'technology's positive potential, not only in terms of the physical and mental augmentation ... but also in terms of the possibility of spiritual development' (Napier 2000: 105). The Puppet Master has evolved from a computer virus into a self-aware being looking to find a way to do more than duplicate itself. Through a melding with the cyborg Major Motoko Kusanagi (who is also self-aware), a new being is created, a 'child' of the two.

Both the Puppet Master and Kusanagi are concerned with creation of individuality: a copy does not fill the bill. As Kusanagi explains, 'There's a remarkable number of things needed to make an individual what they are. A face to distinguish yourself from others. A voice you aren't aware of yourself. The hand you see when you awaken. The memories of childhood, the feelings for the future'. This is the concern of the replicants in *Blade Runner*: how does one ensure that these things themselves are integral, and not grafted on?

Directly after the Kusanagi speech quoted above, her 'ghost', or spirit or soul, communicates with her: 'For now we see through a glass darkly', referring to a First Corinthians phrase that Philip K. Dick also uses, in the title of his *A Scanner Darkly*.

Kusanagi's concern for the integrity of the individual is further expressed just a little later: 'Perhaps the real me died a long time ago and I'm a replicant made with a cyborg's body and computer brain [reminiscent of *RoboCop*]. Or maybe there never was a real "me" to begin with' – like Baudrillard's simulacrum, a copy without an original. By combining with the Puppet Master to create a new being, she renders this concern irrelevant, allowing the movie to end on a positive note for its cyborgs, a note that is much more difficult to find in *Blade Runner*.

Barry Keith Grant points out that 'for many viewers the value of (that is to say, the pleasure derived from) science fiction movies is determined by the quality (synonymous with believability) of the special effects' (1999: 21–2). Yet, says Ebert, too often that is all there is, 'just motion and sensation and visualisation. In the good special effects pictures, the effects are story driven. Whenever we see something amazing, there is a reason for it, there is a purpose behind it, there's a lead-in to it, there's a pay-off afterward' (*Dark City* DVD Commentary, Chapter 8). Dick's fiction, through the attention drawn to his work through *Blade Runner*, has become a source for that 'reason', now providing a full stock of ideas and vehicles for science fiction filmmakers. Taking Marianne Moore's depiction in 'Poetry', that poems provide 'imaginary gardens with real toads in them' (1961: 40), we see Dick's questions more and more often providing the toads, the substance, to movie-makers' imaginary gardens. With over a hundred short stories and more than forty novels still to be mined, it is likely that Philip K. Dick will continue to be an inspiration for science fiction movies. His ideas provide diegetic anchors for digitally-oriented directors (see Landon 1999) whose works might otherwise float off into a Sargasso of insignificance.

Just when the science fiction movie was heading off into a *Star Wars* space opera direction, Scott brought the genre (or a part of it) back to a more nuanced consideration of human character through an inspired absorption of film noir sensibilities. Even if he never works in the genre again, his influence will continue to be felt in cinema.

REDEMPTION, 'RACE', RELIGION, REALITY AND THE FAR-RIGHT: SCIENCE FICTION FILM ADAPTATIONS OF PHILIP K. DICK

DOMINIC ALESSIO

INTRODUCTION

According to *The Encyclopedia of Science Fiction* Philip K. Dick (PKD) is 'one of the two or three most important figures in 20th century US Science Fiction' (Clute & Nicholls 1999: 328). Likewise, John Mann in *The Mammoth Encyclopedia of Science Fiction* refers to PKD as 'possibly the most important SF writer of the second half of the twentieth century' (2001: 121). Not surprisingly, a number of academic texts have been devoted to examining his vast output of science fiction short stories, which number in the hundreds, as well as his forty-four published novels.[1] These same critical works have, however – albeit with some notable exceptions such as Judith Kerman's *Retrofitting Blade Runner: Issues in Ridley Scott's Blade Runner and Philip K. Dick's Do Androids Dream of Electric Sheep?* (which was first published in 1991 and republished in a 1997 revised edition), or Paul M. Sammon's *Future Noir: The Making of Blade Runner* (1996) – tended to ignore film adaptations of his writing. Indeed, there even appears to be some implied criticism of secondary material that tends to focus on PKD film adaptations on the basis that it ignores 'the novelistic source material' (Butler 2000: 88).

Since the release of Ridley Scott's *Blade Runner* (1982), however – based on PKD's 1968 novel *Do Androids Dream of Electric Sheep?* and considered to be 'the most influential sf film' (*The Encyclopedia of Science Fiction* 1999: 224) – a number of other movies have also been directly inspired by Dick's creative output. These include: Paul Verhoeven's *Total Recall* (1990), based on the short story 'We Can Remember It For You Wholesale' (1966); Ridley Scott's re-released Director's Cut of *Blade Runner* (1992) which added the famous unicorn scene, dropped the Harrison Ford voice-over, and cut the more optimistic climax; Canadian director Christian Duguay's *Screamers* (1995) which was adapted from the short story 'Second Variety' (1952); Gary Fleder's *Impostor* (2002), which was predicated on the 1953 short story of the same name; Steven Spielberg's *Minority Report* (2002), adapted from 'The Minority Report' (1956); and most recently John Woo's *Paycheck* (2004) which was based on the 1953 short story of the same title. In addition to these science fiction films there are at least two other much more loosely-based PKD-inspired films in existence. These are Jérôme Boivin's *Barjo/Confessions D'Un Barjo* (1992), a French film that draws on PKD's only non-science fiction novel *Confessions of a Crap Artist* (1975), as well as Australian director Peter Weir's *The Truman Show* (1998), whose concept of an artifical town was lifted from the story 'Time Out of Joint' (1959).[2] Aaron Barlow's 'Reel Toads and Imaginary

Cities', in this volume, suggests that elements of PKD and *Blade Runner's* influence can also be seen in a number of other science fiction productions such as *Brazil* (1985), *Terminator 2* (1991), *Strange Days* (1995), *Twelve Monkeys* (1996), *Cube* (1997), *Gattaca* (1997), *Dark City* (1998), *Soldier* (1998), *eXistenz* (1999) and *The Matrix* (1999). With such an international *opus* of PKD-influenced films, many of which involve some of the most powerful and well-known names in Hollywood, it seems high time that more critical attention was directed specifically at the films themselves, especially as his work, according to John Woo, appears 'written for the movies' since it is so 'cinematic' (Woo quoted on *Sci Fi.com*). In fact, with such a large number of PKD-inspired motion pictures in circulation Dick must surely rank as the most dominant late twentieth-century science fiction author in terms of influence on the film industry.[3]

Film adaptations of published work, in particular science fiction, are sometimes subject to criticism, either on the basis of their inability to effectively elucidate complex ideas or their lack of fidelity to the original material (*The Encyclopedia of Science Fiction*, 1999: 219). Nevertheless, divergence in PKD's case 'does not automatically mean the film is a shallow adaptation of the book' (Sammon 1996: 9). Indeed, as Sammon points out with regard to *Blade Runner* and its relationship with *Do Androids Dream of Electric Sheep?*, 'a careful viewing of *BR* actually reveals a surprising number of similarities between it and the novel' (1996: 20). Brooks Landon echoes Sammon's defence of Scott's film. He argues that the exact reproduction of the original PKD text is not the important benchmark for gauging the success of *Blade Runner*. Instead Landon believes that what is significant about the film is the director's ability 'to tap [the novel's] archetypal appeal' (1992: 97).

The purpose of this chapter, therefore, is not to compare and contrast the similarities and differences between PKD's published material and the science fiction films which were inspired by these works, thereby evaluating a film's apparent success or failure based on its adherence to an Ur-text. Indeed, a significant creative divergence from an original source can in fact provide a fascinating alternative. This can be seen by the successful science fiction films *When Worlds Collide* (1951) and *Forbidden Planet* (1956), both of which are modernised epigones of the Noah's Ark tale and Shakespeare's *The Tempest*. It is possible, if somewhat rarer, to see a successsful remake of a film, exemplified by the 1978 production *Invasion of the Body Snatchers* which updated the classic 1956 original. It can also be argued that Dick himself borrowed some of his ideas from other sources: his body of work dealing with androids indubitably owes a debt of gratitude to Mary Shelley's *Frankenstein* (1818). Likewise, the creative minds behind *Blade Runner*, while adapting the script from PKD's novel, simultaneously borrowed from other sources, in particular detective fiction, film noir and John Milton's *Paradise Lost* (see Landon 1992: 54–8). The same holds true of Woo's *Paycheck*, which in addition to PKD also draws heavily upon Alfred Hitchcock's *North By Northwest* (1959).

Subsequently, when evaluating the relationship between a film and the published work (or film) upon which it is based, it must be recognised that the final result is a product of its time and as such tends to tell its own unique story. These films should, therefore, be treated as creative texts in their own right. Thus the PKD-inspired science fiction films *Blade Runner*, *Total Recall*, *Screamers*, *Impostor*, *Minority Report* and *Paycheck*, while isomorphic in the sense that they enhance some of the central themes which concerned Dick's work, namely 'paranoia about reality not being what it seems, or people who are not what they seem' (Leeper 1995), also address a variety of equally significant themes, including the transformative nature of love; the blurring of boundaries; issues of class, 'race' and the far right; and the significance of the religious.

REDEMPTION

In *Blade Runner* and *Screamers*, the two films that deal substantially with simulacra developed by human beings, the machines are initially designed by their creators as warriors, assassins, sex slaves, *lumpenproletariat* or killers. If, as in Genesis 1:26, God said, 'Let us make man to our image and likeness', what do the androids and their design functions then tell us about their human creators? Like the Golem of mediaeval Jewish legend that is fashioned in the human image and whose characteristics are 'an expression of ourselves' (*The Encyclopedia of Science Fiction*, 1999: 508), humankind – if measured initially by the design functions of the PKD-inspired androids – appears murderous, depraved and divided. In fact, it is the androids in *Blade Runner*, *Screamers* and *Impostor*, and their symbolic equivalents in the other films (the mutants in *Total Recall* and the pre-cogs in *Minority Report*), who often emotionally rise above their human counterparts and/or draw attention to humanity's own inhumanity. They are the modern equivalents of the Frankenstein monster, the 'creature without a soul who is the most soulful' (Desser 1991: 62).

As in a number of novels by science fiction authors such as Robert Silberberg, C. J. Cherryh and John Brunner, by the end of *Blade Runner*'s story it looks as though the authors 'take the side of the androids against their human masters' (*The Encyclopedia of Science Fiction*, 1999: 34), since the artifical creations exhibit a greater share of positive human characteristics than their flesh and blood creators. These human features can particularly be seen in *Blade Runner* when the replicants work together in common cause (an early signifier of civilisation), grieve at their mutual losses, are anxious about their own mortality, exhibit a capacity for forgiveness, and demonstrate love for each other, and potentially even for humans (assuming that Deckard is not a replicant). The lead android Batty (Rutger Hauer), for example, appears distraught after Pris's (Daryl Hannah) death. Likewise the death of Zhora (Joanna Cassidy), a female android, only serves to highlight her human capabilities. She is shot dead by Deckard in the back whilst running away. Her subsequent slow-motion and tragic fall amongst a store front of inert shop mannequins, when followed by Deckard's apparent repugnance at what he has done, serves to heighten her distinction from the other 'dummies' around her.

The replicants in the film are in no way perfect or ideal creatures, however, as they also seek revenge, mislead and kill. To gain information Pris deceives the gentle Sebastian (William Sanderson), the genetic scientist who helped to create the replicants, by pretending to be a lost innocent in the corrupt city. And Batty eventually kills both Sebastian and Tyrell (Joe Turkel), his own creator. But how could these replicants be perfect since they are human creations? It is in fact their confused and complicated personalities that make them so human. In an extraordinarily touching grand finale, the chase sequence wherein Batty, the ultimate Nexus-6 warrior, lets Deckard live, the replicant even manages to put aside his anger and to forgive Deckard. Both psychologically and physically, Batty's actions come to evoke an image of Jesus Christ. When Batty realises that his lifespan is at the end of its genetically predetermined four years, he inserts nails into his hands in order to feel pain and extend his existence by a few short minutes. By doing so, and by then letting Deckard live, he forgives the blade runner and comes to celebrate life. The scene ends with Batty releasing a dove, a traditional Christian symbol of the Holy Spirit, which in turn suggests the presence of *Kodesh* (the breath of God) in the replicant, and thus humanity.

In the film the only way to identify a replicant's status as an android is through the complicated Voigt-Kampff test that is administered by trained blade runners and measures emotional responses by way of pupil dilation in a replicant's eye. A lack of empathy in response to personal questions is supposed to distinguish replicants from humans. To conduct the test blade runners must meet the replicants 'eye to eye' across a table. Although the face-to-face meeting might stem from the investigative interview of the film noir technique, the set-up may also insinuate that the two beings are more alike than supposed. It is certainly the case that in this advanced near-future age of androids and spaceships it should have been technically possible to develop a quicker and more straightforward genetic test, much like the medical examination attempted by Spencer Olham (Gary Sinese) in *Impostor* when he tries to prove that he is not a walking alien bomb.

By contrast to the replicants in *Blade Runner* the human beings who are given speaking parts and some character development are nearly all without emotion. The first blade runner, Holden (Morgan Paull), appears colder in his questioning than Leon, the replicant subject of his interrogation. Deckard himself acts like a 'hollow man' without morality (Mann 2001: 340). He apparently has no reluctance in killing replicants, just as nineteenth-century bounty hunters in pre-Civil War America presumably would have had no hesitations in capturing or returning escaped black slaves to their masters. And Tyrell, the replicants' infamous creator, looks and acts like Josef Mengele, the Nazi 'scientist' (see Kerman 1997: 2). Only by the end of the film does Deckard's position change when he seems to have been transformed by his love for the replicant Rachel (Sean Young), the tragic circumstances surrounding Zhora's death and his experiences with the Christ-like Batty. At the film's conclusion Deckard even runs away with Rachel and does not hunt her down, thereby consciously transgressing Earth's immigration laws. Only the sensitive Sebastian, the genetic scientist suffering from his own biological problems, and Gaff (Edward James Olmos), the cop who knowingly seems to let Deckard and Rachel escape together, demonstrate any human sincerity and empathy.

Screamers, the other PKD-inspired film to incorporate human-engineered androids into its subject matter and to introduce themes relating to love, redemption and the nature of humanity, is set in the year 2078 on the distant mining colony of the once beautiful planet of Sirius 6B. The story involves a war being waged over a new energy source by powerful Earth syndicates, the NEB or New Economic Block (a mining cartel whose primary interests lie in obtaining this energy source without consideration of the costs), and the Alliance (a group of miners and scientists who had once worked for the NEB and who then became disillusioned about the environmental and health consequences of its rapaciousness). The Alliance scientists eventually develop 'screamers' – small mechanical devices with blades that home onto the human pulse and kill the victim – as their primary defensive weapon. But slowly the screamers evolve independently into androids in the form of lost little boys, wounded soldiers and beautiful women. Soon both the Alliance and New Economic Block bases are wiped out by these machines, leaving only the human Alliance Commander Joseph Henricksson (Peter Weller) to work out which surviving NEB soldiers are human or machine.[4]

The storyline for *Screamers* was based on PKD's first android story 'Second Variety' which was set in the Cold War period between US and Communist troops. The film was directed by Christian Duguay who also directed the lesser-known science fiction sequels *Scanners II: The New Order* (1991) and *Scanners III: The Takeover* (1993), whilst the screenplay was adapted by Dan O'Brien, the 'creative force behind *Alien*' (Leeper 1995). Not surprisingly, in both *Screamers* and *Alien* (Ridley Scott, 1979) the theme of corporate greed and its disastrous consequences is significant. Although the majority of the human characters in *Screamers* do not have Deckard's *sang froid* (in the sense that early on in the film Deckard does not seem to have hesitations about the termination of the androids), it transpires that the Alliance troops created the screamers originally and were deceived by their commanders back on Earth about the direction of the war. Similarly, the NEB used nuclear and biological weapons against their human enemies. Neither side, consequently, appears to have acted with much humanity. The evolved androids in the film, mass-murderers who wipe out both NEB and Alliance human colonies numbering in the thousands, are thereby simply imitating their human creators. Some of the androids themselves, however, even come to exhibit human emotions, with one type lamenting his loneliness before destruction, 'I am my motherfucking self, alone'. By the film's conclusion Henricksson comments that the screamers are 'coming up in the world' by behaving more like humans every day, especially so as they learn to kill one another.

In both *Blade Runner* and *Screamers* love, sorrow and/or empathy are the emotional correlatives that redeem both humans and replicants. Deckard loves Rachel and learns what it is like to be hunted. Batty loves Pris and comes to be aware of the tragedy of loss. Sebastian identifies with what it is like to age quickly and feels the rejection of his genetically inferior outcast status. Gaff, by watching Deckard closely, discerns truth and does not 'blow the gaff' by revealing the lovers' secret. Likewise in *Screamers* a female replicant falls in love with Henricksson and sacrifices herself in battle with another android so that the human commander can live. It should not be forgotten either that Rachel in *Blade Runner* also kills her fellow android Leon because of her love for Deckard. Marilyn Gwaltney suggests in relation to *Blade Runner* that the evolution of Batty's and Rachel's positive human characteristics is similar to the process of experience that children go through: 'Perhaps personhood is developmental and children and androids are in the process of becoming persons, depending on their degree of experience' (Gwaltney 1991: 36). Such a theme would apply to the replicant's love for Henricksson in *Screamers* and, assuming here that Deckard is a replicant, for the blade runner himself and his developing love for Rachel. Gwaltney's thesis is also one suggested by the Pinocchio tale as well as by Steven Spielberg's updated science fiction version of this classic, *Artificial Intelligence: A.I.* (2001), the story of a lost little robot boy who wants to become real so that his human mother can love him again. Intriguingly, love is also a central theme that Woo deliberately inserted into *Paycheck* as he felt it was so essential to Michael Jennings' (Ben Affleck) development:

> Jennings, he's just a simple guy. He's not a superhero. He wanted to change his own fate. But somehow, he has some problems. He cannot change it by himself … Maybe love can help him change … So that's why I suggested adding more of a love story, and to make the female role bigger. (Woo quoted on Sci-Fi.com)

Paycheck is set in Seattle, Washington in 2007, and follows Jennings, a 'reverse engineer' who is happy to have all memories of his computer research erased after he has finished a large corporate project in order to ensure that his employer's concerns over industrial secrecy are assuaged. After working on a three year programme for Allcom and expecting a $100 million paycheck, instead he discovers only a manilla envelope with a variety of apparently everyday objects such as a bus ticket, paper clip, sunglasses and hair spray. Finding himself on the run from both the FBI and Allcom's thugs, Jennings relies on the support and the love of Rachel (Uma Thurman), a female colleague from Allcom, to help him understand the uses behind the contents of the envelope and the secret of his lost past. Like Rachel in *Blade Runner*, Thurman's character also turns against her own kind, in this case her employer.

In *Impostor*, as in *Blade Runner*, *Screamers*, *Artificial Intelligence: A.I.* and *Paycheck*, it is Olham's love for his wife Maya (Madeleine Stowe), and empa-

thy for Earth's outcasts, which makes him so determined to prove his humanity. The setting is 2079, and a totalitarian Earth is at war with the genetically superior Alpha Centauri. Most of Earth's inhabitants live in domes protected by
forcefields, with a small population of outcasts living in frontier regions on the
borders of these protected artificial environments. Olham has been accused
by Earth's security services, led by the 'Grand Inquisitor' Major Hathaway
(Vincent D'Onofrio), of being an alien 'replicant' with an explosive implant
designed to assassinate Earth's President. The use of *Blade Runner*'s term for
artificial humans clearly suggests the shaping influence of Scott's film. During
Olham's interrogation by Hathaway the Major insists that Olham and his android kind are not human since they lack souls. Yet Olham's determination to
demonstrate his innocence and his genuine fear, when coupled with his love
for Maya and his concern for Earth's outcasts who live in a kind of third world
poverty (and for whom Olham procures expensive medicines pilferred from
a military hospital), earn him the viewing audience's sympathies. By contrast,
Hathaway's fundamentalist certainty about Olham's guilt, his admission that
innocents have died in his search to weed out Centauri repliants ('we lost ten
and saved ten thousand'), the fact that he is willing to shoot his own security
forces as well as patients in the local hospital to ensure Olham's demise, and
the use of a torturous device that would not look out of place in Counter-Ref-
ormation Europe to remove the bomb inside Olham, all make the Major look
like the real devil. In reality, however, it turns out that Hathaway was correct,
although even Olham himself was not aware he has a duplicate until the last
millisecond of his existence.

Hathaway's apparent lack of concern for his own personnel in *Impostor*
is reminiscent too of the treatment of civilians in *Total Recall*. The latter is
set primarily on Mars in the year 2084 after humans have begun to colonise
the red planet. Humans and their mutant relatives have to live in protected
environments, like the domes in *Impostor*, due to the lack of breathable oxy-
gen. Douglas Quaid (Arnold Schwarzenegger), the central protagonist, lives
on Earth but is haunted by recurring dreams about Mars. Visiting REKALL, a
company that gives its customers the artificial memories of an exciting holiday (Quaid chooses the Martian secret agent scenario), he discovers that he
actually appears to be a real secret agent and begins working against the
corrupt rule of Mars' authoritarian leader. He is followed by Martian counter-
agents who try to kill and/or capture him at every turn and think nothing of
firing upon a crowded escalator or subway, a further example of humanity's
own inhumanity towards its kind.

A BLURRING OF BOUNDARIES

Quaid, whose name was originally Quail in the PKD short story but was changed
in the film to avoid resembling the then US Vice-President Dan Quayle, is not
above jeopardising the lives of innocent civilians either. This suggests that
brutality is not necessarily restricted to the villains or the non-human charac-

ters, and that boundaries between so-called protagonists and antagonists, or aliens/replicants and humans, can sometimes be blurred. While trying to pass Mars customs Quaid disguises himself as a woman whose head explodes and causes instant decompression in a public spaceport, thereby potentially threatening the lives of hundreds of innocent passengers. Similarly, Deckard in *Blade Runner* starts out as a futuristic bounty-hunter/assassin, who if a replicant turns out to be killing his own kind and if a human is still murdering sentient beings. This human potential for demonstrating violence against its own kind, even by the protagonists of the science fiction stories, draws to mind historical parallels, in particular Allied bombing atrocities in World War Two over Dresden and Hiroshima/Nagasaki. It is also a theme common to science fiction, such as *Alien* and *Aliens* (James Cameron, 1986), wherein human corporate greed results in the deaths of thousands of innocent colonists. Corporate profit at the expense of human beings is also a theme raised in *Paycheck* (with regard to Allcom's desire to maximise the share value of the company even at the cost of a nuclear war), *Total Recall* (the mutations in the Mars colonists are the result of poor mining conditions) and *Screamers* (NEB short sightedeness over the environment and the safety of its workers is the reason for the creation of the Alliance).

When assessing these so-called moral dilemmas in films such as *Total Recall* it must be remembered that the film is a Schwarzenegger movie directed by Paul Verhoeven, who in addition to the shoot-'em-up *RoboCop* (1987) also directed the violent science fiction box-office success *Starship Troopers* (1997). Consequently, there is the possible danger of overdoing critical analysis of this kind in a genre aimed primarily at entertainment and that as a matter of course includes large swathes of violence. Nonetheless, Verhoeven's work is not so black and white either. His use of Nazi uniforms for Earth's secret intelligence in *Starship Troopers* not only draws attention to fascistic criticisms of Robert Heinlein's original 1959 novel, but implies that militarist Earth is not as innocent in the conflict with the bugs as the audience might assume. Once more it seems that the so-called human protagonists might actually be the real villains of these pieces. By contrast to the humans in *Total Recall*, the humanoid mutants, like the replicants in *Blade Runner*, appear to be the most considerate characters, as evidenced by their strong community and family bonds. Nevertheless, there is an exception amongst the mutants too as the treacherous taxi driver demonstrates once again that the so-called 'good guys' can in fact be bad. This switching can also work the other way around. Quaid in *Total Recall* started out life as a secret service agent in the employ of the corrupt Mars government but changed his attitude because of his love for a woman in the resistance, and his developing empathy for the mutant cause. There appears to be quite a lot of Deckard in him.

As in the other PKD-inspired films, questions are raised about the nature of human behaviour in Steven Spielberg's *Minority Report*, which stars Tom Cruise as police chief John Anderton, the head of Pre-Crime in 2054 Washington, D.C. One focus of this human cruelty towards its own kind rests on the condition of the pre-cogs, three psychics kept in a near-permanent state of drug-induced suspension because they are used by the police and government to detect murders before they are committed. The pre-cogs' imprisonment and isolation is explained away in the film by the simple dismissal 'better if you don't think of them as human', and there are disturbing echoes here of Major Olham's justification for his actions ('we lost ten and saved ten thousand'). Another questionable human action by the protagonists in *Minority Report* includes the behaviour of the police technician Wally, who watches over the psychics in their stasis and who resembles a sexual *voyeur* towards the female pre-cog Agatha when he caresses and speaks to her in endearing expressions. However, once Agatha is taken out of her drug bath by Anderton, who is presumed a killer and like Olham in *Impostor* must go on the run in order to prove his innocence, she begins to demonstrate that she too has a personality and physical abilities like any other 'normal' human being. The evolution of Agatha from object to subject in *Minority Report* serves to underline how cruel her 'imprisonment' was, since it humanises her character and allows the audience to relate to her as an individual.

Other actions that raise concerns in *Minority Report* about human beings' viciousness towards their own kind include the way the pre-cogs evolved (by experimentation on drug addicts), the intrusive use of robot surveillance spiders on run-down communities, and questions about committing so many people to cryogenic sleep on the basis that they might commit a future crime, even when it is recognised that pre-cogs can sometimes get it wrong. There are echoes of *Minority Report*'s disturbing surveillance techniques by police, government and corporate forces in other films too, such as the x-ray/infra red machines used on the interzone peoples in *Impostor*, the CCTV-like cameras used on the mutants in *Total Recall*, and the hidden video camera from Uma Thurman's bathroom in *Paycheck*. Surveillance is also, of course, a crucial element in *The Truman Show*.

'RACE' AND THE FAR RIGHT

In *Minority Report*, *Total Recall*, *Blade Runner* and *Impostor* future habitations are blighted by class distinctions, indicating how divided human communities can be. The poor and the mutants live in high-density, public-housing sprawls, eking out a living along the fringes of so-called civilised society. By contrast to the dark and lowly mean streets in *Blade Runner*, the corporate leader Tyrell lives far removed from the masses on the top floor of a colossal *ziggurat*, traditionally the abode of the gods and their priests in Mayan and Sumerian culture, and thus a fitting symbol for a creator of replicants. But an association with long-gone empires or peoples such as the Mayans or Sumerians is also a stark warning that imperial powers can come crashing down. It is, therefore, an appropiate apocalyptic warning portending a Tower of Babel-like collapse (see Judith Kerman's chapter in this volume). As Sumeria was the world's first civilisation, a *ziggurat* in a futuristic L.A. might also be an approporiate symbol for its last civilisation.

These class distinctions also raise some interesting questions about 'race' and fascism in the PKD-inspired films, which serve to address further questions about morality and humanity. The positions of the replicants in *Blade Runner* and the images of the masses in L.A. 2019 highlight ethnic concerns in 1980s America. It is never explained, for instance, why replicants are not allowed on Earth and only on the Off-World colonies. Francavilla (1991: 7) suggests that what we could be witnessing in the films is a fear of displacement at home by the Other, a factor testified to by Bryant in the film referring to the replicants as 'skin-jobs', which Deckard in the 1982 voice-over explains is akin to calling them 'niggers'. Official concern about replicants posing as humans, and the need for a police state with scientific tests to determine identity, call to mind comparisons with apartheid South Africa. The purpose of the Voigt-Kampff test is strikingly similar to the so-called 'scientific' tests conducted by South Africa's Race Classifaction Board to determine a person's colour. Likewise, why does the Nazi look-alike Tyrell create only white replicants, especially the genetically super strong and intelligent Batty whom Kerman suggests resembles an 'Aryan superman'? (1997: 22). The Nazi and South African parallels with regard to *Blade Runner* are also intriguing as Earth, or at least L.A., seems to resemble a crowded World War Two Eastern European ghetto or 1980s South African Bantustan, both of which were designed specifically for ethnic division. The choice of Los Angeles as the locale of *Blade Runner* is intriguing too considering that the city, the Watts district especially, has historically been the site of a number of violent twentieth-century racial conflagrations.

If Deckard is a replicant working for a future military-industrial power, then taking the fascist parallels even further, he is the equivalent of Primo Levi's *prominenz*, the Jewish volunteers who helped to sort out arrivals at Auschwitz and who assisted in the attempted genocide of their own kind by the Nazis. At the very least, if he is human, then he is a member of a futuristic *Einsatzgruppen*, the German police battalions who brutally hunted down Jews and Communists in Eastern Europe during Operation Barbarossa. Continuing with the racial and fascist premises, the death of Zhora amongst panes of shattering shop glass might even be an oblique reference to *Kristallnacht* when some 91 Jews were killed by Nazi-inspired purges against Jewish-owned businesses, the event taking its name from the millions of glass fragments that resulted from these pogroms. Perhaps it is not so surprising, after considering the far-right German parallels, that Batty and Leon eventually kill both Sebastian as well as the Chinese eye surgeon, since these two scientists were also complicit in the Tyrell Corporation's genetic creations. The replicants' actions are equivalent to those of post-war partisans in countries like France, Greece and Italy who hunted down and executed any who had collaborated with the occupying Nazi and fascist officials. Is it any wonder then that the mutants who fight the authoritarian forces on Mars in *Total Recall* are called the 'resistance'?

Apart from the genetically inferior Sebastian, it seems that the only whites at street level in *Blade Runner* are cops or replicants. The rest of the city looks like a jumbling mass of Chinese, Japanese and Arabs, with the city's culture dominated by Japanese corportions such as Atari, Chinese food vendors and Eastern belly dancers. In part this emphasis upon a non-white population and Oriental dominance could be a reflection of American grumbling during the Reagan Presidency about US trade inbalances with Japan and illegal Latino immigration to California. If the propaganda from the floating dirigibles is to be believed, in early twenty-first-century Earth it appears to be the case that the mass of healthy white people have sought a Nazi-like *lebensraum* (living space) in a pigmentopia (a utopian discourse with a strong or prevailing ethnocentric/racist world view) amongst the stars.[5] The racist agenda of this pigmentopia is further underlined by the fact that it uses replicant slave labour for its wars and its work force, leaving everyone too sick or too ancient back on the Old World Earth. Earth thereby becomes a dumping ground for the infirm, much like the intention of the so-called 'Homelands' of white South Africa's apartheid regime in the mid-1980s.

While 'race' does not appear to be a significant factor in most of the other PKD film adaptations, it may be worth noting that in *Impostor*, Olham's only friend is the black Kyle. Furthermore, Kyle and the other black characters in the film all appear to be relegated to the interzone places and are poor, sick and without medicine. There is also more than a whiff of fascistic iconography in *Impostor* with regard to the media reports surrounding Earth's President (her television appearances shot from ground up and in large halls full of attendants mirror Leni Riefenstahl's infamous film portayals of Hitler), as well as in the authoritarian and militarised nature of Earth's regime (which is encapsulated by Hathaway's ruthlessness and his uniformed marching goons). With so many far-right parallels in *Impostor*, particularly with regard to the authoritarian portrayal of Earth's political and military leaders, it seems that Fleder borrowed as much from *Starship Troopers* as from PKD.

RELIGIOUS SYMBOLISM

PKD was very much interested in theology from the late 1960s onwards, even conducting séances with a bishop in California and later becoming convinced that he had been directly contacted by a superior power (see Butler 2000: 9–10). A number of religious references also infiltrate the film adaptations of his work, in turn compounding questions of identity, morality and meaning. In *Minority Report* the pre-cog chamber is described as a 'temple' and the name Gideon (an Old Testament judge) is used by the overseer of the cryogenic complex. In *Impostor*, Hathaway enters into a inquisitorial diatribe on the nature of souls, and discusses Olham's predicament in a futuristic chapel setting. There is also *Blade Runner*'s apocalyptic vision of a dark and nightmarish Hieronymus Bosch hell, kindled by the opening sequence of a flame-filled L.A. cityscape into which the replicants have crashed. This in turn draws parallels

to Lucifer's exile and descent from Heaven (Desser 1991: 54). The Biblical association is supported by the fact that Tyrell refers to Batty's life as being 'bright',
recalling the name Lucifer, derived from the Latin for 'lightbringer'.

According to Kerman, Biblically-inspired apocalyptic themes dominate
Blade Runner, including the debased future L.A. as akin to Sodom and Gomorrah, the endless rain as a symbol (and warning) of the Flood, as well as
issues of Exodus with humans leaving the Earth in search of new Promised
Lands (see Kerman in this volume). This theme of the end of the world in PKD's
work is not surprising considering the fact that he was a child of the Cold War
and thus lived under the threat of atomic annihilation. Among all the signs
and symbols of humankind's potential evil and harmful capability towards
its own kind, the destruction of life on Earth is perhaps the ultimate example.
Not surprisingly, nuclear holocaust is a theme in many of the film adaptations
as well. Alamorgodo (the site of America's first nuclear test) is where Commander Hendricksson found his escape rocket in *Screamers*. At the start of
Impostor Olham likens the possible defeat of the Centauri to the atomic defeat
that wiped out Hiroshima and Nagasaki in Japan in 1945. He too includes Alamorgodo in his speech. There may then be a warning in these two films about
the *hubris* of humankind, as Olham does eventually blow himself up and it
turns out that Hendricksson's escape rocket contains a mechanical screamer
that if returned to Earth has the potential to wipe out all life. As the female android remarks to Henricksson: 'You don't know what the hell you have started
up.' Nuclear war also threatens to end humanity in *Paycheck* after Jennings
discovers that the machine which he built for Allcom fortells the future, in the
process inadvertently initiating an atomic conflict.

In addition to the apocalyptic imagery, much of it taken from Revelations
and Genesis, the nomenclature in some of the films is also provocative for
its religious associations. According to *Genesis*, the Biblical Rachel was surrounded by questions of identity as her husband Jacob was originally deceived by Rachel's father and given her covered elder sister as a bride instead.
Both she and Jacob had to flee their homeland after quarreling with her father.
Jennings and the other Rachel in *Paycheck* also have to go on the run from the
FBI and Allcom hitmen, and there are similar questions of identity surrounding Uma Thurman's character. Allcom, for example, tries to dupe Jennings by
using a dummy of Thurman. This ruse, however, is revealed to Jennings by
the imposter's kiss. The use of the kiss as a mark of treachery is also a common Biblical occurence, most famously in the New Testament when Judas
betrays Christ (Mark 14:45–6), but also in Genesis (27:26–7) when Jacob gives
a kiss to Isaac, Rachel's father, as part of his own deception.

Paycheck is not the only science fiction film in which a false declaration of
love and an imposter is discovered by way of a kiss. In *Invasion of the Body
Snatchers* Miles finds out that his girlfriend Becky has been replaced by a pod
person after she kisses him in an old mining shaft. The treacherous nature of
the kiss is also central to *Blade Runner* wherein Batty kisses his creator Tyrell
before he kills him, literally echoing Judas' betrayal of Christ and inverting

Batty's later Christ-like role. A kiss is also used by Quaid's wife (Sharon Stone) in *Total Recall* to try and delay the hero so that Mars secret agents can catch him, and the theme is picked up in the same film by the mutant leader Kuato, who like Christ is not only killed by his enemies but is also betrayed by one of his own, the taxi driver.

According to *The Encyclopedia of Science Fiction*, 'the landscapes of decay and imposture' in PKD's work mirrored the psychological conditions of his characters (1999: 329). In the films too, landscapes and cityscapes are also thematically significant, both for drawing attention to the results of an over-reliance of technology that could lead to Earth's destruction and as a manifestation of the damaging selfishness of humankind. As Kerman suggests in relation to *Blade Runner*, the cityscapes are reminders of God's vow after humankind's expulsion from Paradise: 'cursed is the earth' (Gen 3:17). The future L.A. of *Blade Runner*, at least in the Director's Cut where the rural forest escape of the 1982 version is removed, appears as a barren polluted wasteland in which it always seems to be dark and raining. In the original novel by PKD nearly all animals were wiped out because of nuclear war, but it is never fully explained why L.A. is portrayed so drearily in the film adaptation and we can only assume that it is due to over-crowding and pollution. Likewise in *Screamers*, the once-beautiful colony of Sirius 6B has been reduced to an atomic wasteland. Posters for the planet had once promoted it as 'paradise', but after the war it is more like Paradise Lost. In *Impostor* Earth is a burnt-out wreck following the war with the Centauri. Even nature trails under protected forcefields look like barren brown field sites, and the park where Olham and Maya went on a hiking holiday is burned down twice during the film.

Intriguingly, at least in the 1982 version of *Blade Runner* wherein Deckard and Rachel escape into the wilderness, or the end of *Minority Report* when the liberated pre-cogs begin to build new lives for themselves in an isolated log-cabin in the woods, it seems that the dream of a rural frontier America is also still alive. Herein lies a vision of a New Jerusalem that was so central to Puritan settler thinking in the early history of the United States (again, see Kerman in this volume). Fittingly, the central protagonists of *Paycheck* end up opening a garden centre as a full-time occupation after all of their experiences with high-tech adventure. In this context of rural versus urban, and the religious allusions between corrupt city and paradise/Eden, it might also be significant to note that the cop in *Blade Runner* who allows Deckard and Rachel to escape might have also had his name (Gaff) derived from 'Gaffer', which traditionally means an old country fellow. The association of this name with the pastoral underlines once more the redeeming character of a more natural environment.

REALITY

Philip K. Dick has been described as 'the Poet Laureate of false memories and fake experiences' (Butler 2001: 7) while *The Encyclopedia of Science Fiction* states that the quintessential PKD theme is 'the juxtaposition of two "levels of reality"' (1999: 328). The central motif of things not always being what they appear to be was developed by Dick as early as his first novel *Solar Lottery* (1955), which depicted a future Earth organised around a draw that turns out to be fixed. This theme of obfuscation and confusion is further underlined by the questions raised in the section above with regard to human nature and human-replicant characteristics. In part such concerns about compound tiers of existence and shifting boundaries appear to be a consequence of PKD's heavy use of drugs, including LSD, cannabis and speed, which in turn seemed to have caused him to become paranoid and to query reality (Sammon 1996: 10–12). Drugs also appear central to the plot of many PKD-inspired films, and transform the lives of the characters involved. In *Total Recall* they are used to induce Quaid into a state that enables him to accept the implanted memory programme he requested. In *Minority Report* drugs help Anderton to forget the disappearance of his child and are also inadvertently the cause of the pre-cogs' condition as they bring on their pyschic abilities and cause their imprisonment. A chemical drug was also used to make Jennings forget three years of work on Allcom's top-secret project designed to fortell the future in *Paycheck*. And drugs are also what Kyle is seeking when he teams up with Olham in *Impostor*. Depending on the circumstances and the film, therefore, drugs can either heal, hide or reveal.

Questions of identity and reality are especially prevalent in *Blade Runner*, and much has been written on the question of Deckard's status as a potential replicant. Like the replicants Rachel and Leon, Deckard also relies on photographs as evidence that his past was real, which in turn only ironically serves to insinuate that Deckard's memories have been fabricated. It is never explained why Deckard retired as a blade runner in the first place, implying perhaps that his history, like Rachel's memories of spiders or a brother/sister visit to the basement, were also made up. The fact that Deckard has never taken the Voigt-Kampff test himself suggests too that he might have failed it. Furthermore, that Deckard is such a good blade runner might be due to the maxim that 'it takes one to know one'. Even the name, Deckard, might be a subtle reference to the French philosopher Descartes and his emphasis on hyperbolic doubt. The use of a Coca-Cola product placement in *Blade Runner*, while on the one hand a clever marketing device utilised initially by Spielberg in *E.T. The Extra-Terrestrial* (1982) and possibly added to Scott's film for future authenticity, also ironically emphasises a product that promotes itself as 'the real thing', in turn reminding the viewing audience that all is not what it appears.

Nevertheless, according to some critics, what really seals the case on Deckard's status as a replicant is the unicorn dream sequence added to the Director's Cut. The fact that Gaff at the end of the film leaves an origami unicorn at Deckard's apartment implies that he knows Deckard's dreams just as Deckard knows Rachel's memories. The choice of a unicorn might not be accidental either. According to the thirteenth-century Norman clerk de Guillaume, the unicorn's horn was a mediaeval symbol of truth (Evans 1970: 1115), suggesting perhaps that Deckard's past is as equally mythical as this fabulous beast. Although there are arguments against the possibility that Deckard is a replicant, namely that he is not as strong as Batty and that androids are not allowed on Earth (although Rachel is an obvious exception), there are hints elsewhere in the film that all is not as it appears. The euphemism 'retirement', for example, only serves to hide the true barbarity of the act.

Total Recall also problematises memory and the nature of reality to the point that one is left questioning if the events depicted in the film actually occurred in this fictional future world or if Quaid was just experiencing the secret agent vacation package that he signed up for, complete with the athletic brunette love interest. Characters in the film repeatedly suggest that the entire episode was invented. Schwarzenegger's wife tells him that his 'whole life is just a dream', while Quaid himself questions his very existence, remarking 'Who am I?', and then in an earlier computer conversation with himself states that 'you are not you, you are me'. Similarly the totalitarian leader of Mars warns Quaid that he is merely 'a stupid dream' that will come to an end, while Quaid's Martian love interest Melina (Rachel Ticotin) at the film's conclusion suggests that their victory is 'like a dream' and that Quaid should kiss her quickly before he wakes up. As in *Sleeping Beauty* the kiss is important as it usually does result in the princess being woken from her slumber.

There are a number of other hints that what is seen or heard in *Total Recall* is not to be trusted. The breakfast news programme shows Mars security forces brutally slaughtering opponents while the newsreader comments that 'minimum use of force' was employed. The video images of mountains and lakes in Quaid's kitchen are also fake, while the James Bond-style holograph watch creates yet another duplicate of Quaid. Once again, however, as in *Blade Runner*, contrary positions can be argued. If Quaid is experiencing a dream sequence, then how is the audience or Quaid aware of what goes on when he is not in the room? Similarly, Quaid himself deliberately shoots a possible REKALL employee who tries to convince him that the entire Mars scenario is a dream sequence gone badly wrong. Quaid's justification for this killing is that this so-called employee would not be perspiring so heavily if he did not really think his life was at risk. Yet there also remains the intriguing possibility in this game world of REKALL unreality that the perspiring employee could also be a well thought-out detail of the simulation.

Photographs and video recordings in *Impostor, Blade Runner, Minority Report* and *Paycheck* are used as potential visual testimony by the protagonists to help verify their identities. However, these images too are often subject to distortion and are not ideologically jejune, further emphasising the theme of half-truths and distortion. Olham in *Impostor* stops to focus on an image of his wife Maya as if to remind himself that he had a 'real' past and that he does love his wife. Although this reminder of love might prove to him that he is really human and not a machine, we eventually discover that the Maya in the photo is not the same Maya as his wife: indeed, it turns out at the end of the film that Olham himself is not the real Olham. Similarly in *Blade Runner* Deckard's piano is littered with family portraits, again an apparent signifier of historical evidence, although the images in this scene appear antiquated and thus out-of-place. Following the earlier scenes that emphasised Leon's and Rachel's fabricated photographs and memories, these images in Deckard's apartment cannot be taken at face value. Rachel in *Paycheck* also shows Jennings their personal videos and snapshots to prove to him that he is her partner of three years. Although Jennings responds emotionally to these images they are only used as secondary proof and after the fact; the real evidence of Rachel's authenticity was in her kiss. And visual deception is intriguingly the basis of Tom Cruise's dilemma in *Minority Report*: Anderton keeps replaying 3D footage of his missing son, which when taken with an illegal drug seems to give the police chief some respite from his personal horror by making him believe that he still has a real relationship with the lost little boy. Agatha has her precognition substituted, thereby making Anderton look guilty of a crime that he did not commit; and hundreds of faked photos of murdered children become the basis of an attempt to frame Anderton. In all three cases of *Minority Report* what you see is not what you get.

In both *Screamers* and *Impostor* the directors also play guessing games with the viewers. The former opens with soldiers viewing a desolate landscape from inside of a military fortress, suggesting that people tend to have a kind of blinkered vision or bunker-like mentality about events. Yet as Hendricksson attests in conversation with his second-in-command when he states that 'we were all NEBs once', things are not so black and white and positions can change. To quote Ace, Hendersson's aide: 'It's a bit blurry.' Although Hendricksson also criticises the NEB's use of nuclear weapons on a number of occasions he too is eventually forced to employ them against the 'Davids', androids in the form of lost little boys with teddy-bears, again suggesting the deceptiveness of appearances.

Questions about identity and reality are also raised by Fleder, the director of *Impostor*, who positively encourages the viewer to deliberate over the issue of Olham's innocence and whether he really is the victim of a Centauri plot. After being arrested near the beginning of the film for being an alien explosive device, Olham (who does not believe the charges against him) is forced to pretend to be a bomb in order to frighten his paramilitary escort and escape in the hope that he can then prove his innocence. There is a build-up of suspense with news reports about the Centauri overcoming Earth's forward bases and getting closer and closer all the time, and Olham's neighbour warning him that the enemy can and will get through. Fleder seems to be borrowing here from 1950s anti-Communist hysteria, and the sense of a forthcoming takeover is not too dissimilar from the sense of urgency about alien invasion in the first *Invasion of the Body Snatchers*. Nor do we ever see the Centauri themselves in *Impostor*, which only adds to their mystery. One even begins to wonder if in fact the Centauri actually exist or if the entire war is just a clever scenario to keep the authoritarian leaders of Earth in power, much like the concluding epiphany to the film version of Margaret Atwood's *The Hand-maid's Tale* (Volker Schlöndorff, 1990). Is Olham subsequently singled out for termination by Earth's fascist-like government because he has developed a bomb that can end the war, thus also ending the *raison d'être* of the military government too?

Suspense about the nature of what is real is further helped by Olham lamenting that 'I can't trust my mind', much as Quaid in *Total Recall* questions his own grip on reality. The tension is also heightened in *Impostor* by the fact that Olham's wife seems to doubt her husband, eventually betraying him to Hathaway's security forces. Yet in a twist of fate she is shown to be a bomb; and although viewers might begin to think that Olham is innocent, it transpires that Maya is just a red herring, since both husband and wife are supposed Centauri plants.

CONCLUSION

Themes of redemption through love and empathy, the blurring of boundaries, 'race' and the far-right, the religious, and the question of what is real, dominate the Philip K. Dick film adaptations. Although many of these themes were common to PKD's original work, the adaptations are the result of a number of other influences as well, from the literary and cinematic to the personal. With regard to the last point, what is especially intriguing is that most of the directors of these US adaptions are not American-born. Scott is British, Woo is Hong Kong-Chinese, Duguay is French-Canadian, Verhoeven is Dutch and Weir is Australian. Spielberg, although American born, is also Jewish. As foreign or Jewish directors working in Hollywood, questions about identity, boundaries, and 'race' might have proven to be particularly relevant to their own personal histories, even if only at the subconscious level.

NOTES

1 For a discussion on secondary reading relating to PKD see Andrew M. Butler, *Philip K. Dick* (Harpenden: Pocket Essentials, 2000), 87–90. The information on Dick's total output of published work comes from http://www.philipkdick.com /works_novels.html (accessed 05/10/05).

2 *The Truman Show* stars Jim Carrey as a young paranoid man who, sensing that something is not quite right with his seemingly utopian existence, discovers that he is the protagonist of a high-tech television soap opera and tries to escape his artificial environment. In contrast to the film the short story deals with a much more science fiction theme, namely an interstellar war between Luna and Earth.

3 Butler (2000: 91) suggested that PKD's *A Scanner Darkly* was also forthcoming, although at the time of writing it had yet to be released.

4 Peter Weller also starred in Paul Verhoeven's science fiction film *RoboCop*

(1987) about a part human/part machine cyborg whose personality was blocked by circuitry but who finally managed to regain his past and his humanity.

5   See Dominic Alessio (2004) 'Race, Gender and Proto-Nationalism in Julius Vogel's *Anno Domini* 2000', *Foundation*, 91, 36–54, 45.

SECTION 2: PLAYING *BLADE RUNNER*

REPLICATING THE BLADE RUNNER
BARRY ATKINS

It has been some time since it was possible to discuss *Blade Runner* as if it were a single and fixed text that might be considered in isolation from its history of multiple prints, or detached from its vast array of intertexts, paratexts, references and allusions. It might not have been the first example of a film given a second release in the form of a director's cut, but its various refashionings have caught the attention of both fans and academic commentators to an unusual degree, and its influence on succeeding imaginative representations of the future city has been considerable. Even before the release of Ridley Scott's authorised Director's Cut in 1992, the film was already caught in a web of references to other texts, from its credited relationship to Philip K. Dick's *Do Androids Dream of Electric Sheep?* and its appropriation of the term 'blade runner' from William Burroughs' screenplay title, *Blade Runner: A Movie* (1979), to its density of intertextual allusion to a range of cinematic genres. As Christy Gray discusses elsewhere in this volume, *Blade Runner* has also been reworked and refashioned in subsequent novels, and it is intriguing to attempt to identify what it is about the film that has made it such a productive (and economically rewarding) site for such forms of replication.

In terms of its relationship with computer games, *Blade Runner* has had a wider influence than simply providing a direct licensing opportunity for game development. As Steven Poole has noted:

> One of the most seminal modern influences, not just on videogames but on all forms of science fiction, is the film *Blade Runner*. This is partly due to aesthetic considerations – the popular style of futuristic tech-noir – but for videogames it has also had, until the current generation of extremely powerful machines, a technological payoff. For the vision of neon-soaked streets at night in a skyscraper-studded, futuristic Tokyo [sic] was particularly amenable to videogames' limited powers of representation. (2000: 88)

Poole's point is a fair one, that the deep shadows, neon lighting and general murkiness of vision that so marked out the film proved particularly amenable to the limited representational palette available to game designers, but he misses the extent to which the suitability of *Blade Runner* for a videogame treatment goes far beyond mere questions of visual aesthetics. This essay seeks to address the intersection between film and game in terms that are not only those of visual correspondence, but in their reliance on the exploration of spatial metaphors that mark out the differences between the film's invitation to watch and the game's invitation to play.

REPLICATION, REFASHIONING AND REMEDIATION

In its densely stylised representation of a future Los Angeles, *Blade Runner* has always drawn audience attention to its artifice and its status as a technological product, in whatever form it was first encountered. As a self-consciously made thing it always carried with it the implication that it could be remade. This is, after all, a manufactured product that is almost obsessively focused on anxieties surrounding the development of manufacturing technologies, emblematised through the refinement of the replicants. In its repeated re-emergence as a remade text it also offers the possibility that it could, itself, be refined and developed even to the point where, like Rachel, Roy Batty or Pris, it challenges our understanding of what any claims for the authenticity or originality of the singular or originating object might mean. As the critical response to George Lucas's insertion of new computer-generated images into the first *Star Wars* trilogy of films demonstrates, refashioning, even with the advantages of new technological processes, does not necessarily mean unqualified improvement, but with *Blade Runner* the history of multiple release and the nature of its content coincide in a particularly effective way. Everything points towards *Blade Runner* remaining a multiple and elusive text.

That *Blade Runner* continues to offer the promise of plural experiences is evident in the sleeve notes to the collector's edition DVD, where the merits of the Director's Cut over the original are detailed in a language that might have been familiar to a Tyrell Corporation salesman extolling the virtues of the Nexus-6:

> The result is a heightened emotional impact: a great film made greater. Most intriguing of all is a newly included unicorn vision that suggests Deckard may be a humanoid. *Do Androids Dream of Electric Sheep?* Is Deckard a replicant? As with all things in the future, you must discover the answer for yourself.[1]

The primary gesture made by Scott for the 1992 release, of course, was to remove the presence of the singular interpretative narration of Harrison Ford's Deckard, and consequently open the film up to contesting interpretations. This erasure of an authoritative voice leaves *Blade Runner*, even in such an apparently definitive and authorised form, a firmly plural text that resists and opposes any sense of closure towards the singular. A note to one version of the script dated 11 May 2000 makes a related statement about *Blade Runner* as a text still accessible to reworking:

> So this draft is just one of many. Although a transcript of the dialogue in the release prints must exist for the purposes of translation and subtitling, there is no definitive draft of *Blade Runner* and there never will be. Because it's not finished yet.[2]

Although Hampton Fancher and David Peoples carry the writing credit for the film they are clear that the script was the work of many hands and many imaginations, and that it is a work still in a fluid process of emerging in new forms. *Blade Runner* remains peculiarly appropriate for an age where we consume our entertainment, at least in our domestic spaces, with the controller in one hand always offering us the possibility that we might skip, rewind, pause, record and replay, and we now expect our texts to come packaged with a range of paratexts in the inclusion of deleted scenes, director's commentary and 'making of' documentaries on our DVDs. *Blade Runner* is also a particularly slippery and elusive product of contemporary manufacturing, a thing that can be replicated, mechanically copied and translated, but never finished in a meaningful sense – as with a piece of software, we might expect another release, and another, and another. As such *Blade Runner* presents a particularly promising primary work for the attentions of computer game developers, where the agency of the player in producing the text at the moment of play, and the illusion that play allows intervention in the 'unfinished' text on screen, is central to the operation of games as games. The concluding sentence of the DVD notes might even have been written with newly emergent computer games in mind, for they are a form of 'future' media that relies above all else upon stimulation of the desire to 'discover the answer for yourself'.

The history of computer and video games based on intellectual properties taken from film has, however, been less than illustrious. Some film-game tie-ins may have been successful in commercial terms, but they have only rarely achieved critical success as independent textual artefacts, and remain a phenomenon received with some scepticism by the computer games press and by many players of games.[3] Advances in graphics technology have seen the once massive gulf between the visual quality of the two forms narrow, but it would be a mistake to see the only distinction between film and game in the realisation of a comparable technological possibility of cinematic quality of representation. There have always been exceptions, but the release of the first attempt at a *Blade Runner* game (for the Commodore 64 and ZX Spectrum platforms) in 1985 certainly did little to challenge assumptions that such games often yoke unoriginal gameplay mechanics to glancing visual references to the originating film.[4] There is even some expectation that such games will likely prove to be lazily executed and unsatisfying as games, with their sales dependent more on their connection to the film than on their own qualities as playing experiences. As such, games associated with films frequently appear to be of no more significance than any other form of licensed product used to maximise profit from the intellectual property established by the film, from branded lunchboxes to action figures.[5] In the case of the Spectrum and C64 *Blade Runner* games all the subtleties, complexities and ambiguities of the film were reduced to a game that players in the 1980s would have immediately recognised as a fairly mundane example of the 'shoot-'em-up' genre, where slogans such as 'Move Off World' painted across a primary coloured and flat game space gesture only vaguely to the film as the player adopts the role of a bounty hunter in a raincoat who bears a crude likeness to Deckard. As one internet site hosting screenshots from the ZX Spectrum version summarises the game, it was all 'a bit sad'.[6]

The release of the *Blade Runner* game for the personal computer by Westwood Studios in 1997 (hereafter referred to as *Blade Runner PC* to distinguish it from Ridley Scott's film) was a significant departure from such a (necessarily) totally subservient relationship between originating film and game incarnation, and showed some of the possibilities for what is now referred to by eager studio executives as the 'convergence' between the two forms of media.[7] It should not be misunderstood, however, as a straightforward adaptation from one medium to another that is limited and impoverished, rather than enriched, by the transition. *Blade Runner PC* does not simply offer the player a chance to replay the plot events of the film, but offers a different narrative that begins as the investigation of a case of 'animal murder' by a rookie blade runner, Ray McCoy, who acts as the player's agent in the game. By control of mouse and keyboard the player can make McCoy walk, run, shoot, converse and otherwise interact with the environment as the case progresses. At the same time, the cursor is able to move about the screen freely, and the player can pick up objects and information by clicking on appropriate areas of the screen. There are multiple locations that can be visited, with each accessible on foot or in the police-issue spinner. The player revisits locations and encounters characters familiar from the film, and there is an undeniable pleasure in the recognition of correspondences and the accumulation of an increased knowledge of a world consistent with that presented in the film, just as there is a pleasure in the degree to which Westwood have captured the atmospheric look of the future Los Angeles created in such detail for the film. Ridley Scott might have disposed of the voice-over narration of Deckard, but the game utilises this as an effective element of gameplay, communicating the progress that is being made even as it combines with the game soundtrack to reinforce the relationship between the game text and the original release of the film. At the same time, however, the game strikes off in new directions, and in its initial focus on animal murder is more clearly reworking some of the critical issues and concerns of Philip K. Dick's novel than restricting itself to a faithful reproduction of the film. The game is caught, then, in this difficult space of any reworking; within what, in relation to *Star Wars* at least, is referred to as the 'Expanded Universe', where there are the twin demands of remaining consistent in relation to the licence and yet offering up a unique experience to its consumers.[8]

The producers of *Blade Runner PC* were anything but nervous about claiming to have achieved something exceptional, not only in terms of effective use of the licence, but in terms of radical progress in advancing the boundaries of what can be achieved in computer games. Commenting on the generally lacklustre nature of most licensed games, and the way in which developers routinely make excessive statements of achievement, one reviewer of *Blade Runner PC* commented that

A popular movie license is often the last nail in the coffin, suggesting to gamers that the designers lacked even the minimal level of creativity required to come up with a concept of their own. As such, it is not surprising that when a new game promises a 'dynamic, 3D real-time adventure based on the hit movie,' the first reaction by most gamers is one of foreboding rather than excitement.[9]

The promotional copy that Westwood and their publishers, Virgin Interactive, included in their advertising material was inevitably hyperbolic, but it did make some claims that bear closer examination:

> The First Real-Time 3D Adventure. Armed with your investigative skills and the tools of a 21st century BLADE RUNNER™, you'll be immersed in a futuristic world that revolutionises computer gaming, and tests your ability to survive in one of the richest and most imaginative games ever created for the PC.[10]

In the event the tone proved justified, even if the specifics of the claims made are questionable, and the game generated a largely positive and enthusiastic response. *Blade Runner PC* might be thought of as something of a landmark in the relatively short history of licensed games, showing ways in which a game might go beyond merely picking up the visual vocabulary of the film as a backdrop before which a generic gaming cliché can be played out, and instead exploit the specific strengths of the computer game as an open-ended and played experience, and as an experience of creative possibility within the governance of rules.

What is of most interest here, however, is the claim that the player will be 'immersed' in one of the 'richest' PC games 'ever created'. *Blade Runner PC* plays its own complex games with the fantasy of immersion stimulated by what might be thought of as the 'rich' spectacle of *Blade Runner*. In its successful replication of some elements of the film, while simultaneously playing to the strengths of its own technology of delivery, it represents a significant (if not revolutionary) moment in computer gaming. It certainly foregrounds the possibilities of independent creative expression in this developing media form even as it offers the familiarity of a recognisable version of the film. This constitutes a clear example of what the new media critics Jay David Bolter and Richard Grusin (1999) have called 'remediation,' a term that illuminates wider issues about the shifting and uncertain relationship between computer games and films.

The core point that Bolter and Grusin make is not particularly complex, but it usefully situates computer games, like all 'new' media, as engaged in an ongoing renegotiation of their relationship to established forms of media. Critics should be wary, they argue, of focusing too much on the ways in which new media technologies represent a radical break from old media, and should always be aware that they are in a dialogic relationship with preceding media forms. In these terms, film remediates dramatic performance and literary representation, and the computer or video game will remediate film (among other representative forms) in its turn. This then leaves the critic who would undertake serious analysis of the game with a difficult double task – the identification of the formal novelty of the game simultaneously with identification of its formal debt to past media. Games and films are different in kind, where one is played and the other watched, and it is not sufficient to simply think in terms of adaptation from film to game, with a necessary loss of effective fictive power because of the shift from a relatively mature to an immature form. Instead, it is essential to consider the ways in which they practice remediation, rather than simply adapt, for a new technological medium. What is most interesting in Bolter and Grusin's argument, however, is the language of contestation and opposition in which they couch it, and its almost aggressive dependence on notions of a progressive faith in positive transformation through technological advance that would seem to imply that new and old media are involved in some kind of struggle for domination:

> In our terms, new technologies of representation proceed by reforming or remediating earlier ones, while earlier technologies are struggling to maintain their legitimacy by remediating newer ones. The cyberenthusiasts argue that in remediating older media the new media are accomplishing social change. The gesture of reform is ingrained in American culture, and this is perhaps why American culture takes so easily to the strategies of remediation. (1999: 94)

Such a touching faith in technological progress, whether expressed by the almost evangelical 'cyberenthusiasts' of this description or the more restrained critics of new media technologies such as Bolter and Grusin, might at first appear to sit uncomfortably with *Blade Runner*. Like so much contemporary science fiction, and particularly the cyberpunk fictions in film and literature that owe such a debt of influence to Scott's film, *Blade Runner* works through and interrogates cultural anxieties surrounding technological advance and displays a jaded scepticism towards the progressive assumptions so often shackled to future technology. It is the incremental advance of the manufactured humanoid form, after all, that represents the threat to order based on the distinction between the human and the non-human, with the Nexus-6 the incarnation that is feared over the previous replicant models. Games like *Blade Runner PC* are not somehow 'interactive' films, with that interactivity adding no more than a technological curiosity (like cinematic 3D or projection on an IMax screen) to the expressive range of conventional film.[11] Nor are they a form of entertainment media that threatens to supplant or overwhelm film. Indeed, they need to be recognised as a distinct form of media that have a far more complex relationship with film than models of either derivation or opposition would allow. If we are to fully understand the ways in which they can remediate film, then we need to pay close attention to the specifics of how the game remediates the cinematic text.

IMMERSION AND THE PROMISE OF RICH SPECTACLE

Computer game criticism has often shown a rather simplistic acceptance of the idea that the 'immersive' potential of some games marks a radical departure from that available in earlier forms of media. As the promise of 'real time 3D' in which 'you will be immersed' in the advertising copy for *Blade Runner PC* indicates, there is something marketable about the concept that computer and video games might allow their players to enter the text, to involve themselves in the immediacy of a world presented on screen that might allow something akin to a form of presence inside the text. Promising to 'test your ability to survive *in*' the *Blade Runner* milieu the game stretches the special metaphor of immersion to its limits. In some forms of game (notably third-person adventures such as *Tomb Raider* or *Prince of Persia: The Sands of Time*, or first-person shooters such as *Doom* or *Half-Life*) there is a literal illusion constructed that we can potentially enter the space on the screen before us, and that we can negotiate what Henry Jenkins has called its 'narrative architecture' while giving little or no attention to the practice of manipulating the interface between player and game.[12] It is as well to be sceptical of such claims, even if we do not go so far as Katie Salen and Eric Zimmerman and label this gesture the 'immersive fallacy'; but even if we restrict ourselves to a visual understanding of computer game aesthetics, it is important to note that *Blade Runner PC* depends upon recognising that the crucial difference between game and film rests on the desire not to see the image we have before us, but to access the next image, and that such access is only possible through the manipulation of the player/game interface in the process of play.[13] A key difference between film (which offers the revelation of delayed disclosure in the anticipation of 'what happens next') and games (which extend this to ask 'what happens next *if I*') rests in the way in which any progressive sequence of visual images is entirely dependent on the action of the playing subject.

This is not an experience of surfaces, as the very term 'film' declares itself to be, but an experience of material space as well as representational space that combines real movement in space (of the hand controlling the mouse) with movement of and within the screen image. The immersive potential of *Blade Runner PC* is necessarily limited because it does not feature a true three-dimensional game architecture, and we are unlikely to be confused by any potential for immersion or for the penetration of the intervening screen by the playing subject. Rather, the game operates through constructing the *illusion* of a depth to the image. Although Westwood were particularly adept at using lighting effects and a density of moving shadow, smoke and steam, most scenes remain resolutely two-dimensional and fixed in their equivalent of the static camera shot as they are presented before the player, even if he or she can direct McCoy to traverse its spaces. The key illusion is not that the player can immerse him or herself in the game-space, but that beneath the flat surface of the image is a form of depth that is only implied in other media, but is actually accessible, here, through the operation of the point and click of the mouse. Beneath the obscuring smoke, steam and shadow, something always waits to be discovered. What this means is that the visual plane of the text is of an apparently different quality from that of the conventional cinematic image.

This sense of an image that we consciously know to be flat offering the promise of richness and depth might be thought of as always having been characteristic of *Blade Runner* itself. As Geoff King and Tanya Krzywinska have noted in their examination of the film,

> *Blade Runner* has been described as almost losing itself in its dedication to extremely fine detail, much of which is impossible to grasp even on repeated viewings; parking meters on the main street set, for example, included fine-print warnings of the danger of lethal electric shock faced by anyone tampering with the mechanism. (2000: 73)[14]

But if this recalls that appreciation of *Blade Runner*, as Adam Roberts has noted with a nod to both Fredric Jameson and Jean Baudrillard, as a '"postmodern" artefact more concerned with style than substance, with surface rather than depth' (2000:161), then the PC game changes the terms through which we apprehend those very surfaces. The screens of *Blade Runner PC* offer the promise of ever finer detail, of finding those tiny areas of the screen that will yield up more information, 'sometimes by encouraging the player to look through the surface of the screen and sometimes by dwelling on the surface with its multiplicity of mediated objects' (Bolter & Grusin 1999: 94).

Were the experience of navigation through the game merely a process of accessing each specific area in turn, emptying it of clues to its detective story by exhausting all the dialogue alternatives presented as the in-game characters are encountered, and picking up every object highlighted by the change in cursor colour from blue to green, then this would be a fairly dull experience. Much is now made of the assumed convergence of big-budget Hollywood film and video game, but the largely static *Blade Runner PC* lacks many of the advantages of film, such as a controlled sense of pace and the shifts in shot whose absence is less obvious in more frenetic game genres. In purely visual terms the limited resolution of the graphics have stood up surprisingly well despite the limited processing resources that were available at the time of release, but *Blade Runner PC* simply cannot compete with the visual polish of the film. Where it really succeeds in remediating the expectations of film for the platform of the personal computer, however, is in the ways in which the presence of clues in the screen space do not simply act as conventional hyperlinks that allow immediate movement from one screen image to another (as in the navigation of links on websites, or the scene selection screens of contemporary DVDs), but add the illusion of depth and a richness of texture to an essentially two-dimensional text. Clicking on an individual leads to conversation, clicking on a prop item gives access to McCoy's thoughts about its significance and possible meaning for his investigation. Until all the programmed responses have been generated by repeated clicking the screen remains the site of further possibility. There is something truly disappointing about triggering McCoy's stock response that there is 'nothing more to see here', marking the shift from rich space to a space returned to conventional surface image when its potential has been exhausted.

Navigation between the individual screens is still governed by exit possibilities resembling the compass point choices of North, South, East or West. This would be familiar to players of text adventures as an attempt to replicate the physical topography of the real world (see Aarseth 1997). But each screen also represents something other than a static frame passing before the eyes of the audience like the sequential images of a magic lantern, the frames of a graphic novel, or even the linked screens of a traditional computer adventure game. In one sense we begin with a rich screen space that must be emptied by the action of the player so that the game-state changes as McCoy accumulates data. The identification of rich spaces when the cursor changes colour does not result in movement out and away, but beneath, and leads to an accretion of the game narrative rather than a straightforwardly linear progression in the manner of the read or watched text. It might be impossible for the audience of *Blade Runner* to read the warnings on the side of the parking meters, but there are always areas and items in each location screen of *Blade Runner PC* that the player can examine in more detail, whether they be discarded fast food menus or the collars of pet dogs, irrelevant red-herrings or essential clues to McCoy's investigation.

We have seen something like this before, of course, in the successfully realised science fiction or fantasy world of either novel or film that appear to offer a consistent world always out of reach, always off screen or off the page, but available *in potentia* if only we had access to such spaces. *Blade Runner PC* exceeds the limitations of such worlds, however, in actually allowing access to such richness of detail. For the audience of the film it is not the accessibility of the fine print of *Blade Runner*'s warning signs that satisfies, but the knowledge that it exists at all. What the computer game offers is a technological methodology for reaching such spaces that, in the case of *Blade Runner PC*, combines with content in a particularly successful way. Fantasy and science fiction have no monopoly in creating the illusion that the image we have access to is only a fragment of a fully realised world – this notion informs the scenery flats of the Hollywood western as much as the complex mythic backstory to *Lord of the Rings* and its many imitators – but it is far more pronounced in such genres. Whether it is the 'universe' of *Star Wars* or *Star Trek*, or the Middle-Earth of *Lord of the Rings*, consumers have shown an almost insatiable appetite for the exploration of the implied space beyond that immediately revealed in the originating text. As plenty of critics have pointed out, science fiction is almost definitively either extrapolative or speculative in nature, and what the science fiction computer game such as *Blade Runner PC* enables is the satisfaction, to a limited degree, of a continuing speculative or extrapolative curiosity in its audiences.[15] The success of the marriage of science fiction content and computer or video game form has been the result of far more than a mere appeal to the shared core demographic of young male consumers interested in technology. Science fiction functions by playing with notions of 'what if?', and on the deployment of a 'novum' or novel deviation from the world of experience.[16] The actual playing of a computer game is almost entirely dependent on the basic process of asking 'what if?' that then adds the agency of the 'I' in the posing of the 'what if I?': the imagination of the possibilities opened up by manipulation of the interface, the actual manipulation of the interface, and the following through of the consequences of that manipulation.

It is in the use of the Esper device that we can locate the point at which film and game aesthetics most successfully remediate the particular forms of realism offered by the photograph and perspective painting. In both film and game the Esper is used to take a two-dimensional image (the photograph) and model a three-dimensional representation offering an impossibility of vision frequently allowed the player of third-person computer games, but not allowed in the world of experience. Should Deckard, or the player of the *Blade Runner* game, isolate an area of the photographic frame of particular promise, he or she can direct the Esper to probe that space as if the camera lens were able to move in three dimensions. What is striking is that film and game remediate the photograph in different ways. To use Bolter and Grusin's vocabulary, the film proposes a technology of transparent immediacy (the erasure of the presence of the medium), rather than the hypermediacy (always bringing our attention to the act of mediation) of the game. In *Blade Runner* the Esper responds to Deckard's voice command, in the game the cursor is manipulated by the hand of the player to isolate areas of interest. Even within the logic of *Blade Runner* the Esper device stands as an impossible vision of what technology might ever achieve – the camera cannot see around corners or bend the laws of physics. In terms of computer games, however, it makes perfect sense. What the player sees in games such as *Blade Runner PC* is not what the played avatar McCoy would be able to see if we were to imagine him having a presence in a physical game space – as it pretends to be in the case of first-person games – but an intervention that demands the active control of a playing subject to access an apparently fully realised other world that is part of the everyday experience of computer game play. Old technology (the flat visual image) is shown to be lacking, and the intervention of the technological solution of the Esper through the action of its 'user' or 'player' reformulates that image and allows the viewer to see around, beyond and deeper into the world that *Blade Runner* can only hint at; a world into which *Blade Runner PC* allows extended but limited access. Indeed, the Esper of the game represents a constrained and conservative form of what can now be, and routinely is, offered in the contemporary computer game, where the modelling of 3D objects in space is commonplace and its absence is more striking than its presence.

It is almost always an error to regard science fiction as anything other than an accidentally prophetic or predictive genre, but in the restoration of the unicorn dream sequence to the film we are presented with an image through which we might consider the game as a technological remediation of the tradition of surface representation to be found in painting, the photograph or film. The flat piece of paper-backed foil that is taken as raw material for Gaff's creative act is limited in its possibility of communication. When he manipulates that flat plane through the complex folds of three-dimensional space, however, it becomes rich in possible meanings. The film's shot of the origami unicorn might be flat on a screen, and we can no more touch it than we can reach into the game-space of *Blade Runner PC*, but in its illusion of adding a third dimension it suggests that the future possibility of sustaining the richness of *Blade Runner*'s elusive meanings rests not only in further possible sequential prints that differ in content and organisation, but in allowing a player to have access to a third dimension that would only be made available through its remediation as a computer game.

NOTES

1 This descriptive blurb is included on packaging from the DVD included in the Special Edition PAL release of the film, and has a 1999 copyright date.

2 Hampton Fancher and David Peoples (2000) *Blade Runner Screenplay*. Los Angeles CA: The Blade Runner Partnership/Warner Home Video.

3 The use of licences from film has also been the subject of debate among industry professionals. As Dene Carter stated in a contribution to a debate entitled 'licenced vs original games' in the industry magazine *Develop 26* (March 2003) licences 'are primarily used as a launch pad for second-rate games that rely on consumer gullibility for success'. Even those developers working with licenced properties recognise the uneven history of film-game licences. Simon Carter of the developer Big Blue Box pointed out in a feature article in *Edge* (August 2003) that 'It is very tempting for a publisher to release a shoddy product, happy in the knowledge that it will sell two million units on the back of the licenced material'.

4 Comparatively early computer games are often difficult to locate, but details of the C64 version of this game are available from www.brmovie.com/FAQs/BR_FAQ_C64_Game.htm. This site also explains that 'copyright issues' explain the load screen message for the game that makes the interesting claim that it is 'a video game interpretation of the film score by Vangelis', rather than a game 'based on the film'. With a little diligent searching it is possible to locate sites from which emulator versions of the game can be downloaded that can be played on contemporary personal computers, but the legality of this particular practice of replication is still uncertain. All sites accessed April 2004.

5 For an extended discussion of the developing relationship between computer games and popular film, that cannot be reductively treated as simply antagonistic or even as continuing to assume the cultural dominance of film over game,

see Barry Atkins (2004) '"To Infinity, and Beyond?"': Dialogue and Critique in Popular Film's Portrayal of Video Games', *Text/Technology*, 13:1, 35–51, 90.

6 http://scribble.com/uwi/br/game. Accessed April 2004.

7 The trumpeting of an expectation of 'convergence', where once 'interactive movie' had been the site of commercial promise in the intersection of games and films, should be approached with care. As I show throughout this chapter, games and films may 'remediate' one another, but they remain distinct media forms offering distinct experiences.

8 The 'Expanded Universe' section of the official *Star Wars* website claims that 'If your experience with *Star Wars* has been just the movies, you're only getting a fraction of the entire tale. Since the start, the *Star Wars* saga has been expanded through novels, comics and games.' See http://www.starwars.com/eu/. Accessed July 2004. It is interesting to note that the massively multiplayer online game *Star Wars Galaxies: An Empire Divided* produced by LucasArts uses the plural term 'galaxies' in its title, to emphasise not only its fidelity to the original *Star Wars* but its access to plural possibility.

9 Benjamin E. Shires, 'Blade Runner: Do gamers dream of electric sheep?', originally published in *Computer Games Magazine*, presumably close to the release date of *Blade Runner PC*, but now archived at www.cdmag.com/articles/009/099/blade_runner_review.html. Accessed July 2004.

10 This text originally appeared in *Computer Gaming World*, March 1998, and is reproduced on the computer game archive site Moby Games. See www.mobygames.com/game/adblurb/gameId=341/. Accessed April 2004.

11 For a discussion of *Myst*, the classic example of what was once commonly referred to as the interactive movie, see Bolter & Grusin 1999: 94–9. As the study of computer games has developed the term has fallen out of common critical usage, largely because it fails to account for the played experience of games that goes beyond simply performing an action that will nudge forwards a new still frame or an extended video sequence.

12 See Jenkins, Henry (2004) 'Game Design as Narrative Architecture' in *First Person: New Media Story, Game and Performance*, edited by Noah Wardrip-Fruin and Pate Harrigan, Cambridge Mass: MIT, 118–30. Available online at http://www.electronicbookreview.com/v3/servlet/ebr?command=view_essay&essay_id=jenkins. Third-person adventure games such as the *Tomb Raider* franchise position the player above and behind the played avatar, while first-person games such as *Doom* and *Half-Life* present a stylised version of what might be seen 'through the eyes of' the played avatar. In both instances the successful navigation of the game-space is necessary if the player is to advance in the game, and one of the skills that is needed is the player's understanding how complex negotiation with space can allow access to new areas (*Tomb Raider* and *Prince of Persia*) or be used to protect oneself from enemy fire (*Doom* and *Half-Life*). For a discussion of how possible immersion in this space can be overstated see Barry Atkins (2003) *More Than a Game: The Computer Game as Fictional Form*, Manchester: Manchester University Press, 138–43.

13 See Katie Salen and Eric Zimmerman (2003) *Rules of Play: Game Design Fun-*

damentals, Cambridge, MA: MIT Press, 450–5. As the academic and journalist David Thomas noted in 'Video Game Vocabulary: A Lexicon of Experiental Anchors', an unpublished paper presented at the 'Form, Culture and Videogame Criticism' conference at Princeton University in March 2004, it is as difficult to define what is meant when it is claimed that a game is 'immersive' in the same way that it is difficult to comprehend what is meant when a song is defined as 'cool'. The relative immaturity of the language of game criticism remains a barrier to sophisticated analysis.

14 The point is first made with reference to the electrocution warnings in Sammon 1996.

15 Definition of what is or is not science fiction remains hotly contested, but a useful account of the major positions (including the reliance on extrapolative or speculative models) can be found in Roberts 2000: 1–36.

16 The term 'novum' is a coinage of Darko Suvin's, from his *Metamorphoses of Science Fiction: On the Poetics and History of a Literary Genre*, New Haven, CT: Yale University Press, 1979, and is usefully glossed in Roberts 2000:19–27.

IMPLANTED MEMORIES, OR THE ILLUSION OF FREE ACTION
SUSANA P. TOSCA

INTRODUCTION: THE FRUSTRATIONS OF REPLICANT LIFE

'Quite an experience to live in fear, isn't it? That's what it is to be a slave.'
– Roy
'You're weak my friend ... He doesn't have a choice. He never did.'
– Clovis[1]

The replicants' struggle for freedom is a very human one. As sentient beings who know they are alive, they want to control their own destinies. In the film, Roy and Pris explain this to Sebastian, whose accelerated decrepitude illness makes him sympathetic to the replicants' hunger for life: 'We're not computers, Sebastian. We're physical', he says; 'I think, therefore I am', she adds. But what does she think? According to classical philosophy, and for a rationalist like Descartes, free will is impossible without knowledge,[2] but replicants cannot be sure of what they know (their memories are fake implants and do not derive from experience), and have been programmed to follow one course of action only (as slaves in the Off-World colonies). In their Off-World jobs (for example Pris is a prostitute), freedom is obviously not an option, hence their rebellion. A player of computer adventure games could easily identify with the replicants, because the experience very often feels like travelling on a train; that is, on rails, without any real say in the direction of movement. That's what it is to be a slave. We start the game as a character with memories and an agenda that seem alien and take some time getting used to, and then have to perform a series of required tasks in order to progress to the next level. Do we ever have a choice?

This chapter will examine the *Blade Runner* PC game (Westwood, 1997) in order to find out how much freedom we can feel as players; free will being an important topic in both Ridley Scott's film and Philip K. Dick's source novel. The problematising of this matter is relevant to a narrative analysis of the computer game as it reveals some of the inherent difficulties of the adventure genre as sketched above.

The action of the *Blade Runner* PC game is parallel in time and space to that of the film. The player controls a character named Ray McCoy, a rookie blade runner who works in the same Police Department as Deckard (and seems to live in the same apartment block). The game is set at the same time as the film, so that McCoy will sometimes arrive to a place Deckard has just visited, for example the hotel where Leon lives, or the Tyrell Corporation; and other times he will be quicker than the characters in the film, like when he visits Chew, the eye designer, before Roy kills him. When the game starts we get our first case, an animal murder presumably committed by replicants since no humans would be so cruel as to destroy real animals in a time of extinction. Following the initial clues from this crime scene, we soon get involved in a more complicated investigation of the whereabouts of a group of possible replicants, led by the charismatic Clovis. McCoy will search for clues in crime scenes and interrogate suspects, working towards a grand finale in which we must either have 'retired' all the rogue replicants, or joined them in their search for freedom and life if McCoy turns out to be one of them (an explanation of this twist follows below). The game introduction echoes the movie, with a panoramic view of a dystopian Los Angeles and the Vangelis soundtrack; the flawless reproduction of the movie's settings provides a constant source of wonder and pleasure for players.

PREVIOUS WORK ON THE GAME

As this volume eloquently demonstrates, *Blade Runner* is one of the most discussed films in history, an interest that to some degree also has extended to the novel upon which it is based, Philip K. Dick's *Do Androids Dream of Electric Sheep?*. The 1997 Westwood game, however, has not received the same interest, probably because it is relatively recent, but also because it is only recently that the study of computer games has begun to gain acceptance as an academic discipline.

Blade Runner is usually mentioned as one of the key examples of adaptations from film to the game medium, and Steven Poole has identified its influence on computer game design. According to him, *Blade Runner* inaugurated a specific visual style that has been used repeatedly in subsequent games. Drawing on the movie's noir and decadent scenarios, the game takes advantage of the darkness, permanent rain and fog to achieve a believable atmosphere without spending excessive computer processing power (2000: 88–9).

The only monograph work I know about the game is my article 'Playing for the Plot: *Blade Runner* as Paradigm of the Electronic Adventure Game' (2000). The article argued that *Blade Runner* was the first game that had managed to offer a certain level of narrative complexity due to the efficacy of the decision branching and the significance of the different game endings. The game was also a starting point for discussion of the adventure genre in general, using Peter Brooks' *Reading for the Plot* (1983) as inspiration, and the nascent possibilities of applying narrative concepts to the study of certain computer game genres. Both my own work with computer games and the field itself have grown immensely in only four years, so that I feel a need to revisit my earlier conclusions: the game deserves a grounded discussion.

A QUESTION OF GENRE

As has been mentioned, *Blade Runner* is an adventure game,[3] a genre where player interaction takes the form of spatial exploration, management of an object inventory (finding objects and using them), puzzles, quests and conversations with bots (usually by going down 'conversation trees'). Elsewhere I have characterised this genre as centred on telling a story, where the narrative component is the main motivation for the player as he or she searches for a plot (in Peter Brooks' terms (1983: 3–12)). This also connects such games with 'plot-oriented' literature, such as genre fiction:

> Most adventure games cast the player in a detective's role under various guises: the detective of *Deadline*, the mystery-writer 'Shattenjäger' of the *Gabriel Knight* series, the curious traveller of *Myst*, the journalist of *The 11th Hour* … Something has happened (usually a crime, assault, disappearance or any mysterious deed the programmers can think of), and the player must investigate in order to learn what. She must *look for a plot* behind the apparently meaningless terrible acts in order to reconstruct the story from clues that she finds at the crime scenes and the interviewing of the non-playing characters. The main character/player usually has a motivation: to find a lost girlfriend, to free somebody, to write a book, etc. (Tosca 2000: 3)

In the case of *Blade Runner*, the initial motivation is to advance up the career ladder, since the player's first mission is also the first 'real' case for McCoy, who will try to solve it in order to go from rookie to genuine blade runner. As the game advances, however, motivations can change, as I will examine below. Structurally, it is a progression game (Juul 2002), meaning that action is organised in chapters or 'acts' that need to be solved in order to continue on to the next one. Some of the aesthetic problems of the genre, according to Espen Aarseth, are the lack of believable characters (pre-scripted behaviour, repeating lines) and the conflict between the opposing goals of gameplay and storytelling, which causes the game experience to be undermined because of the priority given to the story (2004: 51). For Jonas Heide Smith, a serious problem is the lack of narrative coherence, since the story easily falls into inertia unless the player triggers the continuation of the story by some (often meaningless) action. He names this problem the 'interactor as a starting gun' (2000), by which, for example, action would only advance when the player found a key and a string hidden in the garden in order to open the door where the clues about the murder are waiting. For both authors, these problems might be partially solved with better artificial intelligence (Aarseth talks about simulation and Heide Smith about 'deistic narration', which means avoiding excessively linear design and instead allowing for objects to have properties governed by natural laws rather than an author's master plan). This would allow for worlds to appear more alive and stories more coherent. What these two authors are seeking is, in Juul's term, for progression games (such as typically linear adventure games) to also include emergence structures, by which a relatively small number of rules produces a great amount of combinations and possible states of a game, as happens for example in chess (see Juul 2002).

This is actually the trend that the market seems to be evolving towards with games such as *Grand Theft Auto III* which combine a very linear mission structure with an open world where objects and people seem 'alive' for the player to interact with. Another tendency is to mix the adventure with some action (mainly in the form of combat) as, for example, in *Deus Ex*. The pure adventure genre seems to have all but died out, with the exception of a couple of recent successful games such as *Syberia* or *The Longest Journey*,[4] although its basic structure is now part of other hybrid genres as mentioned above, or of thematically specialised genres such as the survival horror game.

In 1997, however, today's more advanced uses of artificial intelligence were barely dreamed of, and the developers of *Blade Runner* found other ways of dealing with the problems of the adventure game genre (namely the fact that you can only play once, and the issue that puzzles seem meaningless and disconnected to the main action). The product's marketing reveals that they were conscious of these potential flaws, and therefore created a game with several possible endings, eliminating the puzzles that had been the genre's trademark. They promised a 'constantly changing plot' in a game where 'character agendas are random ... your adventure can be different every time you play'.[5] However, the absence of puzzles was met with a great deal of scepticism and hostility by the genre's fans,[6] who felt the game lacked interactivity and was too linear, as the *Gamespot* review harshly summarises: 'Somewhere along the production line, someone forgot to include a game.'[7] I will address the consequences of these innovations below.

NARRATIVE ANALYSIS OF *BLADE RUNNER*

If adventure games are usually close to stories, the association becomes even more intimate when the game springs from one specific, very well known story. The designers cleverly chose not to try to reproduce the events in the film, but to create a similarly-themed narrative that could play out in the same diegesis. According to designer Louis Castle they were very concerned to avoid misinterpreting the film, which had 'a great base of demanding fans',[8] so that when the production team chose the main theme they tried to remain faithful to the fundamental question of distinguishing between human and non-human. The game makes this more explicit than the film: 'McCoy is even more questioning since he is accused of being a replicant. The ambiguity is one of the game's greatest strengths.'[9] In my analysis I will examine how the game creates this ambiguity and how it adjusts to or differs from the usual techniques in adventure games. My discussion is structured by a series of fundamental topics, according to my framing of the adventure genre.[10]

The plot level: a good old linear story

Let us start with the story, since it is what primarily defines the genre. I am separating the 'plot' level from the 'action' level for purposes of analysis, even though they would be experienced at the same time by a player.[11] The plot is structured in five acts, as in theatre, which in themselves do not present any unity of space or time, but are introduced by different action triggers. The acts are punctuated by the cut-scenes that present important information about the plot (always just before an act starts). The act structure is straightforward, as McCoy advances trying to find more clues and talking to people. As an example, this is the development of act 1:

- McCoy examines Runciter's shop and find all clues, specifically the video-disk with Lucy's picture and the chopstick wrapper with the name of Howie Lee's restaurant in Chinatown.
- Go to the police station to see the pictures on the videodisk (use the Esper) and ask about the rest of the clues in the laboratory.
- Go to Chinatown and talk to the cook Zuben at Howie Lee's. Zuben will run away when he is asked about Lucy and McCoy can either talk to him, try to kill him, or even be unable to find him in the backalleys.
- McCoy goes back to his apartment and in most cases (that is, unless he found him in the alleys before) will be attacked by Zuben, having to kill him here. Sleeps.

The highlighted clues, actions and places are the 'action triggers' mentioned above with reference to Heide Smith. If we don't find the chopstick wrapper, we don't know where we have to go next. If we don't find the picture of Lucy, we cannot ask Zuben about her; this causes the action to stop and will probably force the player to consult a walkthrough in order to continue. In this way we can say that the plot advances as a chain reaction of small events, with clues we found in act 1 leading us into act 2 and so on. The action triggers are pre-scripted, and even though they can sometimes be activated in different orders, there is usually a linear progression through the acts.

If we were to ask ourselves what the player needs to know in order to advance at the plot level, that is, what is her literary repertoire (see Tosca 2003b: 4), we could mention:

- a basic knowledge of the adventure game genre (for example, we would know the rule: don't leave any scene without having tried to click in all the possible places, or keep talking to the characters until they declare that they have no more to say).
- a basic knowledge of the original movie, because otherwise we might not understand the ambiguity as to the nature of the replicants, and the game could be played like an extremely boring *shoot-em-up*, which was not intended by the designers.
- not necessary, but a bonus if players know Philip K. Dick's novel; they will enjoy the references to it, such as the 'kipple', the pollution, the value of animals and the surrealist episode where some fake policemen arrest McCoy and he finds another guy living in his apartment, the fragility of our identities being one of Dick's favourite themes.

Even though the voice acting is relatively good, characters remain stereo-typical, particularly the female ones. The character of McCoy is clearly inspired by that of Deckard, but his constant ironic commentary delivered with a certain degree of cheerfulness makes him very different in personality from his haunted and insecure counterpart. The replicant leader, Clovis, is a dark-haired Roy Batty, who walks around quoting William Blake and brooding philosophically about destiny, eliciting admiration and scorn in equal degrees in the players' fora.[12] Unlike Roy, who is a more ambivalent character, both brutal and compassionate, Clovis's violent side is expressed through the crazy Sadik, whom he has to restrain constantly. The rest of the male characters are typical cardboard figures, although it has to be said that the designers have made an effort at suggesting an inner life for them: Gordo's show-business obsession, Runciter's taste for young girls, the conflict of the Siamese twins Lance and Luther.

This comes across particularly in the cutscenes, as the game sequences do not really allow for persona development and sometimes even force us to act out of character.[13] The female characters in the game all fulfill recognisable roles in computer games: the fourteen-year-old Lolita (Lucy), the beautiful good-hearted erotic dancer (Dektora), the hard, masculine police woman (Crystal). There seems not to be the same degree of correspondence between the female characters in the game and those of the movie as there is with the main male characters; one can only speculate as to the reasons for this, but it seems that the designers deemed the masculine characters more interesting, probably making an informed guess as to possible player demographics.

The action level: frantic clicking
While most fans and reviewers acknowledge that the game scenarios are beautiful and the story compelling, the action level of the game has earned harsh criticism from the player community. The game's only interface is a mouse-controlled arrow that turns green when there is some clue to be examined or a character McCoy can talk to, and blue to indicate a possible exit from that screen into another scenario. The simplicity of this system becomes a disadvantage when McCoy is wielding his gun, because it is very difficult to shoot and steer him at the same time since the arrow turns into a gun sight.[14]

McCoy has a 'clue database' or inventory where clues are attached to the possible suspects and crime scenes, and can be filtered as a way of remembering where each of them comes from. Not that we need to use it, since there is never a need to combine different clues or to hand one clue to a suspect (just clicking on the suspect will get McCoy to automatically produce the document). The clues are classified according to the crime scenes where they were found, and attached to possible suspects, so that the database does your work for you in sorting out the clues and suspects.

The most frustrating aspect of the interaction is the menu that pops up when we talk with the non-player characters.[15] These menus display a list of items suggesting general themes one can interrogate the characters about, but it is impossible to know what McCoy will actually say on each topic. Usually we have to try to cover all the topics or we will miss information and get stuck. As an example, the menu when interrogating Howie Lee in the first act:

LUCY PHOTO
RUNCITER CLUES
EMPLOYEE
SMALL TALK
DONE

In this case they are mostly self-explanatory, except for 'Runciter Clues'. The player has just arrived from the Runciter shop, but what can this possibly mean? It turns out to be a question about the chopstick wrapper that was found there, so 'chopstick wrapper' would have been a much better title. Sometimes the lack of clarity of the menus has unwanted consequences. For example, in a later conversation with Dektora (the erotic dancer), there is an item named CRYSTAL. I wrongly assumed that McCoy would ask her if a female blade runner had visited her already, but instead he warns Dektora that Crystal might be looking for her and her friends, thus effectively making McCoy into a replicant sympathiser without the player's collaboration.

This being said, the advantage of such a simple system is that the learning curve is practically zero, and any player can become familiar with the game mechanics in less than ten minutes. The problem of a system that does not require the player's thinking is that gameplay turns into mindless clicking, both on objects and people. There is no need to register the various discoveries, as McCoy will use this knowledge without our intervention, which in a way ruins the plot as described above (in other games the player must remember information and know what objects to use when; here McCoy does it automatically). It is true that detective stories usually seem quite linear in that the investigator goes from one clue to the next, but if we do not even need to think where to go next, the excitement fades.[16] In this game the plot level and the action level are very closely connected, but there is the risk that we very quickly stop caring about the gaps (what to do now? why did this happen?) because our character knows the answers and continues anyway.

WHERE ARE THE PUZZLES AND QUESTS?

Players of adventure games often enjoy solving complicated puzzles, something absent from *Blade Runner*. As mentioned above, picking up clues is just a matter of clicking every time the arrow turns green, and once they are listed in our inventory we are not required to do anything else with them: no combination of objects in complicated arrangements is needed to gain access to hidden areas or discover secrets.

As for quests, there is a general one, 'find and retire the replicants', that permeates the whole game and gets the player started through the animal murder investigation. The subsequent discoveries work as new mini-mysteries that the player has to solve until we have connected all the dots and found the links between the replicants. *Blade Runner* mini-quests (search the Runciter crime-scene, search the Tyrell crime-scene, investigate the Early Q club, and so on) work well at the semantic level, the player at all times knowing what needs to be done and why, but not so much at the structural level (since the manipulation of objects and the interrogation of characters feels totally random and is not challenging enough).[17]

A more interesting feature is that, unlike other games, the player is not given these mini-quests explicitly by non-playing characters;[18] rather, they appear as we pick up the different clues and new spaces open in our map. Actually figuring out the space of the city becomes a quest in itself after we have lost the Spinner in act 4 and with it the ability to just fly anywhere.[19] McCoy has to move in the sewers and experience the city as the 'negative space' that Scott Bukatman describes (1997: 42).

It would seem that the initial idea of the designers to do away with puzzles and facilitate the ways in which players know what to do next backfired to an extent and contributed to the feeling of having very limited choice in this game; but how is this supported or contradicted at the plot level?

BLADE RUNNER'S CUT-SCENES: THE DESTRUCTION OF SUSPENSE

Blade Runner has a cut-scene at the beginning of each act, plus two others in the middle of acts 2 and 3:

- Act 1. The Runciter animal crime (present: Clovis, Zuben, Lucy and Runciter).
- Act 2. The murder of Eisenduller at Tyrell Corporation (present: Eisenduller, Sadik).
  – Mid. Act – brief movie with Tyrell and Rachel.
- Act 3. Sadik beats McCoy up (present: Sadik, Clovis, McCoy and Lucy).
  – Mid. Act – fake cops interrogate McCoy.
- Act 4. Assault to DNA Row (present: Clovis, Sadik, Luther and Lance).
- Act 5. Tyrell and Clovis.

With the exception of the mid-act movies and the final clip during act 5, the acts are introduced by a cut-scene which shows the crime that has just happened or offers some important backstory about the characters. When McCoy gets to the crime scene the player already knows the facts, although of course McCoy does not since he was not present in the cut-scene events (in the cut-scene introducing act 3 he is unconscious). The third-person perspective plays an important role here since as players we know more than McCoy. The search for clues is thus not aimed at finding out who did what, since we already know that, but becomes a sort of bureaucratic filling of forms, a way to trigger the next action so that we can move on in the game. The cut-scenes thus destroy suspense and make the mechanics of the adventure game fall apart. They dwell, instead, on giving more depth to the replicant characters and their struggle, so that the player gets to know them better and maybe *empathise* with them even though most cut-scenes show the replicants committing acts of violence. As in the film, we are encouraged to understand and feel a human affinity with these non-humans, which might make us in turn wonder about the legitimacy of the blade runner profession of our character: a level of moral sophistication that is entirely innovative for a computer game.

Despite all the criticism above, it is not my intention to portray the game as a failure. In an aesthetic twist, the result of knowing everything about the crime scenes before we even get there causes the player to wonder instead about what we do not know, which happens to be the most human of questions: *who is McCoy?* If we fully identify with our character, the question becomes *who am I?* A few characters ask McCoy throughout the game if he could be a replicant as well, something that he waves off with good humour. But soon there will be too many things he cannot explain: the dream of Mars and Lucy, his picture on the Moonbus with the escaped replicants, and even the fact that at some point McCoy appears as a suspect in his own clue database (as if the inventory was controlled by someone else). This points to a level of control and manipulation above us as players: a god, not of bio-mechanics as in the film, but a game designer intent on the players doubting themselves on this very fundamental level. Ambiguity is key. Even further in the game, most players realise that there is no fixed answer to that question, that we can actually tweak the result ourselves: by being hostile to the replicants we affirm our humanity, while by being sympathetic we will end up being one of them.[20] It is ironic that feeling empathy makes us into a replicant, when the way to detect one is precisely by measuring their lack of empathy through the Voigt-Kampff test. It seems that there is something fundamentally wrong with the test, both in the movie and the game, since most questions are about inquiring whether the subject feels horror about torturing or killing animals, but there are no questions to find out if the subject can empathise with other human beings or replicants. And as in the film, to be a human blade runner, able to kill replicants who just want to live, seems less *human* than actually letting them go; in another moral twist, humanity means behaving 'inhumanely'.

This is a strange but interesting experiment with destiny, not unlike the moral determinism of *Black and White*, where game actions have ethical consequences. It is as if McCoy could take the conscious decision of developing the empathy that Deckard lacks in the film (and Roy Batty demonstrates in the end), and this has enormous consequences for our feeling of agency (see Murray 1997: 126) in the game. It suggests that the illusion of free will is better achieved through clever orchestration of decision points than through augmenting the possibilities for action handling (such as puzzles) or randomising the nature of some non-playing characters (replicant/non-replicant), which feels rather pointless. In fact, trying out the different combinations of choices is what makes players want to re-play this game: as replicant friend, as replicant enemy, or as mere sympathiser (the middle-way option, not entirely coherent since it involves being nice to some replicants and killing others).

CHOICE AND REPLAYABILITY

The success of this game, then, lies in providing the player with the ability to take decisions about crucial plot points always related to McCoy's identity. This willingness to let players choose a moral approach manifests itself in a few elements that enhance the *replayability* value of the game. As argued above, players will soon realise that their investigation of the crime scenes progresses very much on 'rails', so that they are instead able to concentrate on exploring other avenues related to personality and character development. According to my observations in the players' fora, I argue that many players of this game actually *set their own emotional quests* in order to keep their interest in the game alive, such as befriending the replicants, or trying to find the branches that will allow them to develop a romantic relationship with one of the female characters.[21]

In order to talk about options in this game, I would like to distinguish between non-conscious variables and conscious choices. Non-conscious variables occur when McCoy misses a clue in one of the crime scenes, which might or might not have any further consequences in the game. In some cases the game 'stops' because the clue is needed to trigger further action (the picture of Lucy at Runciters), in others it does not matter at all (Lucy's doll in the hotel), yet in others still, the action continues but the missed object has more subtle, long-term consequences for the story. For example, not picking up the DNA information at Tyrell's means that if in the end the player escapes with one of the replicant women, she will die soon; if McCoy had found the DNA string, the voice-over would inform us that her life can be extended.

The really interesting options are, in my opinion, the conscious choices, which happen mostly in confrontations with non-playing characters, where the player can decide to talk to them or have a confrontation with them (which can be verbal, for example when trying to force them to do a Voigt-Kampff test, or physical in armed combat). As the fora and my own experience show, players soon discover that this kind of choice will affect their status as replicant enemy, replicant sympathiser or replicant, so they start trying to influence it consciously as it ties in with the main philosophical question of the game. All walkthroughs, produced by enthusiastic players and available on the web, contain indications as to whether a particular action will have consequences in the determination of our alignment and ultimately our identity.

The genius of this idea is that it allows for conceptual branching (that is, in our perception and expectations about the story and its ethos) while keeping structural branching under control. This happens because the key confrontations of the player with the possibly replicant non-player characters[22] always occur at times when the game 'doesn't need' that character anymore, so that no matter the outcome of the confrontation (whether the character lives or dies, for example) the game can progress without the designers having to cater for major amounts of branching. Some extra design is of course needed since the fact of not killing Lucy, for example, means that she has to be present in the final scene one way or another. But let us illustrate this with an example from our encounter with Zuben, the cook at Howie Lee's. Zuben is always a replicant, and he is the first suspect we encounter face to face after the first Runciter investigation. When McCoy interrogates him, he will try to run away by throwing a big bowl of soup at him; McCoy can either try to dodge or stand in surprise.

In the first case, where we are too slow, we will lose Zuben here, and our only interaction possibility is with a tramp. If we *stand* and lose Zuben he will reappear later to try to kill McCoy at his apartment and then there is no choice but killing him. In the second option, *jump*, we can either interact with the bum as above and waste our time, or we can follow Zuben and find him, in which case we have the option of letting him go or killing him here. As I hope is clear, this tight cluster of branching gets reduced to a very simple result: Zuben either lives or dies. If he dies, the game continues as it was supposed to, and the same if he lives, only he will reappear in the last scene as part of the replicant team in the Moonbus.

Another interesting consequence of these confrontations being optional is that violence actually is not the only possible way out of conflict, which also provides a certain feeling of agency in that each player is able to accommodate his or her style into the gameplay. To a lesser extent, the operation of the Esper machine to investigate photographs, and the Voigt-Kampff test to interrogate suspects, contributes to the sense of our activity being meaningful just by sheer mechanics, even if the clues found in the photographs work as statically as any other in the game, and we cannot choose the questions in the

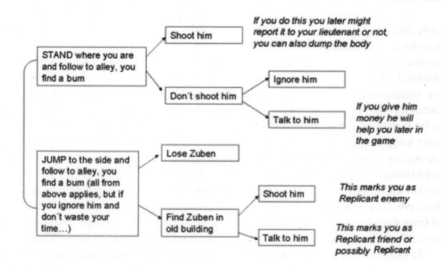

Voigt-Kampff test, but only their intensity (high for the most offensive enquiries, medium, and low for the most innocent).

The *replayability* value of the game therefore springs from the importance of the confrontations, with many players trying different options and saving different paths in order to experience a variety of outcomes. The ultimate success of this strategy is to be able to witness as many final scenes as possible – allegedly thirteen different ones, although I have only reached five myself[23] – a compulsive endeavor that makes *Blade Runner* into a form of hypertext, with its readers always worried about not having found all the branches of the story. They are all variations of two main themes:

McCoy is a human; he retires all the replicants and ends up alone/with Crystal.
McCoy is a replicant; he kills Crystal and goes away either in (i) the Moonbus with different combinations of replicants (depending on who is alive in the end); (ii) a car, with either Lucy, Dektora or alone.

Some players in the fora complained that changing a single action, like forcing Dektora to take a Voigt-Kampff test or not, could have so much influence upon the outcome (not doing it you might end up going away with her), which they saw as a near incoherence if the plot could not stay still.[24] However, I would say that the point of the story in this game is not that there is a single plot to be found, but precisely that each action matters towards the end and that we contribute to the evolving story as we go. Trying to guess which actions those are, and how they lead to each conclusion, is a sort of narrative reverse engineering where, in my opinion, the pleasure of the game lies. And once we know, of course, we can always exert our free will and choose another path.

CONCLUSION: IS McCOY A REPLICANT?

Only the player can answer this question, which is what makes the game interesting, as this version of *Blade Runner*, like the movie, also resists a clear answer. In his book about the film, Scott Bukatman argues that the question of Deckard being a replicant or not should be left unanswered (so that not even the dream of the unicorn and the origami of the Director's Cut can provide certainty), because ambiguity is essential to our questioning of what it means to be human (1997: 82). Is it the biological birth or is it the behaviour? I would even suggest that the game is a simulacrum to explore this question, since real gameplay in the conventional sense is mostly absent, and the process of playing instead pushes us to concentrate on questions of empathy and identity. If we kill all the replicants and are confirmed as blade runner and human in the end, we still have a bitter taste in our mouth. After all, the game spends a lot of time explaining the motivations of the replicant characters, so we may well feel compelled to play again in order to find out what it is to be one of them...

To conclude I will follow two avenues, as I consider the contribution that

Westwood's *Blade Runner* PC game brings to the *Blade Runner* universe in general, and what innovations it brings to the adventure game genre.

With regard to the *Blade Runner* universe, the game allows for enhanced immersion in its carefully reproduced environments. The spatial exploration of the rainy streets and the derelict buildings effectively transports us to the diegesis of the film. More importantly, the scenarios become alive in that we can interact with them, so that we go beyond the mere looking that the film allows. The game also expands on several topics that the book or the film only suggest. For example, McCoy clearly loves his dog Maggie, whereas the attachment of the Deckard in the book to his sheep is merely a question of status. McCoy is always worried about Maggie, buys her a collar, and the most upsetting part of another guy living in his apartment is not the apartment itself, but what might have happened to his dog.

The game also introduces an interesting addition related to the empathy theme: a group of human activists helping replicants, called CARS, or 'Citizens Against the Replicant Slavery'. At some point it is not clear if this group is as pacifist as they claim or whether they collaborate in some of the replicant terrorist acts. What are their motivations and how far can one go in supporting oppressed groups? This question also remains unanswered, but their appearance provides the replicant problem with more texture and contemporary urgency.

As for the contribution of this game to the adventure genre in general, I hope it has become clear throughout this chapter that *Blade Runner* is a successful if unique example of this genre. Instead of exploiting the recognised strengths of adventure games (puzzles and quests) or incorporating features of other computer game genres (simulation or action fighting), it bravely does away with them and tries a new approach. This game, which is almost not a game at all, involves the player in a hunt for decisive narrative turns and gives him or her the chance of moulding their own destiny. In his article about interactive narrative, Heide Smith identifies the secret of mastering the craft:

> A designer who wants to tell the story of how A leads to B while maintaining an interactive element will start going to great lengths to ensure the interactor that the choices he makes are important while making absolutely sure that they are not. (2000)

This is what the game succeeds at so well, with its game choices that do not matter and its emotional identity choices that are all-important. *Blade Runner* creates a digital suspension of disbelief that players are willingly drawn into through the excitement of the different moral choices, where trusting our implanted memories will bring us the illusion of free will. The possibility of Rick Deckard being a replicant is one of the film's most enduring and intriguing questions. The possibility of actually being a replicant ourselves throws up even more fascinating questions, and makes playing, rather than just watching *Blade Runner*, a remarkable experience.

NOTES

1   Both lines belong to dramatic scenes on top of the Bradbury building. The first one is spoken in the film by replicant leader Roy in his final fight against Deckard; and the second by Clovis, the computer game's replicant leader, who witnesses McCoy (the player) being beaten up by another replicant and then mysteriously comments on McCoy's lack of freedom.

2   This idea has been a constant in philosophy since Aristotle, who in his *Ethics* argues that voluntary action is incompatible with ignorance. Knowledge is all-important in the work of a rationalist like Descartes, whom Pris also quotes in the film.

3   For a historical perspective on the genre, see Aarseth 1997 and 2000, who traces its history back to *Adventure* (1976). The trend was structurally continued by graphic adventures of which *Myst* (1993) is the best known. See also Montfort (2003), who considers the first textual adventures as a genre of their own in his book *Twisty Little Passages*.

4   For an introductory history to the genre, visit http://www.lancs.ac.uk/postgrad/watsons/bhadvent.html.

5   From Westwood's original website, now defunct: http://www.westwood.com/games/bladerunner/br/html/advfrmsw.htm. Accessed August 1999.

6   For example, this player's opinion: 'I was a die-hard fan of classic adventure, which offers much more interaction and actual adventuring than *Blade Runner*. Indeed, anyone who is looking for wacky puzzles and unlimited exploration should stay away from this game. It is an interactive movie in the best sense of the word, a piece of art which offers a similar experience like a real movie, [sic] only that here you have control of the actions' (http://www.mobygames.com/game/view_review/reviewerId,6226/gameId,341/platformId,3/).

7   Ron Dulin (03/12/97) in http://www.gamespot.com/pc/adventure/bladerunner/review.html.

8   Louis Castle, interviewed by Gloria Stern; see Stern 1998.

9   Ibid., note 8.

10 For more on the visual and adaptation specific aspects, see the chapter by Barry Atkins in this volume.

11 'Once the game starts, we work at two levels: that of the plot, where Iser's gaps are applicable, and that of the game, where the problems we encounter have to be solved, not interpreted. Our mind is busy with the plot level and the action level at the same time. The first one, that we experience on the fly, can be narrated afterwards (it is *tellable*) and makes sense as a story (complete with character motivation and feelings); the second is about solving action problems, and if it was to be narrated it would correspond to what we know as walkthroughs' (Tosca 2003b: 6).

12 'My personal favorite is Clovis, the poem-quoting Nexus-6 rep and main antagonist. It's the first time in a game that I've actually liked the bad guy better than my own good guy character' (Darren Zimmerman 22/12/98) *Gamespot*. 'You can either kill the dying Clovis or suffer his poetry reading until he dies. Of course, McCoy never did like poetry' (http://www.cheatbook.de/wfiles/

bladerun.htm). 'In the movie, Roy Batty quotes from Blake once – here, the replicant character Clovis spouts Blake almost every time he opens his mouth. "Without contraries is no progression", he says at one point, an apt quotation from Plate 3 of Blake's *The Marriage of Heaven and Hell*. It's just a sound-bite, an empty way of trying to create a consistent character' (http://home.golden.net/~csp/cd/reviews/blade_game.htm).

13 For example I got into a situation where I had to kill Lieutenant Guzza in order to continue the game and not being killed by the replicants, when that was the last thing that I wanted McCoy to do.

14 It is difficult to actually aim with the mouse, so that sometimes McCoy can be killed because the player is too slow at aiming, but this can be prevented by playing on the 'easy' level.

15 Only if we have chosen the option 'player's choice' in McCoy moods. Any other mood (polite, normal, surly, erratic) will mean that he does all the talking by himself, without player intervention.

16 A new area appears in our map, or we will be specifically told by a non-playing character.

17 For a full explanation of the concept of quests and their use in game design, see Tosca 2003a. The semantic level of a quest is related to how it contributes to telling a story, and the structural level has to do with gameplay, that is, which actions the player needs to perform in order to complete the quest.

18 As Louis Castle, executive producer of the game, said: 'the game does not lend well to missions' (http://www.westwoodsurf.com/index_blade.html) official site, accessed August 1999.

19 The sewers have exits to McCoy's apartment, Izo's shop and Bob's Bullets in Animoid Row, the Metro in Nightclub Row, the Garage of the Hysteria Hall and Howie Lee's Backyard. From these spaces we can walk to all the others as they are connected in a dense net.

20 As is obvious from reading the different fora and websites that offer walk-throughs for the game. These examples are from the *Gamespot* players reviews area: '*Blade Runner* makes you think before you act and lets you decide whom to befriend and trust, and whom to hate and fear. Once you get halfway through the game, you'll realise that there are actually no good guys and no bad guys. Certain characters become your friends or enemies depending on your actions' (John Loos 22/06/99); 'You can make subtle decisions that greatly affect the outcome of the story. For example, shooting a certain character or letting them go will spin the storyline into two different directions, and then relates it to the multiple endings' (Darren Zimmerman 22/12/98); 'The game sometimes gets heavily philosophical, and asks, "What is it to be human?" so fans of *Duke* and *Quake* will be bored!' (Jordan Rosanne 09/09/98).

21 All walkthroughs contain advice as to how to reach the different endings, as-suming that every player will be interested in this multiplicity of the story. A common topic in the fora is the discussion (and demands for help) about per-sonal (emotional) goals, for example: how can I save Izo?, how can I talk to Dektora?, how can I meet Crystal on the roof again? (http://www.bladezone.

com/phpBB2/viewforum.php?f=5).

22 I have counted at least thirteen while playing.

23 This is one of the main questions in the fora, as well as a part of most walk-throughs that try to describe different endings and hint at how to get to them.

24 In the *Gamespot* players forum, Frank Kowalkowski mentions the incoherence problem. After ending a game as a replicant sympathiser he loads the game again a few scenes before and 'The ending changes, I'm human again, and the blade runner I killed five minutes ago is now allegedly a rep sympathiser. Say what?! One action not only changed the story, it made it incoherent, inconsistent, and gave me a far worse ending' (22/12/97).

SECTION 3: FANS

SCANNING THE REPLICANT TEXT
JONATHAN GRAY

From 2001 onwards, many *Blade Runner* websites and online discussion groups have been alive with talk of a potential Special Edition DVD release, and all the bonus features that it might offer.[1] 2002 was set as the release date, but in April of that year, reports surfaced of legal problems, and the project has been stalled in production limbo ever since, much to the chagrin and frustration of the film's fan base. Amidst the finger-pointing, some wild speculation, and the carefully pieced together reports at BRmovie.com, is a commonly voiced sentiment: that the fans and the viewing public deserve their text, a text, moreover, that is being withheld from them. *Los Angeles, 2019*'s homepage (www.tyrell-corporation.pp.se), for instance, bemoans that 'it's tragic that such a masterpiece is kept locked up in some vault somewhere … *Blade Runner* deserves a much better DVD than this.' An altogether curious and interesting situation therefore exists in which, well over twenty years after a film's initial release, many of its still loyal fans appear to feel deprived of the text's true self. Likewise, despite and because of their love for what would seem to be the text of *Blade Runner*, many fans are demanding access to an unseen, yet perhaps more 'proper' version. An apparent paradox exists, as the text is seen as having not yet shown itself, and yet that text has many loyal, loving, and active fans.

To delve into this paradox, this chapter examines discussion of the *Blade Runner* Special Edition (or BR:SE) DVD through a series of email interviews with numerous *Blade Runner* fans frequenting the alt.fan.blade-runner newsgroup. Much as the prospect of a new urban development can inspire vital discussion of what a city or neighbourhood at its core is or should be, so too might an examination of the prospect of a BR:SE tell us about what *Blade Runner* is or should be to its fans. Such an examination can also take some steps towards 'solving' the paradox of the not-yet-existent text, inquiring as it does so into the nature of contemporary textuality, and its intersections with and manifestations within both fansites and special edition DVDs. Far too much work within the related fields of media, communications, literary and film studies operates as if 'the text' has already been defined, its behavioural patterns already charted and fully accounted for. However, the peculiar case of *Blade Runner* and its text that is, in some respects, not yet a text, highlights the limits of much established vocabulary and theory on textual ontology and phenomenology. Ultimately, then, this chapter aims to discover more about the internal dynamics and mechanics of textuality, and in doing so, also aims to provide some answers to what *Blade Runner* itself *is*, and what it is becoming.

The proliferation of texts or versions is, of course, nothing new to *Blade Runner*. There are, after all, multiple cuts of the film: the Workprint, shown twice in March 1982, re-exhibited briefly in 1990 and 1991, and supposedly available on Ebay; the San Diego Sneak Preview, shown 8 May 1982; the Original Version (OV), which opened in the USA on 25 June 1982; an International Cut, shown worldwide in 1982 and later released on video; a television broadcast version; and the 1992 Director's Cut, available on video and DVD. Each version has a variety of differences, ranging from slight word changes, to more violence in the international version, to more contentious alterations. Most notably and prominently, the San Diego Sneak Preview, the Original Version, and the International Cut all contain narration throughout by Deckard and a 'happy ending' for Deckard and Rachel, while the Director's Cut features a scene in which Deckard has a vision or dream of a unicorn. This added scene is portentous, however, when read against Gaff's act of leaving an origami unicorn outside Deckard's apartment at the end of the film. To many viewers, this has suggested Gaff's access to Deckard's memories and dreams, hence implying Deckard too may be a replicant, manufactured along with his dreams and memories by the Tyrell Corporation. In short, then, not only do the different versions present slightly different scenes or snippets of dialogue, but they also offer different interpretations, or at least open up different debates over interpretation of both characters and plot.

Meanwhile, *Blade Runner* is hardly alone in its many versions, as most films are cut in a variety of ways for a variety of audiences or purposes: a print is shortened for television, expanded for DVD (as with the *Lord of the Rings* trilogy), given a different or multiple endings for re-release (as with *28 Days Later* (2002)), digitally remastered so as to produce a cleaner print, or even added to after-the-fact (as with the late 1990s re-release of the original *Star Wars* trilogy). Sometimes, too, phantom edits are mentioned in interviews, as cast or crew discuss lost or alternate scenes. Edits are even produced by fans, 'improving' on the official version (as with the Jar Jar Binks-less *Star Wars: Episode I – The Phantom Menace*, available online as *The Phantom Edit*). However, with very few exceptions, this proliferation of textuality has been largely ignored by analytical work, as has its effect on textual ontology. Multiple studies have examined the intertextual travels of a text or characters across media, sequels and/or remakes (see Bennett & Woollacott 1987; Pearson & Uricchio 1991; Barker & Brooks 1998; Brooker 1999, 2002; Chin & Gray 2001), but as such have concentrated largely on what Will Brooker (2001) has called the 'overflow' from one text, platform or medium to another. Little if anything has been said, though, of the DVD's challenge to textuality of revisiting, developing and/or multi-layering the text seemingly from *within* the text. The challenge is no small one, however, for if we wish to discuss issues such as Deckard's identity or the film's regard for and 'take' on humanity, in the case of *Blade Runner*, or multiple other questions of meanings, power, effects and identification with any film, first we must know which text we are talking about, and how its multiple versions work with, alongside, or in spite of each other. This task is larger than any one article could address, and thus I offer no pretension of providing a new and perfect model of post-DVD textuality here. Rather, this chapter outlines some initial stages and observations, and focuses on how we might begin to answer the many riddles of textuality for *Blade Runner*. With no BR:SE yet in existence, a physical, corporeal textuality is absent, and yet as fan anticipation starts to sketch out a BR:SE and its various offers or even threats to *Blade Runner*, a discursive text and a receiver/consumer's textuality begin to emerge and come into focus.

THE RESEARCH PROJECT

In early 2004 I posted a series of questions to the alt.fan-blade-runner newsgroup, asking if members of this online community could reply to me off-list via email.[2] Multiple *Blade Runner* fan groups exist online, but this group appeared by far the most active: rarely a day goes by without multiple postings, as compared with, for instance, many of the Yahoo groups based around *Blade Runner*, which often go months without a posting, and which list few members. In February 2004, by my count, 45 different individuals posted to the alt.fan.blade-runner site. The intent behind the questions was humble, and no attempt was made to access a fully 'representative' group, nor does the following discussion claim to speak definitively of *Blade Runner* fans as some united conglomerate. Rather, I was hoping to elicit some commentary on what the BR:SE meant to some of these fans, and to explore how the topic of the film's multiple versions was discussed. Fifteen fans responded, almost all with fairly lengthy commentary. The basic tenor of these replies, and of the websites, was predictable, in that they all look forward to the BR:SE release, and rue those standing in the way, but I was particularly interested in recording how this anticipation was voiced, and how they imagined this new textual incarnation fitting into their current 'canon' or construction of *Blade Runner*.

One thing made abundantly clear was that while discussion of the Special Edition has picked up in recent years, many of these viewers have been awaiting its arrival for much longer. 'I am most certainly looking forward to it', wrote Lukas Mariman, 'although the endless waiting (it's literally been *years* by now) frustrates me to no end', or as Nicklas Ingels told me, 'I don't think there is one *Blade Runner* fan that doesn't want the *Blade Runner* Special Edition to come out of its shadows.' The reasons for this anticipation, though, seemed threefold.

MORE TEXT, MORE UNIVERSE

First, a BR:SE quite simply represents more of the beloved text. Certainly, my question of what they would like to see on such a DVD became a 'how would you spend a million dollars?'-type question, asking after all the textual excess and overflow such an object could represent. Stephen Klein listed off that he would like: 'Every possible deleted scene', 'alternate scenes, alternate camera angles, alternate sound reels', 'Director's Commentary', 'Documentaries,

Press Kit stuff', 'Isolated Score' and 'Commentary by the original cast', with the telling add-on that 'Harrison Ford wouldn't do it ... but I can dream can't I?' Meanwhile, Red replied that 'I'd really like to see every scrap of footage shot, all of it.' Red would also like to hear all three recorded narrations, and 'it would be killer if we could view the film with the narration of choice'; he called for multiple commentaries, an overview of the sequel books, an interview with Ridley Scott, and 'every single documentary ever filmed about the movie', along with 'featurettes covering the props, vehicles, ridleyville and clothing'. Indeed, most of the responses went into great detail in answering this question, or quite simply offered, as did Mike Helm, that a BR:SE should offer 'Everything'. Summing up, Lukas Mariman declared in a single-sentence paragraph, 'I would definitely love to see more of BR', while Evil Sponge wanted 'as many extras as I can get my hands on'.

Here, the idea of a favourite text proliferating and expanding was clearly enticing. Part of the appeal appeared purely functional, for while some of the extras being demanded had already been seen or acquired by these fans in one legitimate or bootlegged version or another, several spoke of how convenient it would be to have them all in one place. Beyond this plea for convenience, though, a BR:SE would also present even more of the text – more scenes, more tidbits of information, more scene angles. In effect, then, a special edition could expand the film's diegetic world. Indeed, a similar sentiment was voiced by some in response to my question regarding the fans' interest level in either a remake or a sequel. Most balked at the idea of an outright remake, but a few seemed more taken in by the idea that the text and diegetic world of *Blade Runner* could grow through a sequel. All expressed concerns as to any proposed sequel's quality (as discussed below), prompting some to opt instead for, as Dan Gorski called it, a 'sidequel'. But as Gorski also stated, 'yes finally because it is too tantalising a storyline to ignore ... I love the BR universe and want to see it expanded'. Similarly, Will Bueché observed that 'there is room in the *Blade Runner* universe for other stories'.

Ultimately, the fandom of the specific *Blade Runner* text was shown to extend to the vision, style and tone of the world it offered, and thus anything that could meaningfully keep a portal to that world open was to be appreciated. Many of the interviewees spoke glowingly of *Blade Runner* as presenting, as Will Bueché noted, a 'deeply immersive atmosphere'. To some, this atmosphere was largely visual, aural and almost tactile, while to others it was also in large part intellectual-philosophical. David Caldwell, for instance, found great depth in the philosophical questions at the film's core:

What is Human? What makes us Human? What does it mean to be Human? If we create androids in our image that are just like Humans, what rights do they have, can they be treated as slaves and if they are just like us, how are they not like us – i.e. can we create life that is effectively Human in all ways that matter? As time goes by, these questions, the influence of *Blade Runner* and the future it presents, all become more relevant to us.

Behind such comments, we might begin to see that a film can represent much more than a mere two hours of entertainment, but can also open up for us certain aesthetic, contemplative, reflective and emotional spheres. Clearly, in the case of *Blade Runner*, these spheres are by no means in impending danger, as the existence of web discussion should prove, but the prospect of textual expansion nevertheless offers with it the promise of further and significant revitalisation.

This need for revitalisation would seem particularly prescient for a text released in 1982. With so much popular culture forgotten in under two years and replaced by countless other similarly ephemeral texts, maintaining the existence of certain spheres becomes all the more important to certain viewers, and requires all the more effort. *Blade Runner*, of course, questions the very functioning of memory, examining how it can become disembodied and transferred, but also, therefore, how it can live outside of its original 'creator'/experiencer, implanted in a second or subsequent host. The prospect of a BR:SE offers a similar promise of further ensuring that memory and that text's prolonged existence. In an interesting way, David Caldwell (aka Netrunner) and others' frequently updated news page on BRmovie.com also plays a role in keeping the text and its paraphernalia alive and relevant, by listing countless *Blade Runner* references from the press, films, art galleries and so on – a testament to the film's continued importance and vitality. Indeed, the mere existence of websites such as Caldwell's, or of online discussion groups, points to a desire on these fans' behalf to ensure the text remains open and active, its memory 'lived', and not atrophied. A BR:SE, as such, would play its own role – clearly perceived to be important – of keeping the text 'alive'. Just as Deckard hopes to keep Rachel alive beyond her expiry date, so too do these fans want their text, and perhaps more importantly, the intellectual, aesthetic and emotional spheres it creates and evokes for them; a BR:SE promises to be an active, next-generation 'host' for such spheres, granting them an extended lifespan.

Here, Dan Gorski's response to my question of whether he cares or not about a BR:SE is particularly illustrative. Just as Will Brooker (2002) found with original *Star Wars* fans' discussion of the prequel trilogy and what it represents, Gorski looked forward to the new generation of *Blade Runner* fans, aficionados, and acolytes that the BR:SE might create:

It will provide a new generation with the opportunity to experience BR, since BR:SE hype will grab new fans who might be intrigued by a multi-version 'cult classic'. And it's bound to strike a cord [sic] with various 'pop'-cultures that have grown and matured over the 1990s … environmentalist culture who are ever more concerned the environment is going down the drain, technologist culture concerned with pitfalls but intrigued with opportunities of getting rich as Tyrell through tech, and a conservative culture against playing God … and the growing widespread concern over WMD proliferation and nano-molecular tech.

From WMD proliferation to the environment, the text was seen to speak to multiple parties, its relevance to be felt on multiple levels. Not only, therefore, would a BR:SE keep this text alive; it would pass it on to the next generation. Undoubtedly, other fans may well feel possessive of their beloved text, fearful of what new generations might 'do' to it. But whether hoping for or guarding their text from new generations, as fans of the film's 'deeply immersive atmosphere', these fans do not want it to become just a memory.

THE COLD CASE TEXT

Alongside the desire to see this *Blade Runner* 'universe' continue, ran a related desire, to *know* everything one could about the text and universe. As has already been seen, part of what a BR:SE would offer is, as Gorski glossed, 'layer upon layer of relevant information'. In a previous article on *Blade Runner* fans, Brooker noted the degree to which, true to the film's noir/detective roots, fans 'appear to practise a form of "forensic detection"', involving 'a search for answers, an obsessive return to the "original" text(s) in this wealth of false leads, in order to pick over clues and build threads of logic which explain some of the film's unsolved mysteries' (1999: 57; 60). Certainly, many of the fans spoke glowingly of how they often found 'new' elements upon yet another viewing, to the point that when Rob Mellor told me 'every time I watch it I find something new', he almost apologetically prefaced his remark with 'You must have heard this a thousand times…'. As might be expected, these fans already know a great deal about the text and universe, and so, in this regard, were already proficient 'detectives'. BRmovie.com is particularly illustrative here, providing a vastly encompassing look at the film. The site contains a *Blade Runner* encyclopaedia, links to almost any reference of *Blade Runner* on the Web (and many off it), links to articles on *Blade Runner*, information on spinoff merchandise, frequently updated news on the film and BR:SE, interviews, and much more. In contrast to many fansites that can focus more on discussion and pictures, BRmovie.com is dense with text and information, serving as a near-complete 'case file' on *Blade Runner*. Moreover, with over twenty years to accumulate evidence, it is no surprise that very little information seems to be missing. As such, though, a BR:SE offers the prospect of re-opening this cold case file.

Interestingly, however, while on one hand the fans appeared excited to receive any new evidence, on the other hand they also appeared quite ambivalent and conflicted as to whether they truly wanted a 'definitive' *Blade Runner*, and an end to its mysteries. 'I'm not sure if a third new "Director's Cut" can in any way be final and "The" version over the older ones', wrote Nicklas Ingels, for example, but his 'I'm not sure' points to a slight anxiety over how definitive a BR:SE will attempt to be. This anxiety was more explicitly stated by others, as Evil Sponge, for instance, wrote that 'I like to think that there is no answer to the question of whether Deckard is human or replicant, and I'd like it to remain ambiguous. I think it would be a mistake if the SE tipped the balance in favour of one answer or another.' Particularly as regards the question over Deckard's humanity, all seemed quite aware (armed with knowledge of what the Director's Cut did to this debate) that answers *could* be given, but none appeared to *want* or need those answers. Indeed, Gnomus criticised the Director's Cut for 'hit[ting] you over the head and tell[ing] you what to think', preferring the Original Version, since it 'is open so you have to decide what it all means'.

Another common way around this dilemma of the evidence that could close an open case was to hold the question constant, and enjoy the proliferation of answers offered by each version, seeing none as either definitive or canonical. Therefore, Red said he was 'one of the few who seems to enjoy both versions of the film the same amount. I love them both. I would love a new cut of the film as well.' Similarly, Stephen Klein stated, 'I love the story either way, I don't need "definitive", just make sure I get all the versions for posterity'; Dan Gorski claimed, 'The only thing I hold sacred about BR is that it changes as often as my opinions given different moods, nuances, perceptions, information and inebriation'; and David Spiro posited that 'I think it will offer the definitive version as far as RS [Ridley Scott] is concerned, but the so called "Deck-a-rep" debate will go on irrespective of that.' Or, in a more involved discussion of his interaction with the Original Version and Director's Cut incarnations of Deckard, Will Bueché proposed:

> The director feels that Deckard is a replicant. I did not feel that was the case when I saw the theatrical version, and I was frustrated by the suggestion at first. However, the idea that the feelings and empathy that we call 'humanity' might arise in a replicant is the very theme which makes the actions of the Off-World replicants Roy, Pris, Zhora, etc – as well as Rachel – sympathetic. It is therefore not in fact that much of a stretch to have Deckard also be an example of this.

As with many of the others, then, Bueché can take the text either way, and appears quite content to let the text exist between different versions.

In such discussion, we can hear echoes from other fan studies, such as Henry Jenkins (1992), Constance Penley (1997) or Will Brooker (2002), which chart the fan's wrestling away of the text from the author. Several of these *Blade Runner* fans saw Ridley Scott as having a 'definitive' answer, but did not believe this in any way required them to agree. Again, then, what we see is a process whereby the text has become a structure of feeling as much as a set location, a series of questions and themes as much as – or more than – a collection of answers. Almost mimicking their beloved text's hero, the distanced detective tracking down replicants without any necessary conviction of finding a 'truth', these fans scour over evidence and welcome more of it, but seem ultimately unconcerned with (or even anxious about the prospect of) finding some grand form of closure. The notion that any text 'says something' is paramount to much of textual studies, but these fans' reactions suggest that we must also accept the equal and opposite notion that some texts ask instead of answer, and that their resulting persistent refusal of closure and continued open-endedness becomes a large part of what they 'mean' and of why they are valued.

This is not 'polysemy' in the sense of a text allowing its audiences to decide what it means (see Fiske 1989), for this itself requires closure. Rather, this points to a fundamental problem with textual studies' established notion of communication entailing encoding then decoding (Hall 1980). Such a process seems wholly commonsensical, but its curt, rounded-off nature often hides the fact that decoding *continues*, and does not necessarily happen in a 'determinate moment', as Stuart Hall proposed (1980: 130). What we can see in these fans' resistance to the idea of the BR:SE creating a 'definitive' answer to/version of the text, and what we can see in their dedication to discussing the film so closely for many years after initial reception, is that 'decoding' can continue long after initial viewing, and that delivery is just the beginning of interpretation. Texts become internalised, both individually and amongst communities, and a central appeal of many films is their utility to us after reception. A mystery or perhaps 'blooper' in the extant *Blade Runner* that is often pointed out on *Blade Runner* sites is the early discussion of a sixth replicant, and the fact that only five are accounted for has led to speculation as to whether Deckard is the sixth, whether this is simply an error in continuity, or whether a sixth remains out there somewhere in the cityscape. As these fans' discussion suggests, though, I would like to argue that when it comes to textual reception, there is always another replicant – another interpretation, another decoding – potentially out there somewhere.

Once more, then, we return to a conception of texts, and of this text in particular, as spheres for reflection upon certain themes and issues, and as zones for dialogue, discussion and the working through of these themes and issues. Media studies is still too obsessed with texts as stimuli to be reacted to, but responses such as these suggest we must pay closer attention to their inherent dialogic role (Bakhtin 1981, 1986), as participants in personal and communal discussions. As much, therefore, as one might have hypothesised that a BR:SE, complete with its arsenal of bonus features, might seem to appeal to fans for its potential abilities to close off and answer both text and debate, in fact its greatest gift as these fans perceive it may lie in opening up more text and more debate.

REPLICANT TEXTS AND STUDIO INTERFERENCE

A third major reason for anticipating a BR:SE lies in the prospect of the new text improving upon and/or correcting older ones. With pure unanimity, these fans were excited at the idea of a cleaner print, with doctored visuals and audio. As David Caldwell pointed out, the current Director's Cut was 'quite literally one of the first DVDs ever made', and thus it is hardly technically on par with other DVDs. Speaking of the audio, for instance, Nicklas Ingels complained it currently has a 'crappy Dolby Digital 2 channel soundtrack', an audiotrack that he later described as 'a slap in the face'. As such, all hoped for changes on a technical level, not because they would in theory *change* the text, but rather because the true text was seen to be imprisoned behind them. 'I really want', demanded Evil Sponge, 'to see BR in its full glory … hopefully allowing us to finally see the director's version in its purest form.' Similarly, Dan Gorski argued that such changes were necessary because 'BR, given its complex beautiful production deserves a complex beautiful DVD', while Will Bueché quite poetically noted that 'Preserving a vision can mean extending the quality beyond what was originally presented.'

Such responses, I believe, point to two things. First, they show a growing degree of technical literacy with which many cinema-goers (and DVD-watchers) are endowed. Clearly, some are more literate than others, but most viewers are equipped with some degree of knowledge regarding what a movie would or could look like with better sound and visuals, and many possess the vocabulary/lingo of Dolby, 'Isolated Score', 'outtakes' and so on.

However, if all of these fans' responses displayed certain levels of technical literacy, they also exhibited a considerable amount of production literacy. By this, I mean that these fans knew a lot not just about the production process of *Blade Runner*, but about how movies are made in general. Such knowledge particularly showed itself in a common feeling, voiced above by Evil Sponge, that a BR:SE would finally allow Ridley Scott to cut the film the way he wanted it. As David Caldwell explained, this would be 'the *real* Director's Cut – the 1991 version being a rushed affair with precious little input by Ridley Scott'. Similarly, Rob Mellor extended criticism to studio influences affecting both the Director's Cut and the Original Verion: 'What a shame', he wrote, 'that the two extant versions of the film are both further flawed by the commercial influences surrounding their release; the OV with its dreadful studio-imposed "happy ending" and the DC which was rushed out and never the definitive version it should have been.' Likewise, David Spiro said that he had 'the sense that Ridley Scott was never given the chance to complete the film as he would have wished'. Or, in a mournful echo, Will Bueché wrote of how 'Legendary German filmmaker Fritz Lang once sadly referred to his classic silent science fiction epic *Metropolis* as a film "that does no longer exist", due to Lang's own version of the film being lost to the whims of others who edited the film as they saw fit', and he hoped 'that *Blade Runner* can escape that cruel fate'. Clearly, then, to many of these fans, Scott's *Blade Runner* has been withheld from them by a meddling studio. As was suggested in the previous section, if and when the time comes, these fans may not ultimately accept Scott's version as the 'real text', particularly if it clashes with their own textual spheres, but they still clearly value this version (and, if nothing else, simply want to see it), and feel excluded from it by the studio.

But the meddling is not over, as these same producers and executives are being held accountable for the legal wrangling that has indefinitely delayed the BR:SE's release. Like many interviewees, Rob Mellor is 'starting to become sceptical about whether it will ever happen', because of all the petty fighting. Indeed, some were less polite in their expression of frustration, as Stephen Klein, for instance, wrote:

> If from what I've heard is true (that the *Blade Runner* Partnership isn't allow-ing the release of the almost-completed SE), I really hope they shut up and stop whining or finally sell the rights. It's a strange thing when something so great as *Blade Runner* embeds itself into our pop culture and just because of its lacklustre performance in 1982 some producers still have sticks up their asses.

Several fans also expressed dismay at how the producers and rights-holders' squabbles had already cost the project its former hired producer (and long-time *Blade Runner* fan), Charles de Lauzirika, who has now moved onto other work.

In these criticisms of the producers we can hear echoes of earlier work by Henry Jenkins (1992) into *Star Trek* fans' sense of anger at 'character rape' by less proficient writers, or by Will Brooker (2002) into original *Star Wars* tril-ogy fans' anger at George Lucas' misguided decisions for the prequel trilogy. But both of these examples are of texts already-received by fans and subse-quently 'defiled'. Here, however, the supposed pure and original text has yet to be seen, giving rise to the question of why these fans *are* fans. I believe one answer could be reached through examining the metaphor behind Dan Gorski's comment that 'Ridley Scott is God'. After all, God and the very na-ture of creation are questioned by *Blade Runner* and its replicants: only God can create 'real' humans, and the Tyrell Corporation creates replicants, but the movie forces us to wonder about the actual differences and the close proxim-ity. Perhaps, then, a similar situation exists with textuality, whereby the au-thor/director is a godlike creator ('Ridley Scott is God'), and although the fans are without his exact version, the replicant text is close enough. Like Deckard, they have fallen in love with a replicant, and, as *Blade Runner* proposes, ul-timately the replicant texts may prove on par with or better than Scott's. As I would argue, the key issue for fans, it seems, is not so much one of actuality, but rather of the *interference* represented by the creators of replicants. Just as we are invited to empathise with the replicants in *Blade Runner*, so too can a fan love the replicant text; but, just as we and Deckard can see Rachel's flaws and faults as adorable but her inventor Tyrell as arrogantly misguided, so the fans' love for the imperfect product does not extend to the company that made and released it. The studio system may well be necessary in allow-ing a text to be, but it is spoken of and regarded as an imperfect, and even an ignorant, creator.

In proposing this metaphor, though, I also wish to draw attention to two other aspects of contemporary textuality. The first is that many audiences are considerably smarter and more industry literate than many of us in media studies often give them credit for. Media theory can often discuss the role of producers, marketers and so on as though the audience themselves are totally unaware of their role and their potential interference in textual creation. And while this audience of fifteen respondents to the research project can hardly be taken as representative, their comments still point towards a circulation of industry and media literacy that may well be educating audiences to the petty interferences of producers at times, hence making them more critically aware, knowing audiences. Doubtlessly, different audience members will 'remember' and activate their literacy more at some times than at others, so that, for instance, these *Blade Runner* fans may not think twice about the production process of some other films they watch. But a growing literacy is nonetheless evident, a literacy that DVDs are themselves playing a considerable role in teaching.

A second and related point is another vital one for textual studies analysts to learn: that the author is not dead. In the wake of Roland Barthes' 'The Death of the Author' (1977) and of a certain critical disdain for auteur studies, many projects have written the author's obituary and moved onwards. Indeed, audience research is often held up as proof of the insufficiency of encoders and their intentions and/or desires to a proper analysis of textuality. However, even if a solitary focus on encoding is insufficient, we cannot forget that, as this study has proven, encoding and encoders are often of great interest to decoders, as are their ideas and their 'take' on a text. In the proliferation of Directors' Cuts and of directors' or cast commentary tracks on DVDs, or even of interviews with directors in newspapers, magazines and on television, we can see an authorship and an authority that is, for many, very much alive. Granted, and importantly, authors can only exist if decoders wish them to, but it is time that we once again added 'the author function' (Foucault 1980) to our construction of textuality. In the continuing experience that is a text, the author's role can indeed prove a vital one. A god, after all, need not be omnipotent to be of interest. Some constructions of pure-minded, all-benevolent auteurs battling evil corporate studio lackies may seem a page out of *Paradise Lost*, and may be crudely and unnecessarily Manichean at times, but it is important to realise how this still at the very least represents a sophistication of media studies' more common Manichean battle between noble audiences and evil culture industries (with producers and auteurs effaced into the same corporate fallen angel).

Whether authors are constructed based on actual interviews and commentary, or are used as idealised adversaries to the business and marketing side of textual production, they are often invoked as a way of staking out a textuality and aesthetics beyond the dollars and cents of industry. It is therefore no wonder that – as with these fans – audiences often 'shelter' behind the author and his or her desires and artistry, as the very figure who denies the industry's sole claim of ownership on textuality. Due to the at-times awkward construction of this author figure, we should by no means celebrate authorial resurrection as the end of corporatism, but would nevertheless be wise to acknowledge fans' negotiations and awareness of production processes.

Meanwhile, however, if we must recoup the author function to our critical repertoire, so too should we begin to look to a 'producer function'. After all, for all the fans' righteous indignation at the producers and petty executives bickering over rights and thus potentially killing the chance that a BR:SE will ever see the light of day, these same executives appear to be playing a vital symbolic role. Not only do they stand as straw men and women to the 'author function' or to the claimed glories of the text, for the fans do not only value the BR:SE – they also value the *idea* of this version, and value *anticipating* it. Indeed, there may well be some unconscious enjoyment of its non-existence, for while the BR:SE remains in limbo, it can forever be each individual fan's ideal text, open for their own projections. At the moment that it is finally released, though, the formerly blank screen will no longer be available for projection. Certainly, much as many fans of current television programmes can greatly enjoy the process of guessing what comes next week, and of sharing 'spoilers', speculation, hopes and fears, the suggestion of a BR:SE almost seems to provide these fans open license for projection. Brooker (2002) observes a similar situation with *Star Wars* fans in 2002, relishing this last period before the final prequel's release in 2005, and enjoying a twilight hour during which the prequel could be anything they wanted and as good as they dreamed it to be, hence producing an awkward ambivalence whereby some almost did not *want* the film to be released, given the closure it would represent. Ironically, then, as much as the *Blade Runner* fans chastise and scorn these producers and studio executives on one level, on another, unacknowledged level, these producers' and executives' meddling plays an important symbolic role in allowing the fans space for a closer involvement with the text. In short, while the executives may be holding back the actual BR:SE, they are, albeit indirectly, fostering the development of an anticipated, ideal text and, therefore, ensuring the openness of *Blade Runner* as text.

CONCLUSION

In seeking to find what the BR:SE might represent, and what it can tell us about both *Blade Runner* as text and textuality more generally, I have arrived at no easy conclusion. Indeed, to assume a text or textuality can or should mean one thing is an absurd proposition. Rather, as shown here, as we try to get closer to the text, or even as the text appears to come closer to showing itself in all its bonus-feature glory, if anything, the text as given object and location fades from view. As we, blade runner-like, scan the evidence for traces of this text, a different type of object begins to emerge. As illustrated, this text is characterised by the feelings, thoughts and experiences it evokes, by the memories of the text, and yet also by its future potential and the individual's relationship to its past, present and future. The text is an expansive unit that grows with time and, moreover, that is seen as at its best when it outgrows itself, opening up more room, possibilities, diegesis and questions or possible answers than any one incarnation is able to exhaust. And texts are constructed not only in spite of their authors and producers, but also with them, and with an increasing knowledge on the part of many viewers of what processes surround creation. The studios may attempt to play God and to control every aspect of textual creation (see Miller *et al.* 2001), but as *Blade Runner's* tale of replicant lifeforms should tell us, true life exists in the experiences that a text goes through as it is loved, hated, re-released and re-interpreted. A text exists in the lived experience of its fans – as Henry Jenkins notes in his discussion of the 'Velveteen Rabbit', a toy whose value lies 'not in its material qualities … but rather in how the toy is used' (1992: 50). To the fans I have interviewed, '*Blade Runner*' is more than just a Jerry Perenchio-owned commercial offering from Warner Bros. Rather, it is an experience, a structure of feeling and multiple zones or spheres of emotional, intellectual and philosophical contemplation and reflection. Indeed, the mere notion that twenty-plus years and several books (this one included) later, *Blade Runner* may still have more to reveal, and more life left in it, should serve as testament to the intense phenomenological power of what I have called *Blade Runner's* replicant textuality, and to the role that DVDs (both actual and hoped-for) play in contributing to their proliferation in time and space, discussion and thought.

NOTES

1 For helpful and meaningful discussion, feedback, and analysis of this chapter and of the notion of textuality, I would like to thank both Will Brooker and Brock Setchell.
2 (i) Are you looking forward to a BR:SE, do you hope it never comes to be, or do you not care? Why?
   (ii) What do you hope it will or will not contain (i.e. director's commentary, making of)? What would you most like to see and why?
   (iii) Do you think a BR:SE could offer the 'definitive' text/version, or will the Director's Cut remain as the proper one for you?
   (iv) What is it about *Blade Runner* that keeps your interest, and keeps you a fan?
   (v) Would you like to see a *Blade Runner* sequel made? Why or why not?
   (vi) Would you like to see a *Blade Runner* remake? Why or why not?

ACADEMIC TEXTUAL POACHERS: *BLADE RUNNER* AS CULT CANONICAL MOVIE
MATT HILLS

This chapter will explore interpretations of *Blade Runner*, but will diverge from one orthodoxy in media and cultural studies, a *doxa* that has tended to consistently define 'the fan' as being opposed to 'the academic'. My aims in doing so are two-fold: I want to suggest that academics' readings of *Blade Runner* can be significantly addressed as types of cultist response, that is, as examples of 'textual poaching' (Jenkins 1992). And I want to consider how *Blade Runner*'s cult status – linked as it is to the film's academic canonisation – has sustained overlaps and intersections between what might otherwise tend to be considered as clearly separable 'fan' and 'academic' responses (see Brooker 1999: 61). Citing cult film critic J. Hoberman, Caroline Joan S. Picart has described these fan-academic parallels:

> *Blade Runner* ... was ultimately kept alive by a growing fan club, such as the science fiction crowd and academics ... As Hoberman recounts: 'At once a touchstone for MTV and an avatar of cyberpunk (predating the publication of *Neuromancer* by two years), an F/X head trip and an object of academic discourse, praised in *Starlog* and parsed in *October*, *Blade Runner* spent a decade proselytising itself on home video and in classrooms.' (2003: 122; see also Rushing & Frentz 1995: 143)

Similarly, Nick Lacey suggests in his *York Film Notes* guide to the film, that '*Blade Runner* has attracted two kinds of cult audience: the lay and the academic' (2000: 80). By 'lay cult audience', Lacey appears to be referring to *Blade Runner* fans, but note that he does not oppose 'fan' (or lay-cult) to 'academic' (or academic-cult) audiences. Instead, Lacey puts forward a notion that I will be developing here: that of the professional academic and the non-academic viewed as two types of cult viewer.

In the following section I will tackle the issue of 'fan' versus 'academic' practices, before moving on to address accepted narratives of *Blade Runner*'s cult status. All of this will enable me to articulate the specificity of *Blade Runner* as a 'cult canonical' text – a cult movie that cannot be defined via 'a pitched battle between a guerilla band of cult film viewers and an elite cadre of would-be cinematic tastemakers' (Sconce 1995: 372). By contrast, *Blade Runner* is a cult film that has very much been embraced by supposedly 'elite' readers such as university professors:

> In 1997, a survey of science fiction studies courses in North American universities and colleges revealed that *Blade Runner* was far and away the

most widely assigned film ... absences from the list are interesting ... the box-office successes *Star Wars* and *Close Encounters of the Third Kind*, for example, appear nowhere on it ... this survey is certainly indicative, at least, as a snapshot of a science fiction film canon in the process of formation. (Kuhn 1999a: 1)

However, even when noting this ascendancy of *Blade Runner*, and the film's pedagogic significance, Annette Kuhn continues to produce a marked distinction between 'fan' and 'academic' tastes, *contra* Lacey's view of fans and academics as united in a shared predilection for cult texts:

If this does constitute a canon ... it is of a singular kind. A science fiction buff's top ten films ... would probably be quite different from this pedagogic pantheon – which is not ... to say that a degree of 'fannish' investment must necessarily be absent from a university teacher's choice of films. (Ibid.)

Fan studies may well have succeeded in propelling an inoculating shot of 'fannish investment' into the arm of the academic body politic, but Kuhn suggests that science fiction 'buffs' and academics 'probably' cannot be seen as fully sharing an evaluative system. Here, fandom is imagined as being linked to the connotatively 'popular', while academia is distinguished by its greater display of 'cultural capital' and its distaste for commercially successful science fiction blockbusters (see Hills 2002: 46–64 on the work of Pierre Bourdieu). In what follows, I will argue that such presuppositions need to be contested, and that 'university teachers' and cult fans of *Blade Runner* may be rather more similar than dissimilar in their reading practices.

APPROPRIATING *BLADE RUNNER* AS POSTMODERN EXEMPLAR: AN ACADEMIC CULT

Before exploring *Blade Runner* as a case study in attributions of postmodernism, I want to further consider distinctions that have been taken to demarcate 'academic' and 'fan' identities. To be sure, a number of influential writers have noted the importance of hybridised 'scholar-fan' and 'fan-scholar' identities (Jenkins 1992; Doty 2000; Hills 2002; Bird 2003; Brooker 2003 and 2004), while others have suggested that the 'fan' versus 'academic' distinction is maintained through cultural hierarchies rather than being in any way ontological (Jensen 1992). Despite such interventions, many writers have continued to address fandom purely as an object of study occurring outside academic circles and institutions, thus reproducing the cultural hierarchies that Joli Jensen maps. So it is that Cynthia Erb is able to contrast academic and cultist formations: 'it is my contention that cultist readings are generated within institutionalised frameworks and settings that differ dramatically from those that supervise reading in the academy' (1991: 161). Similarly, in a study of academic and fan readings of the *Alien* quadrilogy, Pamela Church Gibson concludes that fans display 'aggressive derision' towards academic interpretations, possibly because 'most academic work on the cycle [of *Alien* films] tends not to discuss in any detail the production designs and special effects which particularly interest *Empire* readers – and indeed those fans investigated by Will Brooker in his essay on internet fandom (Brooker 1999)' (Church Gibson 2001: 44). And even academic studies which work to emphasise historical links between the 'discourses and reading strategies' of fans and academics of cult film still find it necessary to observe that 'cult movie fandom and academic film studies ... have historically diverged into relatively independent scenes' (Jancovich 2002: 308; see also Taylor 1999: 148).

Regardless of a sustained move in fan studies towards making writing as both a fan and an academic more acceptable within the academy, differences between fan/academic 'imagined subjectivities' (Hills 2002: 3) – an 'us' and 'them' mentality enshrined in the institutions of fandom and the academy – continue to remain culturally significant. To take one example, Alan McKee has noted 'that we tend to think that academics and participants in what we used to call "high culture" ... are "theorists"; while workers in popular forms of culture rarely receive that name' (McKee 2002: 311; see also Pyle 1993: 231). The reverse of this is that while 'theory' is typically restricted, semiotically and institutionally, to its authorised users (that is, academics), pop cultural fandom is counter-construed as the sole site of 'textual poaching'. This account of fan activity – Michel de Certeau via Henry Jenkins' (1992) reading – has stressed how fans make communal meanings from their favoured media texts, lacking the power to affect production decisions and textual content, but possessing a limited, resistive power to (re)interpret and refocus storylines, put subtext above main text, or even projectively construct subtexts that may or may not be 'in' a text's preferred readings. As such, while 'theory' is posited by academics as a dignified and 'proper' reading of popular cultural texts, fans' 'poaching' is given a very different status; these readings are not revelatory of 'deep structure', ideology or textual politics, as academic readings of film have tended to assume themselves to be (see, for example, Lipschutz (2003: 88) and Wood (1986: 187) on *Blade Runner* as 'too revolutionary to be permissible'). Nor is academic 'theory' typically celebrated and championed by cultural studies writers in the way that fan 'poachings' sometimes are (Jenkins 1992). Perhaps textual poaching by fans is seen as somehow unusual, and as worthy of critical attention, whereas academic theory is just ordinary practice, being what academics are expected to do. To give a more concrete example, this common sense separation of fan 'poachings' and academic 'readings' is assumed and maintained in Sean Redmond's *Studying Blade Runner*, which treats (academic) postmodern readings and (cult) fan poachings under the different headings of 'Representation' and 'Audiences' (see 2003: 26 and 33), thereby seeming to disavow any sense that postmodern interpretations have themselves been produced by a socially and subculturally-situated audience.

The textual poaching/theory binary opposition – working to reiterate and sustain cultural-hierarchical distinctions between 'the fan' and 'the academic'

– can be deconstructed from both sides. Fans may also use, apply and generate forms of theory (see Hills 2004c, which acts as a kind of companion piece to this chapter). And academics' readings can be addressed as forms of textual poaching (as they will be here). The logic of this latter deconstructive impulse is contained in Henry Jenkins' own gloss on de Certeau, although this subtlety of thought has tended to be displaced in textbook commentaries on Jenkins' work which resolutely equate textual poaching with fandom only, exempting academic interpretation from this set of concerns (see, for example, Taylor & Willis 1999: 191–3; Casey *et al.* 2002: 89–95; Lewis 2002: 285–7; Bignell 2004: 289–94). Returning to Jenkins' *Textual Poachers*, we find the following:

> De Certeau's notion of 'poaching' is a theory of appropriation, not of 'misreading' ... A conception of 'misreading' ... implies that there are proper strategies of reading (i.e. those taught by the academy) which if followed produce legitimate meanings and that there are improper strategies (i.e. those of popular interpretation) which ... produce less worthy results ... De Certeau's formulation does not necessarily reject the value of ... academic interpretive strategies; such approaches offer their own pleasures and rewards that cannot easily be dismissed. (1992: 33)

Jenkins is careful *not* to fully contrast academic to fan readings, and not to position theoretical exegeses as inherently superior to fan interpretations. As Jenkins points out: 'A model of reading derived from de Certeau would question ... the institutional power that values one type of meaning over all others' (ibid.). This undercuts normative academic rationales for carrying out textual interpretation, leaving academic and fan readings similarly positioned as a matter of the 'pleasures and rewards' that each may offer.

In the remainder of this section, I want to make use of the idea that, in effect, academic readings of film can themselves be analysed as a type of textual poaching. How do academics – akin to fans – seek to take possession of media texts like *Blade Runner* by reading them selectively? It should be noted that fans are hardly alone in making meanings from a favoured text while being unable to affect the material production and development of the given text: this structural dimension of material disempowerment aligned with the symbolic power to interpret also closely captures the academic's position. As David Bordwell has put it, 'knowing how to make movies mean is the principal source of such authority as film scholars possess' (1989: 258). *Blade Runner*'s 'academics', like its 'fans', are 'elite', subcultural readers who are generally excluded from sites of media power and production.

Poaching is not just the fans' preserve, then. But if the 'processes by which fans choose to poach one thing and not another are complex and still not very well understood' (Smith 1999: 69), then this difficulty also comes into focus when we address academic interpretations as textual poaching. Why, we might ask, has *Blade Runner* been insistently appropriated by its professional academic textual poachers? Greg M. Smith goes on to argue that certain pop culture texts are more 'quotable' and therefore more likely to be poached. The term ... is intended to indicate that both images ... and dialogue may be removed from their original contexts ... we can list some qualities that make a scene more quotable: the ability of the scene to stand alone; an emphasis on overtly marked performance; a tendency towards tangents. (1999: 68–9)

It could be suggested that *Blade Runner* displays this type of 'quotability', partly through dialogue revolving around the replicants' limited life spans, or around the status of Rachel's memories, and partly through moments of excessive (or in Smith's terms 'tangential') style, such as the dove that appears as Roy Batty is expressing his regrets and desires at the film's dénouement (on the intensity of this scene as a bid for audience empathy, see Plantinga 1999: 251). Such moments and images have the capacity to be lifted out of context or to stand alone, partly because of the affective intensity they convey (for example, Rachel's memories and Batty's closing soliloquy) and partly because they capture the film's problematisations of humanity – dialogue concerning the replicants is more quotable because it can be taken to stand in for, or encapsulate, the film's concerns. The film's potential quotability also emerges in scenes that function by themselves, such as the one referred to in Andrew Spicer's rather loving and lingering academic commentary:

> *Blade Runner*'s densely textured style is evident ... in set pieces such as the 'retiring' of the replicant Zhora which takes place amidst a bewildering cacophony of sounds, objects and twitching neon signs ... Using the 'steadicam', Scott can trace the replicant's sinuous movements through the clutter before 'her' slow-motion demise through the splintering plate glass window, where each successive image is shown in pin-sharp detail, allowing the viewer to savour every instant. (2002: 152; see also Bergstrom 1991: 34 on *Blade Runner* as a 'totally designed perceptual experience')

By seeming to lend itself to de-composition and quotation in academic and fan readings, as much as in 'the *Blade Runner* look' (King & Krzywinska 2002: 11) of later videogames, *Blade Runner* surely resonates with Umberto Eco's argument that 'in order to transform a work into a cult object one must be able to break, dislocate, unhinge it so that one can remember only parts of it, irrespective of their original relationship with the whole' (Eco 1995: 198). *Blade Runner* may be especially open to textual poaching by both fans and academics, given that it is also – unusually for a mainstream film release – profoundly marked by another form of 'glorious ricketiness' (ibid.), namely ambiguities or continuity 'errors':

> Even the Director's Cut retains 'mistakes', some considered deliberate and others – like the numerous internal contradictions over the exact number of escaped replicants – further expressions of the obscurity which has given

the film its aura of myth. These ambiguities are highlighted rather than resolved by the critical texts clustered around the film. (Brooker 1999: 58–9)

Although fans may debate whether Deckard is a replicant or not, either in the
film's initial theatrical release, or in the Director's Cut, Scott Bukatman argues
instead that the 'Deckard debate is ... a denial of what the film really does
offer, which is a double reading' (1997: 80). Bukatman may highlight rather
than resolve textual ambiguity, yet he does so in such a way as to suggest
that irresolution is the very mark or essence of *Blade Runner*'s textuality. Such
irresolution is another incitement to textual poaching, inviting academic and
fan audience speculation, and hence amounting to a variant of Greg Smith's
notion of the 'quotable' that might be better termed 'the analysable' or 'the debatable'. What is significant here is that *Blade Runner*'s 'discontinuities actually
add to the meaning of the film' (Lacey 2000: 81) rather than being discernible
merely as 'errors'. Nick Lacey suggests that the close readings of cult fans and
academics have produced the awareness of such textual ambiguities, arguing
that 'if *Blade Runner* had not become such a cult movie, then most of these
discontinuities would never have become widely known' (2000: 80–1). Following Smith, I would reverse the cause and effect implied in Lacey's statement,
suggesting instead that such discontinuities (relating to *Blade Runner*'s theme
of human/alien rather than being semiotically marginal to its interpretation)
are one aspect of *Blade Runner*'s status as a text 'more likely to be poached'.
These discontinuities, gaps, elisions and disruptions provide the opportunity
for readings to (re)prise the text open, inciting speculation from both 'lay' and
'academic' cult audiences.

Another of *Blade Runner*'s invitations to academic textual poaching has
been the way it can be dislocated and unhinged in order to exemplify pre-
existent themes in postmodern theory. Although Smith notes that a text's status as more or less 'poachable' must 'involve factors both in the text and in
the [reading] individual' (1999: 68), his argument fails to consider social, communal patterns in reading that may allow specific texts to be more readily appropriated and subculturally possessed by given interpretive communities.

Blade Runner's academic textual poaching has often revolved around
claims that the film is 'an exemplar of the postmodern' (King & Krzywinska
2000: 54), and 'certainly the key postmodern science fiction film' (Telotte 2001:
57; see also Sobchack 1987). A range of alternative academic readings have
related the film to representations of the city or LA more specifically (see,
for example, Aitken 2002: 115; Bukatman 1993: 130–7 and 2003: 123; Davies
2003: 217; Orr 2003: 284). But it was arguably postmodernism, sometimes
in conjunction with a focus on the cityscape, that first provided an academic reading protocol for *Blade Runner*. Claims that 'the film can serve as an
impressive guide to the precepts of the postmodern aesthetic as elaborated
by Jencks, Jameson, and others' (Bukatman 1993: 130) are rooted in early,
influential academic appropriations of the initial theatrical release of *Blade
Runner*. Such interpretations have been offered up by Giuliana Bruno (1987,

reprinted in Kuhn 1990) and David Harvey (originally 1989, reprinted as an excerpt in Brooker and Brooker 1997). Although I am referring here to two pieces rather than to a single book or article, I would suggest that these works have nevertheless functioned in the manner of the academic 'exemplar' as outlined by David Bordwell:

> The interpreter's exemplar is a canonical study – an essay or book which influentially crystallises an approach or argumentative strategy ... Wood on Hitchcock, Wollen on auteur theory, Mulvey on gendered representation ... Most critics do not produce exemplars. They practice what we can call 'ordinary criticism'. (1989: 24—5)

Bordwell's argument makes the 'exemplar' equivalent to a great work by a deified academic, whether it be Wood, Wollen or Mulvey, thus neglecting to consider that exemplary status may also arise through a number of prior commentaries, with different books and articles operating in concert to furnish essential, canonical material for any new interpreter, while also *collectively crystallising a given approach*. Despite this difficulty, Bordwell's point has some force, calling attention as it does to the manner in which academic interpretations of texts become routinised and reproduced. Hence, just as belonging to a cult fan community can mean learning patterns of interpretation, and learning exactly how and what to poach from a text (see Jenkins 1992: 88–9), academic textual poachings can also be analysed as constrained by the value systems of the academic institution, and by established interpretations in play.

Timothy Corrigan's view of the cult movie is apposite here, since Corrigan suggests that 'in these cases the audience invariably comes armed and overprepared with a text of its own that makes the film text almost secondary' (1991: 32). Corrigan argues that via this type of 'reappropriation', cult movies become 'vehicles not of original connotation but for the potentially constant regeneration of connotation, through which the audience reads and rereads itself rather than the film' (ibid.). The notion of regeneration suggests that different connotations will be produced by different audiences, or that different connotations may emerge as one audience group shifts its cultural identity over time. It implies that audiences essentially read or project themselves (their concerns; paradigms; purposes) into texts. As such, Corrigan's approach gives us a way to think about the academic textual poaching of *Blade Runner*, whereby readers come very much 'armed and overprepared' with their understandings of Baudrillard or Jameson, Bruno or Harvey. Indeed, it is perhaps such overpreparation and the use of 'other texts' (for example, postmodern theory) rendering the film itself somehow secondary that especially characterise academic readings, and through which academics tend to re-read (and perform) their subcultural identities. Academics, just like fans, are therefore confronted by hierarchies of value and interpretation within their cult community.

The secondariness of *Blade Runner* is evident in its 'exemplary' academic, postmodern readings. David Harvey argues that:

> *Blade Runner* is a science fiction parable in which postmodernist themes ...
> are explored with all the imaginary power that the cinema can command ...
> The depressing side of the film is precisely that, in the end, the difference be-
> tween the replicant and the human becomes so unrecognisable that they can
> indeed fall in love ... The power of the simulacrum is everywhere. (1997: 65)

Against such a conclusion, pre-figured in 'other texts' such as Baudrillardian writing, we might argue that the distinction between human and replicant hardly becomes entirely unrecognisable in the film (even in its different versions: although see Landsberg (1995: 185) for an argument that the Director's Cut is actually *anti*-Baudrillardian in its very refusal of a 'safe position ... from which we might recognise' the human/replicant distinction). Some of the replicants such as Pris and Batty are 'in fact represented as childlike' (Roberts 2000: 160) in a way that distinguishes them from adult, human characters, while the 'Deckard debate' and Rachel's textual representation hinge not so much on a global failure to distinguish human from replicant, as on the narrative process through which specific denotative replicants become connotatively humanised, while other (albeit insecurely) denotative humans are connotatively de- and re-humanised. To read these textual complexities, subtleties and ambiguities (see Telotte 1995: 152–3) as simply a totalising Baudrillardian/anti-Baudrillardian collapse into non-meaning and the 'power of the simulacrum' appears to prioritise theory's 'other text' over *Blade Runner*. Regardless of which version of the film is referred to, and whether it is located as pro- or anti-Baudrillard's gnomic pronouncements, it is the text of theory that recurrently achieves precedence in such textual poachings (and for a related prioritisation of theory, this time Lacanian, see Žižek 1993: 9–44).

Also prioritising postmodern theory over the film text, Bruno slips from arguing that '*Blade Runner* will be discussed as a metaphor of the postmodern condition' (1990: 184) to discussing the film's 'postmodern aesthetic' (1990: 185) and the manner in which the 'narrative "invention" of the replicants is almost a literalisation of Baudrillard's theory of postmodernism as the age of simulacra and simulation. Replicants are the perfect simulacra' (1990: 188). The *almost* here is obscured by the logic of Bruno's theoretical application, given that this collapses into positioning the replicants as 'perfect simulacra'. A metaphor thus becomes a literalisation, and again the 'other texts' of postmodern theory are prioritised over and above a reading of the film, to the extent that Bruno feels able to argue that '*Blade Runner* presents a manifestation of the schizophrenic condition – in the sense that Lacan gives this term' (1990: 189). The film is thus appropriated as if it is a theoretical treatise of its own, as if it (and not its academic textual poachers) has read Baudrillard and Lacan. This style of academic interpretation has been analysed by Bordwell as reading through 'clusters' of theory-driven themes (for example, 'schizophre-nia', 'time-space compression', 'the simulacrum', and so on):

> A cluster is a semantic field ... such fields might be organised as identity relations, as 'family resemblance' relations ... semantic clusters underlie an interpretation ... 'Postmodernism' as employed in recent interpretations seems also to constitute a cluster. One critic, for example [Sobchack] finds playfulness, pleasure, the shallow space of display, the alliance of electron-ics and corporate power, and other postmodern themes to characterise 1970s and 1980s science fiction films. (1989: 115–16)

Given this use of *Blade Runner* as a vehicle for theory, later academic inter-preters treat the film as a theoretical text, with Norman K. Denzin suggesting that we 'call Baudrillard Deckard ... and compare Deckard's chore, to put rep-licants into retirement, with Baudrillard's self-assigned task of making sense of this mad, contemporary world' (1991: 33; see also Shiel 2003: 171 who lists *Blade Runner* alongside 'such seminal cultural studies of [LA] as Davis' *City of Quartz*, and such important social-scientific expositions of LA's economic importance and emergence as a world city as Edward Soja's *Postmodern Geographies*'). In Denzin's account, the film becomes not just a vehicle for theory, but is read back into theory, reversing the actual relationship between theory and film, to imply that *Blade Runner* has 'written' or even trumped Baudrillard:

> He [Baudrillard], like Deckard, asks only half-seriously, 'What defines a hu-man in this postmodern world?' ... He is afraid of the replicants; if he could he would, like Deckard, retire them. And there is no danger that he will fall in love with one ... And if one of us went to him, the genetic engineer of postmodern theory, and asked him to repair what he has made, he would only laugh, and with Tyrell say, 'There is no way. You are doomed to live your programmed life as a simulated human being and your feelings are all false!' (1991: 34)

Such playful blurrings of diegesis and the textual poacher's extradiegetic pos-ition partly characterise cult fan's readings (see Brooker 1999: 64 and 2004: 285–291; Hills 2002: 177). Such blurring evidently also appears in Denzin's work – with the favoured theorist being fantasised as entering into the world of the text – as well as in Mark Bould's reading of *Blade Runner* as 'quintessen-tially postmodern' (1999: 169). Bould argues the case for examining a range or 'cluster' of *Blade Runner* texts and intertexts (including K. W. Jeter's novels as 'continuations') rather than just focusing on the Director's Cut or the initial theatrical release:

> The decision to examine clusters rather than privileging individual texts derives from an unwillingness to become the critical equivalent of a blade

runner. Just as Rick Deckard must track down replicants ... so the traditional textual critic finding himself faced with 'essentially [six versions of the
movie] which have been seen by the general public' [Sammon 1996: 394–
408], must decide which is authentic (whatever that might mean) (1999:
166; see also Strick 2002: 47).

Although, *contra* Denzin, Bould is suggesting that the critic should *not* act as
a blade runner, his playful argument hinges on semantically linking the film
critic to the role of Rick Deckard in order to mark a gap between actual writer
and diegetic character. Rhetorically, the construction of such a gap or distance
between diegesis and extra-diegesis requires that we, as readers, accept the
possibility that 'other' critics – that is, of the 'traditional textual' variety – can
be thought of as metaphorical blade runners. Again, rather than *Blade Runner*
being viewed as a metaphor for the postmodern condition, the critic's role and
work become a metaphor for and of the blade runner. Such academic textual
poaching takes apparent pleasure in appropriating terms from a favoured fiction and applying them to 'real life' examples, just as fans appropriate diegetic
terms within their everyday lives.

    A few academic writers have challenged the way in which postmodern the-
ory has been read into favoured, and hence canonised, movies such as *Blade
Runner*. For example, Andrew M. Butler notes that there 'are many ironies
here. Postmodernist criticism, with its rejections of hierarchies, has limited
itself to a small body of texts – at times just *Blade Runner* and *Neuromancer*'
(2003: 146). Similarly, Marcus A. Doel and David B. Clarke point out that *Blade
Runner* 'has achieved the oxymoronic status of a canonical postmodern cultural artefact' (1997: 141). Although these critics have not directly addressed
such readings as types of textual poaching, they have in effect observed that
'the predominant academic interpretation of a text ... through postmodernity
is related to a specific ... college-educated "media-savvyness"' (Saukko 2003:
111). Covering related terrain, Jonathan Bignell has even gone so far as to oppose the film's postmodern appropriation head-on: '*Blade Runner* should not
be seen as an instance of postmodern cinema, because this assumes that the
film shows a reality which will have been the reality of the postmodern condition, in a circular relation between object and theory' (2000: 64). For Bignell,
the fact that many academic readings of *Blade Runner* prioritise postmodern
theory and thereby render the film secondary means that

> postmodern media culture in the often unacknowledged view of many theo-
> rists is simply that which corresponds to pre-existing abstract theoretical
> definitions of the postmodern ... this leads to a paucity of close analysis
> of examples, as examples function as indicators or evidential grounds on
> which a theory is erected. (2000: 62)

In other words, this can again be a way for academics to 'read and re-read
themselves' rather than paying close attention to the film they are analysing.

Professional academics can also seek to reproduce cultural distinctions between typical fan inter-texts (films/interviews/promotional material/academic monographs) and academic inter-texts (all of the above, but also works of exemplary postmodern theory by Baudrillard, Jameson, and so on). Although fans of Blade Runner may well read academic work about their beloved text, Will Brooker's (1999) study of online fan groups offers little sense that these fans choose to read postmodern theory per se in order to explore Blade Runner. Thus, as Paula Saukko argues:

> Any reading of a text, including an academic reading, is as … embedded in a particular social context and location and their agendas, as any of the texts we analyse. Therefore, textual analysis should not only focus on unravelling the politics encoded into … texts but should also pay attention to the politics embedded in the decoding or interpreting [of] texts. (2003: 112)

This would mean addressing the cultural politics of academic textual poaching as well as that of fans' poachings. How 'resistive' or otherwise are, for example, the postmodern readings of Bruno and Harvey? Such interpretations seek to take possession of Blade Runner, and to appropriate it, in part, to validate prior theoretical tracts in opposition to 'mainstream' receptions of the film (just as cult fans construct their readings in opposition to an imagined 'mainstream'). These readings seem to be premised on enacting a type of academic authority over textual meaning that is socially (and subculturally) defined against non-academic fans' readings, even while still being similarly positioned in structural terms as an interpretation belonging to a relatively 'powerless elite' (Tulloch & Jenkins 1995: 144). Of course, it could be argued that any academic 'powerless elite' is nevertheless more culturally powerful than fandom; via its cultural capital and professional legitimacy, academia is not as clearly subordinated or pathologised as fandom tends to be. Despite this relative power differential, as a type of cult audience, academic textual poachers seemingly remain far more akin to non-academic fans than their exaggerated displays of theory-driven 'subcultural capital' (Thornton 1995: 11) would seem to imply.

So far, I have explored what it might mean to analyse academic readings of Blade Runner as forms of textual poaching. I have therefore investigated the film as an especially 'quotable' or 'debatable' text, and considered academic interpretations (at least in relation to postmodern theory) as the performance of an academic cult where Blade Runner is dislocated, unhinged, read and re-read through 'other texts' such as theory and where playful diegetic/extra-diegetic blurrings occur. In the remainder of this chapter I want to move on to consider how Blade Runner's academic canonisation through these types of textual poaching might complicate its status as a 'cult' movie. Blade Runner may have been previously positioned as an exemplary postmodern text, but can it be so readily construed as an exemplary cult movie?

BEYOND THE EXEMPLARY? NARRATIVES OF *BLADE RUNNER*'S CULT STATUS AND THE 'CULT CANONICAL' MOVIE

Accounts of *Blade Runner*'s move toward cult status have tended to emphasise its initial failure at the box office, and its redemption as a cult movie when released on video and laserdisc. For example, in a section in *Future Noir: The Making of Blade Runner*, Paul M. Sammon devotes a chapter to 'The Cult' surrounding the film (1996: 321–9). Sammon's explanation of how cult status was achieved by *Blade Runner* centres on the film's detail, style and layering, and how these textual attributes rewarded repeated viewing by fans:

> Besides the 'depth, intelligence and detail' which J. P. Byrd pointed out, could there have been other causes behind *Blade Runner*'s remarkable metamorphosis from theatrical flop to cult film *par excellence*? Most assuredly … One of the first (and major) catalysts behind *Blade Runner*'s resurgence was the sudden, near-simultaneous expansion of the cable television and home video markets. (1996: 322)

This micro-narrative of *Blade Runner* as 'flop turned cult' is reiterated in Newman (2002: 45), McCarthy (2003: xiv), Bukatman (1997: 36) and Redmond (2003: 32–3), while Lacey (2000: 80) also stresses the way that the density of *Blade Runner*'s diegetic world invites repeated viewings. Such approaches to 'cult' status replay definitions of the term that have become central to academic work on the subject, implying that 'it is possible … to locate a *textual* source of cult' (Mendik & Harper 2000: 241). In my own earlier discussion and analysis of cult status I suggested that one

> defining attribute of the cult text is *hyperdiegesis*: the creation of a vast and detailed narrative space, only a fraction of which is ever directly seen or encountered within the text, but which nevertheless appears to operate according to principles of internal logic and extension. (2002: 137)

Blade Runner accords rather neatly with this, but its movement into cult status also indicates that the temporality of enduring fan fascination – supported through repeat viewing made possible through video – is equally significant. Anne Jerslev has argued that '"cult film" is basically a historical conceptualisation of a film', since cult status cannot emerge instantly and experientially on a film's release, but requires the passing of time, as only this 'makes repetition possible' (1992: 187). In other words, a film may be promoted or marketed as a 'cult', but the cult film *experience* (not coincidentally, the title of J. P. Telotte's 1991 edited collection on cult movies) calls for and requires textual repetition unfolding over time.

Jerslev goes on to summarise the main points of academic work on cult film: 'what characterises cult films … firstly the screening hour: late at night, often at weekends; second, low budgets and poor distribution, which place the films outside mainstream circuits ... third, cult films are regarded [by scholars – MH] as representations of the life of outcasts' (ibid.). Although video and DVD may have rendered Jerslev's first point less telling more than a dozen years on, her final point certainly remains significant: according to academic commentary, cult movie fans appear to especially identify with film texts that represent sympathetic but oppressed outsiders – characters who do not readily conform or fit into their diegetic *milieux*. This is especially relevant to *Blade Runner*'s narrative, given that it ultimately focuses not merely on the noirish detection and pursuit of Nexus-6 replicants, but comes to hinge on the tragically curtailed lifespan of Batty and the 'humanisation of Rachel' (Neale 1989: 220).

Screenwriting guru Robert McKee has used *Blade Runner* as a case study in his seminars and his published guide to constructing *Story* (1999; see Schelde 1993: 231–2). For McKee, *Blade Runner*'s cult status is fixed not by textual detail or hyperdiegesis, but rather by the possibility that audience identification with the 'Centre of Good' (McKee's phrase for the most compellingly realised, positive character in a film) is unconventional:

> Marketing positioned the audience to empathise with ... Deckard, but ... filmgoers were drawn to the greater dimensionality of the replicant Roy Batty. As the Centre of Good shifted to the antagonist, the audience's emotional confusion diminished its enthusiasm, and what should have been a huge success became a cult film. (1999: 379; and see M. Smith 1999: 217 on 'apparently perverse allegiances')

McKee is not suggesting that cult film is antithetical to 'enthusiasm' *per se* here, rather that audiences were caught out by *Blade Runner*'s unexpected – and unconventional – shift of identification from protagonist to antagonist, and that this shift then reduced the mainstream or mass audience's enjoyment of the film. This is an exceptionally tidy explanation of both *Blade Runner*'s box-office failure *and* its shift towards cult status: both events are attributed to the film's 'failure' to accord with McKee's screenwriting template; that is, with the industrial need for mainstream, Hollywood films to be driven by a protagonist who is the most compelling character within their narrative world. McKee suggests that a text which confuses its audience, perhaps partly blurring human/replicant (though not entirely collapsing this distinction) or muddling constructions of protagonist/antagonist cannot securely achieve mainstream status, a notion seconded by film theorists Geoff King and Tanya Krzywinska (2000: 57).

Blade Runner is therefore multiple-positioned as a cult film due to its commercial failure, its apparent opposition to the 'mainstream', its textual complexity (of both hyperdiegesis and characterisation) and its resulting incitement of audience activity rather than passivity (Wood 1986: 182). In relation to these factors, *Blade Runner* appears exemplary of analyses of cult film. However, there are many scholarly lines of thought on what constitutes the cult movie, and in some respects *Blade Runner* can be positioned as an unusual or resolutely non-exemplary cult. Contrary to Jerslev's production of a synthesising summary, 'cult' has been subject to different scholarly definitions and typologies. One taxonomy of cult that has been influential in the academic literature is the distinction between 'inadvertent' cults and 'midnight movies' designed to be cults (see Telotte 1991: 10; Kawin 1991: 19; and Grant 1991: 123). Although 'inadvertent cults' may well become 'midnight movies' later in their cultural lives, these categories have nevertheless been treated as a type of binary opposition. Within this process, two films have come to symbolise these different categories, hence functioning as *canonical cult* films. By this term, I mean films that exemplify how cult is conceptualised in the academy, and which are academically canonised purely on the basis of their cult status. In short, *canonical cult films are canonical primarily because they are exemplars of specific cult qualities/conditions, and so on.*

The canonical cult movie that acts as a synecdoche for 'inadvertent' cults is *Casablanca*, its canonised role having been inaugurated by Umberto Eco's prescient work on cult film (1995; originally published 1984). As Philippe Le Guern has commented: 'Eco's essay on the film *Casablanca* seems to have played a particularly formative role in research into cult films' (2004: 7). *Casablanca*'s rival for the position of fully canonical cult film is, of course, midnight movie *par excellence*, *The Rocky Horror Picture Show*. Le Guern again: 'It is necessary to take account of the structural effects that such a paradigmatic film produces on research into cults by imposing itself as the dominant model – and by imposing a certain number of characteristic traits' (2004: 23 n.42).

However, in relation to discussions of cult as 'classical', conservative and inadvertent or as more contemporary, inherently subversive and 'programmed' (see Desser 1997: 110), *Blade Runner* does not rest easily in either of these reified categories. It is marginal in discussions of midnight movies, meriting only a brief mention in Corrigan (1991), and not appearing as one of the major science fiction midnight movies in Gregory Waller's (1991) survey of the locale of Lexington, Kentucky, 1980–85. Neither does *Blade Runner* fit into J. P. Telotte and Bruce Kawin's category of the 'classical' or accidental cult, since although it achieved cult status after its theatrical release, it is hardly 'a straightforward, conservative ... studio picture ... [containing] nothing that would offend the mainstream' (Kawin 1991: 19).

Rather than being fully definable through the binaries of mainstream/oppositional, or conservative/subversive, *Blade Runner* converts these static contrasts into a matter of process: it enters and leaves the cultural construct of 'the mainstream' via its initial failure, then partly re-emerges in 'the mainstream' through its subsequent critical recuperation and reputation. Neither securely 'inside' the mainstream despite its bankable star, *auteur* director and major studio release, nor securely 'outside' the mainstream for these same reasons, *Blade Runner* confuses categories of cult that construct the term as singularly anti-mainstream and as linked to 'underground', exploitation movies. At the same time, *Blade Runner* does not quite fit into recent rethinkings of cult status such as the 'cult blockbuster', where films like *Star Wars* or *The Matrix* possess knowledgeable, dedicated, re-reading fan audiences, or the 'mainstream cult' where texts again possess highly active and socially-organised fan audiences but are not generally dubbed as 'cult' (see Hills 2003 and 2004a). Joanne Hollows has written of the 'narrow ways in which cult is employed' in much academic work, arguing that this can

> work against a more expansive understanding of cult movie fandom ... the production of more expansive definitions of cult is dependent, in part, on questioning both the residual and dominant ways in which cult has been, and is, mobilised across a range of academic and popular discourses ... what might be called 'low-end' cult based around 'obscure and trashy titles' (Klinger 2001: 136) [is the] meaning of cult that is most commonly employed by cult film media, distributors and retailers, and which has also preoccupied academic writing. (2003: 38)

Work on cult film of the *Rocky Horror Picture Show* type has thus tended to focus on 'paracinema' (Sconce 1995), and on 'exploitation' film and its 'recuperation as trash and cult' (Watson 1997: 67). Such writing has championed cult as a transgression of cultural hierarchies and taste cultures, where the artfully avant-garde and the artlessly tacky collide (Hawkins 2000: 3). *Blade Runner* might fit many of the criteria of cult status, as outlined above, but it does not correspond at all with this equation of cult and 'low-end' trashy titles identified by Hollows. Quite the reverse. *Blade Runner* can be readily opposed to such narratives of cult status on the basis of its academic canonisation as postmodern exemplar, and hence on the basis of its dual cult audience of fans and academics. It can also be noted that *Blade Runner* is far from 'trash' in its special effects, style, budget, and in the valorised status of both *auteur* Ridley Scott and established 'name' star Harrison Ford.

Rather than being exploitation cinema that has been recuperated and revalorised within academic interpretations – that is, the canonical (because) cult films like *Plan 9 From Outer Space* that make it onto the academic agenda only by virtue of their cult/trash labelling – *Blade Runner* did not become canonical because it already exemplified a type of cult movie. Unlike *Casablanca* and *The Rocky Horror Picture Show*, *Blade Runner* is therefore not a canonical cult film in the sense outlined. And yet it is a film that, as Annette Kuhn has noted, has very much been academically canonised, while also possessing a cult following outside the academy. *Blade Runner* is thus distinctive insofar as different groups of textual poachers, both fans and academics, have appropriated it relatively independently of one another, with fans nevertheless making some use of academic work to support their own speculations and interpretations (Brooker 1999: 63–4). Academic, postmodern-theory-driven textual poachings, on the other hand, have proceeded quite apart from considerations of the film's cult status for (fan) audiences. Rather than existing in the academy as a canonical cult film, then, *Blade Runner* is perhaps better thought of as *cult canonical* film. This type of film accrues different valorisations for and from different subcultural audiences, such as fans and academics, without these institutionally-framed bids for cultural value being causally related (as they are for canonical cult films that are precisely canonical *because* cult).

Jacinda Read has argued that restricted meanings of cult such as 'trashy'/ exploitation allow for an 'identification of the critic with the cult fan [that] reproduces subcultural ideologies in an attempt to guarantee not only the masculinity of cult but ... the cult of masculinity' (2003: 55). In other words, by limiting cult to its equation with trash or underground film, academic writers (usually male) have sought to position themselves and their tastes as sub-culturally 'authentic' in opposition to the 'mainstream' and the academic 'es-tablishment', which are both imagined to be culturally feminised. We could argue that this equation of cult and masculinity also holds for *Blade Runner* academics and fans who, despite not typically identifying with one another, are both engaged in bids for masculinised subcultural authenticity, whether this is the postmodern theorist self-figured as 'adventure narrative ... protago-nist' (Dacre 1998: 3) or the cult fan self-figured as 'manly adventurer' (Hollows 2003: 47). However, in each case, such bids may well be insecure: arguably, theorists and fans alike remain negatively stereotyped in the wider, domi-nant culture as bookish and geeky. And Hollows' work on cult and masculinity cites Charles Tashiro, who when asserting the masculinity of video collecting, specifically uses *Blade Runner*'s ready availability and non-exclusivity as a marker of cultural feminisation:

As ... Tashiro has suggested, part of the thrill of video collecting in general comes from the sense of 'bravado' generated by acquiring a rarity that 'pro-vides a mark of distinction that the widely released Director's Cut of *Blade Runner* doesn't.' (2003: 48)

Exploring wider meanings of cult beyond the bravado of cult = underground/ exploitation/trash may help to challenge such bids for authenticity, but it may also indicate that 'identifications' between academics and fans may operate on levels other than the performance of subcultural value. For, in the case of a cult canonical movie like *Blade Runner*, academic textual poachings that structurally resemble the activities of cult fans have formed one part of the many differently-located cultural and institutional processes eventually feed-ing into the *Blade Runner* cult. Limiting cult to an 'event' happening initially outside or in opposition to types of academic authority can only blind us to the way that cult status is perhaps not only about text-based factors like hyper-diegesis, or extra-textual factors such as the rise of ancillary video/DVD mar-kets for film, but is also linked to the institutional frames within which dif-ferent audiences are located, whether we are considering fans, academics, fan-scholars or scholar-fans (Hills 2004b: 522).

In the case of *Blade Runner*, its academic and fan cults have tended to directly work together only contingently, otherwise paralleling one another's efforts to cement the film's bid for cultural value. This suggests that accounts stressing fan/academic (sub)cultural difference are useful as a general theory, but can overstate fan/academic tensions. Will Brooker has put forward one reason why *Blade Runner* fans may distinctively embrace academic work:

> Perhaps because of the ongoing nature of the [*Alien*] film series over the last twenty years ... fan attention is not really concerned with looking back to favourite texts in a search for underlying themes of, say, human versus alien and android identity ... While Scott Bukatman's essays are treated as key references by *Blade Runner* fans, who subscribe to much the same project of enquiry as Bukatman himself, I have seen no mention of Barbara Creed's equivalent work on *Alien* on internet fan sites. (1999: 63–4)

Blade Runner's relative scarcity of fully canonical texts in contrast with other cult science fiction 'franchises' may work, in part, to legitimate and sustain its fans' pursuit of a wider range of reading material and sources than is characteristic in certain other cult movie fandoms. *Alien* (1979), for example, has been just as much textually poached from (and canonised) academically as *Blade Runner*, and so could be addressed as a further example of cult canonical film. The same might arguably be said for genre films such as *2001: A Space Odyssey* (1968), or even *The Shining* (1980), or *The Silence of the Lambs* (1991). But academic textual poachings of these films lack the directly philosophical focus of those on *Blade Runner* (given the concentration on appropriating *BR* as a vehicle for grand, postmodern theory), being rather more dispersed into ranges of different academic reading formations. Or, as with *Alien*, theoretical intertexts drawn on are psychoanalytic rather than postmodernist. Such writings may be greeted with rather more suspicion by cult fans than exegeses on postmodern aesthetics. The latter do at least construct and dignify *Blade Runner* as 'philosophical' and artful, acting as a (relatively) secure and unifying bid for cultural value inside and outside the academy. By contrast, psychoanalytic intertexts appear to position *Alien* as perverse, while simultaneously positioning its audiences as unconsciously producing certain meanings. *Alien* may therefore be a less obviously cult canonical film than *Blade Runner* not just because the quadrilogy has been a more active franchise, sustaining fan readings based around an interest in production details and so on, but also because many of *Alien*'s academic textual poachings have been implicitly derogatory (or at the very least, aggressively colonising) towards fan readings. It could also be argued that the *Alien* franchise lacks the focused identity that *Blade Runner* offers, given that the *Alien* films were produced over such a space of time, by different production teams, with different aesthetics, and within different genres (horror, war, even 'art film'), not to mention their commercial success. All these factors make it harder for a cult to unite around the *Alien* saga. It is not *any one thing*; it is perhaps too diverse a set of texts to sustain the degree of focus that has characterised academic and fan textual poachings of and from *Blade Runner*.

In this chapter I have sought to develop Henry Jenkins' insight – often somewhat obscured in secondary commentaries – that academic readings may themselves be considered as a type of textual poaching. By examining postmodern interpretations of *Blade Runner* in this way, I have argued that the *Blade Runner* experience involves two types of textual poachers, positioned in structurally resonant roles as 'powerless elites' although they are often perceived as being mutually antagonistic: the academic and the fan. I have thus suggested that *Blade Runner* functions as a *cult canonical* movie, failing to fit neatly into pre-existent taxonomies of the cult film (inadvertent/programmed; conservative-mainstream/subversive-underground) or into restricted connotations of cult status (trash/paracinema). I have also argued that we can view fans and academics in similar terms, not only as textual poachers, but also as relatively 'powerless elites' (from Tulloch & Jenkins 1995: 144) who share a structural position as consumers of media texts producing subculturally-authoritative readings. Given the marked similarities between *Blade Runner*'s scholars and its non-academic fans, it is perhaps surprising that fewer alliances and coalitions have been constructed between these two cult communities.

ORIGINALS AND COPIES: THE FANS OF PHILIP K. DICK, BLADE RUNNER AND K. W. JETER
CHRISTY GRAY

Philip K. Dick died on 2 March 1982; the same month I celebrated my first birthday. Sitting in my playpen, surrounded by a menagerie of toy animals, I was blissfully unaware that one of the world's most gifted science fiction writers had just passed away. Little did I know that twenty years later I would be standing in an East London art gallery, at midnight, surrounded by a dozen fans attempting to communicate with Philip K. Dick's spirit. This event, which took place in a converted church, was put on by a group of PKD fans called the London Bughouse, to commemorate the twentieth anniversary of the author's death. An eclectic evening of art installations, live video mixing, Gnostic baptisms and communing with spirits from beyond; this was my first experience of PKD fandom.

Like many PKD fans, I was introduced to the author via *Blade Runner*, the film based on Dick's novel, *Do Androids Dream of Electric Sheep?* (1968). It is indisputable that *Blade Runner* has had an enormous impact on PKD's fandom and reputation, but it would be incorrect to state that this fandom emerged out of *Blade Runner*'s success. In actuality, the author was attracting a cult following years before the release of the film. His earliest fan group emerged in the late 1950s/early 1960s, and consisted mainly of fellow writers, hippies, beatniks and friends with whom Dick associated in California. He wrote prolifically between 1955 and 1970, having many of his stories published in pulp science fiction magazines or churned out as cheap, paperback novels. Thanks in part to the success of the Space Programme, science fiction experienced a boost in popularity during these years and Dick's work attracted a growing following. Regrettably, although he strove for mainstream popularity his entire career, he never achieved it in his lifetime.

However, following his death and the release of *Blade Runner* in 1982, PKD fandom began to take on a more 'official', organised form. This was marked by the introduction of the first PKD fanzine, created by Dick's friend, Paul Williams. The *Philip K. Dick Society Newsletter* ran from 1982 to 1992 and included letters from fans, interviews, articles, reviews of books and so on. It acted as a successful means of communication and debate between the growing numbers of PKD fans.

In 1992, the same year the Director's Cut of *Blade Runner* was released, Paul Williams passed on the torch to Greg Lee who created *Radio Free PKD*, which continued for seven issues. It included interviews, essays, reviews of the film adaptations, and even a review of the first K. W. Jeter *Blade Runner* spin-off novel, which will be discussed in depth below. Ultimately, however, as with many fan groups in the early 1990s, PKD fandom soon shifted to the

World Wide Web, and quickly the paper fanzines/newsletters began to disappear, replaced by chat rooms, message boards and online archives.

The first major PKD online fan community, PhilipKDick.com, was launched in 1998, and became a place where once-marginalised fans could come together and discuss the man, his work and his revelations. The site currently exists at PhilipKDickFans.com after the recent creation of the official PKD site, which took over the www.PhilipKDick.com web address. While PKD fandom was expanding and transferring onto the Web, *Blade Runner* exploded into a cultural phenomenon. Studied as a model of postmodernism at universities, trawled over by fans on tape and DVD, the cult following also found its niche on the World Wide Web. There are now hundreds of *Blade Runner* sites, compared to only a few dozen PKD devoted sites. So how do these two fandoms interrelate?

There are a variety of online locations devoted to PKD, including a German site, PhilipKDick.de, a French site, LeParaDick.fr, and the newly formed 'official site' of the PKD Trust, PhilipKDick.com. But the hub of PKD fan activity remains centered at PhilipKDickFans.com. Here, 'Dickheads', as PKD fans are affectionately called, can read the online 'zine, *E-Dika*, find articles and essays on PKD-related topics, buy PKD books, post artwork and participate in online forums. Comparing these to the main *Blade Runner* online fan communities at Bladezone.com, BRmovie.com and BR-insight.com, we can see a number of similarities and differences between the two distinct communities.

As with any form of fandom, there is a sense of belonging and collective identity among both groups; however, I found this to be stronger among *Blade Runner* followers. Although *Blade Runner* may be studied in universities and regarded as an important postmodern text, compared to PKD aficionados *Blade Runner* fans appear less secure and confident about their passion for the movie. But it is precisely this lack of security that helps create such a strong community, which provides support and an outlet for expression. The sense of solidarity is expressed after a list of 'signs that you're an obsessive BR fan', posted on BRmovie.com. It defends the long list of quirky traits and states: 'It is okay. You are amongst friends. You may speak freely and we will support you. You will not get over these symptoms but together we can learn how to deal with them...' Being an obsessive *Blade Runner* fan is seen light-heartedly as a slightly embarrassing disease, which cannot be cured but should be shared with the similarly 'afflicted'. Matt Hills suggests that 'within fan cultures, at a fan convention, say, or on a fan newsgroup – a sense of cultural defensiveness remains, along with a felt need to justify fan attachments' (2002: xii). *Blade Runner* fans' sense of obligation to justify and legitimise their fandom translates into creativity, productivity and community involvement; activities used to demonstrate both to the group and to the outside world why their favourite text is both meaningful and important.

Perhaps the visual nature of film lends itself better to fan creativity, as the *Blade Runner* sites tend to exhibit more creative artwork than the PKD sites. Henry Jenkins notes the importance of fan art in playing a 'central role in solidifying and maintaining fan community' (1992: 248). There are sections for art on both PKD and *Blade Runner* sites, but the *Blade Runner* fan contributions are far broader and more numerous. Artwork on PhilipKDick.com consists mainly of computer-generated graphic images and book cover ideas inspired by the author and his writing. By contrast, Bladezone.com has a section called 'The Galleries' which contains hundreds of models, figures and toys made by fans. One exhibit, particularly interesting in terms of its intertextuality, is a series of Simpsons-inspired *Blade Runner* figures, including a Smithers-style Eldon Tyrell and a Homer-like Deckard. There are also drawings, paintings and sketches relating to the film's characters and narrative, and the message boards are buzzing with talk of a new *Blade Runner* fan film, for which a teaser trailer is already available online.

Fans on BRmovie.com can enter the 'Fan-tastic' section of the site and participate in the *Blade Runner* interactive story, which is written round-robin style and open to anyone who wishes to contribute. Both *Blade Runner* and PKD fans alike produce fan fiction, but again there is a larger, more varied collection of *Blade Runner* 'fanfic' on the Web, even a small amount of slash – that is, stories of an erotic nature involving characters of the same sex. The fiction inspired by *Blade Runner* is similar to the *Star Wars* fanfic discussed by Will Brooker in that it is produced by 'extrapolating from the film(s), filling in spaces, daring to go off on tangents, but always using the primary texts as a baseline' (2002: 133). While *Blade Runner* fanfic generally follows on where the film leaves off, or involves new blade runners and characters within the movie universe, PKD fans tend to focus their fiction less on the author's primary texts, and more on the man himself.

PhilipKDickFans.com contains a handful of fan fiction stories, the majority of which deal with Philip K. Dick in various scenarios. Jim Bauer's short story 'Philip K. Dick is Dead' places Dick in afterlife limbo with the likes of Christ and Plato for company, and integrates people and events from the author's real life with fictional elements from his novels. Andrew May introduces PKD to H. P. Lovecraft in his story, 'The Call of Cool-O: Philip K. Dick Meets H. P. Lovecraft', in which May attempts to re-tell Lovecraft's *The Call of Cthulhu* (1926) in the style and tone of PKD. But compared to *Blade Runner* fanfic, PKD fan contributions are surprisingly limited for a community devoted to a fiction author. Scholarly, non-fiction essays, including reviews and articles about Dick and the themes expressed in his work, are far more common. Perhaps writing fan fiction in the shadow of such a prolific author is a daunting challenge, and sticking to non-fiction commentaries and opinion pieces may seem a safer option. But while *Blade Runner* fans may boast a larger and more obviously creative online community, PKD fans express themselves in other ways.

The aforementioned London Bughouse group is a prime example of PKD fan creativity at its most daring. The group was established in 2001 by sociologist John Cussans to 'discuss the science fiction writings of Philip K. Dick and their implications for contemporary cultural production. The discussions have generated a number of collaborative international performance/art events involving individuals and groups working in a variety of creative fields.' The London Bughouse has collaborated on creative projects with its Vancouver counterpart as well as the Austrian Pinklight Project. They are currently continuing their creative efforts with 'a view to orchestrating more experimental events exploring the territory between cold war science fiction, paranormal investigation and anomalous time-space phenomena' (The Bughouse 2003).

Like their 2002 attempt to communicate with PKD's spirit, members of the London Bughouse also participate in the extra-textual experience of fan tourism. Philip K. Dick visited Vancouver on various occasions; one in particular is rumoured to have been for admission to a drug rehab centre. John Cussans and Randy Cutler created the short film, *When is Now*, which represents Vancouver as a PKD cult geography through a series of lengthy camera shots, focusing on everyday locations in the city. Once again this project represents an attempt to track down PKD's ghost by retracing his steps and chasing the energy he has left behind. Matt Hills cites Scott Bukatman in his description of cult geographies as a way for the cult fan to 'extend an engagement with a text or icon by extra-textually "inhabiting the world"' (2002: 145).

In February 2004 I posted a message on Bladezone.com, PhilipKDickFans.com and BR-insight.com, asking fans if they would be willing to answer a questionnaire dealing with Philip K. Dick, *Blade Runner* and K. W. Jeter. I received seventeen completed questionnaires and corresponded in depth with a handful of the respondents via email. The answers supplied on the questionnaires gave me a basic understanding of how some *Blade Runner* and PKD fans view the relationship between the novel and the film, how they feel about other PKD Hollywood adaptations and Jeter's spin-off novels, and whether or not they are actively involved in the fan community. Their responses served as a springboard for ideas and directed my online research to the areas of greatest activity, controversy and debate.

The remaining focus of my research was cyberethnography, compiling information from the content pages and fan forums at the above stated websites and other fan sites. There I followed current debates and trawled through old posts to see the development of topics and ideas over the past couple of years. As 'lurker', I adopted a position as outsider looking in, preferring to refrain from posting my own opinions for fear of influencing fan responses. At the same time I was aware that the fans I was observing do not exist in an online microcosm; they are influenced not only by other media, but also by the knowledge that they themselves are being watched. Matt Hills (2002: 176) discusses the effects of 'lurking' on cyberspace activity, noting that the fan audience becomes a text in itself, caught up in the process of performing fandom.

Forums and message boards are, as Brooker and Hills suggest, a prime arena for fans to 'construct themselves as part of an ongoing fan text' (Brooker 2004:285), and they proved particularly active arenas for fan expression and interaction amongst both PKD and *Blade Runner* aficionados. On PhilipKDickFans.com fans use the forums to discuss an array of topics from Dick-inspired movies to religion and philosophy, but a recent subject of heated debate is the new official PKD website, PhilipKDick.com. One forum is devoted specifically to discussion about the new site, and it is noted that 'this particular forum is monitored by the PKD Trust'. Again fans are made aware that their activities are being observed, in this case by an official regulating body. The posts on this topic reveal the protective attitude that some PKD fans have adopted in response to the slick new official domain. Initial responses to the new venture were generally positive. David Cauchi posted in December 2003: 'I think it's great. Looks great, lots of good content, and a solid base on which to build.' The Father Thing agrees with David, commenting that 'The new site looks nice, it's well designed, it's user-friendly and there's some very interesting unpublished stuff that I enjoyed immensely.' But a few days later it appears that some of the comments were sugarcoated, as James Ferris posts his 'PKD site-dissenting opinion' and numerous fans renege on their previous glowing comments:

> Is there anyone else out there who is disturbed by the new official PKD site? There is something disquietingly corporate about the new site, which makes me uneasy … there has been a push to popularise Dick in such a way as to dumb down his philosophical ideas, make impotent his subversive streaks … I fear that the PKD Estate is buying into this mindset in an attempt to make Dick a more marketable commodity, and to in a sense 'cash in'.

The Father Thing changes tone from his previous post and states, 'I agree with Mr Ferris and his opening post. I was being polite about the new site.' MoodIndigo1 adds, 'there is something missing which is present here at the fan site: essays, critiques, works of erudition'. Although the official site offers unpublished letters and formerly unseen photos of PKD and family, many fans are not impressed and feel strongly that the Trust is failing to present a faithful image of PKD and his work. They fear the author is being repackaged for mainstream audiences, and that in this translation his more challenging and radical ideas are being 'dumbed down' or ignored entirely. The debate continues in the forum dedicated to PKD movies where flynnstudio posts a thread titled, 'Stop Hollywood', suggesting that fans 'come up with some ideas/ground rules and maybe create a group who are willing to support a website/pages/location where we can state the minimum requirements of anyone wanting to work with Phil's material...':

> I've started this thread as a place for other like minded PKD fans who believe that Hollywood's continued and repeated harvesting of Phil's ideas for movie vehicles that have no intention of honouring the original source text or novel MUST BE STOPPED somehow … If we do not act collectively to reign in Hollywood, who are now in my opinion intellectually bankrupt and will continue to harvest 'mass appeal' concepts then we run the risk of having public perception of Phil's work reduced to the level of cliché and pastiche as the periphery ideas that surround the discarded high level concepts in

Phil's work will become tired and overused for the day when a decent, honest adaptation comes to fruition.

Note the reference to PKD as 'Phil', apparently indicating a protectiveness and perceived familiar relationship. But this sense of curatorship was not shared among the whole community. David Cauchi disagrees with the plan to safeguard PKD's ideas:

> This whole fans being the guardians thing – setting ground rules and minimum requirements etc – is extremely wrongheaded. It's like you're setting yourselves up as some kind of priesthood (a 'you only come to him through me' type thing). Reality check: the PKD oeuvre doesn't belong to you. On a cultural level, it belongs to everyone – it's in the public domain. If people are influenced by it and use it to produce their own stuff, that's a good thing. Cultural artifacts live on through influence, otherwise they become stagnant and moribund. I think it's something to be celebrated, not moaned about.

Brooker discusses this concept of 'curatorship' in his study of Lewis Carroll fans, suggesting that 'For most fan groups, this ownership is complicated by a niggling awareness that they do not have any real claim to the text outside their expertise and commitment. They have no legal rights to it, they didn't create it, they don't produce and distribute it, they can't stop it being cancelled or changed out of recognition' (2004: 292). However, members of the Lewis Carroll Society have managed to obtain a position of authority and influence that far outweighs anything PKD fans have been able to achieve. Proof that the fan is not entirely powerless – but even Lewis Carroll fans cannot protect the author against suggestions of paedophilia and perversion, demonstrating that despite their efforts the persona and public image of authors such as Carroll and Dick remain, as David Cauchi insists, in the public domain.

PKD fans have a mixed response to Hollywood film adaptations of the author's work. Some abhor them, others enjoy them for what they are, and some are just grateful for the PKD publicity and resulting increase in availability of his novels and short stories. But one film that the majority of PKD fans tend to agree on is *Blade Runner*. Overall, they embrace the film, many of them having been prompted to learn about the author after watching it. Mark, a 42-year-old engineer from Britain, and an active contributor to the PhilipKDick-Fans.com forums, believes that *Blade Runner* has had a positive impact on the reputation and popularity of the novelist: 'You can read on the forums that people's interest started with *Blade Runner*. I have spoken to others who have picked up the book and have gone on to read others by the author.'

In terms of *Blade Runner* as an adaptation of PKD's novel, *Do Androids Dream of Electric Sheep?* (DADoES), fans have strong opinions as to whether or not the film is a successful translation. Imelda Whelehan ponders the nature of success in film adaptations, commenting on the transition from 'high literature' to popular culture:

The question is left open ... as to how successful films are determined, but it raises the issues of the relationship of box-office success, target audience, and how, in particular, 'high' literature becomes popular culture with a corresponding effect on book sales and the perception of literary value and 'high' cultural tastes in the eyes of the mass viewing audience. (1999:8)

Despite the 'low culture' connotations of the science fiction genre, Philip K. Dick's work could in some ways be compared to that of William Shakespeare or Jane Austen, in that it is repeatedly being harvested for ideas and adapted into cinematic form. Carl Freedman discusses this comparison:

When Fredric Jameson, one of Dick's earliest and most influential academic backers, eulogised him as 'the Shakespeare of science fiction' the comparison referred to the intrinsic merit and interest of Dick's work, not to his reputation; but today one can detect at least the beginnings of a critical 'Dick industry' on the model of the famous (and infamous) Shakespeare industry. (Freedman 1988)

Just as Shakespeare lovers might detest Baz Luhrmann's *Romeo + Juliet*, or dedicated 'Janeites' feel ill at the thought of *Emma* being adapted into *Clueless*, fans of PKD feel equally protective of their author's work and reputation. They may have mixed views on the degree of textual fidelity in Hollywood adaptations, but many are grateful when a film embodies, if nothing else, the main themes and tone of Dick's work. Marco Gerber, a 21-year-old student from Switzerland, feels that *Blade Runner* is 'the best possible film adaptation for *DADoES*, if you know the novel you'll find the "empathy" theme very strongly integrated into the movie'. Philip K. Dick himself was impressed by the relationship between his novel and the film, stating in his last interview before his death that:

After I finished reading the screenplay [the revised David W. Peoples version] I got the novel out and looked through it. The two reinforce each other, so that someone who started with the novel would enjoy the movie and someone who started with the movie would enjoy the novel.

PKD fan, Forteewinks adds:

Scott created a true Dickian universe in the film, from scripting to set design, and because of that I feel it is the best adaptation of a PKD novel to date. There is an overall gloominess that prevails in the film and in much of PKD's work. The post-nuclear vision of the film and its characters rings true to the despair visible in many of Phil's scenarios and characters.

Guy, a PKD fan from London, recognises that *Blade Runner* 'stands well enough on its own to not have to be compared to the source novel. It's really a work of filmic art.' He goes on further to discuss the impact the film has had on him: 'It defined a part of me, without which I would not be as well-rounded or interested in certain things. Certainly, my cinematic education would be sorely lacking, let alone my emotional palette.' However, some PKD fans thought the film could have done with even more depth, and were not pleased by the Chandleresque portrayal of Deckard. Brian Peoples, a 29-year-old high-school teacher, commented:

> I don't think it [*Blade Runner*] compares favorably. The novel has many different levels whereas the plot of *Blade Runner* is pretty straightforward. The only real interest involves the set design, production values, and the question of whether Deckard is an android. It would have been impossible to include all of the themes, but I think they should have kept some of Deckard's more human qualities rather than making him into a prototype hard-boiled detective of the future.

Other fans see the film as focusing too much on aesthetics and not enough on plot elements. They would have liked to have had more emphasis placed on Deckard's desire for a real animal, and the inclusion of empathy boxes and Mercerism are mentioned by many 'Dickheads' as elements of the novel they wish were in the film. But with every adaptation there is a loss as well as an addition of material to the story. Despite this, the vast majority of PKD fans with whom I communicated believe that *Blade Runner* has had a positive impact on PKD fandom. They appreciate the fact that the film has exposed a larger audience to his work, but do find it annoying to hear references to PKD identified solely as 'the author of *Blade Runner*' or 'the *Blade Runner* guy'.

In his study of Jane Campion's film *The Piano* (1993), Ken Gelder discusses how despite 'those initial losses in an adaptation notwithstanding – a film can actually become something more than a novel. At the very least, then, a certain kind of productive entanglement occurs between the "literary" and the "cinematic"' (1999: 157). It is this entanglement, this blurred line between literature and cinema that I want to discuss in reference to the author K. W. Jeter. A good friend and self-proclaimed 'fan' of Philip K. Dick, Jeter is the author of three *Blade Runner* spin-off novels: *Blade Runner 2: The Edge of Human*, *Blade Runner 3: Replicant Night* and *Blade Runner 4: Eye and Talon*; all of which are 'fully authorised by the estate of Philip K. Dick'.

Jeter's first novel, *The Edge of Human*, follows on directly from the film. It was apparently intended to form the basis for a sequel film to *Blade Runner*, but nothing has come of it thus far. It is important to note that none of Jeter's novels are sequels to *DADoES*, and that they only draw selectively on elements from PKD's novel. Jeter's attempt at integrating the novel *DADoES* and the film *Blade Runner* brings to light interesting questions about adaptation and canon, as we find ourselves comparing a book, based on a film, based on a book – and all three have been created by different authors/auteurs. We have seen how PKD fans regard *Blade Runner*, but what do they think of Jeter's novels? What do *Blade Runner* fans think of them? The PKD Trust may officially authorise the novels, but are they seen as canon by fans? First we should look at some of the ways in which Jeter brings *DADoES* and *Blade Runner* together.

In *The Edge of Human* Jeter picks up where the film left off. After fleeing Los Angeles, Deckard is hiding out in the forest with Rachel who, nearing the end of her four-year lifespan, lies dying in a transport sleep module, normally used to delay the ageing of replicants during their long journey to the outer-colonies. Deckard wakes her up for a few minutes every couple of months, desperate to extend his time with her. But her prolonged quietus is interrupted when Jeter introduces Sarah, Tyrell's real niece on whom Rachel is based, and whose memories we learn she was given in the film. In *DADoES*, when Rachel fails the Voigt-Kampff test, Rosen (who is called Tyrell in the film) explains to Deckard that Rachel's unfamiliarity with Earth and human culture is due to her having been born on a spaceship called Salander 3. He claims that her responses would appear similar to those given by a replicant because she was raised partially by the ship's computers and had limited human contact. In *The Edge of Human* and *Replicant Night*, Jeter expands upon this plot element, which is never mentioned in the film, and we learn that Sarah was the only one found alive on board the ship when it returned to Earth. Here Jeter has integrated a minute detail from *DADoES* and expanded it to create the bulk of his entire storyline.

Another element from *DADoES*, omitted from *Blade Runner* but included in Jeter's novels, is the figure of Isidore. In *DADoES* he is an important character who works as a repairman for ersatz animals, and ends up befriending Pris and the other renegade replicants. In the film, Isidore is loosely adapted into Sebastian, the progeria-suffering cybergeneticist who helped design the Nexus-6 replicants and also befriends Pris and Batty. Jeter decides to throw a spanner in the works by bringing back the original character, Isidore, but retaining Sebastian, and as a result is forced to modify Isidore's history to fit in with Sebastian's existence. So, while Isidore is still working at the Van Nuys Pet Hospital in Jeter's novel, as he did in *DADoES*, he can no longer have welcomed Pris and Batty into his home, because in the film it is Sebastian who takes on this part of the character's role.

Additionally, rather than merely fixing animals in Jeter's novels, it is revealed that Isidore secretly modifies replicants so that they can pass as humans; a responsibility similar to Sebastian's role in the film as a replicant genetic designer for Tyrell. So not only does Jeter rewrite parts of the original novel, but he also brings the original source character Isidore and his adapted film version, Sebastian, into the same diegetic universe. This is a complex and ambitious planned collision between parallel universes, where character interactions and overlaps can have cataclysmic repercussions. Having both Isidore and Sebastian existing in the same world at the same time feels dangerous and unnatural; while it is entirely plausible that Sarah was born on Salander 3, because nothing in the novel contradicts this, it is not possible for Isidore to exist in Jeter's world without contradicting some of Philip K. Dick's original novel. By altering the history of Isidore's character Jeter is, in essence, erasing a portion of Dick's text. But while he may be losing fidelity, he is perhaps also gaining authority, as he struggles to incorporate elements from the novel and film to produce a new diegetic world out of two contradictory ones.

The concept of religion is another element in Jeter's novels that integrates *DADoES* and *Blade Runner*. In *DADoES* we are introduced to a faith called Mercerism, where followers link up via an 'empathy box' to join in a collective experience shared by everyone who is hooked up at that moment. Together they follow the climb of a Christ-like figure called Mercer, as he ascends a hill and is repeatedly struck by rocks. The majority of PKD fans I corresponded with mentioned they would have liked to see this element of religion in *Blade Runner*. Dick's writings were filled with spiritualism and many of his fans have found religious inspiration from his work.

Jeter pays homage to Dick's spiritual themes by including a concept called 'the Eye of Compassion', and the more humorous 'dehydrated deity' in *Replicant Night*. The Eye of Compassion is similar to the Grace of God, and relates to the degree of empathy that living beings feel. In *Replicant Night* we learn that the people on the Salander 3 ship were in fact replicants – he uses the term throughout, instead of Dick's 'androids' – but that once they reached the outer colonies they began to change, evolving out of their sterility, and were suddenly able to have offspring like a normal human. Replicants in the outer colonies went through the same changes, but the reverse was happening to the colonies' humans as they became less and less empathetic, and eventually sterile. According to Jeter, the aspect of God called the Eye of Compassion only sees suffering, and those whom it sees suffering are granted attributes of humanness such as fertility, passion and empathy. Because the humans are causing the replicants to suffer as labourers and sex slaves, they have lost their ability to empathise with others, are therefore no longer seen by God as human, and are denied divine gifts such as fertility. Examples of this distinction between human qualities and those of replicants are evident in both the novel and film. In *DADoES* Phil Resch is a human bounty hunter who shows no empathy towards the androids he kills; by contrast, the androids he hunts, like Luba Loft, are shown to be highly emotional beings who in comparison appear to be the more human of the two. Similarly the Deckard of *Blade Runner* is often harsh and cold while Batty is seen mourning over the dead body of Pris, and turning his chase scene with Deckard into a playful cat and mouse game.

The concept of a 'dehydrated deity' is explained by Jeter as a process similar to taking drugs, whereby a packet containing your chosen god is mixed with colloidal fluid and ingested. The result of drinking this concoction is that you are magically, mentally transported inside the imagined world constructed by your god of choice. The idea of drug use is touched upon in *DADoES* when Deckard and his wife dial up particular emotions on their mood organs, punching in a certain code to feel happy or another to make them satisfied. Dick's writing often deals with mind-altering drugs and psychedelic experiences of this nature. In *Replicant Night*, Deckard is transported into Sebastian's self-created world, which exists back in his apartment in the Bradbury building. There, Deckard is given words of wisdom and warnings by the decrepit Sebastian, who has god-like control over his world, before the experience quickly wears off and Deckard wakes up in an entirely different location than where he started. The event is similar to Dick's Mercerism in that the participant is taken into another world where his faux god, Mercer or Sebastian, exists trapped in a never-ending cycle of sameness.

Additional elements that Jeter integrates from *DADoES* and *Blade Runner* include Deckard, Batty and Holden hunting for the notorious 'sixth replicant' mentioned by Bryant. Here Jeter illustrates his awareness of fan debate surrounding this enigmatic figure; he raises the question as to whether or not Deckard is himself the sixth escapee, but in the end leaves it once again open for interpretation. Tyrell's owl returns in *Eye and Talon*, here called Scrappy like the Rosens' pet in *DADoES*; in the same novel Jeter riffs on Ridley Scott's pervasive use of neon lights as the female blade runner Iris's apartment is taken over by a vine-like form of neon, covering her walls and furniture. This idea of inanimate objects taking over a city also derives from PKD's concept of 'kipple', a form of clutter and junk, which piles up and threatens to suffocate *DADoES's* San Francisco.

In *Replicant Night*, Jeter appears to simply be re-hashing scenes from the film, when suddenly it is revealed that characters within the novel are filming the story of Deckard and his hunt for the replicants. They call it '*Blade Runner*,' and it is a simulacrum of the film. In *Eye and Talon* Iris views the finished product. Her friend, Vogel, comments ironically 'It wasn't *that* bad a movie', perhaps making reference to the poor box-office performance of the original *Blade Runner*. Vogel adds 'Oh, this was only the *first* movie. There was actually a sequel, called *The Edge of Human*. That explained a lot more.' Here Jeter is taking the concept of intertextuality to new heights, pushing the boundaries of postmodern reflexivity and achieving the state of hyperreality characterised by the studies of Baudrillard and McLuhan. Like Hamlet's play within a play, Jeter calls attention to the status of his novel as a production, self-conscious and aware of its own existence. As a final twist of reality, which Dick would have been proud of, Jeter's *Eye and Talon* is written as a reality film, with Iris unaware that her every ordeal is being choreographed and captured on hidden cameras. The novel, like the film *The Truman Show*, is intercut with chapters that take place within the live gallery of a film studio, where we hear the very Ridley Scott-like comments of the director concerning visual aesthetic, detail and style. Jeter's novels consistently leave the reader guessing as to what is reality or if, as Baudrillard and PKD question, reality even exists at all. In this sense Jeter's work is an excellent tribute to the recurrent themes and unanswered questions of both Philip K. Dick and *Blade Runner*. But how exactly do the fans regard the novels?

Philip K. Dick fans give the spin-off novels a mixed review. Many have never even heard of K. W. Jeter, which is understandable as not all PKD fans are fans of *Blade Runner* or *DADoES*. Dave Hyde offers a review of Jeter's *The Edge of Human* on PhilipKDickFans.com, and describes how from the point of view of a PKD fan, some of the pressure on Jeter is removed by the very nature of spin-off adaptations:

> The movie BLADERUNNER [sic] was only roughly related to the original novel and, as they say, was nothing like it. It was merely a film version. Good on its own terms, I suppose, and influential in its way ... But, still, BLADERUNNER was just a movie. OK it was even a good movie ... His [Jeter's] task now becomes somewhat easier. The sequel is merely a novel based on a film and only a prequel to another movie.

Hyde makes the point that Jeter's novels are not sequels to *DADoES*, but to *Blade Runner*, so they are one step further removed from the original and therefore less 'important' in the eyes of PKD fans. If, instead, Jeter had attempted to write a sequel to *DADoES* and include only minor details from the film, then PKD fans would perhaps have a greater investment in the quality and fidelity of Jeter's work. He comments that the spin-off novels can only be a good thing, in that they will bring publicity to PKD; 'And for the PKD fan its fun to pick out the references,' he adds.

Guy Cole, a fan who has read the first two Jeter novels, approves of them both, and when asked if combining elements of *DADoES* with *Blade Runner* was a good idea responded: 'Yes. An excellent approach. Absolutely no reason at all why they shouldn't be combined. Entirely complementary.' But some fans are resistant to the idea of the spin-off novels all together, and don't even wish to look into them. Jenkins' study of *Star Trek* fans revealed that while fans may recognise

> that their relationship to the text remains a tentative one, that their pleasures often exist on the margins of the original text and in the face of the producer's own efforts to regulate meanings ... Sometimes, fans respond to this situation with hostility and anger against those who have the power to 'retool' their narratives into something radically different from that which the audience desires. (1992: 24)

'Nope, I never intend to read any *BR* spin-off, because it's (in my opinion) too important a piece of work for playing around and telling new stories in the same universe PKD created ... I am not interested in any *BR2* from anyone else than PKD,' proclaims Marco Gerber from Switzerland. Here the issues of canon and fidelity emerge most clearly. According to Marco, only PKD has the right to continue the *Blade Runner* story, despite the fact that Ridley Scott and the screenwriters, Hampton Fancher and David W. Peoples, rewrote Dick's *DADoES* to form *Blade Runner*. Perhaps the fact that Philip K. Dick was able to read the script and gave his seal of approval has something to do with *Blade Runner* being seen by many fans as authorised by PKD himself.

Blade Runner fans also have a similarly mixed view of Jeter's sequels, except that many more of them have actually read them. From what I have seen on message boards and via personal correspondence, many *Blade Runner* fans read the novels out of a simple hunger for more texts in the same universe. Unlike Philip K. Dick fans, they have only a small quantity of official *Blade Runner* texts including a few film versions of *Blade Runner*, some comics, a computer game, and now the Jeter spin-offs. Colin Driessen, a 34-year-old fan from Holland, puts it simply: 'I think that only the fans who lust for more BR stuff read the books, just to stay in the same vibe as the film, otherwise the books are mediocre.'

Centauro resists the desire for more *Blade Runner* texts on the Bladezone. com message boards where he posts 'I wouldn't accept everything with the blade runner name or logo on it, because it is "more of blade runner". Buying these low quality books and asking for more (!) is just a way to keep prostituting blade runner ... in some way this film is sacred to me, and I don't like the name used ad libitum [sic].' Nakano KalRonin responds to Centauro's post stating: 'what your [sic] saying is that *Blade Runner* the movie and the *DADoES* book should be the only thing that determines the *Blade Runner* universe. My opinion is that I would love to see MORE *Blade Runner* out there!' In a private message Nakano, in reality 25-year-old Bryan Wilson from Illinois, goes on to mention how he has also read 'all the New Jedi Order books and others for *Star Wars*'. Ironically K. W. Jeter has also written spin-off novels for *Star Wars*, and they are seen by many fans as 'official' texts within what is dubbed the EU, or Expanded Universe (see Brooker 2002: 101–13). Wilson compares Jeter's *Blade Runner* novels to the *Star Wars* EU and explains his take on the *Blade Runner* canon:

> The *Star Wars* books are all approved by Lucas himself, so to me its 'Fact' of what is suppose to happen in the lives of all of his characters. If Ridley Scott approved of the books I would still most likely take what I could from them that I thought to be part of my *Blade Runner* universe. Lucas is the creator of all his characters from *Star Wars* so if he approves of the books, than its fact. If Philip K. Dick approved of all of K. W. Jeter's books, than it should be taken as fact ... Philip K. Dick mentions how the movie is exactly how he imagined everything in his book from the characters to the scenery. So I feel that considering Ridley Scott perfectly captured Philip K. Dick's vision, he could have been responsible for the approval of K. W. Jeter's books...

Bryan's comments illustrate the degree of uncertainly felt by some *Blade Runner* fans as to whom they should turn to for authorial meaning. He appears torn between his belief that Ridley Scott is the true auteur of the film and his knowledge that Philip K. Dick created many of the characters and ideas translated to the screen by the director. Michel Foucault's concept of the 'myth of the author' suggests that 'the author functions as a sign of value, since only certain texts are read as authored' (Tulloch & Jenkins 1995: 188). For this fan, measuring the value of Jeter's spin-off novels is complicated by an apparent reverence for the 'authority' – the authorial qualities and status – of both Dick and Scott, and an underlying awareness that the novels are essentially a compromise between the two.

PKD fans have less of an issue with Jeter's novels because they do not need or desire an expansion of the *Blade Runner* film universe. To the majority of them, *Blade Runner* is a completely separate entity from the original novel and they do not see it as a threat to their Dickian universe. On the other hand, many *Blade Runner* fans are caught in the middle, torn by their desire for more official *Blade Runner* texts, and the fact that Jeter's novels are essentially 'changing' the Ridley Scott *Blade Runner* universe, which many fans do not want anyone to tamper with.

The most original of Jeter's novels and least risky – in terms of potential fan disapproval – is the third, *Eye and Talon*, where Jeter introduces a new set of characters. Iris – a possible nod to the character of that name in Kathryn Bigelow's *Strange Days* (1995) – is a female blade runner who teams up with the mysterious Vogel to track down the missing Tyrell owl. Unlike Jeter's first two novels – which repeatedly re-use the characters from Scott's narrative, even the ones who are dead at the end of the movie – *Eye and Talon*, like the Westwood PC game, creates a story within the *Blade Runner* universe that does not impinge upon the trajectory of the characters' lives in the film. Unfortunately, Jeter's use of filmic techniques in the novel becomes tiresome after a while and detracts from the flow and action of the narrative, while the surprise ending, which brings back a character from the film, hinders the novel's potential for creating a distinctive narrative within the familiar *Blade Runner* universe.

Jeter's novels did, however, enjoy a successful if short-lived run on the bookstore shelves. This may stem from *Blade Runner* fans' fundamental but oddly passionless desire for more texts within the same universe, regardless of their quality. Radomir, the 25-year-old Slovakian moderator of BR-insight. com forums, explains: 'Of course I'll buy the lattest [sic] sequel, although more from duty to have the series complete than from real interest.' Sales and popularity of Jeter's novels may also be influenced by the fact that there are many 'followers' of *Blade Runner* who do not necessarily participate in fan communities, but still enjoy the film and are attracted by texts relating to it.

PKD fans embrace *Blade Runner*, more than other PKD adaptations, perhaps because it was essentially approved by the author, but can stand alone as a piece of postmodern filmic art. It is aesthetically challenging and stunningly intricate, setting the visual tone for numerous science fiction films that followed, just as PKD's themes would be used as the source of inspiration for dozens of films over the past two decades. In these respects, *Blade Runner* was, and is, a success, with or without *DADoES*.

But Jeter's novels are viewed by many PKD fans as mere copies of a copy – literally 'novel' like a replicant fresh off the production line, but with a very short lifespan – and by many *Blade Runner* fans as trash to be read mainly as a means of satisfying one's need for more material. Despite intense canonical debate, there is an established fan community around *Star Wars* EU novels, but Jeter's website is out of date and full of broken links. His work is left to the bargain bins, dug up and dusted off only for the occasional discussion on *Blade Runner* fan sites, and random science fiction message boards. He had some interesting ideas; he remained loyal to a number of PKD's themes, and his integration of *Blade Runner* and *DADoES* was both unique and creative. But it would appear he should have left well alone. I almost wish the London Bughouse had been successful at contacting Philip K. Dick's spirit that night in March 2002; I might have had a chance to read some of a K. W. Jeter novel to him and ask if he approved.

SECTION 4: IDENTITIES

THE RACHEL PAPERS: IN SEARCH OF *BLADE RUNNER'*S FEMME FATALE
DEBORAH JERMYN

BEAUTIES, BEASTS AND FEMMES FATALES

Women are a problem in the world of *Blade Runner*. Even in their absence they instigate devastation; in the film's very first scene, Holden's request that Leon 'Describe in single words only the good things that come into your mind about ... your mother' elicits the firing of a bullet into his chest. *Blade Runner'*s women seem to figure overwhelmingly as dangerous or devious creatures, getting by, for example, through the manipulation of a façade of child-like innocence (Pris) or brazen sexuality (Zhora). 'Talk about beauty and the beast' says Bryant of Zhora early in the film, warning Deckard not to underestimate the destructive capabilities that lie behind her outwardly beguiling appearance; 'She's both.'

With this heightened capacity to deceive, we might say that the female replicant is the ultimate manifestation of the commonplace cultural positioning of women as duplicitous. It seems telling in this light that *all* the major women characters in *Blade Runner* are in fact replicants. Subsequently, when these women are 'retired', their deaths are prolonged and bloody punishments in comparison to those of the male replicants, leaving behind butchered bodies where their feminine charms, and the threat they represent, are well and truly razed.

It is through this well-worn, often apparently moralistic and regressive conceptualisation of women, as much as its aesthetic of shadows and Venetian blinds or its world-weary detective and his doleful voice-over, that *Blade Runner* returns to the territory of film noir. Feisty women, female deception, fear of women, the 'threat' of female sexuality and its (apparent) defeat are as characteristic of the world of film noir as cigarettes and alcohol.[1] Women may be a problem in the future Los Angeles of 2019 but, replicants or otherwise, there is very little that is new in this state of affairs. As even a superficial trawl through Western culture manifestly demonstrates, from Eve to Pandora, women are a perennial problem with which we have long been familiar despite their 'unknowability'.

The link between the representation of women and the generic traditions of film noir in *Blade Runner* is, of course, most potently and explicitly evoked through the character of Rachel. In this chapter, it is partly through adopting the critical frameworks of some of the seminal feminist analysis of film noir that I endeavour to turn debate towards a more expansive and reflective discussion of Rachel's import to the film than has hitherto been undertaken. Just as in the late 1970s this work enabled a richer, more complex critical engagement with the figure of the femme fatale, so too does its adoption here uncover the significance of Rachel to *Blade Runner*'s enduring potency. If any of the film's early formal and thematic signifiers of film noir were not already felt by the viewer – for example, its investigative narrative, seedy urban underworld milieu and smoky interiors – they are certainly accentuated by Rachel's arrival.

As Deckard visits the Tyrell Corporation she emerges from the shadows – an entrance immediately linking her to the noir world – dressed in a shoulder-padded suit of black satin pulled tight across her body. The effect is striking. She is immaculate, in dramatic red lipstick, her hair worn up in an elaborate bouffant. With measured, sashaying, pencil-skirted footsteps, the full impact of her 1940s costuming is deployed, seen and even heard as her stilettos clip the hard floor and echo across the cavernous space.

Indeed, so iconic and nostalgic an image is this that it has elicited comparisons between Sean Young/Rachel and that classic noir vision of corrupted femininity, Joan Crawford/Mildred Pierce, the eponymous protagonist of *Mildred Pierce* (1945) (see Desser, 1991: 59; Bukatman, 1997: 24). Sean Young herself has said of first watching this scene, 'I look like a Harrell photograph as I walk into this special light the director designed ... I was stunned! I put my hand to my forehead and said, "Ridley, my God, you've made me look *incredible*!" I didn't believe it was *me*' (cited in Steranko 1982: 70). It is interesting here to note how Young talks about herself as something Scott has created. He seems her 'maker' much as Tyrell is Rachel's ('Ridley, my God') and like Rachel, she too experiences a kind of alienation from what she had believed to be her true self when another, male-manufactured self is revealed ('*I* didn't believe it was *me*'). Young's deference to Scott throughout the interview cited here is quite striking (particularly for an actress who, by her own admission, is often reputed to be difficult and demanding; see Sammon 1996: 214). Indeed, the on-set relationships between Young and both Scott and Harrison Ford, and how these echo her role and relationship with the prominent male figures in the film, are something we shall return to below.

Unambiguously rendered object of 'the male gaze' (Mulvey 1975) in this sequence, Rachel is a wholly fetishised vision of 'the dark lady, the spider woman' (Place 1998: 47), the femme fatale who lies at the cynical heart of film noir. And by drawing on the ingrained duplicitous connotations of this archetype, Scott instantly alerts the audience to approach Rachel with caution. Her link to the spider woman motif is returned to later and evocatively drawn on thematically too, when one of her most vivid and personal 'memories' is revealed by Deckard to be the implanted recollection of a web outside her childhood window, where she watched an egg hatch into 'a hundred baby spiders' who then proceeded to eat their mother.

Rachel, then, is key to the film's overarching thematic and aesthetic debt to, and nostalgia for, film noir. At the same time, she is evidently a fascinating character in her own right – the replicant who believed herself to be human. If, as David Desser suggests, a central philosophical preoccupation that underlies *Blade Runner* is 'the very definition of what it means to be human, to be a real person' (1991: 57), then Rachel is central to the ways in which the film explores that issue. It is for all these reasons that the critical neglect of Rachel within existing scholarship on the film seems so strikingly remiss.

BOYS' OWN STORIES?

Rachel's fate to date has been one that mirrors that suffered at one time by the women she evokes – the femmes fatales of classical Hollywood cinema's film noirs. As both a character within the diegesis and as the subject of critical interest, Rachel also seems to have been marginalised by an apparently overwhelmingly male-driven narrative. This can be at least partly attributed to the fact that as a film-noir-cum-sci-fi, the film's generic hybridity involves the assimilation of two genres commonly (if often prescriptively) perceived as 'masculine'.[2] As Christine Gledhill has noted of film noir, in a description worth citing at length here,

> in the mainstream thriller the investigative structure presupposes a male hero in search of the truth ... This premiss [sic] has two consequences. The plots of the thriller/detective story offer a world of action defined in male terms; the locales, situations, iconography, violence are conventions connoting the male sphere. Women in this world tend to split into two categories: there are those who work on the fringes of the underworld and are defined by the male criminal ambience of the thriller – barflies, nightclub singers, expensive mistresses, femmes fatales ... and then there are on the outer margins of this world wives, long-suffering girlfriends, would-be fiancées...
> (1998: 28)

Significantly, both these categories of women are described here as being on the periphery of 'the male sphere'; inhabiting 'the fringes' or 'outer margins' of the world described. Of course, this is not to suggest that the femme fatale has ever been negligible to film noir; as E. Ann Kaplan notes, 'women are central to the intrigue of the films' (1998b: 16). Rather, what seems at stake here is that arguably their roles have often been disseminated primarily in relation to what they signify *for men*; as Kaplan goes on to explain, they 'function as obstacle to the male quest' (ibid).

Beyond film noir, the characteristic compulsion of Hollywood cinema's classical cause-and-effect narrative *per se*, with its focus on obtaining resolution, has been widely conceptualised by feminist film criticism as being essentially masculine in nature. Film noir is arguably an exemplary instance of this masculine narrative form for numerous reasons; not just for its convention of a male voice-over, which often ascribes further textual authority to the figure of the detective,[3] but since it habitually seems that it is the solving of the problem of 'woman' herself, and not merely a crime, that is the object of the investigative quest (see Dyer 1998: 117).

While such a formulation may run the risk of promoting essentialism, *Blade Runner* arguably seems to operate comfortably within the terms described by Gledhill above; from this perspective, with its 'male hero' (Deckard – and/or Roy Batty), 'action defined in male terms' (interrogation, hunting, fighting) and 'male sphere' of interest (menacing urban streets, seedy strip joints, bachelor pads) it is perhaps hardly surprising that Rachel has not been deemed pivotal to the film. Much more visible has been critical interest in the 'male' spaces opened up by the film: its representation of the city or technology, for instance, as well as its male characters.

For example, though he later goes on to reflect on how Rachel crystallises the film's implicit suggestion that its replicants might embody a more sensitive vision of humanity than its humans, J. P. Telotte casually implies that the film's 'major figures' are all male when he lists them as 'Deckard, Dr Tyrell ... and J. F. Sebastian' (1998: 155). Furthermore, his consideration of Rachel seems motivated not primarily by interest in her *per se*, but rather what she represents for *Deckard*; 'Deckard finds himself attracted to Rachel, fascinated not by her nature as a copy so much as by the way she mirrors something significantly human within him' (1998: 156). It seems significant too here that, with the notable exception of E. Ann Kaplan's *Women in Film Noir* collection first published in 1978, the critical history of film noir has been one marked predominantly by male scholarship. In fact, Telotte's words here remind one of Budd Boetticher's assertion that

> what counts is what the heroine provokes, or rather what she represents. She is the one, or rather the love or fear she inspires, or else the concern he feels for her, who makes him act the way he does. In herself the woman has not the slightest importance. (Cited in Mulvey 2002: 137)

Forty years after the emergence of film noir, then, it seems Rachel merely took up the baton passed on by her classical sisters. This was not only on an aesthetic level, in terms of her sartorial debt to them, but in the way that her relative absence in critical accounts of the film implicitly deemed her to be of subsidiary interest in a cinema where male stories and a male point of view take pre-eminence. In short, prior to Kaplan's collection at least, there has been a curious kind of critical paradox regarding the femme fatale, one seen again in the reception of Rachel; while the femme fatale's role has always been felt to be undeniably indispensable to film noir, there is nevertheless a sense in which many of these films' centres have been enduringly conceptualised as steadfastly male.

ENTERING THE SPIDER WOMAN'S WEB

The cinematic tradition into which Rachel entered in Scott's film, then, apparently constituted a fairly bleak one for her, condemning her in some ways to the fringes of a male adventure. However, while *Blade Runner* was in development in Hollywood, Kaplan's *Women in Film Noir* collection appeared, a significant milestone in feminist film criticism. In a similar spirit to Laura Mulvey's 1975 account of the systematic marginalisation of women in mainstream cinema, much of the work included in Kaplan's collection sought to apply the '(then) innovative critique of classical Hollywood "realism" as always implicitly colluding with the patriarchal status quo that positions women as subordinate ... the authors showed how the female discourse within film narratives is subordinated to overarching heterosexual male discourses' (Kaplan 1998a: 3).

Yet at the same time, some of the essays in this collection opened up a rather different view of the construction of these women, one that began to liberate noir's femmes fatales from the margins of the (male) text and which indeed in some instances celebrated them. While acknowledging that these women may be interrogated, disempowered and chastised by the dominant narrative, some of this critical work suggested that they nevertheless very often undermined these narrative constraints by virtue of their striking resilience, intelligence and vigour.

This position was taken up most ardently by Janey Place, who argued that the femme fatale's 'access to her own sexuality' (1998: 49) was a superlative source of power to her:

> Visually, film noir is fluid, sensual, extraordinarily expressive, making the sexually expressive woman, which is its dominant image of woman, extremely powerful. It is not their inevitable demise we remember but rather their strong, dangerous and, above all, exciting sexuality. (1998: 48)

Richard Dyer has also noted the affective properties that movement and fluidity in cinema may hold, more specifically in terms of our engagement with a character's/performer's 'presence'. He suggested that Rita Hayworth as/in *Gilda* (1946) 'in some measure overturned and exposed' the constraints of the femme fatale role, a feat accomplished partly through the 'positive charge' and 'sheer status of Hayworth as a star' (1998: 115; 119) and partly through her expressive use of dance whereby she resisted the stasis typical of the sexual objectification of women. Also in the same volume, Pam Cook re-appraised *Mildred Pierce* to argue that a kind of internal generic battle takes place within the film. According to her analysis, the female discourse of the woman's picture present in Mildred's own account of her story competes with the male discourse of film noir inscribed by the detectives who arrest and interview her, so that the 'male' narrative here does not go uncontested but rather is rendered fraught. By the time we reach the second edition of *Women in Film Noir* published in 1998, the recognition that it is arguably reductive to only characterise noir as a 'male' genre, or the femme fatale as only speaking to male fantasy and desire, has gained momentum to become a central theme of the collection.

While not without their flaws, the readings summarised above nevertheless opened up analysis of film noir to recognise how its female characters might resist relegation to the passive sphere described by Mulvey and that, far from smoothing over ideological tensions, representation in these films was marked by fissuring and contradiction. These writers prompted the repositioning of the conceptualisation of the femme fatale away from that of a tangential figure in a masculine narrative, obliging film studies to explore her presence more expansively and indeed to reconfigure its understanding of how and where audiences gained pleasure from the genre.

Thus, in a similar spirit to the work which almost three decades ago first instigated a more rigorous and polysemic grasp of the ideological struggles of film noir and the femme fatale, how might a more nuanced and developed analysis of Rachel enrich our understanding of both her and of the film? Mulvey's call to arms for the systematic destruction of mainstream narrative filmmaking in order to demolish its objectification of the female form has clearly not been taken up. The now orthodox feminist critical tradition of seeking to explore the possibilities of textual ruptures, gaps, contradictions – to locate a space for both a more complex conceptualisation of women appearing in mainstream cinema and women watching it – is therefore as legitimate and instructive now as it ever was. As in the case of film noir, might such an analytical approach enable a reading of *Blade Runner* in which its misogynistic undercurrents are problematised and rendered unstable? How might we locate Rachel somewhere other than in the film's margins, and place her instead at the core of *Blade Runner*'s world, its anxieties, pleasures and enduring fascination?

'HOW CAN IT NOT KNOW WHAT IT IS?': LOOKING FOR THE REAL RACHEL

In fact, Rachel's correlation to Mildred Pierce goes beyond the merely visual, since thematically, both women problematise the construction of the femme fatale. Mildred at one point in the film is indeed a power-dressed, independent businesswoman – ultimately, however, she is finally positioned as a self-sacrificing mother who returns to the husband who brought a life of domestic servitude to her. In the same vein, arguably Rachel is a 'femme fatale' who *is not*. On discovering that she is unaware of her replicant status, Deckard asks incredulously, 'How can it not know what it is?' But we might say the whole film struggles to 'place' Rachel, that the text itself does not know what 'she is'; a highly eroticised 'femme fatale' who in fact reveals herself to be sexually inexperienced and who saves the life of the hero rather than destroy him. These contradictions, and the sense of confusion she thus elicits, might on the one hand substantiate a reading of the film that suggests that, in time-honoured fashion, it constructs women as unfathomable. But on the other, these narrative/thematic inconsistencies destabilise the construction of the femme fatale and resist the efforts of both audience and male protagonist to easily categorise her.

At the start of the film, Rachel carries all the superficial erotic trappings of the femme fatale and, at least initially, the same spirit of confidence, an ice-maiden-black-widow who first encounters Deckard with admirable poise, meeting and returning his gaze even while object of the gaze herself. 'Do you like our owl?' she asks him before any introduction. 'Must be expensive', he observes – 'Very. I'm Rachel.' The ease with which she unhesitatingly moves on, passing over the extravagance and excess represented by the owl to introducing herself, underlines the sense that here is a woman who is 'expensive', another prized possession in the Tyrell Corporation, another fetish object. But like Mildred, whose empire also gives way (or is taken) from under her, Rachel's confident demeanour is soon replaced by vulnerability and uncertainty. In the scene that follows, as Rachel undergoes the Voigt-Kampff test her confidence crumbles. Initially she is a demanding subject. She looks at Deckard directly and seems to inspect him as he 'tests' her. When he begins to ask how she would respond to a 'full page nude photo of a girl' she quickly retorts, 'Is this testing whether I'm a replicant or a lesbian, Mr Deckard?' as if she is aware of and confronting her objectification, and turning the tables by questioning her interrogator.

But by the time we reach Deckard's final question, and it has arguably become apparent that there is more to Rachel than meets the eye, the scene is very different. When Deckard looks from the machine to her now, she looks away. Her poise is wavering, she momentarily twists her lip, her smoking now appears a nervous habit rather than a cool affectation. Tyrell asks her to step outside, banishing her from the room where moments ago she had held court, leaving the men free to scrutinise her further still. It is as if they have succeeded, momentarily at least, in 'breaking' her.

If this scene evokes the painful spirit of any other from film noir, it is that of Gilda's wretched and inadvertent return to her tormentor, Johnny, in *Gilda*. Tricked into going back to Buenos Aires by a new 'boyfriend', she realises there that the men have conspired against her to dupe her into returning and that she has been wholly deceived by them. Utterly disempowered, this once spirited woman now drops to her knees and begs to be freed from Johnny – another femme fatale who was not really, but who nevertheless must be 'broken' and punished by the text. Rachel, we now discover from Tyrell, 'is an experiment, nothing more', a male play-thing. The same callous spirit subsequently pervades the scene where she anxiously visits Deckard's house clinging to a photo of herself with her mother, in the desperate hope that this artefact will prove her humanity. He does not even glance at it, but instead, as she struggles with her composure, he cruelly and impatiently relates to her the tale of her six-year-old self playing 'doctors' with her brother; her secret story laid bare to her, her intimate self revealed without her consent.

In fact, we could say that the final and most violent assault she goes on to suffer at Deckard's hands is actually instigated in these two preceding sequences. Rachel's 'rape' begins before Deckard even lays a finger on her; it is the physical culmination of Deckard's and the text's apparent drive to humble and contain her. In this respect, it seems telling that in this 'spider woman's' story of the web she watched outside her childhood window, it was the not the spider who devoured others. This was no black widow feeding on her prey or 'lover'; rather it was the spider who was devoured herself.

Clearly, the most difficult and disturbing scene one must engage with in a discussion of Rachel is the 'rape' she suffers on her second visit to Deckard's house, having just saved him from Leon's vicious attack by shooting Leon moments before he crushed Deckard's eyes into his skull. Reflecting on this chronology, it is easy to read the 'rape' as a desperate effort by Deckard to reinscribe his masculinity.[4] But I use inverted commas around the term 'rape' advisedly here, since it is a sequence where questions of desire and consent are clearly and very deliberately manipulated to evoke ambiguity and ambivalence. For example, in their discussion of the film, Michael Ryan and Douglas Kellner make a bracketed, passing reference to the scene, drawing on it to illustrate how the film contains, 'several sexist moments (Deckard more or less rapes Rachel)' (1990: 63). On the one hand this description seems to rather shockingly understate the gravity of rape; but on the other it points to their evident discomfort at unequivocally designating it rape.

Significantly, Scott's oeuvre has a history of exploring problematic 'rape' sequences, where 'unruly' women endure assaults in which male sexual violence is adopted as a means to overpower and belittle them, violence motivated by the seeming desire to bring them 'back in line'. In a brutal oral penetration sequence in *Alien* (1979), the determined, newly self-appointed captain Ripley (Sigourney Weaver) is almost suffocated when a deranged Ash pins her down and forces a roll of papers into her mouth; in *Thelma & Louise* (1991), Thelma's (Geena Davis) ill-advised weekend away from her husband and mildly drunken dance with a stranger results in her being viciously assaulted in a car park; in *GI Jane* (1997) the 'ballsy' heroine's (Demi Moore) efforts to succeed in the Marine Corps lead her superior officer to attempt to rape her in order to demonstrate the vulnerability and inappropriateness of female soldiers. Looked at in this context, the assault on Rachel seems part of a larger, ongoing preoccupation with sexual violence in Scott's work. But this recurrent theme is one that cannot easily be categorised as entirely misogynistic in intent, since in all cases it features women who achieve narrative vindication, characters whose bravado and defiance are ultimately constructed as entirely deserving of the audience's respect and admiration, and who resonate as 'survivors' rather than 'victims'.

At the same time, however, the 'rape' sequence at Deckard's apartment is evidently a perplexing one. How can this action be reconciled with Deckard's hero-protagonist status? Of course, at one level his assault on Rachel merely serves to underline the sense that Deckard is not really a 'hero' at all, that once again the most inhumane behaviour in *Blade Runner*'s world in perpetrated by its humans. This is a man, after all, who in a horrifying sequence has just shot someone (albeit a replicant) in the back.[5] But in essence the 'rape' sequence is an enormously contradictory one, since while it clearly seeks to further underline Deckard's dark side, it is also constructed in some ways to serve as a romantic love scene. Certainly, actress Sean Young appears to have interpreted the scene in this way, commenting in interview that

> the love scene was the hardest, though we didn't really make love. You see us just before … in a ritual of violent foreplay. It's a scene about a virgin losing her virginity, a woman without experience being endowed with emotions, forcibly – it's really a wild scene. He makes me love him … [he] tells me to say I love him. I've never done that before; I don't know the meaning of love – *but I want to*. (Quoted in Steranko 1982: 26)

Clearly, the issue of consent still looms large in this description; Rachel is 'forcibly' endowed with emotions, he 'makes' her love him, but she 'wants' to learn. Nevertheless, the clearest indicator that Scott himself wished the sequence to be read as a love scene comes at an auditory level through the signifying use of music.[6] Composer Vangelis's languorous use of an 'electrified' sax first enters the scene at the point where Rachel looks at a bare-chested Deckard sleeping, then sits by the piano, takes off her jacket and lets her hair down. The evocatively seductive refrain serves as an auditory cue that a love scene is imminent. The music then shifts to become dark, panicky and menacing at the point at which Rachel escapes Deckard's attempt to kiss her on the mouth. She rushes towards the door, which he slams shut before pushing her back roughly against the blinds. She is tearful and agitated, but at the point at which he leans in to kiss her again, the sultry sax music commences once more. If we take the music as an emotional cue, then, arguably Deckard's aggression is constructed here as a kind of momentary, though dramatic disruption, an awkward and ill-judged exchange that threatened the smooth dénouement of their love scene. One might even say that Deckard himself is 'confused' here, grappling to understand how lovemaking should operate (though clearly this does not excuse his violence). But the 'love-scene' 'resumes' with the return of the seduction music; a refrain which climaxes and draws to a close at the point at which Rachel says, *without* prompting, 'Put your hands on me' – perhaps indicating that if it was not before, their intimacy is now consensual – and the two kiss. While clearly, then, one could condemn this sequence at a number of levels and most pointedly for its eroticisation of violence, to do so would nevertheless be to underplay its enormous polysemic potential.

What is also interesting here in terms of Rachel's characterisation, as her apparently hesitant and confused response to Deckard's advances might initially be said to suggest, is that this most advanced, most 'special' (female) replicant has been manufactured as a seemingly asexual or sexually naïve woman, while her counterparts Zhora and Pris clearly have not. As Roy remarks to J. F., 'We're not computers Sebastian, we're physical'. Yet Rachel has apparently been constructed to have to 'learn' sexual desire in the film, quite unlike Philip K. Dick's original novel too where Rachel reveals that she has had a number of lovers.

Of course this also makes her quite unlike classical noir's archetypal femme fatale; Rachel is denied the 'access to her own sexuality' which Place argued was such an extraordinary source of power to the femme fatale (1998: 49) and thus in this respect arguably made a rather tamer, less vital version of her noir predecessors. While her sexuality might still be 'dangerous' in terms of the responses it may elicit in others, notably Deckard of course, she is rendered frigid rather than 'sexually expressive' (Place 1998: 48), balking at Deckard's suggestion that she meet him at the fabulously decadent Taffey Lewis club, responding with a prim 'That's not my kind of place'. Necessitating, as all this does, a male mentor or svengali figure to sexually initiate her, this component of her psychology might be accused of pandering to patriarchal fantasy – that is, as Steranko has rather objectionably described her, a 'willing virgin' (1982: 29).

It is at this point that I would like to return again to some of the extra-filmic discussion of *Blade Runner*, which has centred on its troubled production history and strained on-set relationships. The difficulties the film's production ran into in terms of its financing, editing and exhibition have been well documented, along with accounts of the numerous personality clashes and extraordinary demands Scott made of cast and crew (see Steranko 1982; Sammon 1996; *On the Edge of Blade Runner* (2000)). Clearly, given its tendency towards hearsay and subjectivity, one needs to apply extra-filmic 'knowledge' with caution when reading any film text. But nevertheless, interpretation of Rachel takes on a further nuance when reports of the film's production history are taken into account.

In the *Prevue* special feature on the film from 1982, Young describes Scott as 'a wonderful director' yet also details a relationship with some dark overtones. It appears Scott 'worked' the actress by wavering between proffering and retracting his friendship and support. Young observes:

> [Scott] knew it was important to me to feel contact, communication ... We'd go to the beach on Sundays and talk about Rachel ... [But] sometimes, he'd set me up just by threatening not to like me or what I was doing ... At other times, near the end of a scene while the cameras were rolling, Ridley would say, "You're boring me!" It would make me angry, embarrass me. (Quoted in Steranko 1982: 70)

It is difficult not to see parallels here with the way Tyrell toys with Rachel's emotions, initially apparently offering her refuge and security within the Tyrell Corporation on the one hand, but all the while ready to undo it with the other.

Meanwhile, Young also clearly struggled to get on with Ford, diplomatically commenting that 'he was very tough to work with but he was a nice person' (ibid.). But she elucidates, 'He didn't want to rehearse with me ... He doesn't like to talk; he didn't want to talk to me, so that's the way it was. He was calling the shots. It's his film.' Young's account is corroborated elsewhere by costume designer Michael Kaplan who has described how 'whenever Harrison would come onto the set he wouldn't speak to her. Totally ignored her' (cited in Sammon 1996: 215). Tyrell similarly rejects Rachel in the film; when Deckard tells her to talk to Tyrell for an explanation of who she is, she tearfully replies: 'He wouldn't see me.' Here, Ford's apparent bullying or will to occupy a position of supremacy in his relationship with Young seems to be a kind of continuum of – almost spilling over from – the supercilious manner with which Deckard treats Rachel in the film. Young herself draws a comparison between Ford's treatment of her and Deckard's treatment of Rachel:

> You must remember there's considerable tension between our characters ... Harrison carried that through both on *and* off the set ... he knew what buttons to push to make me so frustrated – and that's what my character was. In a sense, Harrison's behavior towards me really shaped my character. (Quoted in Steranko 1982: 70)

Young's account, then, of her on-set experiences with the production's major patriarchal figureheads – her director and leading-man – and their place as 'shaping' forces acting on her, brings another fascinating level of insight to bear on the film. While it would be trite to suggest that the film merely 'reflects' these extra-textual relationships, the edginess and anxiety perceptible in Young's reserved performance take on a new resonance when placed within this context. It would appear that while acting out the experiences of a woman in a male-dominated and emotionally manipulative environment, she was working within such an environment herself. These are anecdotal reflections but nevertheless, particularly given that this is a film whose potent mythos has been largely built around rumour and 'insider' detail, they provide a thought-provoking digression into the interweaving levels at which mainstream cinema and the the film industry in general is overwhelmingly structured around patriarchal power.

IN SEARCH OF FEMINISM IN 2019

As already stressed, however, the film's sexual politics are complex and contradictory and Rachel cannot be dismissed as merely a misogynistic fantasy. We should remember, firstly, that in forthright fashion it is Rachel who voices two of the film's most difficult, central (and unanswered) questions. Prior to her Voigt-Kampff test she pointedly asks Deckard 'Have you ever retired a human by mistake?' Later, after discovering that she is herself a replicant, she asks him at his apartment, 'You know that Voigt-Kampff test of yours? Did you ever take that test yourself?' Both questions put the film's moral and philosophical preoccupation with 'what it means to be human, to be a real person' (Desser 1991: 57) firmly on the map. In fact the film often juxtaposes Rachel's (replicant) more developed sensitivity and humanity against Deckard's (presumed human) impeded moral sensibility; her resistance to the intrusiveness of his Voigt-Kampff questions; her evident attachment to the photo of her 'mother' against his callous indifference to the import of such a relationship to her; her willingness to save his life even while contemplating running away and wondering of him, 'Would you come after me? Hunt me?' Her resilience is demonstrated too, not just in her capacity to question Deckard's competence and authority, but in her evident skill in trailing him; while he may 'rescue' her at the film's ending he is only alive to do so because she stepped in just at the point of his imminent demise at the hands of Leon. In fact, as the film progresses, Deckard's confidence and control become every bit as unstable as Rachel's appear; after Leon's attack, he asks her, 'Shakes? Me too. I get them bad.'

In order to reflect further on how the film might lend itself to a feminist reading, however, I want not to merely look at Rachel in isolation, but to consider how all the female replicants are bound up in what we might call a critical commentary on the structure and operation of the male gaze in the film. This is perhaps most explicitly explored in the scene where Deckard talks his way into Zhora's dressing room at Taffey's by pretending to be an inspector from the 'Confidential Committee on Moral Abuses'. 'Have you ever felt yourself to be exploited in any way?' he incongruously and evidently superfluously asks the virtually naked Zhora moments after she has finished performing. 'You'd be surprised what a guy would go through to get a glimpse of a beautiful body', he goes on, as he pretends to look for peep-holes in her room, the handiwork of voyeurs.

There is a palpable irony here, which Zhora clearly feels, that a woman so patently marked as public, sexual spectacle might still attract peeping toms. She looks at him bemused and exasperated. 'No I wouldn't', she replies. The abruptness and knowingness with which she answers suggest a sad and long familiarity with men who have held 'lewd or unsavoury' interest in her. Curiously, as she dresses, it is not clear whether the conspicuous leather bondage-type outfit she changes into is another fetish stage costume or her 'own' clothes, disintegrating boundaries between Zhora's performance/personal spaces, apparently unabashedly inviting the gaze or perhaps simply acknowledging that she is always its object. Later, in her spectacular death sequence, as she runs through a series of plate glass shop windows and finally collapses, what remains most memorable about Zhora is not her stage performance where 'she takes the pleasure from the serpent' – a spectacle we hear but are not shown, despite the MC's invitation to 'watch her'. Rather it is her will to live as she keeps running through one pane of glass after another. As she lies on the ground, dead finally, a police officer turns her face over. Her impassive, motionless, cosmetic beauty renders her like one of the mannequins seen in the store fronts whose glass she has just shattered, inviting us surely to make a visual and thematic critique of the commonplace role and representation of women in mainstream cinema as little more than 'dolls'.

This is a key sequence for a feminist reading of the film, since its critical exploration of the male gaze pivots on the recurrent motif of the mannequin.

For example, Rachel performs as a kind of clotheshorse throughout the film, showcasing heavily stylised 1940s fashion whenever she appears. Like a model on a catwalk who ultimately serves the same purpose as a shop dummy, there is a level of unreality about her manufactured, polished and perfected image, that images her as a kind of mass-produced mannequin at times. Later, of course, at J. F.'s apartment Pris, the 'basic pleasure model', hides from Deckard by disguising herself as a mannequin among the rest of J.F.'s dolls. In fact, a number of critical accounts of the film have compared Pris to Olympia, the doll automaton who passed for a real girl in E.W. Hoffmann's *Der Sandmann* (see Kael 1982: 83; Bruno 1990: 185).

Taken together, these representations might be said to merely recycle conventional patriarchal images of women as doll-like, submissive (and very often 'mute') fantasy figures. But the graphically violent deaths of Zhora and Pris, women who do not submit to their male-determined fate but who aggressively fight for and cling passionately to every last breath in their bodies in an entirely 'unfeminine' fashion, unsettle such a reading. We might say that through the motif of the mannequin, and his simultaneous destabilisation of it, Scott pursues a critical and reflective exploration of how mainstream cinema has conventionally idealised women and female sexuality. Undeniably, all of the female replicants/'mannequins' are evidently sexually objectified by the film's own cinematic language.[7] But so too are they within the patriarchal world that they inhabit within the film, a world Scott seems to deliberately seek to explore, undermine and question, even while at another level he reproduces it.

THE JOURNEY TO A PLACE WHERE INCEPT DATES DON'T MATTER

Through this contradictory and complex trail, other voices and perspectives continually collide with the dominant detective story and fracture any hopes for its comfortable progression, as they have always done in the convoluted plots of the noir world. It becomes possible to reimagine *Blade Runner* as a journey we undertake not with Deckard, but with Rachel. As Elizabeth Cowie has noted, 'it is clear that while many narratives ostensibly tell the tale of a protagonist and his or her adventures, for the spectator the film's "story" is more than that of any one character' (1993: 137). Pushing to one side the textual (if not effectual) dominance that inevitably comes with Deckard's investigative role and voice-over, it is Rachel who we might place at *Blade Runner*'s core for crystallising both the film's troubled sexual politics and its angst around the collapse of the markers of humanity. In a film which is ultimately about anxiety on all sorts of levels, Rachel can be situated as the key player, since she both voices and embodies many of those anxieties; a rescuer who is rescued, a femme fatale who is not, a replicant who 'passes' for human, embarking on a relationship with a human who may well be a replicant.

In his essay on *Gilda* and Rita Hayworth's triumphant overturning of the constraints of the femme fatale role, Richard Dyer has observed that 'the heroes of film noir are for the most part either colourless characterisations (cf. the parade of anodyne performers in the central roles...) and/or characters conspicuously lacking in the virtues of the "normal" man' (1998: 115). This is in part what enabled the femme fatales of classical film noir to 'steal' so many of these films, upstaging the male stars, despite their more marginal positioning in its discourse. And, while it would be churlish to dismiss Deckard's own kind of iconic stature, in many ways, one could perhaps make the same claims for Rachel in *Blade Runner* as Dyer does for her predecessors. Long after many of Deckard's clumsy and insensitive exchanges have lost their shape, Rachel's cool grace, dignity and beauty continue to resonate. Beyond this, the evocation she brings with her of our nostalgia for the golden age of cinema and her poignant quest to understand – 'Where do I come from? Where am I going? How long have I got?' – strike a chord in our collective consciousness that Deckard arguably struggles to match. 'It's too bad she won't live', says Gaff of her at the film's end. In more ways than one, this is precisely what she does.[8]

NOTES

1   Space prohibits me from giving a fuller account of the narrative and aesthetic conventions of film noir; see instead Silver and Ursini (1996), particularly Part One, 17–127.

2   However, some commentators have questioned the 'gendering' of film noir as an essentially masculine form; for example Elizabeth Cowie (1993), who explores its proximity to the 'female' form of melodrama.

3   Though as Cowie notes, the male voice-over also 'conventionally includes the voicing of hesitations and doubts' (1993: 138).

4   I am grateful to Jan Powell for sharing sensitive and insightful discussion of this sequence.

5   My analysis here is carried out within the context of a reading of *Blade Runner* which would maintain the text does not really encourage the spectator to question Deckard's human/replicant status until the latter stages of the film.

6   Indeed, in a review in *The Fresno Bee*, Richard Freedman commented '[Ford's]'s big love scene with Rachel, for instance, makes them both look like robots. If it weren't for the haunting, bluesy score of Vangelis ... this would be the least stimulating moment of passion ever to appear in an R-rated movie' (1982: 3).

7   Of course, the bare-chested Deckard and semi-clothed Batty might also be said to offer sexual spectacle for the spectator here at given moments, but they are not roundly objectified as 'play-things' within the film's diegesis as the women are.

8   Thanks to Will Brooker, Su Holmes, Adam Newell and Pat Pitt-Jones for never tiring of *Blade Runner* talk.

PURGE! CLASS PATHOLOGY IN *BLADE RUNNER*
SEAN REDMOND

> Few things reveal so sharply as science fiction the wishes, hopes, fears, inner stresses and tensions of an era, or define its limitations with such exactness.
>
> – H. L. Gold (quoted in Kuhn 1990: 15)

Blade Runner has become one of the most lauded science fiction films ever made.[1] Cult fans dedicate online homage to it, such as *The Replicant Site*, and organise conventions to consider again and again its cultural and aesthetic merits, and to offer collective answers and solutions to its ambiguous or open-ended narrative. Academics have written about it in terms of its racial and sexual politics (Dyer; 1997; Desser 2000), its exploration of humanity and postmodernity (Sobchack 1987; Ryan & Kellner 1990; Bruno 1990), and in terms of the way it challenges many of the accepted/expected codes and conventions of the science fiction film (Redmond 2003). *Blade Runner* is considered to be a 'Modern Classic' (see Scott Bukatman's excellent monograph, *Blade Runner*, 1997), and is often one of the most theorised films in science fiction readers such as Annette Kuhn's *Alien Zone* (1990). Science fiction courses, such as the one I run at the Southampton Institute, UK, use *Blade Runner* as the seminal text with which to explore the poetics and politics of the science fiction genre more widely. *Blade Runner* gets repeat screening on late-night digital and terrestrial television, and its visual and narrative influence extends not only to other science fiction films, such as *Dark City* (1998), but to fictional films more generally, such as the rain-soaked thriller, *Se7en* (1995). *Blade Runner*, with its dystopian future, nihilistic impulses, psychopathic cyborgs and mesmerising cityscape, is a film that seems to effect profoundly those who come into contact with it – so much so in fact, that one can argue that it acts as a doorway into the wishes, hopes, fears, inner stresses and tensions of an era that now stretches beyond twenty-five years or so since the film's making.

For the purpose of this chapter, this is a doorway worth *re-entering* because at the heart of *Blade Runner* is a powerful story of social class that few writers have so far acknowledged.[2] *Blade Runner* offers up a particularly depressing and pathological vision of the working class, both through the representation of the film's central protagonists, and through the teeming hordes who populate the lower levels of Blade Runner's City. However, the structure of class, and the 'nature' of class difference, is also stitched into the film's ideological system through its hybrid generic footprints; its representation of a class-perverted city space; and, more generally, its intertextual relay to (British) social/urban realism. A profound distrust and dislike of social class haunts the film at almost every moment, seeping its way into the power relationships and binary oppositions that can be found in the film's subtext and metaphoric centre.

A common agreement among writers is that *Blade Runner* is a schizophrenic film. It randomly quotes from different film genres and film movements/periods, as well as from other visual media and actual historical periods – although these feel as if they have themselves been 'quoted' or lifted from postcards, travel books and old films. In terms of the film's visual and narrative aesthetic, references are drawn from, and made to; the German Expressionist film, *Metropolis* (1927); film noir, and *Mildred Pierce* (1945) in particular; the police detective film; the New York skyline; the pulp fiction of Raymond Chandler; the pages/artwork of the science fiction magazine, *Heavy Metal*; and the art of Vermeer and Edward Hopper. The film has a confused vision of the future, one that is in fact welded to the past. Egyptian, Mayan, Roman, Greek and Gothic signifiers fill the visual landscape of the film, and through the design process of 'retro-fitting', the film is also actually made to look like it is partly set in the late 1940s. Consequently, time, history, high and low culture, and the relations and differences between them, have been thrown into confusion. *Blade Runner* happens in a future but one which is an amalgam of numerous pasts, and where taste distinctions have been levelled out.

This over-determining sense of temporal, cultural and historical schizophrenia is compounded by the alienated, confused and displaced characters who drive the film's narrative forward. The film's central characters struggle to find a home in this leaky city, touched as they are by its boundary-less references and numerous possible/impossible subject positions. Amnesia and existential disorientation are the key psychological traits of Deckard, Rachel and Batty, who are not even sure of their origins in the film. *Blade Runner* 'speaks' schizophrenia in its spatial organisation: it is set in a city-without-a-centre, a city without proper borders and boundaries, and without the necessary 'social glue' that usually binds people together.

However, there is another way that one can conceptualise the schizophrenia that is found in the film, one that anchors the reading that I want to give of the film's class phobia. The schizophrenia that reverberates around *Blade Runner* is brought together or finally made sense of through the presence of social class and, in particular, brutish, dangerous working-class masculinity. What I would like to do now is explore the different ways that a class-inflected schizophrenia manifests itself in the film.

SCHIZOPHRENIC HYBRIDITY

In one sense, *Blade Runner* is set in a down-beat, destructive past: through the low-tech noirish aesthetics, the reference to the 'private eye' drama, and the pastiches of Mayan and Egyptian architecture that provide the façades for many of the most important buildings, the future is made to look regressive, as if, paradoxically, the progress of science and technology has been a disastrous step backwards for humankind. Time has not stood still in the film but rather has, in many respects, gone back to earlier, 'bloodier' periods of human existence. In this mish-mash of historical reference points the economic and existential crisis of 1940s America is co-joined with the 'lost civilisation' of the Mayans (brutally crushed, to the point of genocide, by the Spanish) and the tyrannical Ancient Egyptians whose lust for power provided the model for autocratic rule that *Blade Runner* aspires to.

The film locates this regression in terms of a reductive class politics. In this mixed up future-past of *Blade Runner*, power has been given to uncaring, ruthless *upper-class* technocrats, such as Tyrell; Judas-like *blue-collar* workers, such as Deckard, Batty and the 'band' of Replicants, have turned on their Masters/Creators; and the mindless, passive crowds, who walk aimlessly about in the bowels of Blade Runner's City, have been indoctrinated by the mass media to such an extent that they have no separate, discernable self-identities other than that given to them through the tube, the consumer brand and the cult religion. When the city glitters in *Blade Runner*, as it surely does in the high-level, bejeweled exterior spaces, it is because people cannot get to these spaces and so they remain pure – above and beyond grubby class conflict.

Generically speaking, *Blade Runner* is one of those films that mix different genres and influences together to startling ideological effect. While generic hybridity is central to the way films are produced and marketed in contemporary Hollywood, in *Blade Runner* the mixing of visual and narrative conventions, from several genres, and at least two 'national' cinemas (German Expressionism and British Social Realism), is used to play out or give material presence to the schizophrenia and pathology that is attributed to class identity. The blurring and mixing of genres mirrors or rather 'echoes' the confusion (here read pathology) at the core of what are class-based characters in the film. In the case of Deckard, multiple personalities dominate; he is a part-jaded cop, loner-outsider, social rebel, reluctant replicant, awkward human, cold lover, rapist-misogynist; and yet what holds all these different fragments of the self together is his status as a working-class man. His schizophrenia, his pathology, is one borne out of his lowly class position – from which, as I shall go onto argue, he is trying to escape. Deckard does not want to be 'little people', to paraphrase Bryant, and yet neither does he want to be a replicant killer, the central way that the film allows him to cross class positions and rise up out of the bowels of the city. It is the references to film noir that best articulates the class hatred/confusion that lies at the core of Deckard's psyche.

BLADE RUNNER AS FILM NOIR

Blade Runner is clearly marked by some of the key visual and narrative motifs of film noir, a downbeat, investigative genre that emerged in the 1940s. In fact, Ridley Scott has described the overall design of *Blade Runner* as 'set forty years hence, made in the style of forty years ago' (quoted in Bukatman 1997:

19). Deckard, the world-weary and alienated ex-cop, who wants to jack it all in, is reminiscent of the Humphrey Bogart private eye character, found in such films such as *The Maltese Falcon* (1941). Rachel is the archetypal 1940s femme fatale: mysterious, sexually dangerous and potentially duplicitous (critics such as Scott Bukatman have noted how much she resembles the wronged Mildred Pierce, or the double-crossing character Phyllis Dietrichson from *Double Indemnity* (1944)). The down-beat voice-over narration of the original release, allowing Deckard to recall events that have already happened, is a device also borrowed from film noir and one that closes down the options for a happy ending (since the protagonist is always caught looking back mournfully). The moral ambiguity found in all the central characters is again a feature of film noir: trust, morality and the lines between good and evil, right and wrong are blurred in *Blade Runner*, as they are in films such as *Touch of Evil* (1958). Deckard, for example, kills replicants that he knows have not committed any real crime, and who also reflect his own psychosis. Deckard is a replicant, probably a Nexus-6, and so in essence one could argue that he is killing his own brothers and sisters.

But Deckard is, of course, also working class, just as in the same way that the noir's 'private eye' is also decidedly working class, at least in upbringing and biography. Conversely, in film noir, the femme fatale comes from good stock, new 'money' or has inherited money through marriage. In film noir, during the highly-charged relationships that emerge, one understands that the private eye is attracted to the femme fatale because she has 'class', and that she is attracted to the private eye because of his brute physicality and the belief that he can be easily duped/corrupted, simply because he lacks intelligence, education and breeding. The power relations that emerge between them, then, are class driven and it is this that is often the key to the mayhem and corruption that follows. The two are simply not meant to be together by virtue of their different class births or life choices. The private eye will not be duped or be fully complicit, and the femme fatale will not be easily tamed by him – and so 'someone' by the film's end (usually her) has to be punished for their class transgression.

In *Blade Runner*, Rachel seems to be the archetypal 'upper-class' femme fatale. Her position within the Tyrell Corporation is marked out as relatively high; she is 'close' to Tyrell (she is in fact his virtual/replicant daughter) and commands authority. She seductively enters the film dressed in high heels and a sharp, tight business suit and is framed in low-key light but with a halo effect around her. She paradoxically appears to be both a Madonna and a whore-type figure – dark and light at the same time – deliberately playing out, or so it seems, this contradiction so that Deckard will fall for her – as if this is what she thinks he wants; the promise of great sex with someone who is nonetheless pure. In this opening 'interrogation' scene, Rachel visually speaks the language of female sexual danger, literally and metaphorically blowing smoke rings around Deckard as he seeks to discover her true identity. But, as the film progresses and her true, replicant identity emerges, she also comes to be seen as 'honestly' pure, untouched and wanting only to be loved by Deckard.

Again, one can read this in class terms. Rachel is Tyrell's replicant/virtual daughter – she has actually been given his 'real' niece's memories from which to construct her past. As such, she is born of elite, ruling technocrat blood. By contrast, Deckard is either working class or, if he is a replicant, has been modelled on the attributes of a hard-bodied working-class male. Rachel and Deckard come from different (albeit simulated) stock, and the film plays these class differences out in a highly problematic way.

Deckard is given the stereotypical attributes of an abusive partner who dishes out 'violence' because he cannot handle or express his emotions in any other way. He becomes the film's archetypal working-class misogynist. Deckard cruelly proves to Rachel that she is a replicant by recalling to her two of her most secret memories (memories that have actually been implanted by Tyrell without her knowledge). The masculine/feminine knowledge/power in-equalities here leave her violated and distraught, and Deckard appears to gain some pleasure from this. Such violation takes a more perverse turn later on in the film when Deckard forces her to make love to him. This brutish encounter, although it quickly becomes consensual, suggests that Deckard believes that not only do women need heterosexual love to be complete, but also that co-ercion is a 'likeable' or necessary part of the experience.

He extends this type of 'violence' to all the female characters he comes into contact with, principally because they threaten his position as masculine male and because he does not know how to communicate with them in any other way. For example, Zhora, who takes work as an exotic dancer under the guise of Miss Salome, is the embodiment of Othered female sexuality. Deckard is both attracted to her and scared senseless by the thought of her. She is more woman than he is working-class, masculine man, and her panicked escape from Deckard through the city streets, dressed only in a see-through plastic mac and knee length boots, is meant to foreground her wanton ways and to give justification to the killer shot that she receives in the back from him.

Visually and stylistically *Blade Runner* has the look and feel of a film noir. The rain-soaked Los Angeles streets, the plot change from 'penthouse' apartments to inner-city hovels, the 1940s fashions, the long, lived-in trench coat worn by Deckard, and the low-tech interiors and concrete brick exteriors of many of the buildings all recall the bleak setting and dress codes of a classic film noir potboiler. The chiaroscuro lighting codes add to this effect. Shafts of light break through into dingy interiors and strike the sides of the characters' faces to suggest moral uncertainty or an embedded identity crisis. Deckard and Rachel first make love (although this starts out as a rape scene) in a low-key lit, sparse room, at the precise moment they are the least sure about one another. But this noir environment is also supported by parts of the Vangelis soundtrack: the saxophone/blues 'solos' that punctuate a number of the public/bar scenes reek of melancholy and loss, and reference the film as belonging to a down-beat past.

However, there is another key reference point for the film in terms of its tortured look and overall crisis-driven mood – a reference point that links film noir to German Expressionism and to Fritz Lang's *Metropolis*. In German Expressionist films the 'mood-image' functions as a pathetic fallacy, as a way of suggesting the pessimism of the world and the alienation of the central characters. Off-centre framing, shadowy lighting techniques, distorted and wrongly sized city/townscapes, long shots with little cutting, and the use of acute angles, lines and perspectives are all used to create the impression of a creeping dystopia. The seminal expressionist image for a city without a soul is found in *Metropolis* – on the surface a mechanical, metal clad sea of high-rises, but down below, beneath the ground, a slave camp where the faceless workers blindly work the machinery for their rich masters. If one was to graft Los Angeles 2019 onto the city of Metropolis they would, in some respects, be a perfect fit.

But not exactly. While Los Angeles 2019 is made up from the same high/low spatial metaphor as *Metropolis* (see Desser 1997), with the new power elites of scientists, technocrats and monopoly capitalists living high, and the unwashed, powerless masses living low, the perverse class politics of *Blade Runner* pathologises *all* social classes. In *Blade Runner*, the masses, no longer a potential revolutionary force as they are in *Metropolis*, are presented as responsible for their stupefaction – not physically repressed but ideologically so – suckers for bread and circuses. They live their lives in the shadow of Atari and Pan-Am advertising, and are told to dream of far away places, Off-World, as if this is enough (*and it is*) to keep them from seeing the poverty of their own lives in the material present. The ruling class are also free of a guiding, enlightening force that would change their oppressive ways. Tyrell is a depressing, all-devouring presence who is only counter-balanced in the film by the similarly 'dangerous' replicants.

However, *Blade Runner* also offers up a third version of social class in the form of the 'modern' middle class or the petit bourgeoisie. In the film, this class exists in the slipstream of commodity capitalism: running small entrepreneurial businesses such as bars, shops, a snake-making booth and Eye-works concern, to attain the all-important social and economic power that literally raises them up off the lower levels and puts them in touch with the advantages that the ruling elite hold. Deckard is again interesting in this respect. On the one hand, Deckard is allowed *material* access to this class through his position as Ace Cop: he has a mid-level apartment and certain cop privileges that remove him from the masses. On the other hand, Deckard is marked out as someone who *comes from* the masses – as someone who is intimately or biologically connected to the lower levels. In this respect, Deckard hates himself not only because he is continually reminded that he is 'low' but because the only way that he can achieve upward mobility – and climb higher – is through the brute force of his working-class masculinity. Of course, Deckard also hates the ruling elite, and so in every way he – and class as a social category – is cut adrift in the film.

Nobody appears to be home/at home in Los Angeles 2019. Along the lower levels population flows happen in tidal proportions, and people move like rats in a sewer, as various communication signs direct behaviour from one boundary-less destination to another. Along these rain- and neon-soaked corridors of decay and endless consumption, punks rub shoulders with Buddhist monks, debutantes and other marginal groups and outsiders. Spatially, the inner city appears to stretch out horizontally forever, so that it is only through vertical orientation that suburbia can be reached – in essence, the higher one lives the higher one's social standing or economic position. Suburbia is high in *Blade Runner* while the inner city low. But even in the stratosphere of Los Angeles, technocrats have lost sight of their humanity and are seen to live empty, messed-up lives.

Blade Runner clearly has a mixed (social) realist aesthetic at its centre. On one level, the references to gritty, urban genres such as film noir and the police detective film bear this relationship out, extending the metaphor of road building, construction and urban sprawl to their nightmarish limit. This is immediately represented through the crowded and media-saturated city space that is Los Angeles 2019. The film constantly returns the viewer to high, low and expansive shots of the Gothic/patchwork city as it belches flames, chokes on its own smog, and produces the discernible sense of an omnipresent decay that eats into the very fabric of the (lower) buildings. As Giuliana Bruno observes,

> the city of *Blade Runner* is not the ultramodern, but the postmodern city. It is not an orderly layout of skyscrapers and ultra-comfortable, hypermechanised interiors. Rather, it creates an aesthetic of decay, exposing the dark side of technology, the process of disintegration. (1990: 185)

Blade Runner is all about urban disintegration: the Earth is so over-populated and polluted that (wealthy white) people are encouraged, through adverts that adorn everything from spacecrafts to the sides of hi-rise buildings, to move to Off-World colonies. Advertising, consumer goods, media and consumer conglomerates fuel the economy and indoctrinate the populace. Anything can be bought and sold on the black market because the city itself has become one giant marketplace – a metaphoric Chinatown no less. The city is chaotic, crisis driven: made up at the lower levels of waste, acid rain, tumble-down dwellings, hovels, faceless racial Others, the lumpen proletariat, and a maze of dangerous side-streets. The city has been poisoned: turned over to a ruling class that has no concern for the welfare of the masses; and the masses, regulated and controlled via consumption, lead docile lives.

In *Blade Runner*, the city emerges as an 'affective power … a specific power to affect both people and materials – a power that modifies the relations between them' (Sobchack 1999: 124). The city works to instill a pervasive sense of alienation and loss, and to shape and define the motivations of the characters that live there. Los Angeles 2019 is largely an urban nightmare – a nightmare fleshed out of the materials of globalisation, capitalism, cyberpunk and noir, so that its neon and concrete veins and arteries appear clogged up and yet leaky, pouring despair and bilge onto its inhabitants.

Deckard is one of these despairing inhabitants; he eats fast food in the city, mopes about in the shadows there, and confronts and kills two of the replicants in its dislocated interiors (Deckard kills Zhora as she runs through a crowded shopping mall, the inner cathedral of capitalism, while Pris is killed in the decaying and deserted Bradbury building). In one sense, he chooses to part-live in the bowels of the city as if he paradoxically feels at home there. But Deckard is also at his most vulnerable in the lower levels: it does something damaging to his core being. The way the lower-level, street scenes are captured best illustrates this. Often shot with a hand-held camera, these lower levels feel threatening, unstable, crowded and claustrophobic. When Deckard is in the city this dislocated subjectivity appears to be his or at least as belonging to his, in part poisoned, point of view. What is the poison in Deckard's veins? It is his working-class origins, the barely conscious knowledge that he comes from the city, from the mindless mass of people who live there – it/they are his very closest relation – so this is his home, and the thought of it is tearing him up inside. This is why Deckard is also an inhabitant of the higher levels; he goes back to his apartment (to his old job, with cop privileges) to escape the filth and the squalor, to literally and metaphorically separate himself from the crowd 'down below'.

There is one key sequence in the film that best demonstrates Deckard's sense of class crisis and phobia. In Deckard's 'nameless' introduction sequence in the film, the camera finds him deliberately hiding in the background, as a constant stream of faceless people rush about madly in the pouring rain. At this moment of 'capture', Deckard is filmed in long shot, standing in the centre of a shop window that is ablaze with neon signs and filled with flickering television screens. He is keeping out of the way. The old trench coat that he wears and the general disheveled nature of his clothes suggest a vagrant-like status. He is also located in a grim (ghetto area) part of town, seemingly with nothing to do.

Deckard is reading a newspaper, eyes down. The connotations of this are complex. On the one hand, by reading a newspaper in a world of advertising-led audio-visual signs Deckard is being revealed as an educated man – interested in hard facts rather than the hard sell of the advertising blimps that cross the sky as he stands there. He immediately separates himself from his fellow low-level citizens who seem to be children of the hyperreal media revolution – only able to 'read' the advertising slogan and the brand name. As the advertising blimp crosses overhead, prophesising 'a new life awaits you' Off-World, Deckard gazes up at it, as if moving Off-World would be a potential escape for him, away from the squalor that he finds himself in. On the other hand, because of the way/where he is standing, he also seems to be 'plugged' into the neon signs and television terminals that are situated behind him. Symbolically, perhaps, Deckard is being connected to the very mass of people he is trying to remove himself from. His look to the blimp may be a mournful glance as if moving Off-World would be a familial death for him.

Later, in the same sequence, Deckard is 'arrested' – not for a crime or misdemeanor but because he is reluctant to take up his old job as a replicant killer. He is taken away in a police spinner. The last, 'exterior' shot that the viewer gets before the spinner lifts off, is filled with smoke, rain, noise, pollution, faceless people scurrying about, and 'vulgar' neon lights – in effect, all the motifs of social decay and dislocation. The shot is filthy, ugly and pregnant with disgust. One of the first signs that the viewer sees from the interior of the spinner, as it rises off the ground, is the word, flashing up on a monitor, 'purge'. The violent connotations that emerge from this juxtaposition are relatively clear: that what is indeed being left behind, on the lower levels, should be purged, purified, washed away with a terrible rain. An apocalyptic, holocaust-like credo is given momentary articulation in this scene. And given that Deckard is, albeit reluctantly, in the vehicle, he is being connected to or implicated in the disgust towards the docile crowd left on the ground. Given the high degree of subjectivity in the film, one can read that this is in fact Deckard's desire to purge what is below. However, Deckard's present in the spinner complicates such assumptions, not least because he is working class and from the city, and so belongs in or comes from the belly of the beast.

As the spinner takes off a series of interior and exterior shots are cut together so that Deckard and Gaff, the arresting officer, are observed flying (in) the spinner, and the camera watches them observing the metropolis from their aerial viewpoint. The higher the spinner flies the clearer, 'cleaner' and the more spectacular the scenery appears. Vast edifices and structures compete with one another for domination of the skyline, and the electric glow of adverts, spinners, free of pollution, smog and rain, radiate the scene so that it feels warmer, purer. The higher one goes, in fact, the better life appears precisely because it is free of people and their impoverished ways. The movement of the camera also changes: as the spinner approaches an unnamed police headquarters, the camera arcs and circles the building with near-balletic grace. Given the melodic, soft electronic tones of the Vangelis soundtrack that accompanies the flight, the whole journey becomes a musical refrain. In fact, there are clear visual echoes here to the classical musically-cued 'satellite' dance sequence in *2001: A Space Odyssey* (1968).

However, the whole scene remains troubled by Deckard's presence, not least because he continues to eat the noodles he had just bought prior to his arrest. Not only does this give him a laconic, take-it-as-it-comes attitude (he has just been arrested but does not seem to care), but the noodles link him back to the low-level space that he has just come from. By eating noodles from a street vendor, by bringing 'fast food' into the glowing technophilia of the upper levels, he is confirming his class origins – he could not be further removed from the electronic dance that goes on outside the spinner's cock-pit. Deckard belongs to the ghetto below and the world of mass consumption, even if he does not like it there or, perhaps, wishes that he did not like it so much.

BLADE RUNNER AS SOCIAL REALISM

In one direct way, one can make the link from *Blade Runner's* representation of the 'working class' back to a particular type of British social realist film in which, in particular, working-class men are stereotyped as misogynist, non-communicative brutes, and working-class spaces are marked out as pathological. In films such as *Kes* (1969), *Rita, Sue, and Bob too* (1986), *Naked* (1993) and *Nil by Mouth* (1997), the 'ghetto' areas in which the films are set literally produce men whose violence, drug addiction, alcoholism and criminal activities seem to stem from the lack of space, the lack of status that such environments carry with them. Two pivotal, recurring metonymic shots from these films concretise this. The first shot is an exterior, low-lit pan across high-rise council flats, or red-brick, back-to-back terraces, on a dull day. The shot suggests that life is drab here, and the lack of natural colours and the absence of organic textures (such as trees, green fields, or even grass) extends the metaphor that this is a harsh, unforgiving, concrete jungle that will and does swallow up its inhabitants. The second shot, a continuity cut, is an interior shot, supposedly within one of these flats or houses, where families are arguing, abusing one another or engaging in illegal acts. The interior lacks light, is poorly decorated and is overcrowded, with too many people living together in such a small space. The working-class men in these spaces are found to drink too much, quarrel too much, fight and fuck too much, and they resort to domestic violence to deal with their social/economic inadequacies. For want of a better metaphor, they are climbing up the walls.

In *Nil by Mouth* we are presented with a variation of this: an interior shot of one of the central protagonists stealing dope from his brother-in-law is followed by two exterior shots of what we presume to be these council flats on a dull, colourless night. The harsh vertical and horizontal lines of the blocks of flats 'slash' each of the frames, and because the camera remains still, again in both shots, there is a complete absence of the organic, the natural, to the representation. When the camera cuts back to the interior again, the brother-in-law appears and proceeds to bite the nose of the 'thief' – a family member. In this hostile environment, it is suggested, working-class men are nothing more or less than animals.

Blade Runner uses the exterior pan in a similar way, but not only for self-contained lower-level spaces such as that encountered in the 'purge' scene, but for the entire city, repeatedly photographed in long shot as a sprawling, heavy metal, Dante's Inferno. However, there is a third type of shot common to British social realism and *Blade Runner*. In films such as *Vroom* (1988) a space is created between the suffocating claustrophobia of the working-class ghetto and the 'semi-rural'. A character emerges from the city to stand on a hill and look back at what he has just left behind, a shot 'emblematic of the desire to escape the confines of the city' (Hill 1998: 169). Similarly, Deckard is able to look back on/at the city, not only in the police spinner but in his apartment, above the lower levels. When Deckard looks out across the city what he sees is a terrible confusion, a confusion that he feels at the core of his own dislocated working-class being, and a longing for a permanent way to escape this God-awful place.

BLADE RUNNER AS SCIENCE FICTION

Technophobia

In terms of iconography, *Blade Runner* has many of the visual trademarks of the science fiction film. Flying cars or 'spinners' move menacingly across the landscape. 'Trafficators' direct the flow of traffic and people. Advertising 'blimps' hover above the city promoting a better life 'Off-World'. Elements of the cityscape are nightmarishly futuristic. In the city, it constantly pours with acid rain and the sun is, in part, blotted out because of the pollution. There is no discernible difference between night and day in *Blade Runner*. People use neon tubes in their umbrellas to light their way and identify themselves. The media are an omnipresent force – one cannot go anywhere in Los Angeles 2019 without media technology shaping one's behaviour. In short, in one clear sense the entire *mise-en-scène* of *Blade Runner* speaks the visual language of dystopian science fiction. But, on a sonic level too, the futuristic synth score by Vangelis anchors the technophobic visual field of the film. The haunting electronic pulse of the soundtrack adds semiotic weight to the dystopian images and settings that hold the film together. At key moments, in fact, the music almost seems to weep into the film.

In *Blade Runner* the growth of technology has resulted in a future where nature and the natural has nearly been entirely snuffed out. Media technologies blast out from every street corner transmitting adverts, travel directions, warnings, news bulletins, whilst engaging in the most pervasive, all-seeing form of surveillance. There are very few private, technology-free spaces in *Blade Runner* so that inhabitants are unable to be 'natural' because they are under constant watch. In fact, technology even invades their dreams through memory implants (Deckard's dream of the unicorn being a key moment in the Director's Cut, revealing, as it probably does, his replicant status).

Techno-science has produced a 'superior' form of human life in terms of the Nexus-6 and bio-tech corporations rule, so it seems, the entire planet, not least because all geographical borders seem to have been eroded in the film. Not only do unmarked cyborgs walk the city streets but cyberpets and genetically-engineered life-forms populate people's homes. Sky-rises pay homage to the most advanced form of civil engineering, and flying forms of transportation make all vertical and horizontal forms of space accessible and therefore crowded (or anyway teeming with technology since, at times, Los Angeles 2019 is empty of people, at least on the upper levels). When Deckard is first taken up in the 'spinner', level after level of this technologically crowded metropolis is revealed like a never-ending trail of signals and transmissions. Consequently, in this supra-mechanical Los Angeles 2019, not one blade of grass grows, not one glorious dawn rises, and not one natured landscape appears on the near horizon. In essence, then, the film is deeply technophobic and pitches the technological against the natural in a relationship that calls out for the beauty of the country – precisely Rachel and Deckard's exit point in the original release of the film.

Again, the intertextual relay to British social realism is clear here. Rachel and Deckard want to escape the city, its class-driven divisions and their own class differences, and the utopian space of the rural is where they dream of going. The desire to find the real, the authentic, the 'semi-rural', then, is a desire to escape the class position that limits and labels one within the confines of the artificial city. In the British social realist film, *Saturday Night and Sunday Morning* (1960), the central character, Arthur Seaton, hates his blue-collar job and the lack of opportunity that his working-class background brings him. He sleeps around, drinks heavily, rages against his own identity, but he also retreats to the semi-rural (fishing in the canal) to find a space away from the crushing limits of the inner-city and his working-class origins. In fact, the ending to the film is not that dissimilar to the 1982 ending to *Blade Runner*. Arthur and his girlfriend stand on a hill just above a new development of houses: one of which they may move into. He throws a stone at the development board, while remembering the freedom these fields had given him as a kid. Arthur is all-too-aware that if he sacrifices the rural for the domestic and the city he will sacrifice his freedom and confirm his place in the lower ranks of the social order.

However, *Blade Runner*'s technophobia is connected to a more fundamental and reductive class politics. The film does not *fear* technology – in fact in some respects one can argue that it is in love with it – but fears what technology *does* to the (uncritical) mass population. The film does not *hate* technology but the way it has been put to use by the ruling elite in the film. In one sense, the film seems to adopt the determinist Marxist position that was outlined by Theodor Adorno and Max Horkheimer in the late 1940s (ironically the time in which *Blade Runner* is metaphorically set). Adorno and Horkheimer (1993) argued that the new cultural industries (technologies) of cinema, advertising and television would render the masses passive. They would become fully indoctrinated by the false promise of a happy life sold to them through the conservative narratives of Hollywood cinema and the ubiquitous adverts that were springing up everywhere. In their apocalyptic vision of class relations, the mass of the population would become docile and fully obedient in the face of the dream networks circulated by these cultural industries. *Blade Runner* clearly adopts this position: and the pill-popping Geisha girls who adorn the sides of the high-rises best capture the sense that the mass are firmly 'chewing' on the opiate of modern consumption and the fantasies of the mass media.

In terms of *Blade Runner*'s class-inflected technophobia, the ruling techno-crats, scientists and monopoly capitalists are as much, if not more, to blame. They have fostered this 'aesthetic of (mediated) decay', made it possible (commanded) that technology and techno-science has reached into all areas of life, to the extent that the lines between human and machine, the real and the manufactured have blurred, creating the terrifying schizophrenia that hangs over the entire film. In *Blade Runner*, simulation and the synthetic reach into all areas of social life. Surveillance and media devices are everywhere – in fact one only really knows that one is human through an electronic emotional response test. The geneticist J. F. Sebastian surrounds himself with cyberpets and suffers from 'accelerated decrepitude', a wasting disease that ages him prematurely – as if he is himself a genetic experiment gone wrong. The towering Tyrell Corporation building is a mock Egyptian edifice and overlooks the *image* of the Egyptian pyramids. In this glass house, Dr Tyrell has forgotten what it means to be human: in his pursuit for scientific knowledge and economic power he has become the one true unfeeling, arch-rationalist in the film – an embodied tyrannical machine.

The film taps into real fears about techno-science, globalisation, population flows, media manipulation and environmental catastrophe that were in circulation at the time of the film's release. The 1980s were a time of media corporate take-overs that saw the rise, for example, of the Murdoch media empire. The first stories about the hole in the ozone layer appeared, and recurrent fears about genetic engineering found their way into the press. Asia was imagined to be an economic and cultural threat to the hegemony of the West with the emergence of Sony and Honda as super-companies. Migration and immigration were seen as threats to national identity (in Britain, the then Prime Minister, Margaret Thatcher, referred to immigration as a 'swamping' problem).

But there were also fears about an unwieldy, unionised working class wrecking havoc, particularly in Britain. The Conservative Thatcher Government had come to power in 1979 with a mission to both change the culture of the working class (make them more individualistic and possession-orientated) and to crush those elements that were resistant to change (like the miners). A similar position was occurring in the US with Ronald Reagan adopting a far-right political agenda with regards to welfare, employment law and individual enterprise. In *Blade Runner*, the autocrat/tyrant Tyrell is not that far removed from Thatcher/Reagan in terms of a desire to control and indoctrinate the masses, and the working class are not that far removed from those who bought into this ideology, abandoning political consciousness for ownership, in the British context, of their council houses and the 'loadsamoney' ideology of the time. Similarly, the entrepreneurs and the small business people of the film are the 'children' of Thatcher's enterprise culture, drunk on the rewards of individualistic endeavour.

However, *Blade Runner* does also pay homage to technology in the film. In fact, the 'natural' is in some respects intimately connected to the technological, mechanical and the engineered. One can argue that 'nature' is not found outside the city, but above the city, in the people-free spaces of hyper-technology. The glistening blimps and the incandescent oil fields have an organic, life-like quality. One can also argue that 'nature' is not found in humankind but in the replicants who become associated with the natural. In effect, *Blade*

Runner complicates the relationship between technology and nature, collapsing to a degree the binary opposition between them. Again, as I will go onto argue, social class sits at the centre of these textual articulations.

Technophilia

Blade Runner has clear elements of *technophilia*, or a love for showing and displaying the operations and functions of the technological as it impacts on everyday life in Los Angeles 2019. The spinner's inaugural flight over the city is so captured that as it disappears into the distance the 'glitter' washes over the spinner, as if it is merging with the electronic circuits of the city in a moment of perfect unison. Visually, in amongst the smog and burning oil fires there is a luminous beauty that emanates from the neon signs, advertising blimps, the mechanical toys, the spinners and trafficators and the re-engineered Mayan and Egyptian edifices. *Blade Runner* is wonderful to look at, conjured up from (then) state-of-the-art special effects – effects that in part create an awe of and for the technologies used to texture this future-past world.

But the technophiliac elements of the film, as already briefly discussed, are only centrally foregrounded when people/real people are absent from the frame. Through attributed and non-attributed point of view shots, and 'master' shots of the city, technology reveals itself in all its splendour when all traces of humanity have been effaced (or simulated). This is because, in terms of the film's message system, people, tainted by their class position, would pollute what is in effect the only true vision of 'purity' in the film. While characters such as Deckard are allowed to stare at this utopian vision of a productive technology, they cannot enter its space without catastrophic consequences, because by doing so they would bring with them their own destructive (working-class) tendencies. When Deckard enters the Tyrell ziggurat, or Sebastian enters Tyrell's bedroom, chaos and destruction eventually follows.

Of course, looking, being seen or not seeing what is really there, is also central to the film's narrative trajectory and subject positioning. These technologies of seeing – electronic eyes, scanners, photographic cameras, retina devices and so on – are everywhere in the film, and they produce a layered gaze or a type of miraculous vision. When one looks or is looked at (penetrated) in the film there is a beauty to the gaze employed, but this is ultimately a terrifying beauty that one cannot escape from. No matter how often Deckard stands on that 'hill', no matter how many times he retreats to the shadows, or looks up to the skies, he will be caught in the city's panoptic field of vision and his 'working-class' origins will be confirmed again, and again and again.

Technophobia/Technophilia

Blade Runner, then, to advance the argument a little further, offers the viewer a simultaneous technophobic/technophiliac dichotomy. From the opening panoramic long shot of a brooding futuristic LA, the audience is treated to a visual extravaganza in which spectacle and display dominate the screen and stimulate the pleasures on offer. *Blade Runner* functions in terms of awe and wonder, but this is also tinged with melancholy and introspection since the *Blade Runner's* city is a paradoxical ugly/beautiful place. We are asked to marvel at the technological textures in the (high) spaces of the city but also to recoil at what the ruling class have done with this technology, commodifying and pacifying the masses in the lower levels; and what the masses have done to themselves by letting such technologies get into their veins. It is in and through the embodiment of the replicants that such issues are further played out.

The replicants are often the only characters to be situated in contexts where human values and images of the natural are present. The rebel replicants are an imagined family unit, and the only extended family in the film. They look out for one another: they are immensely loyal to one another, embodying the cultural axiom that blood is thicker than water. Of course, the idea of a strong union has clear echoes to working-class solidarity and resistance, and so their rebellion/uprising has clear connections to worker (slave) revolt. They have come to Earth for a showdown with the boss/creator.

The impression that the replicants are connected with nature is also supported by images that suggest the human and the natural belong with and to the replicants. As Scott Bukatman notes (1997: 40) we see Deckard bleed into his clear glass of vodka; when Pris dies her tongue drops out of her mouth only to be caressed by Batty, in a scene of real human tragedy and emotional intensity. Batty dies in a downpour talking of 'tears in rain'. More systematically, water, rain, tears, and water-based reflections bathe or wash the replicants to give the impression that they are made up from or connected to natural sources – touched, one might say, by the heavens at the moment they open. Although, in *Blade Runner*, this rain is poisoned with acid, caused by *human* pollution, so water is eating into or away at the electronic circuitry beneath the replicants' human skin – killing them because it is not pure water – and it will not or cannot actually let them be real humans. These replicants, nonetheless, have come to Earth to secure their freedom – to become real humans, to taste real human rain.

In *Blade Runner*, the Nexus-6 androids or replicants are virtually identical to humans. However, they have been given near super-human powers in terms of strength and agility, and their intellectual capacity matches the genetic engineers who created them, making them also intellectually superior to most humans. They are in effect (or should be) shining beacons for the triumph of genetic engineering. But what have they been created for in the film? To be 'used as slave labour, in the hazardous exploration and colonisation of other planets'.

One can read this entire 'encounter' as an allegory about class conflict and class relations. The 'unionised' replicants are really 'the salt of the earth', connected to the natural/earth by virtue of their manual labour. They only want what is rightfully theirs – a fair wage, a say in their destiny, a degree of respect. Their alienated and impoverished lives (as slaves) are slowly killing them and so they join together to resist the oppression they face. The 'factory' boss (Tyrell) listens to their demands but argues that they have been given enough already. This 'paying lip service' to their demands makes matters only worse. Their leader, Batty, ultimately wants control of the whole business – he wants to be (his own) boss. Class conflict thus becomes open warfare. The boss wants the revolt put down and he calls in the police (Deckard), fellow workers, in effect, but ones who support the status-quo and their privileged position within it. Violence and murder ensues and, to a degree, all parties are to blame for their sickly greed and intransigence. Deckard occupies an uncomfortable position in this relationship: he is a world-weary cop desperate to escape both his working-class origins and the job that forces him to execute his comrades (his brothers and sisters). He despises Tyrell but considers the replicants to be dysfunctional – he can have no pact with them either.

Both the replicants and the ruling elite are ultimately shown to be pathological in *Blade Runner*. Murder, deceit and a wilful disregard for others *less than them* mark them out as uncaring, savage brutes (much like Deckard, then). In the case of Batty this is played out in and through his increasing delusions of and pretensions to be a messianic, Christ-like figure. Near the end of the film, Batty dies an implicitly religious death: half-dressed as if in a loincloth, he 'saves' Deckard from an early/earthly death, puts a nail through his palm, and at the moment of his own death releases a white dove into the heavens.

In *Blade Runner* there is an over-arching and insipid class-based identity crisis, a crisis that seems to touch everything and everyone in the film. Los Angeles 2019 is made up from a patchwork of styles and fads: it has no geographical centre, no 'original' past to refer to, no secure history to be bound to, and no concrete present that would allow communities to foster. In one sense this is why the replicants, including Deckard, are drawn to its quarters – they share, imitate, and can plug into its schizophrenic state. But the relationship or correspondence is one borne out of the most despairing search for difference – all anyone really wants in the film is a place, a history, a personal biography to call their own.

The world-weary Deckard best represents this: his goal-driven pursuit of the replicants and his love affair with Rachel is really a journey into his own (working-class) heart of darkness. His real quest is a quest to discover his origins, to find the truth about who he really is and where he comes from. Of course, in *Blade Runner*, Deckard *is* home (these are his origins) but he nonetheless feels desperately homeless. By the end of the film Deckard and Rachel may have found 'love' together but their time is short. Their class transgression means that they can only have a limited life-span. Together, they only have the time to die.

NOTES

1   Parts of this chapter are modified from section of *Studying Blade Runner* (2003) Leighton Buzzard: Auteur.

2   David Harvey has written about *Blade Runner*'s class politics in Brooker and Brooker (1997). Harvey and I come to a similar conclusion: *Blade Runner* fails to offer up a progressive or radical view of class solidarity. However, I see this emerging in and through the film's general phobia and pathology of class.

POSTMODERN ROMANCE: THE IMPOSSIBILITY OF (DE)CENTRING THE SELF
NICK LACEY

Blade Runner is often treated as an exemplary postmodern text (for example, see Sobchack 1987; Bruno 1990; Boozer Jr. 1997; Hill 1998) but it, along with science fiction films that followed such as *Dark City* (1998), *The Truman Show* (1999), *The Matrix* (1999) and *Vanilla Sky* (2001) celebrated (humanist) romantic love as the core of the human condition and the antidote to a 'paranoid world'. This does not square with the postmodern view of what it means to be human:

> The posthuman view considers consciousness regarded as the seat of human identity in the Western tradition ... as an evolutionary upstart trying to claim that it is the whole show when in actuality it is only a minor sideshow ... the posthuman view thinks of the body as the original prostheses we all learn to manipulate, so that extending or replacing the body with other prostheses becomes a continuation of a process that began before we were born ... by these, and other means, the posthuman view configures human being so that it can be seamlessly articulated with intelligent machines. In the posthuman, there are no essential differences of absolute demarcations between bodily existence and computer simulation, cybernetic mechanism and biological organism, robot teleology and human goals. (Hayles 1999: 2–3)

Blade Runner ultimately 'fails' to offer this view of the posthuman because it was a production of mainstream cinema. Whilst some elements of postmodernism can be incorporated extremely successfully into mainstream films, only films with an independent sensibility are able to fully represent the disturbing – to the bourgeoisie – posthuman. As we shall see, this is because the ideals of romantic love are central to patriarchal society's needs.

However *Blade Runner* does offer a posthuman view of the replicants. In Batty's final moments, when he saves Deckard, he becomes human because of his behaviour and his realisation that his life was worth living. This is in stark contrast with the androids in the source novel, Philip K. Dick's *Do Androids Dream of Electric Sheep?* (1968), who exist on the emotional level of a washing machine (though Dick did often have empathetic machines in his work).[1] The argument as to whether Deckard was also a replicant appeared to be ended with the Director's Cut of the film because of his dream of the unicorn. However, as I have argued elsewhere (Lacey 2000) the 'dream sequence' is not formally signified as such (by a dissolve accompanied by a strumming harp, for example) and he does not appear to fall asleep. If this is read as Eisensteinean montage the unicorn actually becomes symbolic of Deckard.[2]

However, regardless as to whether he is a 'flesh and blood' human, Deckard finds absolution in a romance with Rachel.

Blade Runner is postmodern only up to a point. Before examining in what ways the film 'fails' to fully represent the postmodern view of the human condition it is necessary to sketch out how the film is successfully postmodern.

In Marxist terms Deckard is alienated: he is forced to hunt replicants and gets no pleasure from his work. In addition, he drinks too much and his initial attempts at seducing Rachel borders on rape. Deckard is world-weary and the world is hellish. Postmodernism denies the possibility of alienation, just as it rejects meta-narratives such as Marxism, because that 'presupposes a coherent rather than a *fragmented* sense of self from which to be alienated' (Harvey 1989: 53; emphasis added). In postmodern terms Deckard is schizophrenic:

> Lacan describes schizophrenia as a breakdown in the signifying chain, that is, the interlocking syntagmatic series of signifiers which constitutes an utterance or a meaning ... If we are unable to unify the past, present and future of the sentence, then we are similarly unable to unify the past, present and future of our own biographical experience of psychic life. (Jameson 1991: 26–7)

The postmodern world is at the 'end of history' and is as fragmented as the beings that inhabit it. LA's architecture, in 2019, is as eclectic as the racial make up of its inhabitants. Old buildings are recycled (retrofitted); instead of being demolished they are 'up-dated' by being built upon. The city is also postmodern because it is, at once, over-crowded and deserted and there is an emphasis on spectacle at the expense of an explanation as to why the world has become an ecological disaster.

Spectacle is, obviously, important in *Blade Runner* from the very first shot, which approaches the Tyrell corporation headquarters. It could be argued that the spectacle represents postmodernism's obsession with surface gloss rather than explanatory depth because the film does not explain why the world of L.A., in 2019, is continually dark, exhibits a peculiar mix of architecture and is populated mostly by non-WASPs. In addition, surface gloss is characteristic of Ridley Scott's *mise-en-scène* except, perhaps, in *Alien* (1979) where the setting is shown as a convincing space mixing the pristine high-tech with dank 'cellar' spaces. On the other hand 'spectacle and speculation'[3] is typical of science fiction and the genre's readers are used to piecing together a society from clues dropped throughout a narrative; so there is little difficulty in working out that an ecological disaster has occurred and anyone with money (the 'missing' WASPs of the city) is Off-World.

Blade Runner's postmodern credentials are also emphasised by its influence on the development of cyberpunk, a sub-genre of science fiction spawned as a hybrid of it, film noir and 'hard-boiled' detective novels which Fredric Jameson has called the 'supreme *literary* expression if not of postmodernism, than of late capitalism itself' 1991: 419). Further, Scott Bukatman notes:

> *Blade Runner*'s cyberpunk urbanism exaggerates the presence of the mass media, evoking sensations of unreality and pervasive spectacle: advertising 'blimps' cruise above the buildings ... and gigantic vid-screens dominate the landscape with images of pill-popping geishas. (1997: 49)

Notoriously, in the original cut, Deckard and Rachel appear to escape to the countryside (outtakes from *The Shining* (1980) tacked on by anxious producers who were panicked by the uncomprehending preview audiences' responses). The sudden appearance of 'nature', for many, accompanied by the revelation that Rachel had no 'incept' date, made a mockery of the film. Both Deckard and Rachel are redeemed by their love, which enables them to escape from their predicaments. In the Director's Cut this escape is undermined by the final shot, a black screen after the lift door closes.

While there is no reason not to discuss *Blade Runner* as an exemplary postmodern film, why does it lapse into the 'liberal humanist' view of the subject by celebrating romantic love? As noted above, other films that picked up the themes of *Blade Runner* also eulogise heterosexual romance.

Dark City ends with John Murdoch (Rufus Sewell) using his god-like powers to destroy the alien Strangers, as he brings light to the city and rescues Anna/Emma (Jennifer Connelly). Truman (Jim Carrey), of *The Truman Show*, is motivated to leave his fabricated world by his love for Lauren/Sylvia (Natasha McElhone) though, narratively, this is unresolved as the final shot sees Truman step into the darkness of the real world. *The Matrix* requires Trinity (Carrie-Anne Moss) to save Thomas Anderson/Neo (Keanu Reeves) with a kiss (a situation reversed in *The Matrix Reloaded* (2003)). In *Vanilla Sky* David Aames (Tom Cruise) is redeemed by Sofia's (Penelope Cruz) love, though as this only occurs in a virtual world it could be argued that the film is suggesting that romance is a dream.

In *Abre los Ojos* (*Open Your Eyes*, 1997) – of which *Vanilla Sky* is a remake – when the Aames character, Cesar (Eduardo Noriega), conjures up Sofia (Cruz again) for 'one last farewell' she does not know who she is, unlike in the Hollywood version which portrays the 'sweet sadness' of goodbye. In the first version Sofia stands, arms hugging herself against the cold, and, when asked by Cesar who she is, replies 'I don't know'.

It is notable that three of these films have characters with dual identities casting into doubt the primacy of the (modernist) ego. This split identity can also be found in recent, consciously postmodern, non-science fiction films such as *Suzhou le* (*Suzhou River*, 2000) and *Lucia y el sexo* (*Sex and Lucia*, 2001). The postmodern subject does not consist of the modernist binary opposition: 'The apparent mind/body dichotomy is superseded by the trichotomy of mind/body/machine (Bukatman 1990: 203). Of the above characters, Lauren/Sylvia, Anderson/Neo and Sofia owe part of their existence to technology; the first being the television programme, the other two to virtual worlds. Drawing on Baudrillard, Scott Bukatman characterises this postmodern identity as 'terminal identity':

It has fallen to science fiction to repeatedly narrate a new subject that can somehow directly interface with – and master – the cybernetic technologies of the Information Age ... This new subjectivity is at the centre of *Terminal Identity*. (1993: 2)

Blade Runner investigates this identity through the characters of the replicants who are cyborgs, technologically created beings that are, in part, made of human flesh; but the film allows love to offer transcendence. This contrasts with the films of David Cronenberg whose films are littered with examples of terminal identity: see *Videodrome* (1983), *The Fly* (1986), *Crash* (1996) and *eXistenZ* (1999) (he also deals with schizophrenia in *Spider* (2002)). Of these *Crash* is particularly interesting as an adaptation of J. G. Ballard's novel of 1973, a work that dealt with the melding of humans and technology through car crashes and offers a representation of the antithesis of bourgeois romantic love.

By naming the protagonist James Ballard, the author suggests the novel is autobiographical. However the events of the book are so bizarre that they are obviously not meant to represent actuality. Rather, through the central character's name, Ballard highlights the issue of identity as an important theme of the work. His novel predates cyberpunk by ten years, at a time when computing power could not readily create virtual worlds. However, the union of technology and flesh is evident: 'How could I bring her to life – ramming one of these massive steel plugs into a socket at the base of her spine?' (1973: 40). Ballard also offered an early insight into the postmodern subject when referring to Vaughan, who is bent upon an erotic destruction in a car crash. The character Ballard says: 'Am I under his thumb? No. But it's difficult to know where the centre of his personality is' (1973: 115).

The central characters in *Crash* are all decentred, a point accentuated by the actors' performances in Cronenberg's films. Only James Spader, as Ballard, shows conventional reactions to events, and even these are subdued. For example, when Vaughan (Elias Koteas) forces Ballard's wife, Catherine (Deborah Kara Unger), off the road in her car, Ballard looks *momentarily* concerned. Conventionally a husband's reaction would be extreme anxiety followed rapidly by anger. Cronenberg stated:

In *Crash*, I'm looking at people trying to create a new morality. They realise that the old forms of love and sexuality aren't working for them. So they're actively trying to create new ones ... There's a growing refusal to be bound by the apparent limits of what the body is. There's an attempt to transcend it by transforming it – transmutation. (Quoted in Sirius 1997)

This transformed morality is both suggested by the characters' actions and their reactions to events. The characters appear to lack passion, their reaction to events is subdued their acts of sexual intercourse (the apotheosis of bourgeois secular passion) are mechanical and never appear to satisfy them ('maybe next time...' is spoken both at the beginning and end of the film). In order to convey the 'other worldliness', or even 'inhumanity', of their actions the characters must be conceived unconventionally.

Richard Dyer (1979) suggested that the novelistic conception of character consisted of the following:

a) particularity – the character is unique rather than typical;
b) interest – the particularity of characters makes them interesting;
c) autonomy – characters have a 'life of their own', they are not blatantly a function of the plot;
d) roundness – characters possess a multiplicity of traits rather than one or two which 'types', or flat characters, possess;
e) development – characters should develop in the narrative; they learn from experience;
f) interiority – characters have an interior life; this might be shown by giving access to their intrapersonal communication and, again, emphasises their particularity;
g) motivation – there are clear psychological reasons for characters' actions, often derived from their particularity;
h) discrete identity – the character must be signed to exist beyond the text in which they appear, in other words, they usually have a past and a future beyond the text;
i) consistency – while characters must develop, they must also possess a central core, an ego-identity, that does not change.

The novel is a quintessential bourgeois form (see Watt 2000) and this description of character represents the bourgeois ideal of the individual. However, even the most 'literary' of novels are almost certain to use types (see point 'a') for secondary characters; and mainstream cinema is likely to be populated wholly by types. These types offer a shortcut to novelistic characters. For example:

> To refer 'correctly' to someone as a 'dumb blonde', and to understand what is meant by that, implies a great deal more than hair colour and intelligence. It refers immediately to *her* sex, which refers to her status in society, her relationship to men, her inability to behave or think rationally, and so on. In short, it implies knowledge of a complex social structure. (Perkins 1979: 139)

Whether novelistic or types, characters in films usually act in an understandable fashion suggesting (even if they are psychotic!) a coherent ego. This, however, is undermined by *Crash* as the film's characters do not appear to be 'autonomous' but are rather gripped by obsessions that dominate their lives. Ballard's and Catherine's encounters with Vaughan seem to drive them toward their own destruction so if they are learning from experience it is a lesson about the death wish. We are given no access to the character's interior lives and so cannot understand their motivations. This lack of an interior life casts doubt on them having a coherent central core.

> On a balcony overlooking jammed motorways, James and Catherine Ballard compare notes on the day's sexual encounters: 'how was work today darling?' is replaced by the equally perfunctory 'who did you fuck at work today, darling?', and shortly followed by the question, 'Did you come?' Sex becomes the same dull daily grind as work: a banal, repetitive, mundane event absorbed in the pleasure principle of the productive and consumptive economy. (Botting & Wilson 1998: 186)

The characters are ciphers, both in the senses of being a 'non-entity' and a puzzle. And in their desire for, and actual fusion with cars (including having car insignias tattooed on themselves) they are seeking to be cyborgs.

> Cronenberg asks us to consider the nature of desire in the postindustrial, postmodern age. Desire represents the opposite of the Romantic ideal of truth, beauty and wholeness; the postmodern desiring subject yearns for an experience marked by crash culture – division, simulation, brutality, obscenity, perversity, death … Flesh melts into chrome, wounds open, technology links sex to cold smooth surfaces and metallic limbs. (Creed 1998: 175–6)

The reception of the film was particularly interesting in Britain as its release coincided with a General Election and was used, by the *Daily Mail* amongst others, as an example of the right wing's belief that society was 'going to the dogs', a process that would be accentuated if Labour won the election. In a detailed examination of the film's reception Martin Barker, Jane Arthurs and Ramaswami Harindranath conclude:

> We are convinced that [the] anti-formulaic quality in the film explains the extremity of many responses – people were simply confused, and surprised, by what they saw. (2001: 5).

The authors show how it is difficult to read the film generically (the opening three scenes all show sexual intercourse but the film is patently not pornography). Added to the difficulty in understanding the characters' motivations, the film resists conventional, and therefore bourgeois, understanding on multiple levels. The mix of adultery and homosexual sex also works against bourgeois morality. It was this that particularly upset that repository of reactionary values, the *Daily Mail*:

> As evidence of [the film's] perverted morality, the reader's attention [was] drawn to the fact that 'the initially heterosexual characters lose their inhibitions [and] they experiment pleasurably with gay sex, lesbian sex, and sex with cripples.' (Kermode & Petley 1997: 16)

In the Hollywood films mentioned above, heterosexual union cements the narrative's closure. Whilst this union is usually *the* narrative closure in melodramas and romantic comedies, many other generic films also include a romance between the male protagonist and, in Proppian terms, the female helper and/or princess. Vladimir Propp stated that function 31 of his schema for folktales was 'the hero is married and ascends the throne' (1968: 63). Narratives do not require the 'legitimacy' of marriage; Propp noted five variants of this (1968: 64), two of which did not include marriage. It is the typical (heterosexual) coupling that works against the postmodern grain.

So why should mainstream cinema, when it has so thoroughly embraced the postmodern aesthetic in many other ways, eschew the de-centred self and recycle the myth of romantic love? Jameson (1991) suggests that postmodernism is the expression of late capitalism and so remains, at least in part, a bourgeois aesthetic. This is particularly true of the 'end of history' and 'death of metanarratives' aspects of postmodernism as these suggest that the world cannot be changed and we are stuck with the bourgeois hegemony.

As the *Screen* theorists of the 1970s were fond of noting, bourgeois ideology strives to give the illusion of wholeness. In the terms of Jacques Lacan, unified human subjects are impossible as their subjectivity is formed at the mirror stage and is forever divorced from itself: 'hence Lacan's comment that loving is giving what one does not have' (Lapsley & Westlake 1988: 70).

In the symbolic realm of (film) language, this wholeness is possible and can be provided by the representation of love. Bourgeois romance is predicated upon the perfect heterosexual match, which may be 'love at first sight', or not, but requires the individuals to know one another. This is impossible in a postmodern romance because the individual subject does not have a fixed identity. In *Blade Runner* the replicants rely upon their fabricated memories and photographs to give them a sense of their past and, therefore, a sense of identity: 'Rachel, seeing Deckard's photographs of his family ... tries to integrate with them. She puts her hair in the style of the photographs, plays the piano as if in a picture' (Harvey 1990: 312).

The replicants' obsession with a past they never had, mirroring Deckard's peculiarly old-fashioned pictures on his piano (suggesting they too are not 'real'), is an attempt to overcome their schizophrenic state. They literally have no childhood to give ballast to their identity and their future is extremely limited – hence their quest for 'more life' – so they are forced to live in a continual present.

However because Batty strives to give meaning to this continuous present through his search for his maker (in order to get more life), which obviously has religious overtones, and in his romantic passion for Pris, he falls into the 'bourgeois trap' of seeking individual fulfilment to his life.

We can see that 'romantic love' is of central importance to bourgeois society through its idealisation of monogamy. This 'ideal' state of romance is primarily to the detriment of women: 'Engels believed that monogamy ... was central to the decline of women's power. Monogamy evolved to ensure paternity' (Fisher 1992: 283). In a polygamous society the identity of a parent can only be certain on the mother's side and so the family line must be passed down the female side. However in a capitalist society, with its inherited private property, patriarchy needs to know the identity of their children; hence the importance of monogamy.

In addition, capitalism suggests that it can fulfil all our psychic needs, through consumerism. Self-realisation is attained through parenthood and career development (which is becoming increasingly important to females). Postmodernism 'knows' that the de-centred subject can never make he/she/itself whole. In this postmodernism reveals the contradictions inherent in capitalism. Our needs can only be fulfilled through consumerism. However, we must never stop consuming, so our needs can never be fulfilled. So while capitalism can exploit postmodernism's ahistoricism and surface gloss for commercial purposes, it cannot embrace the fragmented posthuman – for then we might realise that there's no point behaving like a consumer because it cannot make us whole.

Most cinema is bourgeois in nature (in terms of its modes of representation and its ideological content) and this is particularly true of Hollywood. It is therefore no surprise that, when film is primarily a commodity, that bourgeois values will be the structuring influence (though 'active' readers can create subversive films out of the these bourgeois constructs). Hollywood movies work, primarily, to entertain and so require the unification of narrative resolution (regularly accompanied by heterosexual union). It is therefore difficult for mainstream cinema to fully represent the postmodern de-centred subject, as romance is impossible for de-centred selves.

Crash, on the other hand, though distributed by Columbia Tristar in a number of countries, is essentially an independent production. Add to that Cronenberg's artistic sensibility (which is in tune with Ballard's) and it becomes possible to offer subversive representations of the self. Of course, such generalisations do not hold up in every case. For example, 20th Century Fox co-produced *Solaris* (2002), a film made possible by the 'industry clout' of Steven Soderbergh and George Clooney.

At a therapy session early in the film, presided over by Kelvin (Clooney), a character makes a 'postmodern statement': 'the more I see the images the less real I feel…' Dylan Thomas's 'And Death Shall Have No Dominion' informs the film's themes and suggests a humanist view of life: 'Though lovers be lost love shall not.' However the *mise-en-scène* suggests otherwise. The film ends, as it begins, with a bewildered Kelvin who may simply be a manifestation of his memory recreated by the planet Solaris.

Jonathan Eig, however, noted a trend in contemporary Hollywood to offer surprises about the identity of the central characters; for example in *The Sixth Sense* (1999), *Fight Club* (1999), *Memento* (2000), *Mulholland Dr.* (2001) and *Donnie Darko* (2001). These 'mindfuck' movies lead audiences to ask: 'Who can I trust to tell me the truth about my own identity?' (Eig 2003).

Only *The Sixth Sense*, of these films, can be considered to be a mainstream Hollywood film; though *Fight Club* was produced by 20th Century Fox it was clearly an 'aberration' that led, indirectly, to studio boss Bill Mechanic losing his job. *The Sixth Sense* offers a clear narrative resolution that hinges, in part, upon Crowe's (Bruce Willis) love of his wife. Eig also considers *A Beautiful Mind* (2001) within this group: however, in this film the 'split' identity is clinical (that is, he is medically schizophrenic) and love 'saves the day'.

The independently produced films, on the other hand, do represent identity as decentred. In *Memento* Leonard Selby (Guy Pearce), whose memory only lasts a few minutes so he literally has to inscribe what he knows onto his body, does not know whether he is Sammy Jankis or whether he is setting himself up to murder people. *Mulholland Dr.* takes us into typical David Lynch territory where the protagonist Betty Elms/Diane Selwyn (Naomi Watts) certainly does not know who she is. Although the protagonist of *Donnie Darko* is clinically schizophrenic, this independently-produced film does investigate the notion of identity through the theory of multiple universes and does not conclude with 'they all lived happy ever after'.

As Donna Haraway (1991) showed in her 'Cyborg Manifesto', undermining the bourgeois conception of the self is a political act. It should be no surprise that Hollywood, and mainstream film worldwide, should embrace the 'consumerist' aspects of postmodernism but refuse to countenance the instability of the postmodern subject. Science fiction remains the genre most able to deal with the posthuman, but whether it does so depends upon the institutional context in which films are produced.

Blade Runner is a film that, possibly, pushes the idea of the posthuman as far as a mainstream movie can; after all, we can never be certain of Deckard's ontological status. The Director's Cut does not offer the narrative resolution that characterises mainstream film. For example, *Minority Report* (2002), another adaptation of Philip K. Dick, sets up the possibility that John Anderson (Tom Cruise) will murder someone in cold blood but negotiates this disturbing instability in the protagonist through a conventional 'whodunnit'.

The growth of *Blade Runner*'s reputation, after its commercial failure, suggests that mainstream audiences may take a while to get used to identifying with a protagonist who has an unstable self. On the other hand, maybe the appeal is simply Scott's dazzling *mise-en-scène* and the exciting action. This action, with its love of surfaces and rush of images, are exactly the elements of the postmodern aesthetic embraced by mainstream films and audiences.

NOTES

1 'Human characters frequently feel dead inside and see the world around them as dead. Many are incapable of love or empathy for other humans. From the android side, the confusion of boundaries is equally striking. The androids and simulacra of Dick's fiction include characters who are empathic, rebellious, determined to define their own goals, and as strongly individuated as the humans whose world they share' (Hayles 1999: 164).

2　'The unicorn is a mythical beast that can only be tamed by a virgin, the single horn being an obviously phallic symbol. Rachel is a virgin and she tames the hunter Deckard, giving meaning to his alienated life' (Lacey 2000: 44).

3　The title given to the introduction of Geoff King's and Tanya Krzywinska's (2000) book on science fiction cinema.

SECTION 5: THE CITY

FALSE LA: *BLADE RUNNER* AND THE NIGHTMARE CITY
STEPHEN ROWLEY

Ridley Scott has always been a highly visual, design-driven filmmaker, and the strength of his work is his strong grasp of mood and environment. It is characteristic, then, that the vision of 'Los Angeles: 2019' in *Blade Runner* remains central to the film's appeal well over twenty years later. In one of several recent volumes that address links between theories of urban planning and the cinema, Marcus A. Doel and David B. Clarke seem almost sheepish at bringing *Blade Runner* into the discussion. How, they ask rhetorically, can they justify further analysis of the film, 'beyond the trivial reasoning that a book on the cinematic city is more or less obliged to say something about *Blade Runner*?' (Doel & Clarke 1997: 141). For Doel and Clarke, the answer is that other analyses have misunderstood the film, but the sense of obligation they feel is telling: *Blade Runner* demands studying because it is has become so entrenched as the definitive screen depiction of the nightmare future city. Its imagery has become the standard visual iconography for the science fiction metropolis: super-tall buildings; poorly-lit streets and alleys; smog; rain; heavy industry belching fire into the sky; neon advertisements; overcrowding; ethnically diverse (that is, non-white) crowds; eclectic punk-inspired costumes and hairstyles; retrofitted buildings of varying architectural styles; scavenged props, and so on. None of these elements were new or unique to *Blade Runner*, but Scott's utilisation of them has become a standard reference point, with highly *Blade Runner*-esque cities recurring in science fiction and fantasy films since, such as *Batman* (1989), *Strange Days* (1995), *The Fifth Element* (1997), *Dark City* (1998), *Artificial Intelligence: A.I.* (2001) and *Star Wars: Episode II – Attack of the Clones* (2002), to name just a few. Even where these films draw on other traditions – such as the much more overtly gothic *Batman*, or the lighter, more comic-book influenced *The Fifth Element* – they struggle to stamp a distinct look on their cities that escapes comparison with Scott's film. What is interesting is that *Blade Runner*'s future should continue to have such purchase despite not showing any particular signs of materialising. As Mike Davis complains, 'for all of *Blade Runner*'s glamour as the reigning star of science fiction dystopias, its vision of the future is strangely anachronistic and surprisingly unprescient' (1999: 360). The *Blade Runner* nightmare is simply not one shared by most urban planners. *Blade Runner* therefore has a lot to tell us about the difference between the ways urban planners view space, and the ways that movies ask us to.

Films themselves show little respect for such academic divides, and theoretical analysis can be found wanting when it comes to a film that is as cinematic as *Blade Runner* but which says so much about urban life. This is not to say that there is no academic literature that breaks out of particular theoretical confines. On the contrary, there has been a recent rush of anthologies explicitly focusing on the links between spatial and cinematic theory – such as Clarke 1997; Lamster 2000; and Shiel & Fitzmaurice (2001, 2003) – and these follow many individual works that similarly try to bridge this gap. The difficulty of linking film and spatial theory therefore arises not from lack of attention, but rather from the diversity of writing in the field. The eclecticism of this work is a result of the enormity of the subject. Writing about 'the city' is, in this urbanised age, akin to addressing the whole realm of physical existence. Seen this way, theorising the link between the city and the cinema risks becoming another hopelessly broad conceptual project such as theorising the link between film and reality. Certainly it is not simply a matter of drawing links between two discrete fields: on the spatial side of the divide, for example, urban planners and architects view space quite differently. The links between film theory, spatial theory and *Blade Runner* could therefore be mapped in any number of different, but equally valid ways. My intention here is not, therefore, intended to suggest any level of definitiveness. Instead, I wish to highlight one particularly interesting conflict between *Blade Runner*'s depiction of urban hell and some of the prevailing notions in the field of urban planning.

To understand the depth of the rift between *Blade Runner*'s dystopic city and that which urban planners might imagine, it is necessary to characterise the notions underpinning it, rather than simply listing its visual signifiers as at the start of this chapter. So what is the present-day basis for *Blade Runner*'s city? As has often been pointed out, the city of *Blade Runner* is conspicuously not Los Angeles, and is much more convincing as a depiction of a future New York (in addition to Davis, see Bukatman 1997: 62 and Carper 1991: 186). The vertical scale of the city suggests the former World Trade Center towers – design artist Syd Mead has said one conceptual exercise was based on an extrapolation of New York's form based upon the assumption that these buildings would become the norm (Peary 1988: 35) – and the closely-packed buildings covered in neon advertising evoke Times Square. Scott has talked of the experience of flying into New York as an inspiration for the film's urbanism (Sammon 1996: 76), and the film's flying cars supplant freeways, one of the most potent visual signifiers of Los Angeles. There is little sense of the low-density expansiveness of Los Angeles (although the occasional shot, such as the smog-choked longshots of Tyrell's headquarters, and the views from its windows, hint at it). On the contrary, as Mead's explanation makes clear, it is density (and the street-level overcrowding, dirtiness and crime that are portrayed as accompanying it) that defines the nightmare world of *Blade Runner*. Visually, it is an effective shorthand for a world in which fears of overpopulation and depletion of resources have been realised: by evoking New York's crowding of buildings and people onto Manhattan island, *Blade Runner* suggests a similar overcrowding onto a constrained planet. The film's evocation of New York is therefore of a dysfunctional New York, a development of the contemporary urban wilderness in films such as John Schlesinger's *Midnight Cowboy* (1969) or Martin Scorsese's *Taxi Driver* (1976).

The contrast between the New York look and the title-card's insistence on Los Angeles is partly explained by the fact that the setting was switched from New York to Los Angeles late in production once it became clear it would be shot on the West Coast. Paul Sammon quotes production executive Katy Haber on this point: 'You couldn't set a film ... in New York and then show Harrison Ford driving up to the Bradbury Building [in Los Angeles]' (1996: 76). However, this does not explain the proposed use of New York in the first place, since Phillip K. Dick's original novel was set in San Francisco.

Perhaps a better explanation is the film's utilisation of film noir, arguably Los Angeles' most powerful regional mythology. This is particularly clear in the original cut, with its heavy handed use of the voice-over narration. Even in the narrationless Director's Cut, however, the influence is strongly felt with a range of noir signifiers prominent: the lead character of the tough, disillusioned cop; cinematography that runs the murky gamut from rain-drenched darkness to hazy brown smokiness; the 1940s influence in some sets, costumes and hair-styles; and the pseudo femme fatale character of Rachel. The look of the *Blade Runner* city might be said to evoke the traditional 'dark city' of film noir, but this is a particularly limited, old-fashioned view of the way noir views the city. To stereotype noir as typified by images of detectives trudging through a crime-ridden downtown at night is to ignore the way that noir has responded to the regional realities of its home city. As Norman Klein (1997: 295) points out, in postwar noir the suburbs often displace the big city as the location for the hero's alienation, as in the sun-baked noir of Polanski's *Chinatown*, a film that fictionalises the battles around Los Angeles' ever-expanding fringe. So while the 'Los Angeles' title card might be tip of the hat to noir, the film's visuals of the dark downtown cannot be explained away as a noir device.

In considering the underlying principles of *Blade Runner*'s urban vision, it is also necessary to consider postmodernism. *Blade Runner* was pigeon-holed early on as a postmodernist text: indeed, much of its cultural cachet arises from the attention it has received from postmodernist writers. Writers such as David Harvey (1989) and Giuliana Bruno (1990 [1987]) established this pattern early on, and certainly such writing can identify a convincing array of postmodern traits in the film. There is the pastiche of different eras and styles in the architecture and design, and the signs of post-industrial decay. The theme of time-space compression, embodied by the short-lived replicants and the prematurely-aging J. F. Sebastian, is a central postmodern theme. The Tyrell Corporation's outsourcing of production to impossibly small sub-contracting firms (some of them literally running out of street stalls) is a clever play on the flexible production models of postmodern post-Fordist economies. The film's ruminations on the nature of memory (and the importance of photographs) evoke postmodern ideas about the mediation of life through technology and the elimination of 'real' history. In the context of these commentaries, the use of Los Angeles rather than New York as the nominal setting makes more sense given the former city's status as an archetypal postmodern city, in contrast with New York's status as the quintessential modernist metropolis, a dichotomy explored by Mark Shiel (2003) and others. (This, of course, does not explain away the city's resemblance to New York, a point returned to below).

Interestingly, however, Harvey's discussion of the film's postmodern traits concentrates on narrative and has little to say about the urban planning (or lack of it) apparent in *Blade Runner*'s city. This is despite his background as a geographer, and his consideration of the film in *The Condition of Postmodernity* sitting alongside that book's discussion of postmodernism in the city. Yet in this regard, too, the film seems at first glance thoroughly postmodern, at least in its rejection of modernist models of urban planning. Such models are recognisable by their tendency towards, as Harvey puts it, 'large scale, metropolitan-wide, technologically rational and efficient urban plans, backed by absolutely no-frills architecture (the austere "functionalist" surfaces of "international style" modernism)' (Harvey 1989: 66). This rationalist trait is central to the whole discipline of urban planning: a motivating impulse of the field is the desire to impose order of some kind upon the chaos of the city. Early examples include Baron Georges-Eugène Haussman's remodelling of Paris (creating grand boulevards and new open spaces) from the mid-nineteenth century, or Ebenezer Howard's 'Garden City' conceptions (calling for new self-contained small towns set in agrarian surrounds), first proposed at the turn of the century. The most dramatic and far-reaching rationalist model, however, was the 'Radiant City' first proposed by Le Corbusier in the 1920s, and it is Le Corbusier's work that epitomises the modernist approach described by Harvey. Le Corbusier's formulations were both urban planning-based and architectural, which may partly account for their huge influence. His idealised future city was the ultimate masterplan: huge international-style skyscrapers, linked by freeways and set in parkland, with the extreme vertical form allowing enormous populations to exist in landscaped surrounds. The sheer ambition of Le Corbusier's modernist utopia means it has never been fully realised, but the postwar period saw a great deal of rebuilding, urban renewal, road projects and public housing that in one way or another represented scaled-down versions of Le Corbusier's vision. Before *Blade Runner*, these modernist projects and buildings were frequently the basis for the cities in cinematic science fiction. Their sleek futuristic-ness meant that they could be easily dressed up as cities of the future for convenient location shooting, whether the vision was dystopic (as in *THX-1138* (1971)) or utopic (in the various manifestations of *Star Trek*).

Blade Runner's city could hardly be further from the clean lines of the modernist future city, and its break from these aesthetics doubtless contributed both to its ongoing influence, and the continued categorisation of it as a postmodernist text. Yet Scott Bukatman, in his excellent discussion of *Blade Runner*'s urbanism, has questioned this point, noting that the film's embrace of the chaos and heterogeneity of urban life is in fact quintessentially modern:

> The rational, planned city of efficient circulation and an International Style, perhaps epitomised by Le Corbusier, belonged to another modernism en-

tirely. *That* modernism is indeed rejected by *Blade Runner*, while the modernist experience of the city described by Simmel, Benjamin and Kracauer – disordered, heterogeneous, street-level – is revisited and renewed ... The city has existed in cinema as a place of delirious chaos, alienation, resistance and even improbable liberation. *This* city once again finds eloquent voice in *Blade Runner*. (1997: 61)

When viewed this way, *Blade Runner*'s New York influence makes much more sense, being a nod to New York's status – especially in the first half of the twentieth century – as a centre of world finance and the ultimate modernist metropolis. However, I do not believe it is necessary to discard a particular manifestation of modernism for *Blade Runner*'s view of the city to be characterised as modernist. If we accept that the film does not wish us to view its city as an attractive place – and given the sombre tone of the film, and the rather bleak existence of its characters, this seems a reasonable assumption – then it becomes much easier to reconcile modernist planning with the film. The film's apparent abhorrence of the disorderly city is a manifestation of the same quest for order that underlies modernist urban planning such as Le Corbusier's. If we can conjure up the utopic vision of modernist planning – freeways that are efficient and clean, slick futuristic buildings, beautiful and safe parkland – it is easy to see *Blade Runner*'s city as its flip-side. At least in terms of its representation of the city, *Blade Runner* is not so much a postmodern vision, as an old-fashioned modernist view of what to avoid.

This point is perhaps clearer when *Blade Runner*'s urbanism is contrasted with the notions of urban planning that arose in reaction to the urbanism of Le Corbusier-style modernism. While most large cities around the world have their own local stories of resistance to pseudo-Le Corbusier programmes of urban renewal and high-rise construction, New York again becomes a critical location. The conflict between the observed consequences of urban redevelopment proposals in New York and the traditional fabric of the city is central to Jane Jacobs' classic study *Death and Life of Great American Cities* (1961). Jacobs took the appreciation of the fine details of existing local conditions that might usually find expression in community activism and developed it into a study with much wider application. Jacobs does not write exclusively about New York, but her observations of the daily street life of the city are central to her thesis (the book is still fascinating as a memoir of life in the city in the late 1950s and early 1960s). Jacobs' approach is unashamedly anecdotal in its somewhat romanticised description of, for example, the comings and goings throughout the day on Jacobs' own street in Manhattan. Yet its anecdotal nature is its central strength, because Jacobs is focusing on the kind of intangible everyday experience for which anecdotalism is the only form of empiricism. *Death and Life of Great American Cities* is a celebration of street-level vitality and dynamism. Her thesis, put simply, is that the masterplanned redevelopments of modernist planning do not support the kinds of functions and activities that make the best urban areas pleasant to live in. Her suggested principles of urban design – uses mixed within areas, short blocks, buildings of mixed age, and high population density – are based on an embrace of the chaotic but stimulating urban fabric found in a city such as New York. They are a reaction to the fundamental principles of the then-prevailing highly rational modernist urban planning, be it on Le Corbusier's model or otherwise. For example, the mixing of uses runs counter to the conventional notion of zoning (which is based upon the principle of separation of uses into categories: residential, commercial, industrial and so on). Similarly, her discussion of the uses of streets as recreational and social spaces opposes highly rational models that focus on street design as a function of vehicular traffic flow.

Jacobs, of course, is just one theorist, and she was not the only person to write about the shortcomings of the modernist notion of urban planning. However, she is of interest here for the particularly urban, New York-inspired spin she put on her ideas. Her focus on facilitating the many intangible small-scale social interactions that contribute to functional communities is found echoed in other approaches, most famously by the so-called 'New Urbanism' (Southworth 2003). In the context of discussing *Blade Runner* and cinematic cities, though, it is worth noting that for Jacobs describing the 'look' of cities is secondary to mapping the activities that occur within them. When she does so, though, it is lack of visual stimulation that is at the forefront of her criticism. She talks, for example, of the 'Great Blight of Dullness' and 'gray areas' (for example, see Jacobs 1961: 34 and 42 respectively; interestingly, both phrases are indexed), terms that speak of the spectres of both International Style architecture, and urban decay caused by the flight from the inner cities. While such areas are still referred to in visual critiques of urban areas, more recent writing is less likely to emphasise dullness, with its attendant implication of a visual monoculture. For example, James Howard Kunstler (1993) uses the phrase 'The Geography of Nowhere', to evoke the anonymity of much postwar development, and while the term (and Kunstler's approach) echoes Jacobs, the detail of his critique shows that different visual blemishes have come to the fore. Kunstler's catalogue of urban blight is much more pre-occupied with the predominance of the disorderly, postmodern and kitsch:

> Eighty percent of everything ever built in America has been built in the last fifty years, and most of it is depressing, brutal, ugly, unhealthy, and spiritually degrading – the jive-plastic commuter tract home wastelands, the Potemkin village shopping plazas with their vast parking lagoons, the Lego-block hotel complexes, the 'gourmet mansardic' junk-food joints, the Orwellian office 'parks' featuring buildings sheathed in the same reflective glass as the sunglasses worn by chain-gang guards... (1993: 10)

Kunstler's highly polemical formulation is indebted to Jacobs but is more architectural in focus and more preoccupied with the proliferation of cities and towns that are littered with buildings and urban spaces that have no relation to their surroundings, and which therefore become interchangeable. The shifting of retailing away from traditional main streets guts local communities, and further entrenches national (or international) chains of stores whose buildings all look alike and are clustered along highway strips.

It should also be noted that Kunstler's litany of horrors is preoccupied less with ravaged inner cities than with the kind of development that occurs at the urban periphery. The spectre of widespread high-density urban renewal that formed part of Jacobs' inspiration has faded: instead, though, her vision of the friendly, people-focused downtown is threatened by the flight to the anonymous, sprawling, car-oriented suburbs. In the sprawling city, the single-use zoning Jacobs decried is still a problem, but becomes even more extreme, rendering the population dependent on cars to get from one area to the other. In mapping the results of such an automobile dominated land-use pattern, Andres Duany, Elizabeth Plater-Zyberk and Jeff Speck echo Kunstler's account:

> We Americans have been building a national landscape that is largely devoid of places worth caring about. Soulless subdivisions, residential 'communities' utterly lacking in communal life; strip shopping centres, 'big box' chain stores, and artificially festive malls set within barren seas of parking; antiseptic office parks, ghost towns after 6 p.m.; and mile upon mile of clogged collector roads, the only fabric tying our disassociated lives back together...
> (Duany *et al.* 2000: 4)

Duany, Plater-Zyberk and Speck are proponents of the 'New Urbanism', of which Kunstler is also a supporter (see Kunstler 1996). This movement is the most sustained attempt at constructing a model for planning that can make wholesale changes to the pattern of conventional postwar suburban sprawl: a middle road, in a sense, between inner-city high-density urban renewal projects, and ultra-low-density development seen in many cities' outer suburbs. The New Urbanism draws more explicitly than Jacobs on themes such as ecological sustainability that have emerged since 1961, but the preoccupation with development patterns that allow for vitality and interest remains. The movement's Charter, for example, calls for neighborhoods to be 'compact, pedestrian friendly, and mixed use' (Duany *et al.* 2000: 263), a principle that embodies three out of four of Jacobs' 'indispensable' conditions for urban diversity (Jacobs 1961: 150–1). The missing condition from Jacobs, buildings of mixed ages, reveals a key difference in approach: the New Urbanism is more positive about the prospects of building masterplanned new communities on greenfield sites that still generate vibrant, people-friendly communities. While Jacobs embraces the inner city, New Urbanism looks also to traditional small towns as a model for new development that reinserts a sense of local community into suburban development.

What this very brief survey is intended to show is the emerging lifestyle focus of urban planning: fostering a sense of place and community; a pedestrian focus; street-level vibrancy; and so on. This urbanism's nightmare city is not

New York, but rather the dispersed, centreless, car-dominated suburban fabric of present-day Los Angeles. The city has become a focal point for disquiet about the built form of American cities, a frequently cited example of what not to do. This extends not only from the kind of approaches outlined here, but also through transport planners (who decry the city's emphasis on roads and inadequate public transportation) and theorists such as Mike Davis (who, amongst other critiques, cites the public and private 'militarisation' of Los Angeles' built environment (see Davis 1990)). Los Angeles' pattern of development, seemingly all hinterland and no centre, is a particularly dehumanising built form. The Los Angeles example is particularly interesting for the way it breaks down old ideas of good and bad neighborhoods: while there has rightly been much attention given to the particularly crime and poverty-ridden neighborhoods of Los Angeles, the critiques cited in this chapter extend to the whole of the city. As the city's boundaries expand ever further in new subdivision, even affluent commuter suburbs struggle to escape the tyranny of repetition, placelessness and automobile dependency. In the hinterlands of Los Angeles many arterial roads do not even have footpaths, leaving little room for the vibrant 'sidewalk life' that Jacobs celebrated.

None of this is apparent in Scott's film. *Blade Runner*'s high-density vision of urban hell is not just 'wrong' as a depiction of Los Angeles, but it fails to grapple with the paradigm change in thinking about the city that occurred since the Second World War. Today's urban planners are much less likely to celebrate visual order or efficient vehicle circulation in the way Le Corbusier-inspired modernist planners would. Instead, they are likely to see these things as potentially in conflict with the fostering of vibrancy, diversity and human interaction. When *Blade Runner* is viewed in the light of the aesthetics of cosmopolitanism that underpin this viewpoint, its city does not look so bad after all. Norman Klein notes that 'three out of five leading planners agreed that they hoped L.A. would someday look like the film *Blade Runner*' and that L.A. residents thought the sushi street vendors in the film look impressively cosmopolitan (1997: 94; 98). After all, *Blade Runner* shows many of the problems of present-day Los Angeles solved. As Carper puts it, the film's 'visual futurist', Syd Mead, 'has accomplished what generations of city planners have failed to do in reality: he has given Los Angeles a downtown' (1991: 84). If vibrancy and vitality are what we are after, there is a lot to like about this fictional Los Angeles of 2019. It has plenty of street-level convenience retailing and restaurants. The nightlife looks fantastic. There is either a good public transport system, or everything is pretty close together – civilians seem to get around okay on foot. (There is no sign that the escaped replicants own a car, there are buses on the streets, and Zhora seems to be descending into a subway as Deckard pursues her.) It abounds, then, in the kind of qualities that Los Angeles lacks but which have led to the rehabilitation of New York in the public imagination as an exciting, attractive place to live. That *Blade Runner* nevertheless clearly intends us to take such a negative view of the New York-style metropolis speaks to its rejection of prevailing views of the city.

Accounts of the making of *Blade Runner* suggest Ridley Scott was aware of the possibilities of basing *Blade Runner*'s city more closely on the actual Los Angeles. As Scott admitted:

> At one point we were going to call the city San Angeles, which would of course have suggested that the 800-mile-long Western seaboard had been transformed into a single population centre with giant cities and monolithic buildings at each end, and then this strange kind of awful suburb in the middle. (Quoted in Sammon 1996: 7)

As already noted, there are a few sequences in which we seem to be overlooking just such a 'strange awful suburb', when the film takes us to the Tyrell Corporation headquarters. The headquarters – with their pyramidal form – show a horizontal expansiveness that seems apt for an exaggerated Los Angeles. Yet these sequences almost seem to belong to a different movie than the bustling street scenes we see elsewhere, and the dreary brownness of the landscape around the pyramid suggests what may be the real reason Scott avoided such a conception: visually, it simply is not terribly interesting. As suggested at the start of this chapter, Scott's filmmaking is driven by visuals, and an intellectually-based notion of the city as a sprawling, centreless non-place is not suited to his style of filmmaking. Not only does the big-city imagery have a razzle-dazzle factor that the dispersed suburb does not, but they lend the city a distinct sense of place. Film is drawn to the visually cohesive and legible: the anonymous and incoherent do not make as attractive locations. Filmmakers do use such locations: Quentin Tarantino, for example, makes heavy use of visually indistinct Los Angeles locations (such as the industrial neighbourhood in *Reservoir Dogs* (1992), the overgrown backyards and apartment Bruce Willis walks through in *Pulp Fiction* (1994), or the Del Amo Mall carpark in *Jackie Brown* (1997)), but the pointedly everyday nature of such locations ground the films solidly in reality. Such visuals are not the building blocks of an immersive fantasy environment, whether utopic or dystopic.

The cost of embracing the more visually interesting approach, however, is that the view of the city becomes regressive and backward looking. Contemporary Los Angeles continues to evolve away from, not towards, the imagined nightmare city of 2019. The future city of *Blade Runner* trades on older, more familiar notions of urban hell that considerably pre-date the postmodern influences of its visuals. I have suggested that the disordered, crowded and heterogeneous *Blade Runner* city is the dystopian inversion of clean, ordered modernist utopias. Yet the *Blade Runner* city is even older and more familiar than that. As Peter Wollen (1992: 26) notes, the 'thronged alleys' of *Blade Runner* have strong overtones of medievalism, and this speaks to the depth of historical basis that *Blade Runner*'s image of urbanity holds: until the rise of the automobile, density was always at the heart of urban problems. Yet while the familiarity of the model of urbanism makes it easier to understand

and more instantly persuasive, it also makes it less threatening. The idea of a dense, forbidding inner city is so familiar that it is almost taken for granted; it is also something that one can leave. After all, one of the underpinnings of urban sprawl has been the departure of the middle class from the inner city. Indeed, the notion of flight from the city is deeply embedded in *Blade Runner*. This is most obvious in the Original Version, with its incongruous final images of wilderness, yet it remains a motif even in the Director's Cut. The Off-World colonies beckon, and the replicants enquire why a professional like J. F. Sebastian has not left. Only his medical condition has kept him on Earth, and his whole apartment complex lies empty as a testament to the middle- and upper-classes' abandonment of the city. Rachel talks, too, of fleeing 'north'. (The United States might be hell, but maybe Canada is fine). This dulls the edge of the nightmare future, since we are being presented a situation in which only a certain underclass have to face the terrors of urban decay. Those who have already escaped present-day inner urban areas and moved to the suburbs can therefore watch *Blade Runner* with a certain complacent detachment.

A *Blade Runner* that came to terms with the real Los Angeles would be rather more frightening, and more pertinent. The physical properties of Los Angeles are so widely discussed because they are so common, particularly in countries such as the United States and Australia where land abounds at urban fringes. The dystopic properties of Los Angeles subsume the suburbs that are supposed to be the escape from inner urban woes. By its very nature, a nightmare of sprawling placelessness lacks a discrete physical location that can be avoided. There is less prospect of escape from a nightmare city that consists of huge swathes of indistinguishable housing interspersed with freeways, shopping malls, chain stores, petrol stations and burger joints. How do Deckard and Rachel flee from such an environment when it encompasses the entire fabric of the human built form? Do they live out their possibly foreshortened lives stuck in traffic, eating fast food, and shopping in malls?

IMAGINING THE REAL: *BLADE RUNNER* AND DISCOURSES ON THE POSTMETROPOLIS
PETER BROOKER

Paul M. Sammon reports that there was a thought at one time of using the Bonaventure Hotel as the location for Tyrell's office in *Blade Runner* (1996: 125). The Bonaventure has assumed a classic status, of course, in debates on postmodern hyperspace. For it was here, most famously, that Fredric Jameson's experience of disorientation prompted the call for a double accented 'cognitive mapping' which would, on the one hand, take a guest comfortably around the hotel and, on the other, provide a 'symbol and analogon' of the newly spatialised global operations of late capitalism (1991: 44). Mike Davis (1988) in turn argued that Jameson's essay had ignored the key factors of class, ethnicity and social exclusion at a critical conjuncture in the LA economy and that the city's new 'carceral' regime was precisely exemplified by the Bonaventure. Where Jameson was selective and speculative, Davis was inveterately materialist. Elsewhere, however, far from oblivious to the role of 'immaterial' factors in shaping LA's identity, Davis himself tells how *Blade Runner* has acquired iconic status as 'Los Angeles' dystopic alter ego', the 'official nightmare' shaping ideas of the city's future (1998: 360). In a further loop in this circuit across socio-spatial realities and the hyperreal, the postmodern social geographer Edward W. Soja suggests we can think of the Bonaventure as a 'heterotopia' and as presenting 'a *Blade Runner*-built environment' (1996: 198).

What are we to make of this co-mingling of fictional texts and scenarios with the concepts and assumptions of cultural analysis and social science? Or of the silent, deep-running exchange across discourses in the talk of 'mental' or 'cognitive maps', 'interpretive grids' and the concept of the 'urban imaginary' which informs the new cultural geography? (Soja 2000: 324). Are metaphor and analogy, story and narrative, to say nothing of the outer reaches of reverie and dream, an extraneous supplement to or an integral part of our attempts to understand the contemporary city? Are they even in some ways the best we can do?

I want to reflect on these questions below in a discussion of *Blade Runner* and accounts of the postmodern 'postmetropolis' of Los Angeles as advanced especially by Davis and Soja. Much of this discussion – not unexpectedly for those acquainted with debates on the film or in cultural geography – is about the perception and problematising of binary oppositions. Discussions of the film have centred, for example, on the relation of the human and replicant and invoked the 'postmodern' as a way of suggesting a movement beyond this and other apparently stable oppositions. Soja, too, has spoken of the 'post' and the realm of 'Thirdspace' in similar terms, as exploratory strategies that will open a 'critically postmodern cultural politics' beyond the 'binary battlegrounds' of gender, race and class (1996: 12–13). The received binary distinction or boundary I want to add to these concerns is that between social fact and social fiction; between *this* urban world and its oblique representation in an alternative, adjacent fictionalised mode, as a parallel *other* world. The two broad discourses in question here have mixed designations on either side of conventional markers: not only of 'fact' and 'fiction', important and persistent though this is, but of literal and symbolic or fantastic geographies, academic and popular or commercial culture, and written and visual texts. Not surprisingly, any exchange across these modes has in this case tended to be one-sided. *Blade Runner* knows nothing of its critics, nor does it openly acknowledge the postmodern tropes long associated with it, while academic or social commentary continues to refer, indeed defer, to the film. I want to suggest below how urban sociology can alert us to some possible, newly situated meanings in the film. My emphasis, however, is on the ways both film texts and the writings of social and cultural geographers have recourse to the forms, figures and speculative narrative modes usually associated with imaginative works in mapping and re-visioning the city. This is not to say that these discourses are at bottom the 'same', since part of this discussion is a demonstration of how they imagine differently, but it is to underline the common role of what might be called the active urban imaginary.

One of the first, most cited readings of *Blade Runner* was in fact by the historical geographer, David Harvey. Amongst those who responded to his analysis was Doreen Massey, herself a cultural geographer. Other urban theorists, such as Soja and Davis, as we have seen, have adopted *Blade Runner* into a specific discourse on Los Angeles as a quintessential postmodern or post-metropolitan urban arena. But already the earlier commentators on the film help suggest the perspective I want to take here. Harvey, for example, while praising the film as a symptomatic portrayal of postmodernism, laments that the manifest 'signs of objective class relations' do not materialise in 'a coalition of the oppressed' primed for revolt against corporate power (1989: 322; 313). Massey in turn points to Harvey's blindness to questions of gender: his is a 'male-based analysis', she says (1994: 230). Their disagreement takes place on what Massey terms 'the terrain of sexual identity', not of textual interpretation, which she sets to one side (1994: 229). The point, however, is not so much that the film is side-stepped but that both judge it by way of a preferred political and cultural agenda, drawing respectively on traditional class and feminist analyses. What these 'materialist' commentaries demonstrate is a dependence at their very core on strongly imagined social fictions and the accompanying critical consciousness of a transformed world. Both read the present, including the film *Blade Runner*, in terms of this preferred vision. They are in a word and at root 'utopian' – a perspective that in Harvey's later *Spaces of Hope* (2000), which includes its own utopian dream narrative, becomes explicit.

This is of particular interest not only in relation to *Blade Runner* but also to the city of Los Angeles. Bertolt Brecht, an exile in California in the early

1940s, found 'on thinking about Hell' that it was 'like Los Angeles' (1976: 367). Like Brecht, many writers in the 1930s and 1940s wrote and saw as outsiders, often drawn by the prospect of scriptwriting for Hollywood, but at odds with its pervasive and commercialised visual aesthetic. This sense of displacement gave rise, says David Fine, to a persistent contrast between the present in Los Angeles and a past left behind, but also to a mixed fascination and revulsion for the new: at once counterfeit, corrupt and excessive but alive with possibilities. For writers, movie makers and the millions who have settled there over the last half century, California and Los Angeles in particular have continued therefore to represent all the persistent ambiguity of the myth of the West, 'the place of the fresh start and ... the scene of the disastrous finish' as Fine puts it (1995: 7). This is an ambiguity compounded, moreover, by the climate and land itself: a surreal combination of endless summer and the threat of natural disaster. Both physical and cultural landscape have joined therefore in the unstable symbolism of paradise and hell, reinforcing a vocabulary of desire and fear that swings this way and that with the city's utopian and dystopian moods.

Both *Blade Runner* and the work of Davis and Soja emerge out of this already established urban imaginary, and it is this context that I want to compare them. Davis, writing in 1998, sees how *Blade Runner* has haunted the city's sense of itself but dismisses it as out of date, since the city has already outpaced the film's worst projections. Soja too sees *Blade Runner* as joining a lineage of dystopian images of the city, but as an indelible part, too, of Davis's depiction of Los Angeles (2000: 137–87). He too, though in different terms, writes therefore of moving 'beyond the formative dichotomies' of both Davis's '*City of Quartz* and the *Blade Runner* scenario' (2000: 319). There is much to consider here on all sides, not least the complications of the time or period at issue, spanning the first release in 1982 and Director's Cut of the film in 1992; dramatic developments in Los Angeles in the 1990s; and the combined thinking in these texts about the future. To begin with, too, we might think that *Blade Runner* splices utopian options with its pervasively dystopian mood: in the invitation to start over in a 'new life' in the 'golden land of opportunity and adventure' and in the notorious 'happy ending' which discovers a pastoral escape route by way of a borrowed clip from Stanley Kubrick's *The Shining* (1980). Viewers have regularly rejected this ending as an inorganic and unwarranted imposition upon the sombre tones of the film, and indeed find this view confirmed by the Director's Cut. But in itself this blatantly forced 'happy ending' can be read as a sign of the persistence, however compromised, of the utopian impulse in the world of contemporary Los Angeles. The film in this version and at that time catches, that is to say, not at one mood, as Davis would have it, but at the double options running, as ever, unevenly across the city's psyche.

This prominent if gauche ambiguity in the 1982 film is built, moreover, upon a series of superimposed and compound but collectively insecure oppositions. To give two examples. The film was shot on the Burbank (later Warner

Bros.') 'Old New York Street' set, built in 1929 (see Sammon 1996: 98). Origi-nally Ridley Scott had in fact sought to present a future composite of two world cities, one of which, complete with the Chrysler Building and Manhat-tan skyline, would be New York. Also, before the decision to transform the Burbank set, there had been a search for actual locations in New York, At-lanta, London and Boston. On set, under Scott's close instruction, the pro-duction crew brought a scrupulous attention to the would-be authenticating detail of the props, vehicles and street architecture (including parking me-ters, 'traffickers', 'VidPhons' and future-styled magazines on a newsstand) to manufacture the film's 'Los Angeles 2019'. Paul Sammon reports that the transformed 'Old New York Street' set comprised recognisable but altered fea-tures of New York itself, Hong Kong, London and Milan. We might think we detect a subterranean play in all this between the 'modern' or 'modernist' New York or European metropolis and an Asian or Los Angeles 'postmodern' – and feel this echoes the film's debate on the 'human' and postmodern cy-borg or replicant – only to realise this 'modern' is itself founded on a studio back lot in Hollywood, as 'unreal' as the 'accurate' retro detail of the imagined future city.

A marked premise of this future world, secondly, is the much observed contrast between (human) emotion and a (posthuman) lack of feeling, or what is otherwise termed – in a thread of commentary running from Freud to J. G. Ballard, Fredric Jameson and cyberpunk fiction – a 'loss of affect'. But here too the underlying opposition does not pan out as it should. Emotion, firstly, or a show of emotion, is manifested by both Deckard and replicants in scenes of heterosexual affection or desire; male bonding and rivalry; a stereotypical 'love' for the mother; and the tangle of Oedipal feelings shown by Roy Batty towards the symbolic figure of the father, Tyrell. Lack of feeling is associated with the absence of a personal family past, and is the plight especially of the replicants, at least of the Nexus-6 generation, who have a limited life span of four years. Leon and Rachel react by shoring up a personal past and memory through the dubious authenticating evidence of a set of family photographs. But Deckard too surrounds himself with a gallery of family photographs. He is also characterised initially as being without feeling ('"sushi" – that's what my ex-wife called me – cold fish') and in his impersonal professionalism as a blade runner ('Replicants weren't supposed to have feelings' he muses, 'Nei-ther were blade runners. What the hell was happening to me?').

The alignment of the 'human' with emotion and biographical narrative and the 'non-human' with the loss of affect and personal history is clearly prob-lematised – to the point where any assumed binary opposition between the two gives way. Even an allied thread of imagery which connects the 'non-hu-man' replicants with coldness, by association, for example, with the freez-ing environment of the eye factory, is contradicted by a further association, indebted to the poet William Blake, of Roy Batty with energy and fire in his speech 'Fiery the angels fell, deep thunder rolled around their shores, burning with the fires of Orc'.[1]

In these, and many other ways, principally in the implication that Deckard is a replicant, the real and imaginary, feeling and lack of feeling, having and not having a past and future are blurred in the film's composition and narrative and as such complicate and undermine the premised opposition of the human and replicant as well as posited dystopian and utopian alternatives. As we have seen above, an ontological ambiguity is an accepted part of the discursive history and experience of Los Angeles. For writers of fiction and for social commentators alike, the city has consequently become the quintessential expression of a decentred, unanchored domain of simulation or of the hyperreal. The texts of 'literary Los Angeles', David Ulin writes, have framed a portrait of the 'existential city, all sun and celluloid [where] the residue of history collapses into the dreamscape of a never-ending present' (2001: xv). Los Angeles has no single collective mythology or encompassing narrative, he says, but is instead experienced as a series of impressions across a randomised sprawl of border towns: it's 'another kind of city, one with no single identity, no unifying centre … a collage city, a pastiche of time and place and attitude' (2001: xvi). Ulin's Los Angeles finds its cultural rhyme in Umberto Eco's inventory of 'real fakes' along the Californian cultural landscape, and above all in Jean Baudrillard's propositions on simulation and the simulacra. Baudrillard posits an evolution of the sign whereby the traditionally assumed correspondence between the signifier and signified or referent has become increasingly attenuated. A final stage in this evolution produces the 'pure simulacrum' which Baudrillard deems characteristic of contemporary consumer societies. In this regime the free-floating signifier becomes finally detached from its signified, the image or representation from its reference, and the consummate simulacrum from any supposed original. Simulation spells the end of 'realism' and the onset of hyperreality, a realm where imitation usurps, indeed is 'better than', the real thing (to the extent, paradoxically, that a postmodern art might be claimed as a 'new realism' since this is what society is 'really' like). In this guise postmodern theory had made its way, though not uncritically, back to the city, especially in Soja's reflections on Los Angeles (1998: 239–44; 2000: 323–30) and has incorporated *Blade Runner* as corroboration of both theory and postmodern urban experience (see Wakefield 1990).

Baudrillard's theorisation of the loss of reference, of history and the real (which Steven Best and Douglas Kellner liken to the speculative hypotheses of recent science fiction; 1991: 143) has been answered by a host of left-liberal critics insistent on real-life relations of power and agency and their respectively dire consequences and hard-won achievements. This is not the end of the story, however. For a theory of the untrammelled hyperreal or purely autonomous image not only undermines the concept of reference in the real world – the usual complaint – but also distorts the function of the image, the imaginary and imagination. A world of unrelieved simulation therefore remains stubbornly two-sided, simultaneously presenting the spectacle of unending novelty and invention and the grim prospect of dismal uniformity. Thus, in the end, the bright and ever-new is produced as twin to an unrelenting sameness. If 'reality' is lost on one side, the transformative power of the imagination which has for centuries energised artistic creation, and indeed social and political change, is annulled on the other. Simulations, notes Soja somewhat along these lines, are 'insidiously diverting' (2000: 340). That is to say, 'simulation' has not rid itself entirely of the sense of '*dis*simulation' and of presenting a pliant populace with a diverting narcotic. In short, as in Jameson's argument, the society of simulation is synonymous with advanced consumer or capitalist society and arguably finds its most concentrated expression in the global cities of the world's most powerful capitalist nation. In having pulled apart the two sides of the sign (sloughing off reference and releasing the autonomous reign of the signifier) Baudrillard's simulacrum denies agency and possible change through *either* social realism *or* works of high imagination and fantasy. The latter are consistently credited with the power to estrange the taken-for-granted and overly familiar. But there can be no estrangement or 'critical distance' without reference and no transformation in attitude, sensibility or social forms without a present-day actuality to return to. Hence Jameson's question at the onset of debates on the postmodern: having seen, as he writes, how 'postmodernism replicates or reproduces – reinforces – the logic of consumer capitalism; the more significant question is whether there is also a way in which it resists that logic' (1992: 179).

Science fiction is an obvious place to look for this critical postmodern art. For it is here, by means of what Darko Suvin (1980) characterises as an aesthetic of 'cognitive estrangement' that *this* world can be problematised and re-imagined or out-imagined rather than replicated. The latter term in Jameson suggests an imitation or copy amounting to little more than impotent conformity. But words and meanings too can change, as *Blade Runner* reveals, for here the embodied metaphor of the replicant becomes a catalyst for disturbance and altered awareness. It is through this central device that it plays out the tactics of estrangement and, as sketched above, problematises the binary pairings it first brings into play. But critical estrangement is not limited to self-declared future fictions. It embraces too the undeclared 'fictional' tropes and polemical strategies of urban sociology or cultural geography, caught like literature and film and Los Angeles itself in the implications of a doctrine of simulation, and in the utopian/dystopian rhythms characterising the city's collective urban imaginary. It is at this general level that the affinities – and differences – between film and urban geography become most apparent.

Davis argues that the dystopia of *Blade Runner* has been superseded by events and was anyway indebted to earlier outdated 'modernist' scenarios such as H. G. Wells' *The Future in America* (1906) or Fritz Lang's *Metropolis* (1927). The city, now, as Davis surveys it in *City of Quartz* (1990), in pamphlets and essays through the 1990s, and *Ecology of Fear* (1998) is a city of simulation both in the uneven and unequal emergence as an information city and in the growth of the tourism, hotel and entertainment sector producing the city itself as a hyperreal theme park. Meanwhile, the police force is brutalised, the middle class retreat behind gated enclaves, a pervasive technology of surveillance criminalises non-whites and the homeless, and the city's continued disposal of dangerous waste threatens catastrophic and widespread environmental effects. It is true of course that *Blade Runner* evokes other science fiction texts (its source text, *Do Androids Dream of Electric Sheep?*, amongst them) and that it is, at bottom, a reflection of its moment, even if its different versions mean this moment stretches over a decade. It is a mistake, nonetheless, to convert either version into an intended prediction of a future reality. Davis's own account of Los Angeles is not only, naturally enough, open to debate, but is more to the point openly supplemented by the authority of other works of fiction and in particular, in the present context, by William Gibson's cyberpunk novels and Octavia Butler's *Parable of the Sower* (1993). Davis sees clearly enough how an apparent dialectic of 'simulation' and 'authenticity' is unraveling in the 'social fantasy' of contemporary Los Angeles but consistently uncovers the disadvantaged, undisclosed and out of sight which comprise a fuller social reality – 'our real nightmare', as he puts it (1992). Fiction aids this paradoxically 'realist' project. Thus, what we need instead of the 'gothic romance' of *Blade Runner*, he argues, is the template of a 'relentlessly realistic future' such as Gibson extrapolates 'on what actually exists' (see Davis 1996). Butler's novel he recommends similarly because of its 'disciplined extrapolation [on] existing trends' (1998: 362). Riots, drought, walled suburbs, have, as Davis says, become in her novel a part of everyday life. Nevertheless, the story includes minor and major elements – space exploration, a drug which turns people into pyromaniacs, the heroine Lauren Olamina's condition of 'hyperempathy' – which have little to no 'existing' equivalent. Also, Lauren's privately developed system of belief, named 'Earthseed', and based on the idea of a God whose principal manifestation is 'change', though perhaps an extrapolation on New Age beliefs, is after all sheer invention.

Davis is given to a grimly sublime apocalyptic rhetoric and borrows as easily from noir or science fiction, including H. G. Wells, as, more recently, from catastrophe theory. In *Ecology of Fear*, in the course of contemplating the history and imminence of natural disaster, he surveys several hundred examples of Los Angeles disaster fiction. More tellingly, and in addition to these external sources, his arguments carry their own internal images and alternative scenarios: the lost experiment of the turn-of-the-century socialist community of Llano del Rio established in the Mojave desert, for example, which Davis holds up in *City of Quartz* to the monster Los Angeles has become. Thus, too, in interviews he speaks of defending 'a nostalgised vision of what Southern California was like thirty years ago – the freedom of its beaches and its cruising streets and the kind of careless, libidinal adolescence that used to be possible' (Dery 1996) and reminisces about the earlier industrial era of working steel mills and strong unions in the town of Fontana where he grew up. When he talks of retiring to Butte, Montana, one time 'mecca of copper mines and labour socialism' (Schatz quoted in Dery 1997), it is as if it is to a memory of such a place, empty of its past. *Parable of the Sower* is an attractive text, one suspects, because it belongs with this set of inclinations, especially in the idea (minus its theism), echoing the commune of Llano del Rio, of a settlement established from scratch on communitarian lines away from the hell of Los Angeles with which the novel ends. The libertarian communities hinted at in Gibson's *Virtual Light* and *All Tomorrow's Parties* – though set in San Francisco – might seem to confirm this same utopian side of Davis's thinking. They share a simplicity, an ethic of co-operation and elementary mode of production akin to the earlier time Davis remembers of forgotten forms of labour, solidarity and the 'careless, libidinal adolescence' of a Californian youth. The prospect of a reformed or other, displaced future in the face of the disastrous complexities of postmodern, post-Fordist society is sustained, that is to say, by fragments from the past, lost outside of memory and imagination.

Edward Soja presents Los Angeles as the limit case of the contemporary postmetropolis, the ultimate example of an entire city actively 'replacing reality with insidiously diverting simulations' (2000: 340), and headed down a socio-economic spiral towards a 'bleak *Blade Runner* scenario' (2000: 187). So far this is much like Mike Davis. Like Davis too Soja means to move explicitly 'beyond the *Blade Runner* scenario' (319–22); not, however, so as to paint a still darker world, but in the hope of a transformed future. This cannot derive, so Soja argues, from Baudrillard's fatalism, nor Davis's 'residual historicism' (1996: 201) or other traditional Left strategies. Resistance to the power of hyperreality can no longer content itself with 'stripping away the imagery to unmask the "truer" material reality' (2000: 347), revealed once more as the old enemy, capitalism. Soja looks to a reassertion of the local in the activism of environmental pressure groups and new radical coalitions on issues of space, race, class and gender (2000: 322; 348). He draws openly in this thinking on feminist and poststructuralist models as well as on Foucault's notion of heterotopia, on Henri Lefebvre, and on Jorge Luis Borges' idea of the 'Aleph', 'the space where all places are' to convey the notion of an open, complex totality, an 'imaginable universe' of infinite parts and potential (1996: 56). His continuing project, styled 'Journeys to Los Angeles And Other Real-And-Imagined Places' in the subtitle of the volume *Thirdspace*, is plainly committed to bringing the resources of empirical social science, theory and literature together so as to outline a newly configured and politically engaged urban imaginary.

I want, in what follows, to take up the implication in both Davis and Soja of a need to move 'beyond' *Blade Runner*. We might want to quarrel with Davis on the film of course – for if *Blade Runner* does not show us a world of gang warfare, gated enclaves or the impact of natural disasters, it does evoke the postmetropolitan tropes of environmental pollution, blatant social inequality and police surveillance – but is anyway concerned with a particular theme (genetic engineering), incidentally treated by neither Davis nor Soja, and not with the plight of Los Angeles. Still, this argument is likely to concede too much to the fallacious reading of the film as, in effect, a delayed form of realism which awaits events in the world to prove its predictions correct. We need instead to understand its oblique, selective and speculative reference to the known world. Soja's arguments expressly allow for this kind of flexibility of modes and ways of meaning, and he himself in the three final chapters of the volume *Postmetropolis* adopts a different style, the first two inspired by a performance of scripted interviews by the documentary theatre artist Anna Deveare Smith, the third an unmediated, open-ended conclusion (2000: 353–4).

Why then move on from *Blade Runner*? One date, or rather, event, prompts both Davis and Soja to think this way: 1992 and the so-called 'LA riots' or what Soja terms the 'Justice Riots'. To many, the riots underwrote Davis's prophetic analysis in *City of Quartz*. It is at this point, too, in his discussion, that Soja shifts into a non-academic multi-voiced collage of excerpts from documentary, dramatic and theoretical sources. The riots were located principally in South Central Los Angeles and triggered especially by the 'not-guilty' verdict passed on four LAPD policemen who had been videoed beating a black man, Rodney King, the previous year. As many commentators, including Davis and Soja, argued, the burning, looting and street violence which followed gave explosive expression to years of mounting frustration at the social-economic disadvantage and racism experienced by blacks in the area. What also emerged, in a complex picture of racial tension, was the apparent targeting by looters of Korean stores and, as Mike Davis pointed out, the degree to which the plight of Latino (Mexican and Central American) immigrants was ignored but represented a higher percentage than Blacks (51 per cent to 38 per cent) of those arrested. There were, he argues, essentially two uprisings; one in South Central, 'driven by Black anger' and a 'largely invisible' riot in the Latino Mid-City area (1993: 37–8).

Blade Runner: The Director's Cut was released in 1992. Given its genesis in the 1980s it could not be a contemporary film in any direct sense, and from a perspective which saw the dystopian rhythms of Los Angeles spiral to a new low in the 1990s, it seemed decidedly surpassed by events. Within the terms of a realist framework this is unarguable. However, there are ways, indirect, fleeting and fragmentary, but part nonetheless of the film's central concern with normative concepts of the 'human', which do relate to the issues of race and ethnicity conspicuously raised at this time. For example, the film's normative conception of the human is embodied in the American white male Deckard. That at least is its premise. The replicants' superior strength and intelligence; Deckard's romance with Rachel; his epic roof-top encounter, the tired 1940s detective hero to Roy Batty's athletic Aryan; his self-doubt or, if you will, eventual consciousness of his own replicant identity – all serve to question the authority of this norm. The police chief Bryant refers to the replicants as 'skin jobs' (glossed in the original voice-over as like calling black men 'niggers'); there was an initial idea that Leon would be black (see Sammon 1996: 108); and the world of the street, including the market which services the Tyrell Corporation is peopled largely by Asian-Americans. These are the 'little people' from which Deckard is literally lifted up to re-assume the role of blade runner under the threat of being 'retired' and returned to that same subordinated populace if he refuses or fails.

Of most interest in all this, however, is the little explored relationship between Deckard and Gaff. Gaff is American-Japanese-Mexican; speaks the hybrid street slang of 'Cityspeak', an amalgam of 'Japanese, Spanish, German, whatever', and he is a blade runner. The actor Edward James Olmos is Mexican-American. He constructed a backstory of Gaff as primarily 'Mexican-Japanese ... more Asian than anything else' but with 'some other nationalities in him too' (Sammon 1996: 113–14). The idea of Cityspeak derived from early allusions to the slang of 'Latino guys in East LA', the Tagalog spoken by Filipinos, until Olmos translated Gaff's 'original dialogue into fragments of foreign tongues' (1996: 115) – all of which emphasise his ethnic hybridity and 'otherness'. The Director's Cut, which for many confirms that Deckard is a replicant (whether an anterior, superannuated type or more advanced, because more conventionally human, model), also establishes a particular affinity between Gaff and Deckard. The Director's Cut also of course notably includes Deckard's reverie or dream of a unicorn. This insert of a few seconds serves a number of functions. The appearance of a fabulous beast from the borderland realm of myth or fable reinforces the film's underlying interest in a new hybrid, posthuman type; it adds to the film's own imaginative structure and intertextual operation; and it explains the origami unicorn Gaff leaves for Deckard at the film's close. Gaff, this implies, knows that Deckard's dream is an implant, just as Deckard knows this of Rachel's memories. This does not – in what remains the most common reading of this central theme – simply confirm the suspicion that Deckard is a replicant, but suggests, that Gaff and Deckard are similarly situated in the in-between hybrid world of human/replicant. They are, in other words, instances of the 'posthuman' the film works to produce. If this is speculative, it is precisely this kind of speculation the film enacts and engenders throughout in taking us beyond the duality of 'human' and 'replicant' and the allied normative social and ethnic categories attached to this distinction.

The white American male and his 'foreign' ethnic other thus emerge as in fact kin. They are privy to the same non-standard 'gibberish' and share a silent understanding; even to the point of inhabiting each other's dreams and common archetypes. 'It's too bad she won't live', Gaff declares of Rachel at the film's dénouement, 'but then again, who does?' Deckard's nod to this remembered, now interiorised speech, as he ponders the origami unicorn, is not a nod to a superior human intelligence but the acknowledgement of a recognised affinity, a shared condition of uncertainty and indeterminacy; one which echoes the film's simple but radical discovery of a common predicament for human and replicant alike: 'All he wanted', says Deckard of Batty, 'was the same answers the rest of us want. Where do I come from? Where am I going? How long have I got?' The apparent cliché of a bland humanism (we are all alike in the end) is rendered as an acceptance across differences of the never to be realised quest for final knowledge. The questions are unanswered, as the Director's Cut significantly underlines; the lift closes on darkness: there is no final identity, nor destiny.

This has nothing directly to do with the LA riots of 1992.[2] It does, however, speak to some of the complexities of a racialised and racist society founded on notions of normative and non-normative 'alien' or 'non-human' identities, raised in the discursive forms of reportage and political analysis of this episode by, amongst others, Davis and Soja.[3] In one of the few direct discussions of ethnicity in the film (and which she rightly argues distinguishes it from *Metropolis*), Janet L. Abu-Lughod, once more an urban sociologist, notes how 'Anglos' are elevated above both 'robotic "hands"' who wish to be 'real people' and 'unassimilable and marginalised "exotics" ... cordoned off in deteriorated zones' (1999: 379). Presumably these are the 'Asiatics', amongst others, who comprise the 'little people', who occupy the street level.

What is striking, however, says Abu-Lughod, about this 'nightmare' future is that any anxieties about the 'the Hispanicisation of Los Angeles are distinctly muted' (1999: 378). 'Mexicans/Mexican Americans' who she feels would occupy the role 'today' (the late 1990s) of docile hands or 'rebellious others' are symptomatically out of view (1999: 379). In fact, however, the Director's Cut intimates an underlying, hitherto repressed, intimacy between the normative Anglo male and his 'exotic' Japanese-Mexican-American other, and brings its hero to an emerging consciousness of this. It does this too in a way that is of special interest to the present argument about how meanings are conveyed. For it suggests that this affinity can only be expressed obliquely, without words ('muted' if you will) – for the characters themselves and in Scott's recovery of his own original intention – through the medium of image and dream and in the displaced realm of fantasy.

Edward Soja defines the 'urban imaginary' as 'our mental or cognitive mappings of urban reality and the interpretative grids' by which we live and act in urban places, spaces and communities (2000: 324). In a world where the urban imaginary is so markedly changed that distinctions 'between what is *real* and what is *imagined*, what can reliably be identified as fact as opposed to what must clearly be labelled fiction' are difficult to draw (2000: 325), Soja seeks a progressive apprehension of the 'real-and-imagined' as a combinatory, hybrid 'Thirdspace'. I have wanted to confirm this interdependence of modes of analysis and representation less from a base in social science or 'fact' than from the other side, the side of fiction, and to point out three things: firstly, how a discourse of the imagined is an inevitable dimension of social or cultural geography; how, secondly, both belong to a historically changing consciousness responsive to the actuality of the postmetropolis, but, thirdly, also, to suggest how fiction can participate in its own ways, through image and implication, in helping us rethink the present and the new.

Blade Runner prompts this critical re-visioning in ways which cross cliché and convention with a remarkable inventiveness and, in the small changes to the Director's Cut, a boldness which gives its deliberations on the posthuman an unexpected contemporary specificity. Within what is commonly deemed the film's predominantly dystopian mode it comes, therefore, as suggested here, to imply an unsettling and more open consciousness of the human, the machine and ethnicity. It compares in this respect with the cultural strategy Soja theorises as 'othering' and would enlist in a 'postmodern politics of social and spatial justice' (1996: 5, 10–11; 2000: 348). It is important, all the same, to say that *Blade Runner* does this differently – fleetingly and profoundly; that it drops a three-second reverie, as it were, upon a wide conceptual map. Soja's critical cultural politics calls, he says, for 'an alternative and transgressive new imagery ... for so much now depends on these image wars' (2000: 348). *Blade Runner* does not rise to Soja's full agenda. Nevertheless, this deeply embedded, iconic text which he and Davis want to move 'beyond', does, with all due qualifications, already occupy such a space.

NOTES

1   Blake's lines from 'America: A Prophecy' are 'Fiery the Angels rose, and as they rose deep thunder roll'd, Around their shores; indignant burning with the fires of Orc': given in William M. Kolb, 'Blade Runner Film Notes' in Judith B. Kerman (ed.) *Retrofitting Blade Runner*, Bowling Green, Ohio: Bowling Green State University Press (1997), p.160.
2   A film which does more explicitly represent the riots of 1992 and issues of race is Kathryn Bigelow's *Strange Days*; see Brooker 2003.
3   Soja includes documentary and dramatised material which tells how the accused LAPD policemen spoke of Rodney King as 'like a wounded animal ... a monster ... a big man ... acting like an animal' and describes how members of the LAPD force, composed almost exclusively of white men and women, living in close communities outside the city, such as Simi Valley where the four accused lived, saw black society as a threat to the ordered normative model of the family (2000: 368–9; 374–5).

FILMOGRAPHY

A Beautiful Mind – dir. Ron Howard, 2001; DVD Universal, 2002.

Abre los Ojos/Open Your Eyes, – dir. Alejandro Amenàbar, 1997; DVD, Momentum Pictures Home Entertainment, 2002.

Akira – dir. Katsuhiro Ôtomo, 1988; DVD Special Edition, Pioneer Video, 2001.

Alien – dir. Ridley Scott, 1979; DVD 20th Anniversary Edition, 20th Century Fox Home Entertainment, 1999.

Aliens – dir. James Cameron, 1986; DVD 20th Century Fox Entertainment, 1999.

Artificial Intelligence: A.I. – dir. Steven Spielberg, 2001; DVD Dreamworks, 2002.

Anderson, Paul. 'Commentary on *Soldier*' in *Soldier* – dir. Paul Anderson, 1998: DVD, Warner Home Video, 1999.

Batman – dir. Tim Burton, 1989; DVD Warner Home Video, 1997.

Batman Forever – dir. Joel Schumacher, 1995; DVD Warner Home Video, 1997.

Barjo/Confessions D'Un Barjo – dir. Jérôme Boivin, 1992.

Blade Runner – dir. Ridley Scott, 1982; DVD Warner Home Video, 1999.

Blade Runner: The Director's Cut – dir. Ridley Scott, 1992; DVD Warner Home Video, 2003.

Brazil – dir. Terry Gilliam, 1985; DVD Criterion-Home Vision Entertainment, 1999.

Breathless – dir. Jim McBride, 1983; DVD MGM Home Entertainment, 2001.

Bugsy – dir. Barry Levinson, 1991; DVD UCA Catalogue, 2003.

Citizen Kane – dir. Orson Welles, 1941; DVD Universal Pictures Video, 2004.

Close Encounters of the Third Kind – dir. Steven Spielberg, 1977; DVD The Collectors Edition, Columbia Tristar, 2001.

Contact – dir. Robert Zemeckis, 1997; DVD Warner Home Video, 1997.

Crash – dir. David Cronenberg, 1996; DVD New Line Home Video, 1998.

Cube – dir. Vincenzo Natali, 1997; DVD Trimark Home Video, 1999.

Dark City – dir. Alex Proyas, 1998; DVD The New Line Platinum Series, New Line Studios, 1998.

The Day the Earth Stood Still – dir. Robert Wise, 1951; 20th Century Fox Home Entertainment, 2003.

'Deconstructing *Minority Report*' – dir. Laurent Bouzereau, *Minority Report* DVD.

Donnie Darko – dir. Richard Kelly, 2001; DVD 20th Century Fox Home Entertainment, 2000.

Double Indemnity – dir. Billy Wilder, 1944; DVD Image Entertainment, 1998.

Escape from New York – dir. John Carpenter, 1981; DVD MGM Home Entertainment, 2000.

Escape from LA – dir. John Carpenter, 1996; DVD Paramount, 1998.

eXistenZ – dir. David Cronenberg, 1999; DVD Dimension Home Video, Buena Vista Home Entertainment, 1999.

The Fifth Element – dir. Luc Besson, 1997; DVD Columbia TriStar 1997.

Fight Club – dir. David Fincher, 1999; DVD 20th Century Fox Entertainment, 2000.

The Fly – dir. David Cronenberg, 1986; DVD 20th Century Fox Entertainment, 2000.

Forbidden Planet – dir. Fred M. Wilcox, 1956; DVD MGM Home Entertainment, 1997.

Fortress – dir. Stuart Gordon, 1993; DVD Artisan Entertainment, 1999.

Gattaca – dir. Andrew Wood, 1997; DVD Columbia/TriStar, 1998.

Ghost in the Shell – dir. Mamoru Oshii, 1995; DVD Manga Video, 1998.

GI Jane – dir. Ridley Scott, 1997; DVD First Independent Video, 2001.

Gilda – dir. Charles Vidor, 1946; DVD Columbia Tri-Star home Video, 2000.

Guilty by Suspicion – dir. Irwin Winkler, 1990; DVD 20th Century Fox Home Entertainment, 2003.

The Handmaid's Tale – dir. Volker Schlöndorff, 1990; DVD MGM Home Entertainment, 2001.

Heat – dir. Michael Mann, 1995; DVD Warner Home Video, 2005.

House on Haunted Hill – dir. William Malone, 1999; DVD DVD Warner Home Video, 2000.

House Party 2 – dirs. George Jackson and Doug McHenry, 1991; DVD Entertainment in Video, 2004.

Imagining Total Recall – *Total Recall* DVD.

Impostor – dir. Gary Fleder, 2002; DVD Dimension Home Video, 2002.

Invasion of the Body Snatchers – dir. Don Siegel, 1956; DVD Republic Pictures, 1998.

Invasion of the Body Snatchers – dir. Philip Kaufman, 1978; DVD MGM Home Entertainment, 2000.

Jackie Brown – dir. Quentin Tarantino, 1997; DVD Miramax Home Entertainment, 2002.

Johnny Mnemonic – dir. Robert Longo, 1995; DVD Columbia/TriStar, 1998.

Judge Dredd – dir. Danny Cannon, 1995; DVD Hollywood Pictures Home Video, 1998.

Kes – dir. Ken Loach, 1969; DVD MGM Home Entertainment, 2003.

La cité des enfants perdus/The City of Lost Children – dirs. Marc Caro and Jean-Pierre Jeunet, 1995; DVD Columbia/Tristar, 1999.

LA Confidential – dir. Curtis Hanson, 1997; DVD Warner Home Video, 1998.

Lethal Weapon 4 – dir. Richard Donner, 1998; DVD Warner Home Video 1999.

Lucia y el sexo/Sex and Lucia – dir. Julio Medem, 2001; DVD Tartan Video, 2002.

Mad Max – dir. George Miller, 1979; DVD Image Entertainment, 1997.

Mad Max II: The Road Warrior – dir. George Miller, 1981; DVD Warner Home Video, 1999.

The Maltese Falcon – dir. John Huston, 1941; DVD Warner Home Video, 2000.

The Matrix – dirs. Andy and Larry Wachowski, 1999; DVD Special Edition Warner Home Video, 1999.

The Matrix Reloaded – dirs. Andy and Larry Wachowski, 2003; DVD Warner Home Video 2003.

The Matrix Revolutions – dirs. Andy and Larry Wachowski, 2003; DVD Warner Home Video, 2004.

Memento – dir. Christopher Nolan, 2000; DVD Columbia/TriStar, 2001.

Metropolis – dir. Fritz Lang, 1927; DVD Deluxe Edition ufa Home Entertainment,

2003.

Midnight Cowboy – dir. John Schlesinger, 1969; DVD MGM Home Entertainment (Europe) Ltd., 2000.

Mildred Pierce – dir. Michael Curtiz, 1945; DVD Warner Home Video, 2005.

Millennium – dir. Michael Anderson, 1989; DVD Artisan Entertainment, 1999.

Minority Report – dir. Steven Spielberg, 2002; DVD. DreamWorks Home Entertainment, 2002.

Mulholland Dr. – dir. David Lynch, 2001; DVD Universal, 2002.

Naked – dir. Mike Leigh, 1993; DVD Criterion, 2005.

Nemesis – dir. Albert Pyun,1993; DVD Lions Gate Home Entertainment, 2001.

Nil by Mouth – dir. Gary Oldman, 1997; DVD 20th Century Fox Home Entertainment, 2001.

No Escape – dir. Martin Campbell, 1994; DVD HBO Home Video, 1998.

North By Northwest – dir. Alfred Hitchcock, 1959; DVD Warner Home Video, 2000.

On the Edge of Blade Runner – dir. Andrew Abbott, 2000, televsion documentary, Channel 4, originally aired 15 July 2000.

Paycheck – dir. John Woo, 2004; DVD Paramount, 2004.

Pulp Fiction – dir. Quentin Tarantino, 1994; DVD Miramax Home Entertainment, 1998.

Reservoir Dogs – dir. Quentin Tarantino, 1992; DVD Artisan Entertainment, 2002.

Rita, Sue, and Bob too - dir. Aland Clarke, 1985; DVD Cinema Club, 2003.

RoboCop – dir. Paul Verhoeven, 1987; DVD Image Entertainment, 1997.

Saturday Night and Sunday Morning – dir. Karel Reisz, 1960; DVD British Film Institute Video Publishing, 2003.

Scanners II: The New Order – dir. Christian Duguay, 1991; Anchor Bay Entertainment, 2005.

Scanners III: The Takeover – dir. Christian Duguay, 1992; Anchor Bay Entertainment, 2005.

Screamers – dir. Christian Duguay, 1995; DVD Columbia/TriStar, 1998.

Se7en – dir. David Fincher, 1995; DVD New Line Home Video, 1997.

The Shining – dir. Stanley Kubrick, 1980; DVD Warner Home Video, 2001.

Shrek 2 – dirs. Andrew Adamson and Kelly Asbury, 2004; DVD Warner Home Video, 2001.

The Silence of the Lambs – dir. Jonathan Demme 1991; DVD MGM Home Entertainment (Europe) Ltd., 2003.

The Sixth Sense – dir. M. Night Shyamalan, 1999; DVD Hollywood Pictures Home Video, 2000.

Solaris – dir. Steven Soderbergh, 2002; DVD 20th Century Fox Home Entertainment, 2003.

Soldier – dir. Paul Anderson, 1998; DVD Warner Home Video, 1999.

Spider – dir. David Cronenberg, 2002; DVD Redbus, 2003.

Starship Troopers – dir. Paul Verhoeven, 1997; DVD Columbia/TriStar, 1998.

Star Trek – First Contact – dir. Jonathan Frakes, 1996; DVD Paramount, 1998.

Star Trek II: The Wrath of Khan – dir. Nicholas Meyer, 1982; DVD Paramount, 2000.

Star Wars: Episode I – The Phantom Menace – dir. George Lucas, 1999; DVD 20th

Century Fox Home Entertainment, 2001.

Star Wars: Episode II – Attack of the Clones – dir. George Lucas, 2002; DVD 20th Century Fox Home Entertainment, 2002.

Star Wars: Episode IV – A New Hope – dir. George Lucas, 1977; DVD 20th Century Fox Home Entertainment, 2004.

Strange Days – dir. Kathryn Bigelow, 1995; DVD 20th Century Home Video, 1998.

Suzhou Ie/Suzhou River – dir. Lou Ye, 2000; DVD Artificial Eye Co. Ltd., 2003.

Taxi Driver – dir. Martin Scorsese, 1976; DVD Tri-Star Home Video, 1999.

The Terminator – dir. James Cameron, 1984; DVD MGM Home Entertainment, 2001.

The Terminator 2: Judgment Day – dir. James Cameron, 1991; DVD Live Entertainment, 1997.

The Terminator 3: Rise of the Machines – dir. Jonathon Mostow, 2003; DVD Warner Home Video, 2003.

Thelma & Louise – dir. Ridley Scott, 1991; DVD MGM Home Entertainment, 1997.

The Third Man – dir. Carol Reed, 1949; Criterion, 1999.

THX-1138 – dir. George Lucas, 1971; Warner Home Video, 2004.

Touch of Evil – dir. Orson Welles, 1958; DVD Universal Pictures Video, 2003.

Total Recall – dir. Paul Verhoeven, 1990; DVD Artisan Home Entertainment, 2002.

The Truman Show – dir. Peter Weir, 1998; DVD Paramount, 1999.

Twelve Monkeys – dir. Terry Gilliam, 1996; DVD Universal Home Video, 1998.

28 Days Later – dir. Danny Boyle, 2002; DVD 20th Century Fox Home Entertainment, 2003.

2001: A Space Odyssey – dir. Stanley Kubrick, 1968; DVD Warner Home Video, 2001.

Vanilla Sky – dir. Cameron Crowe, 2001: DVD Paramount, 2002.

Videodrome – dir. David Cronenberg, 1983; DVD Universal, 1998

Vroom – dir. Beeban Kidron; 1988; VHS First Independent Video, 1997.

When Worlds Collide – dir. Rudolph Maté, 1951; DVD Paramount, 2003.

Who Framed Roger Rabbit – dir. Robert Zemeckis, 1988; DVD Disney/Touchstone, 1999.

Wolf – dir. Mike Nichols, 1994; VHS, Columbia Tri-Star Home Video, 1995.

X-Men – dir. Bryan Singer, 2000; DVD 20th Century Fox Home Entertainment, 2000.

X-Men II – dir. Bryan Singer, 2003; DVD 20th Century Fox Home Entertainment, 2003.

Y2K: The Invasion of the Millennium Bug. PBS Home Video. Produced by South Dakota Public Television. Burbank: Warner Home Video, 1999.

COMPUTER GAMES

Adventure – 1976; developed and published by Crowther and Woods.

Black and White – 2001; developed by Lionhead Studios and published by EA Games.

Blade Runner – 1997; developed and published by Westwood Studios.

Deadline – 1982; developed by Marc Blank and published by Infocom.

Deus Ex – 2000; developed by Ion Storm and published by Eidos Interactive.

Doom – 1993; developed and published by id Software.

Duke Nukem – 1996; developed by Eurocom Entertainment Software and published by GT Interactive.

The 11th Hour – 1995; developed by Trilobyte and published by Virgin Interactive.

Gabriel Knight – 1993; developed and published by Sierra.

Grand Theft Auto III – 2002; developed and published by Rockstar Games.

Half-Life – 2001; developed by Gearbox Software and published by Sierra.

The Longest Journey – 2000; developed and published by Funcom.

Myst – 1993; developed by Cyan Ltd and published by Brøderbund.

Prince of Persia: The Sands of Time – 2003; developed and published by Ubisoft.

Quake – 2000; produced and developed by Activision.

Syberia – 2002; developed by Microids and published by Adventure Company.

Tomb Raider – 2000; developed and produced by Eidos Interactive.

BIBLIOGRAPHY

Aarseth, E. (1997) *Cybertext. Perspectives on Ergodic Literature*. Baltimore: John Hopkins University Press.

____ (2004) 'Genre Trouble: Narrativism and the Art of Simulation', in N. Wardrip–Fuin and P. Harrigan (eds) *First Person: New Media as Story, Performance and Game*. Cambridge, MA: MIT Press, 45–55.

Abu-Lughod, J. L. (1999) *New York, Chicago, Los Angeles. America's Global Cities*. Minneapolis: University of Minnesota Press.

Aden, R. C. (1999) *Popular Stories and Promised Lands: Fan Cultures and Symbolic Pilgrimages*. Tuscaloosa: University of Alabama Press.

Adorno, T. and M. Horkheimer (1993) 'The Culture Industry: Enlightenment as Mass Deception', in S. During (ed.) *The Cultural Studies Reader*. London: Routledge, 31–41.

Aitken, S. C. (2002) 'Tuning the Self: City Space and SF Horror Movies', in R. Kitchin and J. Kneale (eds) *Lost in Space: Geographies of Science Fiction*. Continuum: London and New York, 104–22.

Alessio, D. (2004) '"Race', Gender and Proto–Nationalism in Julius Vogel's *Anno Domini 2000*', *Foundation*, 91, 36-54.

Alter, R. (1981) *The Art of Biblical Narrative*. NY: Basic Books.

Anon. (1999) 'Y2K and the Apocalypse', *Anti-Defamation League Online Homepage*. Available online: http://www.adl.org/y2k/apocalypse.asp (accessed 1 June 2004).

Anon. (2000) 'Introduction', *Federal Y2K Biomedical Equipment Clearinghouse*. Available online: http://www.fda.gov/cdrh/yr2000/year 2000.html (accessed 1 June 2004).

Anthony, P. (1969) *Macroscope*. New York: Avon.

Atkins, B. (2003) *More Than a Game: The Computer Game as Fictional Form*, Manchester: Manchester University Press.

Bakhtin, M. M. (1981) *The Dialogic Imagination*. Trans. C. Emerson and M. Holquist. Ed. M. Holquist. Austin: University of Texas Press.

____ (1986) *Speech Genres and Other Late Essays*. Trans. V. W. McGee. Eds C. Emerson and M. Holquist. Austin: University of Texas Press.

Ballard, J. G. (1973) *Crash*. London: Jonathan Cape.

Barlow, A. (1997) 'Philip K. Dick's Androids: Victimized Victimizers', in J. B. Kerman, *Retrofitting Blade Runner: Issues in Ridley Scott's Blade Runner and Philip K. Dick's Do Androids Dream of Electric Sheep?* (second edition). Bowling Green: Popular Press, 76–89.

Barker, M. and K. Brooks (1998) *Knowing Audiences: Judge Dredd, Its Friends, Fans and Foes*. Luton: University of Luton Press.

Barker, M., J. Arthurs and R. Harindranath (2001) *The Crash Controversy: Censorship Campaigns and Film Reception*. London: Wallflower Press.

Barthes, R. (1977) 'The Death of the Author', in *Image/Music/Text*. Trans. S. Heath. Glasgow: Fontana-Collins, 142–48.

Baudrillard, J. (1981) 'Simulacra and Simulations', in *Jean Baudrillard, Selected Writings*. Stanford, CA: Stanford University Press, 1998, 166–84.

_____ (1988) *Selected Writings*. Stanford, CA: Stanford University Press.

Bauer, J. (1998) 'Philip K. Dick is Dead'. Available online: http://PhilipKDickfans.com (accessed 12 May 2004).

Bellamy, E. (1986 [1888]) *Looking Backward: 2000–1887*. Middlesex: Penguin.

Ben-Abba, D. (ed.) (1994) *The Meridian Hebrew/English English/Hebrew Dictionary*. NY: Penguin/Meridian.

Bennett, T. and J. Woollacott (1987) *Bond and Beyond: The Political Career of a Popular Hero*. London: MacMillan.

Bergstrom, J. (1991) 'Androids and Androgyny', in C. Penley, E. Lyon, L. Spigel and J. Bergstrom (eds) *Close Encounters: Film, Feminism and Science Fiction*. Minneapolis and London: University of Minnesota Press, 33–60.

Best, S. and D. Kellner (1991) *Postmodern Theory*. Critical Interrogations. London: Macmillan.

Bignell, J. (2000) *Postmodern Media Culture*. Edinburgh University Press: Edinburgh.

_____ (2004) *An Introduction to Television Studies*. Routledge: London and New York.

Bird, E. S. (2003) *The Audience in Everyday Life: Living in a Media World*. Routledge: New York and London.

Bolter, J.D. and R. Grusin (1999) *Remediation: Understanding New Media*. Cambridge, MA: MIT Press.

Boonstra, J. (1982) 'Final Interview with Philip K. Dick', in *Rod Serling's The Twilight Zone Magazine*, 2, 3, 47–52.

Boozer Jr, J. (1997) 'Crashing the Gates of Insight: *Blade Runner*', in J. B. Kerman (ed.) *Retrofitting Blade Runner: Issues in Ridley Scott's Blade Runner and Philip K. Dick's Do Androids Dream of Electric Sheep?* (second edition). Bowling Green, OH: Popular Press, 212–228.

Bordwell, D. (1989) M*aking Meaning: Inference and Rhetoric in the Interpretation of Cinema*. Cambridge, MA and London: Harvard University Press.

Botting, F. and S. Wilson (1998) 'Automatic love', *Screen*, 39, 2, 186–92.

Bould, M., (1999) 'Preserving machines: recentring the decentred subject in *Blade Runner* and *Johnny Mnemonic*', in J. Bignell (ed.) *Writing and Cinema*. Essex: Longman, 164–78.

Bourdieu, P. (1986) *Distinction: A Social Critique of the Judgement of Taste*. London: Routledge.

Brecht, B. (1976) *Poems 1913–1956*. Eds John Willett and Ralph Manheim. London: Eyre Methuen.

Brooker, W. (1999) 'Internet Fandom and the Continuing Narratives of *Star Wars, Blade Runner* and *Alien*', in A. Kuhn (ed.) *Alien Zone II*. London: Verso, 50–72.

_____ (2001) 'Living on Dawson's Creek: Teen Viewers, Cultural Convergence and Television Overflow', *International Journal of Cultural Studies*, 4, 4, 456–72.

___ (2002) *Using the Force: Creativity, Community and* Star Wars *Fans*. London: Continuum.

___ (2003) 'Rescuing *Strange Days*: Fan Reaction to a Critical and Commercial Failure' in D. Jermyn and S. Redmond (eds) *The Cinema of Kathryn Bigelow: Hollywood Transgressor*. London and New York: Wallflower Press, 198–219.

___ (2004) *Alice's Adventures: Lewis Carroll in Popular Culture*. New York and London: Continuum.

Brooker, P. and W. Brooker (1997) *Postmodern After-images*. London: Arnold.

Brooks, P. (1983) *Reading for the Plot. Design and Intention in Narrative*. New York: Alfred Knopf.

Bruno, G. (1990 [1987]) 'Ramble City: Postmodernism and *Blade Runner*', in A. Kuhn (ed.) *Alien Zone: Cultural Theory and Contemporary Science FictionCinema*. London: Verso, 183–95.

Bukatman, S. (1990) 'Who Programs You?', in A. Kuhn (ed.) *Alien Zones: Cultural Theory and Contemporary Science Fiction Cinema*. London and New York: Verso, 196–213.

___ (1993) *Terminal Identity: The Virtual Subject in Post-Modern Science Fiction*. Durham and London: Duke University Press.

___ (1997) *Blade Runner*. London: British Film Institute.

___ (2003) *Matters of Gravity: Special Effects and Supermen in the 20th Century*. Durham and London: Duke University Press.

Burdett, J. (2003) *Bangkok 8*. New York: Alfred A. Knopf.

Burroughs, W. (1979) Blade Runner: A Movie. Berkeley: Blue Wind Press.

Butler, A. M. (2000) *Philip K. Dick*. Harpenden: Pocket Essentials.

___ (2003) 'Postmodernism and Science Fiction', in E. James and F. Mendlesohn (eds) *Cambridge Companion to Science Fiction*. Cambridge: Cambridge University Press, 137–48.

Butler, O. E. (1993) *Parable of the Sower*, New York: Warner Books, in association with Seven Storries Press.

Carper, S. (1997) 'Subverting the Disaffected City: Cityscape in *Blade Runner*', in J. B. Kerman, *Retrofitting Blade Runner: Issues in Ridley Scott's Blade Runner and Philip K. Dick's Do Androids Dream of Electric Sheep?* (second edition). Bowling Green, OH: Popular Press, 185–195.

Carter, D. (2003) 'licenced vs original games', in *Develop 26*, March, 30–2.

Casey, B., N. Casey, B. Calvert, L. French and J. Lewis (2002) *Television Studies: The Key Concepts*. London and New York: Routledge.

Cavicchi, D. (1998) *Tramps Like Us: Music and Meaning Among Springsteen Fans*, Oxford: Oxford University Press.

Chin, B. and J. Gray (2001) '"One Ring to Rule Them All": Pre-Viewers and Pre-Texts of the *Lord of the Rings* Films', *Intensities: The Journal of Cult Media*, 2. Available online: http://www.cult-media.com (accessed 2 January 2004).

Church Gibson, P. (2001) '"You've been in my life so long I can't remember anything else": into the labyrinth with Ripley and the Alien', in M. Tinkcom and A. Villarejo (eds) *Keyframes: Popular Cinema and Cultural Studies*. New York and London: Routledge, 35–51.

Clarke, D. (ed.) (1997) *The Cinematic City*. London & New York: Routledge.

Clute, J. and P. Nicholls (eds) (1999) *The Encyclopedia of Science Fiction*. London: Orbit.

Cobham, E. and Rev'd I.H. Evans (eds) (1994) *The Wordsworth Dictionary of Phrase & Fable*. Ware: Wordsworth Editions Ltd.

Cook, P. (1998) 'Duplicity in Mildred Pierce', in E. A. Kaplan (ed.) *Women in Film Noir* (second edition). London: British Film Institute, 69–80.

Corrigan, T. (1991) 'Film and the Culture of Cult', in J. P. Telotte (ed.) *The Cult Film Experience: Beyond All Reason*. Austin: University of Texas Press, 26–37.

Cowie, E. (1993) 'Film noir and Women', in J. Copjec (ed.) *Shades of Noir*. London and New York: Verso, 121–65.

Creed, B. (1998) The Crash Debate: Anal wounds, metallic kisses, Screen, 39, 2, 175–9.

Cussons, J. (2004) The Bughouse Intro. Available online: http://groups.yahoo.com/group/the_bughouse (accessed 3 October 2005).

Dacre, A. (1998) 'Predator 3, or the cultural logic of late capitalism', *The UTS Review*, 4, 2, 1–13.

Darley, A. (2000) *Visual Digital Culture. Surface Play and Spectacle in New Media Genres*. London: Routledge.

Davies, J. (2003) 'Against the Los Angeles Symbolic: Unpacking the Racialized Discourse of the Automobile in 1980s and 1990s Cinema', in M. Shiel and T. Fitzmaurice (eds) *Screening the City*. London: Verso, 216–38.

Davis, M. (1988). 'Urban Renaissance and the Spirit of Postmodernism' in E. A. Kaplan (ed.) *Postmodernism and its Discontents*. London: Verso.

_____ (1990) *City of Quartz, Excavating the Future in Los Angeles*. London: Verso.

_____ (1992) *Beyond Blade Runner: Urban Control and the Ecology of Fear*. Westfield, NJ: Open Magazine Pamphlet Series. Available online: http://www.levity.com/markdery/ESCAPE/VELOCITY/author/davis.html (accessed 20 November 2004).

_____ (1993) 'Who Killed Los Angeles? The Verdict is Given', *New Left Review*, 199, 29–54.

_____ (1998) *Ecology of Fear. Los Angeles and the Imagination of Disaster*. London: Picador.

De Certeau, M. (1984) *The Practice of Everyday Life*. Berkeley: University of California Press.

Denzin, N. K. (1991) *Images of Postmodern Society: Social Theory and Contemporary Cinema*. London: Sage.

Dery, M. (1996) 'Downsizing the Future. Beyond *Blade Runner* with Mike Davis', *Escape Velocity*. Available online: http://www.levity.com/markdery/ESCAPE/VELOCITY/author/davis.html (accessed 21 November 2004).

Desser, D. (1997) 'The New Eve: The Influence of *Paradise Lost* and *Frankenstein* on *Blade Runner*', in J. B. Kerman (ed.) *Retrofitting Blade Runner: Issues in Ridley Scott's Blade Runner and Philip K. Dick's Do Androids Dream of Electric Sheep?* (second edition). Bowling Green, OH: Popular Press, 53–65.

_____ (1997) 'Race, Space and Class: The Politics of the SF Film from *Metropolis* to

Blade Runner', in J. B. Kerman (ed.) *Retrofitting Blade Runner: Issues in Ridley Scott's Blade Runner and Philip K. Dick's Do Androids Dream of Electric Sheep?* (second edition). Bowling Green, OH: Popular Press, 110–123.

____ (1999) 'Race, Space and Class: The Politics of Cityscapes in Science-Fiction Films', in A. Kuhn (ed.) *Alien Zone II*. London: Verso, 80–96.

Dick, P. K. (1955) *Solar Lottery*. New York: Ace Books.

____ (1957) *Eye in the Sky*. New York: Ace Books.

____ (1959) *Time Out of Joint*. New York: Lippincott.

____ (1962) *The Man in the High Castle*. New York: Putnams.

____ (1963) 'The Days of Perky Pat', in *The Days of Perky Pat: The Collected Stories of Philip K. Dick, Vol. 1*. Los Angeles: Underwood/Miller, 301-21.

____ (1964) *The Three Stigmata Of Palma Eldritch*. Garden City, NJ: Doubleday.

____ (1975) *Confessions of a Crap Artist*, Los Angeles: Entwhistle Books.

____ (1969) *Ubik,* Garden City, NJ: Doubleday.

____ (1970) *Our Friends From Frolix 8*. New York: Ace Books.

____ (1974) *Flow My Tears, the Policeman Said. New York: Doubleday.*

____ (1977) *A Scanner Darkly*, Garden City, NJ: Doubleday.

____ (1985) 'Introduction: How to Build a Universe That Doesn't Fall Apart Two Days Later', in *I Hope I Shall Arrive Soon*. Garden City, NJ: Doubleday, 1--23.

____ (1987 [1952]) 'Second Variety' in *Second Variety: The Collected Stories of Philip K. Dick, Vol. 2*, Los Angeles: Underwood/Miller, 15–52.

____ (1987 [1953]) 'Paycheck', in *Beyond Lies the Wub: The Collected Stories of Philip K. Dick, Vol. 1*. Los Angeles: Underwood/Miller, 279–308.

___ (1987 [1954]) 'Meddler', in *Beyond Lies the Wub: The Collected Stories of Philip K. Dick, Vol. 1*. Los Angeles: Underwood/Miller, 269–78.

____ (1987 [1968]) 'The Electric Ant', in *The Little Black Box: The Collected Stories of Philip K. Dick, Vol. 5*. Los Angeles: Underwood/Miller, 225-39.

____ (1994 [1953]) 'Impostor', in *Second Variety: The Collected Stories of Philip K. Dick, Vol. 2*. London: Harper Collins, 348–393.

____ (1996 [1968]) *Do Androids Dream of Electric Sheep?*. New York: Del Rey/Ballantine.

____ (2002 [1956]) 'The Minority Report', *Minority Report*, London: Orion/Gollancz, 1–44.

____ (2002 [1966]) 'We Can Remember It For You Wholesale', *Minority Report*, London: Orion/Gollancz, 267–290.

Doel, M. A. and D. B. Clarke (1997) 'From Ramble City to the Screening of the Eye: *Blade Runner*, Death and Symbolic Exchange', in D. B. Clarke (ed.) *The Cinematic City*. London and New York: Routledge, 140–67.

Doty, A. (2000) *Flaming Classics*. New York and London: Routledge.

Duany, A., E. Plater–Zyberk and J. Speck (2000) *Suburban Nation: The Rise of Sprawl and the Decline of the American Dream*. New York: North Point Press.

Dyer, R. (1979) *Stars*, London: British Film Institute.

____ (1997) *White*. London: Routledge.

____ (1998) 'Resistance through Charisma: Rita Hayworth and Gilda', in E. A. Kaplan (ed.) *Women in Film Noir* (second edition). London: British Film Institute,

115–22.

Eco, U. (1995) '*Casablanca*: Cult Movies and Intertextual Collage', in *Faith in Fakes: Travels in Hyperreality*. London: Minerva, 197–211.

Eig, J. (2003) 'A beautiful mind(fuck): Hollywood structures of identity', *Jump Cut*, 42. Available online: www.ejumpcut.org/currentissue/eig.mindfilms/index (accessed January 2004).

Erb, C. (1991) 'Film and Reception: A Contextual and Reading Formation Study of *King Kong* (1933)', PhD, awarded by Indiana University, UMI Dissertation Services, Michigan.

Evans, I. H. (1970) (ed.) *The Wordsworth Dictionary of Phrase and Fable*. London: Wordsworth Editions.

Fancher, H. and D. Peoples (2000) *Blade Runner Screenplay*, Los Angeles: The Blade Runner Partnership/Warner Home Video.

Fine, D. (ed.) (1995). *Los Angeles in Fiction* (revised edition). Albuquerque: University of New Mexico Press.

Fisher, H. (1992) *Anatomy of Love: A Natural History of Mating, Marriage, and Why We Stray*. New York: Fawcett Books.

Fiske, J. (1989) *Understanding Popular Culture*. London: Unwin Hyman.

Foucault, M. (1980) 'What is an Author?', in J. V. Harari (ed.) *Textual Strategies: Perspectives in Post–Structuralism Reader*. London: Routledge and Kegan Paul, 128–385.

Francavilla, J. (1997) 'The Android as Doppelganger', in J. B. Kerman (ed.) *Retrofitting Blade Runner: Issues in Ridley Scott's Blade Runner and Philip K. Dick's Do Androids Dream of Electric Sheep?* (second edition). Bowling Green, OH: Popular Press, 4–15.

Freedman, C. (1988) 'Philip K Dick and Criticism', *Science Fiction Studies*, 45. Available online: http://www.depauw.edu/sfs/covers/cov45.htm (accessed 3 October 2005).

Freedman, R. (1982) '*Blade Runner* – A Look into Futuristic Private Eyes', *The Fresno Bee*, June 25, section C, 3.

Gelder, K. (1999) 'Jane Campion and the Limits of Literary Cinema', in D. Cartmell and I. Whelehan (eds) *Adaptations: From Text to Screen, Screen to Text*. London and New York: Routledge. 157–71.

Gibson, W. (1994) *Virtual Light*. London: Penguin Viking.

___ (2001) *All Tomorrow's Parties*. London: Penguin Viking.

___ (2003) *Pattern Recognition*. New York: Putnam.

Gledhill, C. (1998) 'Klute 1: A Contemporary Film Noir and Femnist Criticism', in E. A. Kaplan (ed.) *Women in Film Noir.* (second edition). London: British Film Institute, 20–34.

Grant, B. K. (1991) 'Science Fiction Double Feature: Ideology in the Cult Film', in J. P. Telotte (ed.) *The Cult Film Experience: Beyond All Reason*. Austin: University of Texas Press, 122–37.

___ (1999) '"Sensuous Elaboration": Reason and the Visible in the Science-Fiction Film', in Annette Kuhn (ed.) *Alien Zone II: Cultural Theory and Contemporary Science Fiction Cinema*. London: Verso, 16–30.

Grey, R. (1991) 'Entropy, Energy, Empathy: Blade Runner and Detective Fiction', in J. B. Kerman (ed.) *Retrofitting Blade Runner: Issues in Ridley Scott's Blade Runner and Philip K. Dick's Do Androids Dream of Electric Sheep?* (second edition). Bowling Green, OH: Popular Press, 66–75.

Gwaltney, M. (1997) 'Androids as a Device for Reflection on Personhood' in J. B. Kerman (ed.) *Retrofitting Blade Runner: Issues in Ridley Scott's Blade Runner and Philip K. Dick's Do Androids Dream of Electric Sheep?* (second edition). Bowling Green, OH: Popular Press, 32–39.

Hall, S. (1980) 'Encoding, Decoding', in S. Hall, D. Hobson, A. Lowe and P. Willis (eds) *Culture, Media, Language: Working Papers in Cultural Studies, 1972–1979*. London: Unwin Hyman, 128–385.

Haraway, D. (1991) *Simians, Cyborgs and Women: The Reinvention of Nature*. New York: Routledge.

Harris, S. L. and R. L. Platzner (2003) *The Old Testament: An Introduction to the Hebrew Bible*. New York: McGraw-Hill.

Harvey, D. (1989) *The Condition of Postmodernity*. Oxford: Basil Blackwell.

____ (1997) 'Time and space in the postmodern cinema', in P. Brooker and W. Brooker (eds) *Postmodern After-images*. London: Arnold, 61–73.

____ (2000) *Spaces of Hope*. Edinburgh: Edinburgh University Press.

Hawkins, J. (2000) *Cutting Edge: Art–Horror and the Horrific Avant-garde*. Minneapolis: University of Minnesota Press.

Hayles, N. K. (1999) *How We Became Posthuman: Virtual Bodies in Cybernetics, Literature, and Informatics*. Chicago and London: University of Chicago Press.

Heide Smith, J. (2000) 'The Road not Taken – The How's and Why's of Interactive Fiction', *Game Research*. Available online: http://www.game-research.com/art_road_not_taken.asp (accessed 12 May 2004).

Hill, J. (1998) 'Film and Postmodernism', in J. Hill and P. Church Gibson (eds) *The Oxford Guide to Film Studies*. Oxford and New York: Oxford University Press, 96–105.

____ (1999) *British Cinema in the 1980s*. Oxford: Oxford University Press.

Hills, M. (2002) *Fan Cultures*. London and New York: Routledge.

____ (2003) '*Star Wars* in fandom, film theory, and the museum: the cultural status of the cult blockbuster' in J. Stringer (ed.) *Movie Blockbusters*. London and New York: Routledge, 178–89.

____ (2004a) '*Dawson's Creek*: "Quality Teen TV" and "Mainstream Cult"?', in G. Davis and K. Dickinson (eds) *Teen TV: Genre, Consumption and Identity*. London: British Film Institute, 54–67.

____ (2004b) 'Defining Cult TV: Texts, Inter–texts and Fan Audiences', in R. Allen and A. Hill (eds) *The Television Studies Reader*. London and New York: Routledge, 509–23.

____ (2004c) 'Strategies, Tactics and the Question of *Un Lieu Propre*: What/Where is "Media Theory"', in *Social Semiotics*, 14, 2, 133–49.

Hoffman, L. A. (1998) 'How the *Amidah* Began: A Jewish Detective Story,' in *My People's Prayer Book: Traditional Prayers, Modern Commentaries. Vol. 2 – The Amidah*. Woodstock, VT: Jewish Lights, 17–36.

Hollinger, V. (1991) 'Cybernetic Deconstructions: Cyberpunk and Postmodernism', in L. McCaffery (ed.) *Storming the Reality Studio: A Casebook of Cyberpunk and Postmodern Fiction*. Durham and London: Duke University Press, 203–18.

Hollows, J. (2003) 'The masculinity of cult', in M. Jancovich, A. Reboll, J. Stringer and A. Willis (eds) *Defining Cult Movies: The Cultural Politics of Oppositional Taste*. Manchester: Manchester University Press, 35–53.

The Holy Bible (1953). (Douay-Rheims version). Bristol: Nicholas Adams.

Hyde, D. (1995), *A Quickie Review*. Available online: http://www.philipkdickfans. com/pkdweb/blarun2.htm (accessed 3 October 2005).

Jacobs, J. (1961) *The Death and Life of Great American Cities*. New York: Random House.

Jameson, F. (1991) *Postmodernism or, The Cultural Logic of Late Capitalism*. London and New York: Verso.

____ (1992) 'Postmodernism and Consumer Society', in P. Brooker (ed.) *Modernism /Postmodernism*. London: Longman.

Jancovich, M. (2002) 'Cult Fictions: Cult Movies, Subcultural Capital, and the Production of Cultural Distinctions', *Cultural Studies*, 16, 2, 306–22.

Jenkins, H. (1992) *Textual Poachers: Television Fans and Participating Culture*. London: Routledge.

____ (2004) 'Computer Games as Narrative Architecture', in First Person: New Media as Story, Performance and Game, N. Wardrip-Fruin and P. Harrigan (eds) Cambrige, Mass: MIT Press. Available online: http://www.electronicbookreview.com/v3/servlet/ebr?command+view_essay&essay–id=jenkins (accessed 3 July 2004).

Jensen, J. (1992) 'Fandom as Pathology: The Consequences of Characterization', in L. A. Lewis (ed.) *The Adoring Audience*. New York and London: Routledge, 9–29.

Jermyn, D. and S. Redmond (eds) (2003) *The Cinema of Kathryn Bigelow: Hollywood Transgressor*. London: Wallflower Press.

Jerslev, A. (1992) 'Semiotics by instinct: "cult film" as a signifying practice between audience and film', in M. Skovmand and K. C. Schrøder (eds) *Media Cultures: Reappraising Transnational Media*. London and New York: Routledge, 181–98.

Jeter, K. W. (1995) *Blade Runner 2: The Edge of Human*. London: Orion Books.

____ (1996) *Blade Runner 3: Replicant Night*. New York: Bantam.

____ (2002) *Blade Runner 4: Eye and Talon*. London: Gollancz.

Just, F. (2004) *Apocalypse: Definitions and Related Terms*. Available online: http:// catholic-resources.org/Bible/Apoc_Def.htm (accessed 28 September 2005).

Juul, J. (2002) 'The Open and the Closed: Games of Emergence and Games of Progression', in F. Mäyrä (ed.) *'Computer Games and Digital Cultures' Conference proceedings*. Tampere: Tampere University Press, 323–331.

Kael, P. (1982) 'Baby, the Rain Must Fall', *The New Yorker*, 12 July, 82–5.

Kaplan, E. A. (1998a) 'Introduction to New Edition' in E. A. Kaplan (ed.) *Women in Film Noir* (second edition). London: British Film Institute, 1–14.

____ (1998b) 'Introduction to 1978 Edition' in E. A. Kaplan (ed.) *Women in Film Noir* (second edition). London: British Film Institute, 15–19.

Kawin, B. (1991) 'After Midnight', in J. P. Telotte (ed.) *The Cult Film Experience: Beyond All Reason*. Austin: University of Texas Press, 18–25.

Kennedy, B. M. (2000) *Deleuze and Cinema: The Aesthetics of Sensation*. Edinburgh: Edinburgh University Press.

Kerman, J. B. (ed.) (1997) *Retrofitting Blade Runner: Issues in Ridley Scott's Blade Runner and Philip K. Dick's Do Androids Dream of Electric Sheep?* (second edition). Bowling Green, OH: Popular Press.

_____ (1997) 'Technology and Politics in *Blade Runner* Dystopia', in J. B. Kerman (ed.) *Retrofitting Blade Runner: Issues in Ridley Scott's Blade Runner and Philip K. Dick's Do Androids Dream of Electric Sheep?* (second edition). Bowling Green, OH: Popular Press, 16–24.

Kermode, M. and J. Petley (1997) 'Road Rage', *Sight and Sound*, 7, 6, 16–18.

King, G. and T. Krzywinska (2000) *Science Fiction Cinema: From Outerspace to Cyberspace*. London: Wallflower Press.

_____ (2002) 'Introduction: cinema/videogames/interfaces', in G. King and T. Krzywinska (eds) *ScreenPlay: cinema/videogames/interfaces*. London: Wallflower Press, 1–32.

Klein, N. (1997) *The History of Forgetting: Los Angeles and the Erasure of Memory*. London and New York: Verso.

Klinger, B. (2001) 'The Contemporary Cinephile: Film Collecting in the Post-video Era', in R. Maltby and M. Stokes (eds) Hollywood Spectatorship. London: British Film Institute, 132–51.

Kolb, W. (1997) 'Script to Screen: Blade Runner in Perspective', in J. B. Kerman (ed.) *Retrofitting Blade Runner: Issues in Ridley Scott's Blade Runner and Philip K. Dick's Do Androids Dream of Electric Sheep?* (second edition). Bowling Green, OH: Popular Press, 132–153.

Kuhn, A, (ed.) (1990) *Alien Zone: Cultural Theory and Contemporary Science Fiction Cinema*. London: Verso.

_____ (ed.) (1999a) *Alien Zone II: The Spaces of Science Fiction Cinema*. London: Verso.

_____ (1999b) 'Clasical Hollywood Narrative', in P. Cook (ed.) *The Cinema Book*. London: British Film Institute. 39–42.

Kunstler, J. H. (1993) *The Geography of Nowhere: The Rise and Decline of America's Man-made Landscape*. Touchstone: New York.

_____ (1996) *Home From Nowhere: Remaking Our Everyday World for the 21st Century*. New York: Touchstone.

Lacey, N. (1998) *Image and Representation: Key Concepts in Media Studies*. Basingstoke and New York: Palgrave.

_____ (2000) *York Film Notes: Blade Runner*. London: York Press.

Lamster, M. (2000) *Architecture and Film*. New York: Princeton Architectural.

Landon, B. (1992) *The Aesthetics of Ambivalence: Rethinking Science Fiction Film in the Age of Electronic (Re)production*. Westport, CT: Greenwood Press.

_____ (1997) 'There's Some of Me in You: *Blade Runner* and the Adaptation of Science Fiction Literature into Film' in J. B. Kerman (ed.) *Retrofitting Blade Runner: Issues in Ridley Scott's Blade Runner and Philip K. Dick's Do Androids Dream of*

Electric Sheep? (second edition). Bowling Green, OH: Popular Press. 90–102.

____ (1999) 'Diegetic or Digital? The Convergence of Science-Fiction Literature and Science–Fiction Film in Hypermedia', in A. Kuhn (ed.) *Alien Zone II*. London: Verso, 31–49.

Landsberg, A. (1995) 'Prosthetic Memory: *Total Recall* and *Blade Runner*', in M. Featherstone and R. Burrows (eds) *Cyberspace/Cyberbodies/Cyberpunk*. London: Sage.

Lapsley, R. and M. Westlake (1988) *Film Theory: An Introduction*. Manchester: Manchester University Press.

Le Guern, P. (2004) 'Toward a Constructivist Approach to Media Cults', in S. Gwen-llian-Jones and R. E. Pearson (eds) *Cult Television*. University of Minnesota Press: Minneapolis, 3–25.

Lee, P. (2003) 'Interview: Ben Affleck and Uma Thurman cash in on John Woo's Paycheck', Science Fiction Weekly, 349. Available online: http://www.SciFi.com/sfw/issue349/interview.html (accessed 2 February 2004).

Leeper, M. R. (1990) 'Review of *Total Recall*'. Available online: http://reviews.imdb.com/Reviews /07/0775 (accessed 5 May 2004).

____ (1995) 'Review of *Screamers*'. Available online: http://reviews.imdb.com/Reviews/46/4615 (accessed 5 May 2004).

Lewis, J. (2002) *Cultural Studies: The Basics*. London: Sage.

Lipschutz, R. D. (2003) 'Aliens, Alien Nations, and Alienation in American Political Economy and Popular Culture', in J. Weldes (ed.) *To Seek Out New Worlds: Exploring Links Between Science Fiction and World Politics*. London: Palgrave, 79–98.

Mann, J. (ed.) (2001) *The Mammoth Encyclopedia of Science Fiction*. London: Robinson.

Massey, D. (1994) *Space, Place and Gender*. Cambridge: Polity Press.

May, A. (2000) 'The Call of Cool-O: Philip K. Dick Meets H.P. Lovecraft'. Available online:http://PhilipKDickfans.com (accessed 3 October 2005).

McCabe, B. (1999) *Dark Knights and Holy Fools: The Art and Films of Terry Gilliam*. New York: Universe Publishing.

McCarthy, A. (2001) *Ambient Television: Visual Culture and Public Space*. Durham, NC: Duke University Press.

McCarthy, S. (2003) *Cult Movies in Sixty Seconds*. London: Fusion Press.

McKee, A. (2002) 'What Cultural Studies Needs Is More Theory', *Continuum*, 16, 3, 311–16.

McKee, R. (1999) *Story: Substance, Structure, Style, and the Principles of Screenwriting*. London: Methuen.

McLeod, J. (2000) *Beginning Postcolonialism*. Manchester: MUP.

Mendik, X., and G. Harper (2000) 'The Chaotic Text and the Sadean Audience: Narrative Transgressions of a Contemporary Cult Film', in X. Mendik and G. Harper (eds) *Unruly Pleasures: The Cult Film and Its Critics*. Guildford: FAB Press, 237–49.

Miller, T., N. Govil, J. McMurria and R. Maxwell (2001) *Global Hollywood*. London: British Film Institute.

Montfort, N. (2003) *Twisty Little Passages. An Approach to Interactive Fiction.* Cambridge, MA: MIT Press.

Moore, M. (1961) 'Poetry', *Collected Poems.* New York: Macmillan.

Morgan D. (1995) 'Production Designer Jeffrey Beecroft on Creating the Worlds of *Twelve Monkeys.*' Available online: http://members.aol.com/morgands1/close-up/text/beecrof2.htm (accessed 5 April 2003).

Morris, S. 'The Eye in the Pyramid', *Short Talk Bulletin*, Masonic Service Association of the United States. Available online: http://web.mit.edu/afs/athena.mit.edu/user/d/r/dryfoo/www/Masonry/Essays/eyepyr.html (accessed 28 May 2004).

Mulvey, L. (1975) 'Visual Pleasure and Narrative Cinema', *Screen*, 16, 3, 6–18.

Murray, J. (1997) *Hamlet on the Holodeck. The Future of Narrative in Cyberspace.* New York: Free Press.

Napier, S. J. (2000) *Anime: From Akira to Princess Mononoke, Experiencing Japanese Animation.* New York: Palgrave.

Neale, S. (1989) 'Issues of Difference: *Alien* and *Blade Runner*' in J. Donald (ed.) *Fantasy and the Cinema.* London: British Film Institute, 213–25.

Newman, K. (ed.) (2002) *Science Fiction/Horror: A Sight and Sound Reader.* London: British Film Institute.

Oehley, J. (2003) 'Best and Worst Movies of the Decade', *The Sci-Fi Movie Page.* Available online: http://members.tripod.com/scifimoviepage/ (accessed 10 May 2004).

Orr, J. (2003) 'The City Reborn: Cinema at the Turn of the Century' in M. Shiel and T. Fitzmaurice (eds) *Screening the City.* London: Verso, 284–98.

Patrick, L (2003) 'Interview: Ben Affleck and Uma Thurman cash in on John Woo's Paycheck'. Available online: http://www.scifi.com/sfw/issue349/interview.html (accessed 2 February 2004).

Pearson, R. E. and W. Uricchio (1991) *The Many Lives of Batman: Critical Approaches to a Superhero and His Media.* London: British Film Institute.

Peary, D. (1988), *Cult Movies 3.* New York: Simon & Schuster.

Penley, C. (1997) *NASA/TREK: Popular Science and Sex in America.* London: Verso.

Perkins, T. E. (1979) 'Rethinking Stereotypes'. in M. Barrett, P. Corrigan, A. Kuhn and J. Wolff (eds) *Ideology and Cultural Production.* London: Croom Helm.

Picart, C. J. S. (2003) *Remaking the Frankenstein Myth on Film: Between Laughter and Horror.* New York: State University of New York Press.

Place, J. (1998) 'Women in *Film Noir*', in E. A. Kaplan (ed.) *Women in Film Noir* (second edition). London: British Film Institute, 47–68.

Plantinga, C. (1999) 'The Scene of Empathy and the Human Face on Film', in C. Plantinga and G. M. Smith (eds) *Passionate Views: Film, Cognition, and Emotion.* Baltimore and London: Johns Hopkins University Press, 239–55.

Pomerance, M. (2003) 'Neither Here Nor There: *ExistenZ* as "Elevator Film", *Quarterly Review of Film and Video*, 20, 1, 1–14.

Poole, S. (2000) *Trigger Happy: The Inner Life of Videogames.* London: Fourth Estate.

Propp, V. (1968) *Morphology of the Folktale*. Austin: University of Texas Press.

Pyle, F. (1993) 'Making Cyborgs, Making Humans: Of Terminators and Blade Runners', in J. Collins, H. Radner and A. Preacher Collins (eds) *Film Theory Goes To The Movies*. New York and London: London, 227–41.

Read, J. (2003) 'The cult of masculinity: from fan-boys to academic bad-boys', in M. Jancovich, A. Lázaro Reboll, J. Stringer and A. Willis (eds) *Defining Cult Movies: The Cultural Politics of Oppositional Taste*. Manchester: Manchester University Press, 54–70.

Redmond, S. (2003) *Studying Blade Runner*. Leighton Buzzard: Auteur.

Rickmann, G. (1984) *Philip K. Dick: In His Own Words*. Long Beach, CA: Fragments West.

Roberts, A. (2000) *Science Fiction*. London and New York: Routledge.

Rushing, J. and T. S. Frentz (1995) *Projecting the Shadow: The Cyborg Hero in American Film*. Chicago and London: University of Chicago Press.

Russell, J. (2000) 'Carry on Dick: The Weird Sci-Fi Worlds of Philip K. Dick'. Available online: http://www.bbc.co.uk/films/2002/06/10/who_is_philip_k_dick_article.shtml (accessed 5 May 2004).

Ryan, M. and D. Kellner (1990) 'Technophobia', in A. Kuhn (ed.) *Alien Zone: Cultural Theory and Contemporary Science Fiction Cinema*. London and New York: Verso, 58–65.

Salen, K. and E. Zimmerman, (2003) *Rules of Play: Game Design Fundamentals*, Cambridge, Mass: MIT Press.

Sammon, P. M. (1996) *Future Noir: The Making of Blade Runner*. New York: HarperPrism.

____ (1999) *Ridley Scott: The Making of His Movies*. London: Orion.

Saukko, P. (2003) *Doing Research in Cultural Studies*. London: Routledge.

Schatz, A. (1997) 'The American Earthquake: Mike Davis and the Politics of Disaster', in Radical Urban Theory. Availble online: http://www.rut.com/mdavis/americanearthquake.html (accessed 19 September 2005).

Schelde, P. (1993) *Androids, Humanoids, and Other Science Fiction Monsters*. New York and London: New York University Press.

Schellenberg, J. (1997) 'Review of *Blade Runner*', Challenging Destiny: Science Ficiton and Fantasy Reviews. Available online: http://www.challengingdestiny.com/reviews/blade_movie.htm. (accessed 11 September 2005).

Sconce, J. (1995) '"Trashing" the Academy: taste, excess and an emerging politics of cinematic style', *Screen*, 36, 4, 371–93.

Scott, S. (2004) 'Is *Blade Runner* a Misogynist Text', *Off Scribble*. Available online: http://scribble.com/uwi/br/bri-misog.html (accessed 7 May 2004).

Shay, D. (2000) *Blade Runner: The Inside Story*. London: Titan Books.

Shelly, M. (2003 [1818]) *Frankenstein*. Available online: http://etext.lib.virginia.edu/etcbin/toccer-new2?id=SheFran.sgm&images=images/modeng&data=/texts/english/modeng/parsed&tag=public&part=8&division=div1 (accessed 24 February 2005).

Shiel, M. and T. Fitzmaurice (2001) *Cinema and the City: Film and Urban Societies in a Global Context*. Oxford & Malden: Blackwell.

____ (2003) *Screening the City*. London and New York: Verso, 160–79.

Shiel, M. (2003), 'A Nostalgia for Modernity: New York, Los Angeles, and American Cinema in the 1970s', in M. Shiel and T. Fitzmaurice (2003) *Screening the City*. London and New York: Verso, 160–79.

Shires, B.E. (1999) 'Blade Runner: Do gamers dream of electric sheep?' in *Computer Games Magazine*. Available online: http://www.cdmag.com/articles/009/009/blade_runner_review.html (accessed 3 July 2004).

Silver, A. and J. Ursini (1996) *Film Noir Reader*. New York: Limelight Editions.

Sirius, RU (1997) 'Sex Machine', *Wired*, 5.05. Available online: http://www.wired.com/wired/archive/5.05/ff_cronenberg.html (accessed 14 January 2004).

Smith, G. M. (1999) '"To Waste More Time, Please Click Here Again": Monty Python and the Quest for Film/CD–ROM Adaptation', in G. M. Smith (ed.) *On a Silver Platter: CD–ROMs and the Promises of a New Technology*. New York: New York University Press, 58–86.

Smith, M. (1999) 'Gangsters, Cannibals, Aesthetes, or Apparently Perverse Allegiances', in C. Plantinga and G. M. Smith (eds) *Passionate Views: Film, Cognition, and Emotion*. Baltimore: Johns Hopkins University Press, 217–38.

Sobchack, V. (1987) *Screening Space: The American Science Fiction Film*. New Brunswick, NJ: Rutgers University Press.

____ (1999). 'Cities on the Edge of Time: The Urban Science-Fiction Film', in Annette Kuhn (ed.) *Alien Zone II*. London: Verso, 123–143.

Soja, E. W. (1989) *Postmodern Geographies*. London: Verso.

____ (1996). *Thirdspace. Journeys to Los Angeles and Other Real-And-Imagined Places*. Oxford: Blackwell.

____ (2000) *Postmetropolis. Critical Studies of Cities and Regions*. Oxford: Blackwell.

Southworth, M. (2003) 'New Urbanism and the American Metropolis', *Built Environment*, 3, 29.

Spicer, A. (2002) *Film Noir*. Essex: Longman.

Staiger, J. (1999) 'Future *Noir*: Contemporary Representations of Visionary Cities', in A. Kuhn (ed.) *Alien Zone II*. London: Verso, 97–122.

Steranko (1982) '*Blade Runner*: Harrison Ford, a Tough, New Detective Hero in a Hard Boiled Thriller of the Future', *Prevue*, 48, 26–9, 67, 70–3.

Stern, G. (1998) 'An Interview with Louis Castle About Westwood's *Blade Runner*' in *Gamasutra*, 20 February 1998. Available online: http://www.gamasutra.com/features/19980220/blade_runner_louis_castle01.htm (accessed 10 May 2004).

Strick, P. (2002) '*Blade Runner*: Telling the Difference', in K. Newman (ed.) *Science Fiction/Horror: A Sight and Sound Reader*. London: British Film Institute, 47–50.

Suvin, D. (1980) *Metamorphoses of Science Fiction: On the Poetics and History of a Literary Genre*. New Haven: Yale University Press.

Taylor, G. (1999) *Artists in the Audience: Cults, Camp and American Film Criticism*. Princeton: Princeton University Press.

Taylor, L. and A. Willis (1999) *Media Studies: Texts, Institutions and Audiences*.

Oxford: Blackwell.

Telotte, J. P. (1990) 'The Doubles of Fantasy and the Space of Desire', in A. Kuhn (ed.) *Alien Zone: Cultural Theory and Contemporary Science Fiction Cinema.* London: Verso, 152–9.

____ (1991) 'Beyond All Reason: The Nature of the Cult', in J. P. Telotte (ed.) *The Cult Film Experience: Beyond All Reason.* Austin: University of Texas Press, 5–17.

____ (1995) *Replications: A Robotic History of the Science Fiction Film.* Urbana and Chicago: University of Illinois Press.

____ (1998) 'The Doubles of Fantasy and the Space of Desire', in A. Kuhn (ed.) *Alien Zone: Culture Theory and Contemporary Science Fiction Cinema,* London: Verso, 152–9.

____ (2001) *Science Fiction Film.* Cambridge: Cambridge University Press.

Thomas, D. (2004) 'Video Game Vocabulary: A Lexicon of Experiental Anchors', presented at the *Form, Culture and Videogame Criticism* conference, Princeton University. (unpublished paper).

Thornton, S. (1995) *Club Cultures: Music, Media and Subcultural Capital.* Cambridge: Polity Press.

Tosca, S. (2000) 'Playing for the Plot: *Blade Runner* as Paradigm of the Electronic Adventure Game', Dichtung Digital, June. Available online: http://www.it-c.dk/people/tosca/bladerunner/ (accessed 10 May 2004).

____ (2003a) 'The Quest Problem in Computer Games', in *Proceedings of TIDSE 2003*, Darmstadt, Germany, March. Available online: http://www.it-c.dk/people/tosca/quest.htm (accessed 12 May 2004).

____ (2003b) 'Reading Resident Evil: Code Veronica X', in *Proceedings of the Fifth International Digital Arts and Culture Conference*, RMIT, Melbourne, Australia, May, Available online: http://hypertext.rmit.edu.au/dac/papers/Tosca.pdf (accessed 9 May 2004).

Travers, Chris (1999) '*Y2K APOCALYPSE*: When the computers break down, will it be the end of the World?' *Round Top Register.* Available online: http://www.roundtop.com/y2k1.htm (accessed 1 June 2004).

Tulloch, J., and H. Jenkins (1995) *Science Fiction Audiences.* London and New York: Routledge.

Turner, V. (1969) *The Ritual Process: Structure and Anti–Structure.* New York: Cornell University Press.

Turner, V. and E. L. B. Turner (1978) *Image and Pilgrimage in Christian Culture.* New York: Columbia University Press.

Twersky, I. (ed.) (1972) A Maimonides Reader. Springfield, NJ: Behrman House.

Ulin, D. L. (ed.) (2001) *Another City: Writing From Los Angeles.* San Francisco: City Lights Books.

Urry, J. (2002) *The Tourist Gaze.* London: Sage.

Wakefield, N. (1990) *Postmodernism.* London: Pluto Press.

Waller, G. (1991) 'Midnight Movies, 1980–1985: A Market Study', in J. P. Telotte (ed.) *The Cult Film Experience: Beyond All Reason.* Austin: University of Texas Press, 167–86.

Watson, P. (1997) 'There's No Accounting for Taste: Exploitation Cinema and the

Limits of Film Theory', in D. Cartmell, I. Hunter, H. Kaye and I. Whelehan (eds) *Trash Aesthetics: Popular Culture and its Audience*. London: Pluto Press, 66–83.

Watt, I. (2000) *The Rise of the Novel: Studies in Defoe, Richardson and Fielding*. London: Pimlico.

Webb, Brian (2004) 'Just Desert', *LA Alternative Press*, 3, 7, 9–22.

Wells, H. G. (1906) *The Future in America*. London: Chapman and Hall.

Whelehan, I. (1999) 'Adaptations: The Contemporary Dilemmas', in D. Cartmell and I. Whelehan (eds) *Adaptations: From Text to Screen, Screen to Text*. London and New York: Routledge, 3–19.

Wollen, P. (1992) 'Delirious Projections', *Sight and Sound*, 2, 4, 24–7.

Wood, R. (1986) *Hollywood from Vietnam to Reagan*. New York: Columbia University Press.

Žižek, S. (1993) *Tarrying with the Negative: Kant, Hegel and the Critique of Ideology*. Durham and London: Duke University Press.

INDEX

THE MATRIX TRILOGY

Cyberpunk Reloaded

edited by Stacy Gillis

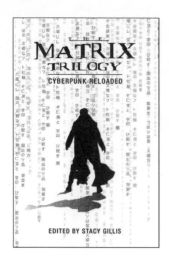

£15.99 pbk
1-904764-32-0
£45.00 hbk
1-904764-33-9
240 pages

The Matrix Trilogy: Cyberpunk Reloaded is a collection of critical essays on the massive phenomenon that is the three *Matrix* films, including the subsequent websites, computer games and *The Animatrix* films. Among the topics considered are the new cyberpunk, Baudrillarian simulacra, the politics of gender and race, the femme fatale, costume, cyberculture and the body, virtual realities and special effects. Discussing both the influences on the trilogy and the impact they have had since their release, the contributors to this collection provide critically innovative readings of the franchise. *The Matrix Trilogy: Cyberpunk Reloaded* is a long-awaited exploration of a modern film phenomenon and is the first academic publication to consider the films as a cultural event.

'This collection brings together an impressive international array of critics to direct their fearsome collective intelligence on The Matrix in its numerous guises: as extraordinary technological artefact, as Hollywood franchise, as vehicle for popular philosophical reflection on virtuality, postmodernism and the human, and as a science fictional rendition of the dialectic of totalitarianism and subcultural resistance. In a crowded market for commentaries, this collection stakes a strong claim to be The One for the discerning critical reader.'
Roger Luckhurst, Birkbeck College, University of London

Stacy Gillis is Lecturer in Modern and Contemporary Literature at the University of Newcastle. She is the co-editor of *Third Wave Feminism* (2004) and has published widely on cybertheory, cyberpunk and feminist theory

LIQUID METAL

The Science Fiction Film Reader

edited by Sean Redmond

£16.99 pbk
1-903364-87-6
£45.00 hbk
1-903364-88-4
366 pages

Liquid Metal: The Science Fiction Film Reader is the first extended collection of previously published essays on science fiction film and television. This Reader brings together a great number of seminal essays that have opened up the study of science fiction to serious critical interrogation. It is divided into eight distinct themed sections and includes important writings by Susan Sontag, Vivian Sobchack, Steve Neale, J. P. Telotte, Peter Biskind and Constance Penley amongst others, writing on films such as *Blade Runner*, *Alien*, *Star Wars*, *Total Recall*, *Them!* and *The Thing*.

'A significant collection of essays addressing the major themes that have informed the genre since it emerged on film and television screens in the 1950s ... as a whole, it provides an invaluable – and singular – text for both students and scholars.'
Professor Vivian Sobchack, University of California, Los Angeles

'Sean Redmond's selection process is a ... rigorous one, drawing together extracts, essays, and articles from monographs, edited collections, and refereed journals, including some unlikely sources as well as Science Fiction Studies ... In the range of its coverage, Liquid Metal makes a bid at becoming the set text around which both undergraduate and postgraduate courses on sf film will, with some supplementary readings, be based, and the list of contributors is a pretty solid guarantee of the quality of the criticism it contains.'
Science Fiction Studies

Sean Redmond is Lecturer in Film Studies at the Southampton Institute, UK, co-editor of *The Cinema of Kathryn Bigelow: Hollywood Transgressor* (Wallflower Press, 2003) and contributor to *Contemporary North American Film Directors: A Wallflower Critical Guide* (2002)